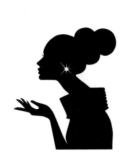

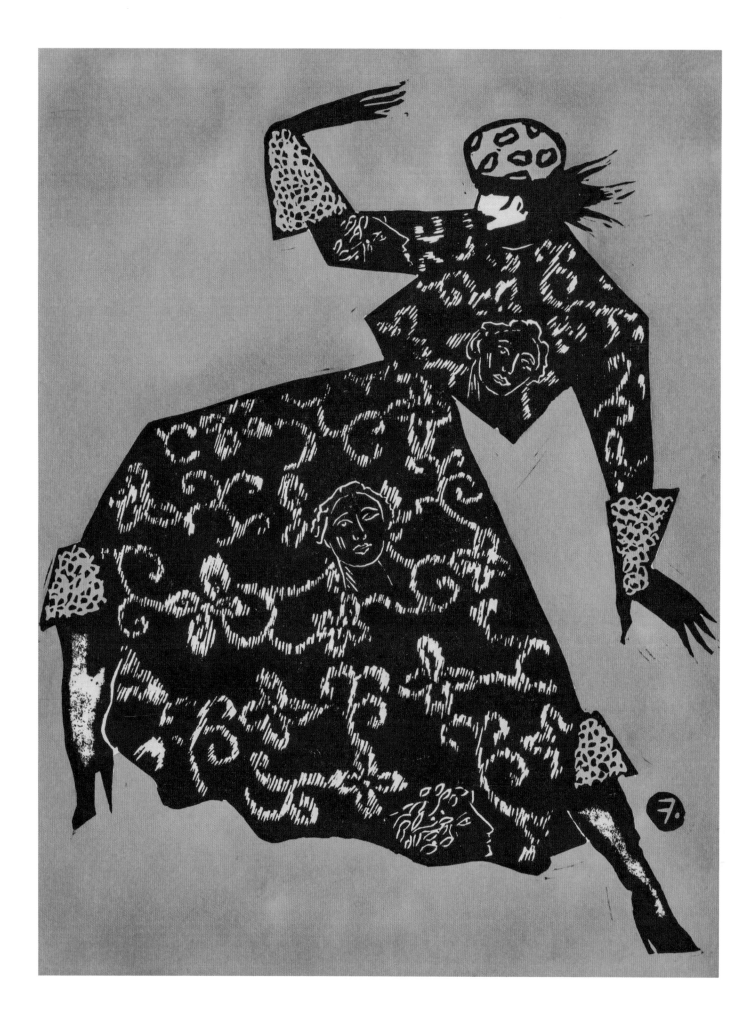

Ed. Julius Wiedemann

Illustration Now!
FASHION

TASCHEN

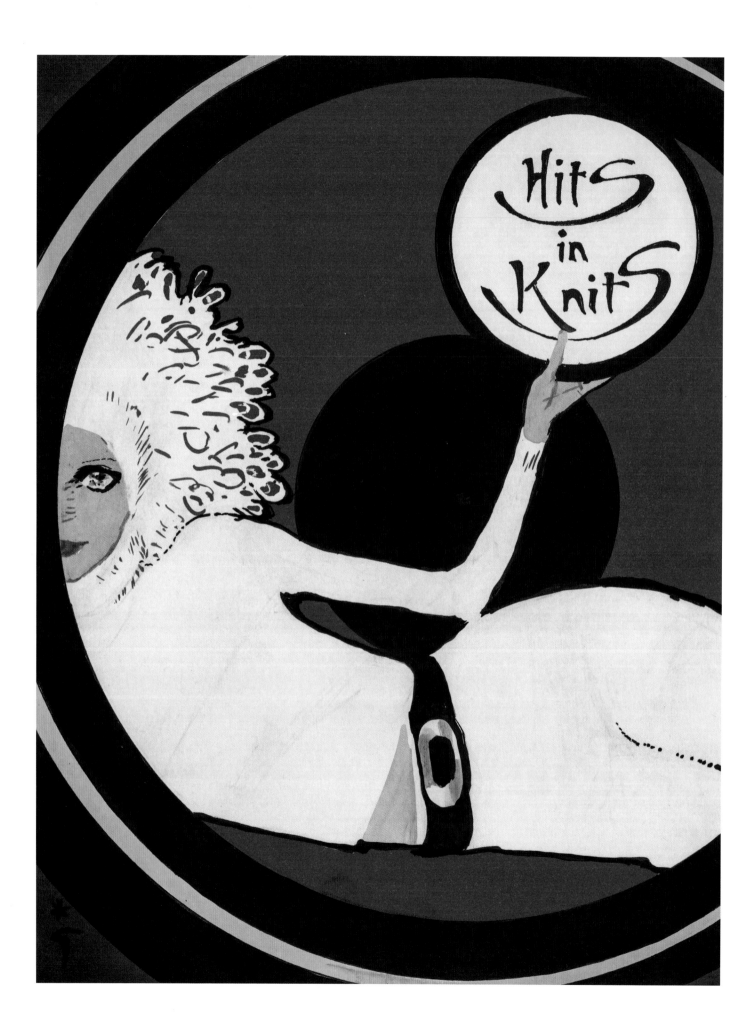

Contents
Inhalt/Sommaire

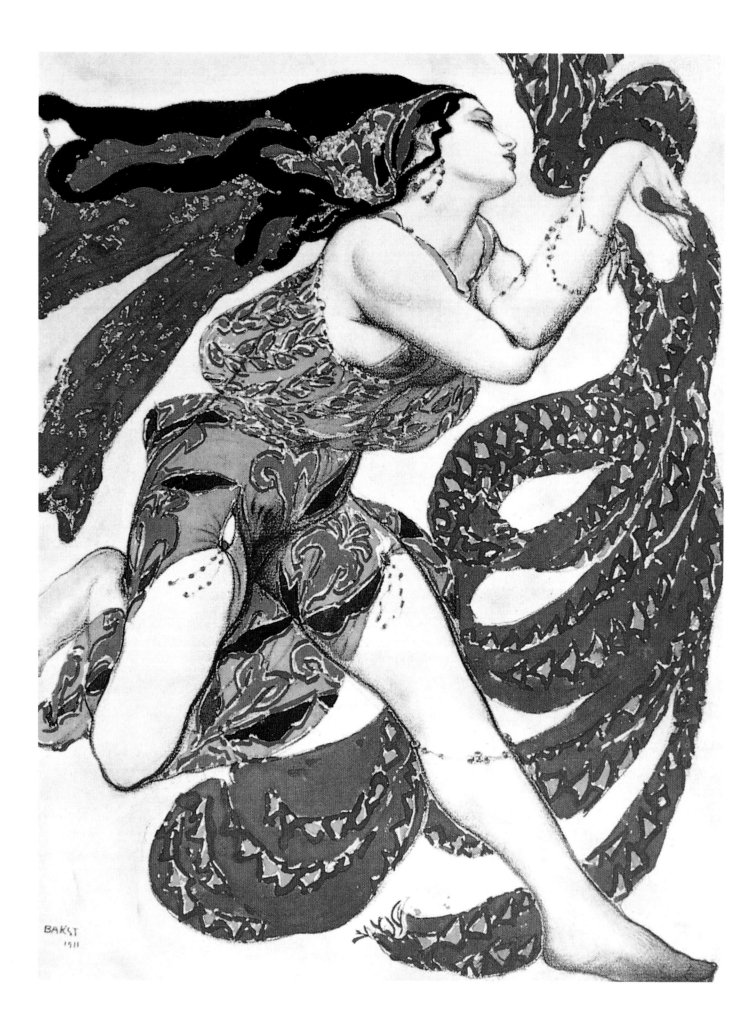

Fashion Lines

by Steven Heller

Not every artist can *do* fashion and not every fashion artist *does* fashion well. There are tough standards to uphold and great legacies to honor—including those of Leon Bakst, Paul Iribe, Charles Dana Gibson, J.C. Leyendecker and Antonio Lopez. Fashion illustration is not as effortless as the best illustrators make it appear. It is one thing to draw inanimate objects for a catalog and quite another to paint models alluringly without resorting to facial or body clichés. Fashion illustration requires the unique ability to wield pen or brush in such a way that it not only captures nuance through gesture but also can readily transform the graphic representation of a garment, accessory or cosmetic into an object of desire. When models are used, they must be as come-hither as Marilyn Monroe yet as reserved as the Mona Lisa.

These are tall orders for the average illustrator, which is why although there are artists without any fashion experience who have been known to dabble now and again with fashion illustration, the true fashion illustrator is often dedicated to a single métier. But here's the inelegant elephant in the room: Since photography is the quintessential medium for conveying fashion's allure—and some great fashion photographers are more artfully adventurous than some illustrators—where and how does illustration play a role?

Fashion illustrations have been in vogue since the birth of modern clothing design around the turn of the 20th century. The designers themselves produced some of the earliest illustrations in order to visualize their creations before cutting a piece of expensive fabric. In those years, before photography was as widespread as it has become, studio illustrators were hired to depict from actual garments every detail of, say, a lady's frock or a gentleman's waistcoat. Such artwork was usually found gracing the pages of the various mail-order catalogs—like Sears Roebuck—that provided customers who lived far from the big cities with the stay-at-home means to purchase the latest styles. Early fashion magazines, including the original *Harper's Bazaar*, were laden with stiff wood-engraved renderings of actual women and men wearing their finest and looking their best. The artists' goal was to manufacture an ideal.

Objective representations of clothing are no longer the purview of fashion illustrators, except in certain art-directed instances (like vintage Banana Republic and J. Peterman catalogs) where realistic illustration is a conceit. Rather, illustration's purpose now is to create moods, emotions and experiences of the kind that can only be achieved through a human hand pressing against paper or canvas with ink or paint, wherein the fluidity of a line or the starkness of a tone or the serendipity of a smudge adds to the allure. And there is a lot of leeway here: Abstraction and realism are acceptable. Impressionist and Expressionist styling are embraceable. Distinct and eccentric mannerisms are electable as long as they imbue the clothing with the air that distinguishes one line from another, or even one season from another.

There is some truth to the belief that fashion illustration is merely about capturing momentary trends. Yet the most successful artists are stylistically and methodologically consistent—trends emanate from earlier trends just as much as they echo them. By adding their unique graphic signatures to a particular collection they give the brand its validation. As you peruse this book replete with many approaches and personalities, look carefully at what the illustrator has tried to impart and how it was accomplished. Some of these images invoke personal styles as testimonials, while others create an aura through their art. In either case watch how skillfully these artists have done their jobs.

Modelinien

von Steven Heller

Nicht *jedem* Künstler gelingt auch Mode, und nicht *jeder* Modekünstler macht gute Mode. Man muss strengen Standards genügen und sich großer Vorgänger als würdig erweisen, etwa Leon Bakst, Paul Iribe, Charles Dana Gibson, J.C. Leyendecker oder Antonio Lopez. Die Modeillustration gelingt nicht so mühelos, wie es bei den besten Vertretern des Genres den Anschein hat. Es ist eine Sache, leblose Objekte für einen Katalog zu zeichnen, doch etwas völlig anderes, Gesicht und Körper von Models verlockend zu gestalten, ohne auf Klischees zurückzugreifen. Modeillustration bedarf der einzigartigen Fähigkeit, gestische Nuancen mittels Stift oder Pinsel einzufangen. Zusätzlich aber verwandelt sie Kleidungsstücke, Accessoires oder Kosmetikartikel in Objekte der Begierde. Kommen Models ins Spiel, müssen sie so aufreizend erscheinen wie Marilyn Monroe und so reserviert wie die Mona Lisa zugleich.

Ganz schön viel verlangt für den durchschnittlichen Illustrator. Das ist auch der Grund, warum sich zwar immer wieder mal Künstler ohne Modeerfahrung nebenbei mit Modegrafik beschäftigen, doch der wahre Modeillustrator widmet sich oft ausschließlich diesem einzigen Metier. Um die eine Frage jedoch kommt man nicht herum: Wenn Fotografie das wesentliche Medium ist, um die Reize der Mode zu vermitteln (und einige hervorragende Modefotografen sind kunstvoller und kühner als manche Illustratoren), welche Rolle bleibt der Illustration?

En vogue sind Modeillustrationen seit den ersten Tagen des modernen Fashiondesigns, also seit Beginn des 20. Jahrhunderts. Einige der frühesten Illustrationen schufen die Designer damals selbst, um ihre Entwürfe zu visualisieren, ehe sie ihre Schere an die teuren Stoffe setzten. In jenen Jahren, bevor die Fotografie überall verbreitet war, beauftragte man Studioillustratoren, um jedes Detail eines Kleidungsstücks darzustellen, etwa von einem Damenkleid oder einer Herrenweste. Solch künstlerische Darstellungen zierten gewöhnlich die Seiten der verschiedenen Versandkataloge, etwa jenem von Sears Roebuck. Damit konnten Kunden fernab der großen Städte bequem von Zuhause aus die neueste Mode erwerben. Die ersten Modemagazine, darunter auch *Harper's Bazaar* in seinen Anfängen, steckten voller steifer Holzstichdarstellungen realer Frauen und Männer in feinstem Zwirn, die möglichst gut aussehen sollten. Ziel des Künstlers war hier, ein Ideal herzustellen.

Die objektive Darstellung von Bekleidung ist nicht länger Hauptaufgabe der Modeillustration, außer als gezielter Art-Directing-Gag (wie etwa in den Vintage-Ausgaben der Kataloge von Banana Republic und J. Peterman). Illustrationen unserer Zeit stellen sich vielmehr die Aufgabe, Stimmungen, Emotionen und Erfahrungen entstehen zu lassen, die nur gelingen können, indem Menschen mit eigener Hand Tinte oder Farbe auf Papier oder Leinwand aufbringen, wo flüssige Linien, krasse Farbtöne und zufällig gelungene Kleckse den Reiz verstärken. Es bietet sich ein breiter Gestaltungsspielraum: Abstraktion wie auch Realismus sind okay, es lässt sich impressionistisch oder expressionistisch verfahren, oder man entscheidet sich überdies für ausgeprägte und exzentrische Manierismen – alles, solange dadurch Kleider von jenem Flair durchdrungen werden, das Produktlinien untereinander oder auch Saisonen voneinander abgrenzt.

In der Feststellung, bei Modeillustration gehe es vornehmlich ums Aufgreifen vorübergehender Trends, steckt ein Körnchen Wahrheit. Doch die erfolgreichsten Künstler sind stilistisch und methodisch konsistent – Trends entstehen ebenso aus früheren Trends, wie sie sie widerspiegeln. Indem Künstler einer Kollektion ihre unverwechselbare bildliche Signatur verleihen, schenken sie der Marke Gültigkeit. Schauen Sie sich dieses Buch mit all seinen vielfältigen Ansätzen und Persönlichkeiten aufmerksam an und stellen Sie fest, was genau die Illustratoren vermitteln wollten und wie ihnen dies gelang. Manche Bilder legen in ihrem persönlichen Stil Zeugnis ab, während andere durch ihre Kunst eine bestimmte Aura schaffen. Achten Sie in jedem Fall darauf, wie geschickt die Künstler ihre Arbeit erfüllen.

Lignes de mode

par Steven Heller

Tous les artistes ne peuvent pas forcément *faire* de la mode, et tous les artistes de mode ne le *font* pas forcément bien. Il y a des précédents difficiles à égaler et des œuvres imposantes auxquelles il faut rendre honneur – notamment celles de Leon Bakst, Paul Iribe, Charles Dana Gibson, J.C. Leyendecker et Antonio Lopez. L'illustration de mode n'est pas aussi facile que les grands illustrateurs peuvent nous le faire penser. Dessiner des objets inanimés pour un catalogue est une chose, mais représenter des mannequins séduisants sans stéréotyper les visages ou les corps est autrement plus difficile. L'illustration de mode requiert un talent unique, celui de manier le stylo ou le pinceau de façon à non seulement exprimer la nuance dans le geste, mais aussi à transformer la représentation graphique d'un vêtement, d'un accessoire ou d'un produit cosmétique en objet du désir. Lorsque des mannequins sont utilisés, ils doivent être aussi aguichants que Marilyn Monroe, mais aussi réservés que Mona Lisa.

Ce sont des défis de taille pour un illustrateur lambda, et c'est pourquoi, bien qu'il y ait des artistes sans expérience dans la mode qui tâtent de l'illustration de mode de temps à autre, le véritable illustrateur de mode se consacre souvent entièrement à cette activité. Mais il y a un problème dont personne n'a envie de parler : puisque la photographie est le véhicule de la mode par excellence – et certains grands photographes de mode sont plus aventureux artistiquement parlant que certains illustrateurs – quel est le rôle de l'illustration, et quelle est sa place ?

Les illustrations de mode sont en vogue depuis la naissance de la mode moderne, au début du XXᵉ siècle. Ce sont les créateurs eux-mêmes qui ont dessiné les premières illustrations, afin de visualiser leurs créations avant de tailler dans le coûteux tissu. À cette époque, avant que la photographie ne devienne aussi répandue qu'aujourd'hui, les studios embauchaient des illustrateurs pour dessiner les plus petits détails des vêtements à partir des modèles réels. Ces dessins ornaient habituellement les pages des différents catalogues de vente par correspondance – comme Sears Roebuck – qui permettaient aux clients éloignés des grandes villes de se procurer des articles des dernières tendances sans quitter le confort de leur foyer. Les premiers magazines de mode, et notamment le *Harper's Bazaar* original, étaient truffés de gravures sur bois qui donnaient une représentation amidonnée d'hommes et de femmes réels sur leur trente-et-un. L'objectif des artistes était de fabriquer un idéal.

Les illustrateurs de mode ne cherchent plus à donner une représentation objective des vêtements, sauf dans certains cas où l'illustration réaliste est une prise de position qui relève de la direction artistique (comme les catalogues vintage de Banana Republic et J. Peterman). Aujourd'hui, l'objectif de l'illustration est plutôt de créer des ambiances, des émotions et des expériences que seule une main humaine appliquant de l'encre ou de la peinture sur du papier ou une toile peut créer, où la fluidité d'une ligne, la force d'une couleur ou le hasard d'une tache ajoute à la séduction. Et il y a ici beaucoup de liberté : l'abstraction et le réalisme sont acceptables. L'impressionnisme ou l'expressionnisme sont envisageables. Tous les maniérismes et toutes les excentricités sont concevables, du moment qu'ils confèrent au vêtement un air qui distinguera une ligne d'une autre, ou même une saison d'une autre.

Certains pensent que l'illustration de mode n'est rien de plus que l'art de fixer des tendances éphémères, et ce n'est pas faux. Pourtant, les plus grands artistes font preuve de cohérence dans leur style et leur méthode : les tendances émergent des tendances qui les précèdent, tout autant qu'elles leur font écho. En ajoutant leur signature graphique unique à une collection particulière, ils valident la marque. Lorsque vous feuillèterez cet ouvrage qui regorge de démarches et de personnalités différentes, observez attentivement ce que l'illustrateur a essayé d'exprimer, et comment il s'y est pris. Certaines de ces images emploient le style personnel comme une véritable lettre de recommandation, tandis que d'autres créent une aura grâce à leur art. Dans tous les cas, vous ne manquerez pas de remarquer l'immense savoir-faire de ces artistes.

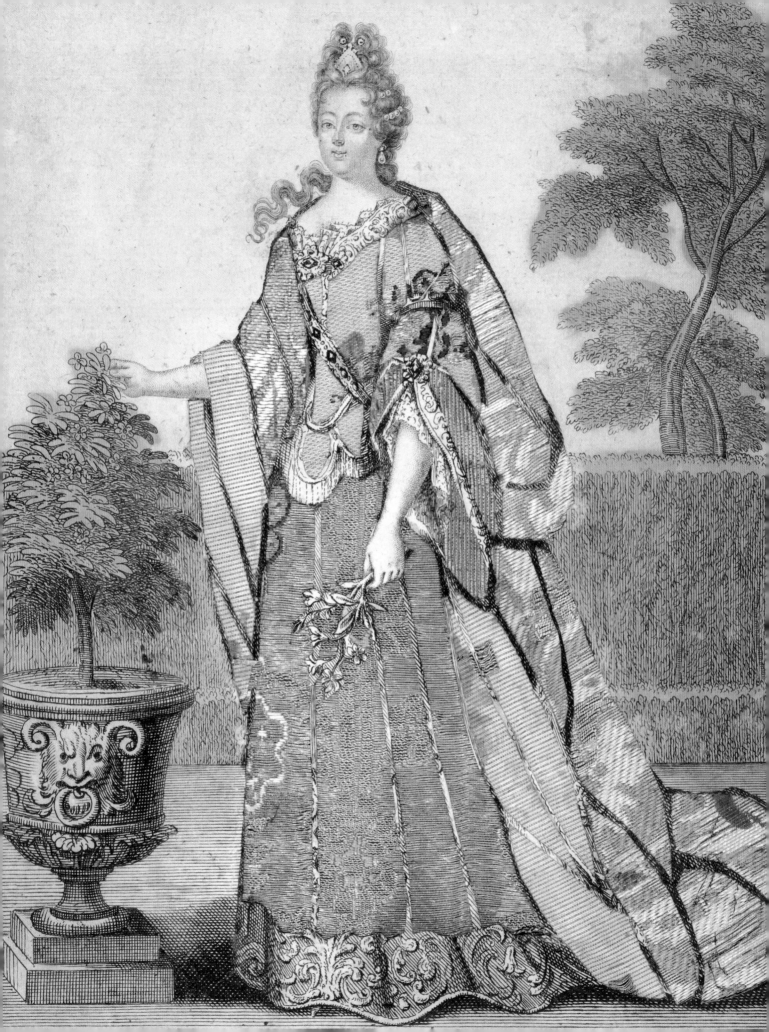

Depictions of Style

A History of Fashion Illustration

by Adelheid Rasche

Fashion, when considered as a social phenomenon, is very much fed by our fascination with the new. It is the fruit of an interactive relationship between a cast of actors, a stage, and an audience. Trend-setting individuals parade their outfits in conspicuous locations where they are seen as models by interested observers and imitated as a result.

It wasn't until the early 17th century that fashion trends began to spread internationally. Because of France's commercial and cultural supremacy, the nobility and upper middle classes across Europe tried to keep pace with the French royal court. Visitors to France spoke of the lustrous silks of Lyons, the delicate lace of the northern provinces, and the stylish cutting of Parisian tailors and dressmakers. With its strictly organized trade guilds and a commercial system providing special protection for home-produced goods, France indisputably led Europe in the production of luxury goods, as it did with its fashion industry.

Banquets, balls, outings to the theater, and even promenading were opportunities for those who moved in court circles to flaunt their modish outfits and accessories. At the time, these were all made exclusively by hand, either singly or else in very small numbers. Anyone who could not get to Paris, the center of the fashion world, had to rely on letters and journalism for information, but above all on visual images. As a result, printed fashion plates quickly became a much sought-after commodity throughout the courts of Europe.

As early as the 1620s, there appeared in Paris two series of such images which could be regarded as the first fashion illustrations. These etchings and copper engravings by Jacques Callot and Abraham Bosse enjoyed wide circulation (p.12). They featured full-length portraits of noblemen and women of the day who appeared to the observer to be standing on a stage. The focus was on their fashionable finery and posture, and any representation of them as individuals was purely secondary.[1]

During the reign of Louis XIV, large numbers of prints emerged showing distinguished-looking people wearing the latest fashions, reflecting the splendor of the royal court. They included engravings based on drawings by Nicolas Arnoult, Robert Bonnart, and Antoine Trouvain, which became famous right across Europe (p.10). They depict full-length, static, single figures against a backdrop of interiors, parks, or cityscapes. It is clear from these images that fashion illustrations always reflected contemporary trends in art—we only have to think of the full-length portraits by Anthony van Dyck or Diego Velázquez.

Another equally influential forerunner of today's fashion plates was the series entitled *Galerie des Modes* (1778–1787), published in Paris barely a century later. With more than 340 hand-colored engravings it is the most comprehensive fashion document of the French Rococo era. Reminiscent in style of the paintings of François Boucher and Nicolas Lancret, the series attracted a rich assortment of contributions from such well-known artists as François Watteau and Claude-Louis Desrais (p.13). They included elegantly arranged genre scenes set in the open air, statuesque single figures seen from in front or behind, beautifully detailed views of hats and hairstyles, as well as charming still-lifes put together with fashion accessories. Many of the tableaux displayed in the *Galerie des Modes* still find an echo in 21st-century fashion illustrations.

In the 1780s, the first fashion magazines established illustration as a recognized facet of the fashion trade. At this time, two styles predominated. As well as the luxury and courtliness of Parisian trends, which some saw as refined but others as fussy and flamboyant, many followed the simple, rational tastes of the British bourgeoisie. Both styles are represented in elegant, hand-colored drawings in the *Cabinet des Modes* (1785–1793) (p.14).

Moreover, fueled by the far-reaching changes brought about by the French Revolution, around 1800 the world of fashion witnessed equally dramatic changes of silhouette in both masculine and feminine attire. Examples included semi-transparent, Grecian-style, chemise dresses for women and skin-tight trousers for dashing young men. Here, for the first time, we see a clear correlation

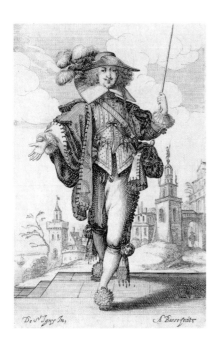

Abraham Bosse, 1629
Le Jardin de la noblesse française

→   François Watteau, c. 1780
Galerie des modes

p. 10   Robert Bonnart, c. 1687
La reine de Portugal

between radical change in fashion and innovation in the fashion illustrator's art. Philibert-Louis Debucourt's drawings in *Modes et Manières du Jour* (1798–1808) and Horace Vernet's series *Incroyables et Merveilleuses* (1810–1818) can be considered high points in French fashion illustration of the time (p. 15). In their work, both artists intermingle elegance with wit, vivacity with slapstick humor, and the minuscule with the monumental. Today, their engravings are sought-after collectors' pieces.

Things were kept much simpler by those illustrators working for the increasing number of fashion magazines that sprang up across Europe in the course of the next few years, some of which went on to survive for decades. Their illustrations were based more on Paris's leading fashion publications than the original garments. If the more or less legal practise of copying led to the unstoppable decline in genuinely artistic fashion illustration, amidst the abundance of mass-produced images the work of certain talented French illustrators nevertheless still stood out. Among them was Jules David (p. 15), who for decades provided illustrations for *Moniteur de la Mode* (1843–1913).[2] His painstaking, atmospheric, and densely detailed fashion plates were not only perfect representations of the latest trends, but also reflected bourgeois values. References to contemporary art—from portraits by Jean-Auguste-Dominique Ingres, by way of Franz Xaver Winterhalter's group paintings of European royalty, to Impressionist figure paintings—are unmistakable.

The advent of photography, which printing technology could handle with relative ease by the end of the 19th century, meant there was now serious competition in the field of fashion illustration. To begin with, a number of interesting combinations emerged. For example, drawings could be made to look like photographs, or actual photographs painted over in color (p. 16). Even so, during the Belle Epoque, fashion plates remained faithful to 19th-century notions of artistic presentation.

It was only in 1908, when the resourceful Paris couturier Paul Poiret collaborated with the young graphic artist Paul Iribe

to publish the album *Les Robes de Paul Poiret racontées par Paul Iribe*, that fashion illustration suddenly stepped into the modern age (p. 18). As would be the case in the second Poiret album, published in 1911 with drawings by Georges Lepape (p. 19), Iribe found sophisticated and versatile ways of blending together different styles. Both artists took elements of the Classic and Empire repertoire and were also inspired by the Ballets Russes, which was then taking Paris by storm. At the same time, they incorporated some of the ideas of the Arts and Crafts movement and borrowed from the much-admired British style of children's book illustration.

The enormous success of both Poiret albums guaranteed full order-books for the younger generation of graphic artists. Even today, André Marty and Georges Barbier's visuals for *Modes et Manières du Jour* (1912–1921), published annually in Paris, still stand among the very best examples of artistic fashion illustration (pp. 20 & 21).[3] In the same decade, work of similarly high quality was being produced by German illustrators in Berlin, a city with a thriving fashion industry. In their contributions to leading fashion magazines like *Die Dame* (1912–1942), *Der Kleiderkasten* (1915), *Styl* (1922–1924) or *Die deutsche Elite* (1924–1930), female artists such as Lotte Wernekink (p. 24) and Julie Haase-Werkenthin (p. 22) took ideas from the Expressionist movement in art, picked up others from the art of Japan, and others still from the aesthetics of 1920s cinema.

International competition from American magazines like *Harper's Bazaar*, which first appeared in 1867, and *Vogue*, founded in 1892, had a positive effect on fashion illustration. Always full of new ideas, the versatile Erté worked for *Harper's Bazaar* (p. 26) for more than 20 years. *Vogue* provided work for many great fashion illustrators, such as Georges Lepape, Eduardo García Benito, and Christian Bérard, whose pithy, atmospheric drawings appeared either on the cover or as picture spreads inside the magazine, each bearing the artist's own unmistakable signature (p. 27).

Since the 1950s the photograph has been the predominant form for fashion plates. Nevertheless, fashion illustration remains

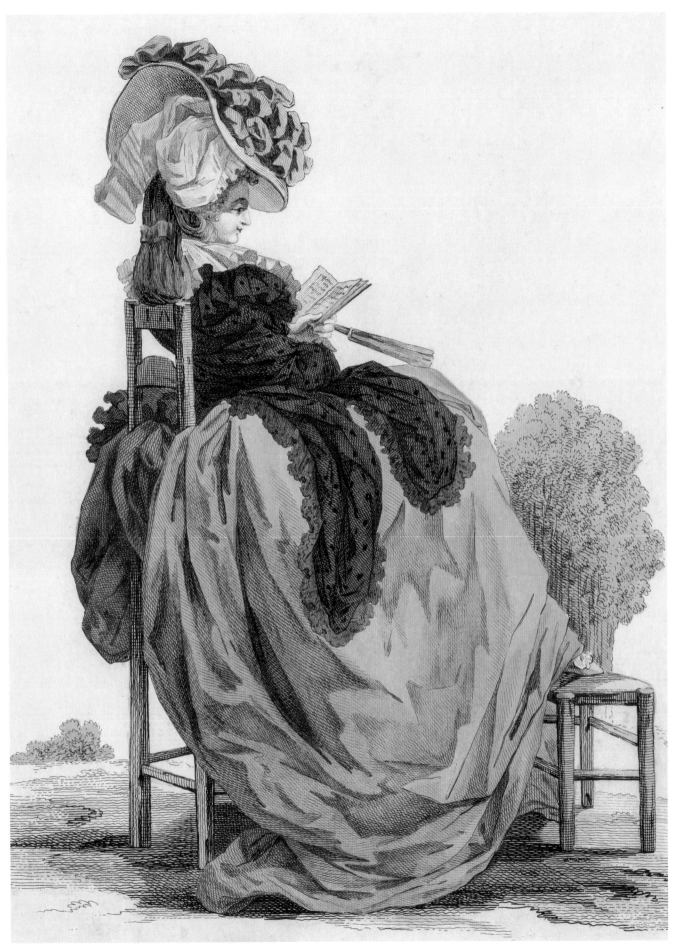

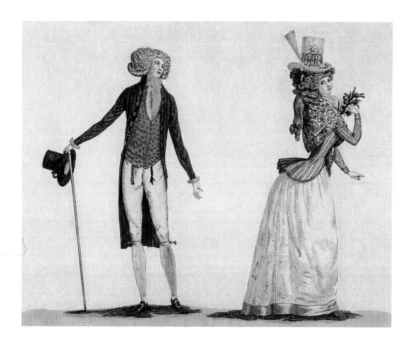

Unknown artist, 1790
Cabinet des modes

→ Jules David, 1870
Moniteur de la mode

→→ Horace Vernet, 1820
Incroyable no. 3

a dynamic means of expression embracing a whole range of artistic styles. In France, Bernard Blossac, René Bouché, and Eric (Carl Erikson) were the most frequently published illustrators, famed for their classically elegant drawings. The two most outstanding personalities in the field were undoubtedly René Gruau (p. 4) and Antonio Lopez (p. 28). Gruau acquired a good deal of his pictorial vocabulary from Henri de Toulouse-Lautrec and the school of Japonism, and in turn left his mark on succeeding generations of graphic artists. Lopez's world of "modern rococo extravagance through line, form and color"[4] was a force for the radical modernization of fashion illustration in New York and Paris from the mid 1960s onwards, and also introduced elements of Pop Art and psychedelia.

When the Paris-based magazine La Mode en Peinture (1982–1984) came on to the market the fashion world discovered a new generation of artists who, as well as engaging in their own projects and in advertising, were also involved with fashion.

As a tangible product, fashion is transient. Designed, manufactured, sold, and worn in fixed cycles, it is invariably subject to a time factor. Even so, its visual presentation as drawings, in print, as collages, paintings, photos, or movies, lends it a certain degree of longevity. Throughout the life-cycle of fashion, visual images play a crucial role. At the start of the creative process they serve as inspiration. The initial sketches record the designer's ideas. Technical drawings provide details of how the item will be produced, while in-house visuals document the finished product. Then the fashion illustration comes into play. Just like the photographer, the illustrator is the first to bring the finished garment to life, presenting the outfit in a way that emphasizes its special features, accentuates proportions and colors, analyzes the various details, and sometimes even adds something new.

As René Gruau put it so succinctly: "Drawings are as free as the imagination."[5] Unlike the photographer, the illustrator does not necessarily have to concentrate only on the model. Even when making the first sketches in the studio, during a fashion show, or working from already-published photographs, the illustrator has a whole host of possibilities. Completely independently, the illustrator can translate what can be seen into their own visual language, with new coloration, or with deliberate reductions in size. The illustrator has a free hand.

When five of Germany's best-known fashion illustrators were featured in the December 1955 edition of the magazine Kristall (1948–1966), they pinpointed the advantages of the artistic fashion plate. "It shows the broad outline of up-to-the-minute styles in exaggerated form. It gives artistic expression to the spirit of fashion. It emphasizes new lines and doesn't pay much attention to the model. Drawings of this kind help people to have a genuine understanding of fashion."[6]

The selections in this book convincingly demonstrate the sheer creative scope of fashion illustration. Many illustrators prefer particular artistic techniques—Molly Bartling favors classic drawing, Fredrik Tjernström silhouettes, Cem Bora collage, Minni Havas photographs, and José Luis Merino prints. Fashion illustrations, such as those by Jean-Philippe Delhomme, can tell stories in the same way as comic strips. They can be satyrical and entertaining. Many fashion illustrators resort to historical examples of their craft, such as Anja Kröncke with her references to Art Nouveau and Tanya Ling who borrows from the Expressionists.

In her book published in 2000, Laird Borrelli divided contemporary fashion illustrators into three categories—"sensualists," "gamines and sophisticates," and "technocrats." "Sensualists impress us" with the "delicate, supple silhouettes" of Alterio, the minimalism of Mats Gustafson, the clear woodcut contours and concept art of Berthoud (p. 2), and the unmistakable characters of Mattotti (p. 25)."[7] Ann Field is yet another illustrator who can be added to this list of Borrelli's. Artists such as Ruben Toledo, classified as being among the "gamines and sophisticates," rely on caricature and engaging exaggeration, while "technocrats," like Autumn Whitehurst, feature cyber-girls and Pop-Art figures in surreal and hyper-realistic settings.

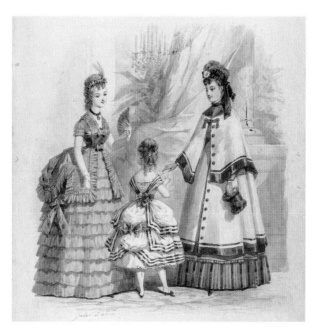
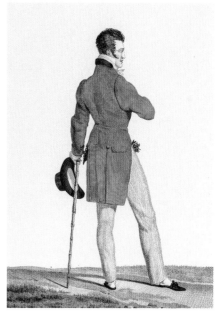

Other fashion illustrators, Sandra Suy for example, stand out for their idiosyncratic approach to the pictorial content and their psychological insight into their subjects. Recently, some illustrators, including Elisa Mazzone, have gained recognition for the ultra-realism in their work.

The following overview of contemporary, international fashion illustration impressively demonstrates the sheer vitality and scope of the genre. It can be realistic or abstract, personal or universal. It can be about product presentation or about creating a fantasy world. Fashion illustrations awaken the emotions, using a multitude of cultural references to speak to the viewer, and to relate stories about beautiful things and interesting people. Let's accept this invitation to the world of fashion!

Born in Salzburg (Austria), the art and fashion historian Adelheid Rasche has since 1990 been in charge of the Fashion Image Collection—Lipperheide Costume Library, part of the Art Library, National Museums in Berlin. She has curated numerous exhibitions, edited and written specialist books, and served on judging panels. She is an expert on fashion illustration and a consultant to the fashion industry on its historic cultural heritage.

1. As early as the second half of the 16th century, so-called "costume books" focused on the clothes worn by people of different nations and different social status. The artists who provided the pictures for these widely circulated publications concentrated far more on regional differences than on the latest fashion trends.

2. Others included Paul Gavarni, who contributed drawings to *La Mode* (1829–1862), as well as the sisters Laure Noël, Anaïs Toudouze, and Héloise Colin, who provided illustrations for *Le Follet* (1829–1892) and other publications.

3. The graphic artists Paul Iribe, Georges Lepape, Charles Martin, Georges Barbier, and André Marty, as well as Umberto Brunelleschi, Étienne Drian and Pierre Brissaud, all published illustrations using the costly pochoir process in the *Journal des Dames et des Modes* (1912–1914) and in the influential *Gazette du Bon Ton* (1912–1925).

4. See Roger and Mauricio Padilha, *Antonio Lopez – Fashion, Art, Sex & Disco.* New York 2012, p. 9.

5. René Gruau in an interview to mark his 90th birthday in *Süddeutsche Zeitung Magazin*, February 5, 1999, p. 33.

6. *Kristall*, December 1955 p. 39f. The artists featured were Antonia Hilke, Elisabeth Charlotte von der Horst, Walter Voigt, Regina May, and Gerd Hartung.

7. Ingrid Loschek in Laird Borrelli, *Illustrationen der Mode. Internationale Modezeichner und ihre Arbeiten.* Munich 2000, p. 9.

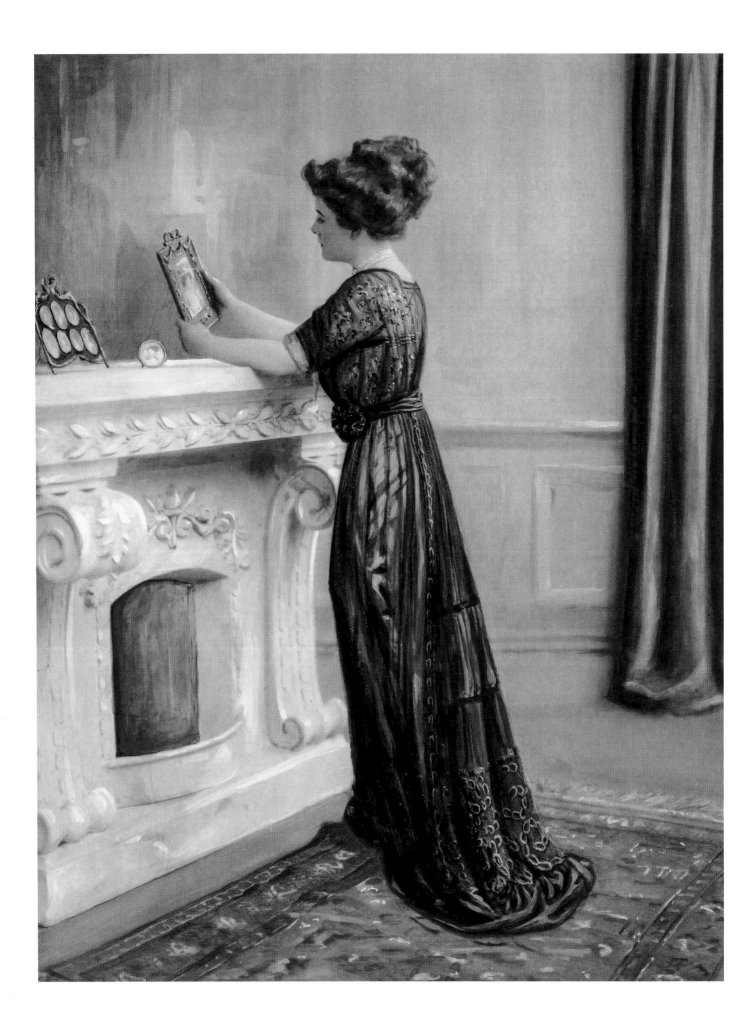

Zeitbilder des Stils

Zur Geschichte der Modeillustration

von Adelheid Rasche

Mode, verstanden als gesellschaftliches Phänomen, lebt vom Reiz des Neuen. Sie braucht das Zusammenspiel von Akteuren, Schauplätzen und Publikum, um sich zu entfalten: Trendsetter zeigen sie an gefragten Orten und werden von interessierten Betrachtern als Vorbilder wahrgenommen und imitiert.

Die internationale Verbreitung von Modetrends, wie wir sie heute kennen, tauchte erstmalig im frühen 17. Jahrhundert auf. Dank der wirtschaftlichen und kulturellen Vormachtstellung Frankreichs eiferten Adel und gehobenes Bürgertum in ganz Europa dem Vorbild des französischen Königshofs nach. Frankreichreisende berichteten von den glänzenden Seiden aus Lyon, von den feinsten Spitzen aus den nördlichen Provinzen oder von den raffinierten Schnitten der Pariser Schneider. Ein strenges Zunftwesen sowie der Merkantilismus mit Schutzmaßnahmen für die heimischen Waren brachten Frankreich in eine unangefochtene Spitzenposition in Europa, was die Luxusgüterproduktion und Mode anging.

Modische Kleidung und Accessoires, in damaliger Zeit ausschließlich handwerklich als Einzelstücke oder in geringen Mengen hergestellt, wurden an den höfischen Zentren beim Ball, im Theater, beim zeremoniellen Tafeln oder einem Spaziergang zur Schau gestellt. Wer sich nicht selbst im Modezentrum Paris aufhielt, war auf Berichte und vor allem auf Bilder angewiesen: So wurden Modegrafiken an den europäischen Höfen schnell zu heiß begehrter Ware.

Bereits in den 1620er Jahren erschienen in Paris zwei künstlerische Bildserien, die als die ersten Modeillustrationen angesehen werden können und damals weite Verbreitung fanden. Jacques Callot und Abraham Bosse stellen in diesen Radierungen bzw. Kupferstichen zeitgenössische adelige Männer und Frauen in ganzfigurigen Kompositionen vor, die sich dem Betrachter wie auf einer Bühne darbieten (S.12). Modische Kleidung, Aufputz und Gesten stehen im Mittelpunkt, die Darstellung der individuellen Persönlichkeit tritt in den Hintergrund.[1]

Während der Regierungszeit Ludwigs XIV. entstand schließlich eine große Zahl repräsentativer Kostümbilder, die die Pracht seiner Hofhaltung widerspiegeln. In diesem Zusammenhang sind besonders die Kupferstiche nach Zeichnungen von Nicolas Arnoult, Robert Bonnart und Antoine Trouvain zu nennen (S.10). Diese europaweit vertriebenen Grafiken zeigen einzelne Ganzfiguren in statischer Pose, den Hintergrund bilden Interieurs, Parkanlagen oder städtischer Raum. In diesen Bildern wird bereits deutlich, dass Modeillustrationen stets auch die Kunstströmungen ihrer Zeit reflektieren – hier sind es die ganzfigurigen Porträts von Anthonis van Dyck oder Diego Velázquez.

Ein ebenso einflussreicher Vorgänger der heutigen Modeillustration war die knapp 100 Jahre später in Paris erschienene Grafikserie *Galerie des Modes* (1778–1787). Sie stellt mit über 340 kolorierten Kupferstichen die reichhaltigste Modedokumentation des französischen Rokoko dar. Stilistisch an den Gemälden von François Boucher und Nicolas Lancret orientiert, steuerten zahlreiche bekannte Künstler wie François Watteau oder Claude-Louis Desrais variantenreiche Zeichnungen bei: raffinierte Genreszenen im Freien, statuarische Einzelfiguren in Vorder- oder Rückansicht, Detailansichten von Frisuren und Hüten sowie reizvolle Stillleben, zusammengestellt aus Modeaccessoires (S.13). Viele Kompositionsschemata der *Galerie des Modes* lassen sich in der Modeillustration unserer Zeit wiederfinden.

Die ersten Modejournale in den 1780er Jahren etablierten die Illustration als festen Bestandteil des kommerziellen Modekreislaufs. Zu dieser Zeit dominierten zwei Stilrichtungen: Neben der höfisch-luxuriösen Pariser Mode, die einerseits als raffiniert, andererseits als überladen galt, fand der aus dem englischen Bürgertum kommende Trend mit Leitbegriffen wie Natürlichkeit und Rationalismus viele Anhänger. Die Illustrationen im *Cabinet des Modes* (1785–1793) präsentieren diese beiden Moderichtungen in eleganten handkolorierten Kompositionen (S.14).

Zusätzlich befeuert durch die Umbruchszeit der Französischen Revolution setzte sich um 1800 ein radikaler Silhouettenwechsel in der Mode beider Geschlechter durch, wie etwa die halbtransparenten Chemisenkleider *à la grecque* der Damen oder hauteng

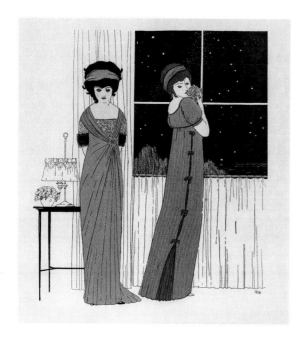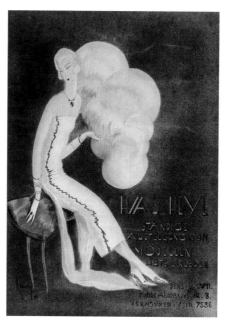

Pantalons für die jungen Gecken. Erstmals lässt sich hier eine deutliche Wechselbeziehung zwischen einem markanten Mode-umbruch und künstlerisch innovativer Modeillustration erkennen: Philibert-Louis Debucourts Grafiken *Modes et Manières du Jour* (1800) und Horace Vernets Serie *Incroyables et Merveilleuses* (1810–1818) sind Höhepunkte der französischen Modeillustration jener Zeit (S. 15). Beide Künstler verbinden in ihren Darstellungen Eleganz mit modischer Information, Lebendigkeit mit Situations-komik, Leichtigkeit mit Monumentalität. Ihre Grafiken sind heute gesuchte Sammlerstücke.

Sehr viel sachlicher arbeiteten jene Illustratoren, die für die wachsende Zahl der in den folgenden Jahren in allen europä-ischen Ländern entstehenden, teilweise über Jahrzehnte publizier-ten Modejournale tätig waren. Inspiration holten sie sich eher bei den Illustrationen der führenden Pariser Modezeitschriften als bei den Originalentwürfen. So entstand im Verlauf des 19. Jahrhunderts eine mehr oder weniger legale Praxis des Kopierens, die zum unaufhaltsamen Niedergang der künstleri-schen Modegrafik führte. Aus der Fülle der Massenproduktion ragten jedoch in Frankreich weiterhin künstlerische Talente heraus, darunter Jules David (S. 15), der über Jahrzehnte die Illustrationen des *Moniteur de la Mode* (1843–1913) lieferte.[2] Seine sorgfältigen, atmosphärisch dicht angelegten Kompositio-nen spiegeln die Schwerpunkte einer Modelinie perfekt wider und verdeutlichen die Werte der bürgerlichen Gesellschafts-kreise. Anregungen aus der zeitgenössischen Malerei – von Jean-Auguste-Dominique Ingres' Porträts über Franz Xaver Winterhalters höfische Gruppenbilder bis zu den Figurenge-mälden der Impressionisten – sind unübersehbar.

Mit der Erfindung der Fotografie und deren technischer Übertragbarkeit in den Zeitschriftendruck im ausgehenden 19. Jahrhundert entstand der kommerziellen Modeillustration eine ernstzunehmende Konkurrenz. Anfänglich bildeten sich interessante Mischformen heraus, etwa nach Fotografien gezeichnete Illustratio-nen oder farbig übermalte Aufnahmen (S. 16). Die überwiegende

Zahl der Modeillustratoren der Belle Epoque blieb jedoch den künstlerischen Gestaltungsideen des 19. Jahrhunderts treu.

Erst als der ingeniöse Pariser Couturier Paul Poiret 1908 mit dem jungen Grafiker Paul Iribe das Album *Les Robes de Paul Poiret racontées par Paul Iribe* veröffentlichte, kam die Mode-grafik schlagartig in der Moderne an (S. 18). Wie im zweiten Poiret-Album, 1911 von Georges Lepape gezeichnet (S. 19), mischte Iribe Stile auf raffinierte und vielschichtige Weise. Beide Künstler griffen auf Elemente des Klassizismus und Empire zurück, ließen sich vom Orientalismus und den damals in Paris umjubelten Ballets Russes inspirieren und integrierten Stilideale der Arts-and-Crafts-Bewegung sowie der hochstehenden englischen Kinderbuchillustration.

Der enorme Erfolg der beiden Poiret-Alben bescherte der jungen Grafikergeneration volle Auftragsbücher. Die Illustrationen von André Marty und Georges Barbier für das alljährlich in Paris veröffentlichte Album *Modes et Manières du Jour* (1912–1921) zählen bis heute zu den Höhepunkten der künstlerischen Modegrafik (S. 20 & 21).[3] Auf vergleichbarem Niveau sind die Werke der deutschen Grafiker dieser Dekaden, die in Berlin ein reiches Modeangebot vorfanden und für die führenden Modejournale wie *Die Dame* (1912–1942), *Der Kleiderkasten* (1915), *Styl* (1922–1924) oder *Die deutsche Elite* (1924–1930) tätig waren. So nutzten etwa die Künstlerinnen Lotte Wernekink (S. 24) und Julie Haase-Werkenthin (S. 22) expressionistische Bildideen, sie griffen Anregungen des Japonismus auf und orientierten sich an der Filmästhetik der 1920er Jahre.

Auf internationaler Ebene wirkte sich die Konkurrenz der amerikanischen Journale *Harper's Bazaar* (seit 1867) und *Vogue* (seit 1892) positiv auf die künstlerische Bildqualität aus. Für *Harper's Bazaar* war der vielseitige Erté mehr als 20 Jahre als ideenreicher Illustrator im Einsatz (S. 26). *Vogue* beschäftigte zahlreiche großartige Modeillustratoren wie Georges Lepape, Eduardo García Benito oder Christian Bérard: Ihre stimmungs-vollen, prägnanten Zeichnungen erschienen als Cover oder

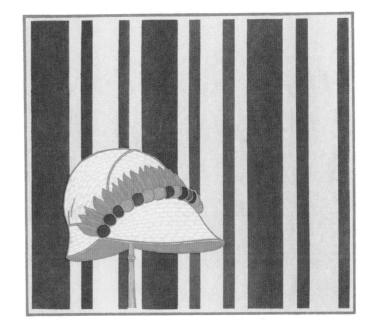

Georges Lepape, 1911
Les Robes de Paul Poiret

← Kenan, 1925
Otto Haas-Heye

←← Paul Iribe, 1908
Les Robes de Paul Poiret

p.16 Studio Reutlinger,
Paris, c. 1910
Dame im Abendkleid

als Bildstrecken im Heft, jede mit unverkennbar persönlicher Handschrift (S. 27).

Seit den 1950er Jahren ist das Modebild insgesamt vom Primat der Fotografie bestimmt, dennoch blieb die Illustration ein lebendiges Ausdrucksmittel in vielfältiger künstlerischer Stilistik. In Frankreich zählten Bernard Blossac, René Bouché und Eric (Carl Erikson) zu den elegant-klassischen und am häufigsten veröffentlichten Zeichnern. Die beiden herausragenden Persönlichkeiten waren zweifelsohne René Gruau (S. 4) und Antonio Lopez (S. 28). Gruau prägte mit seiner am Japonismus und an Henri de Toulouse-Lautrec geschulten Bildsprache ganze Generationen von nachfolgenden Grafikern. Die „in Linie, Form und Farbe moderne Rokoko-Extravaganz"[4] von Lopez modernisierte die Modegrafik in New York und Paris ab Mitte der 1960er Jahre radikal und brachte Elemente der Pop-Art und psychedelischen Kunst mit ein.

Als 1982 das Pariser Magazin *La Mode en Peinture* (1982–1984) auf den Markt kam, entdeckte die Modewelt eine weitere Generation von Künstlern, die sich neben freien Arbeiten und Werbegrafik auch mit Mode beschäftigten.

Mode als materielles Produkt ist vergänglich. In festen Zyklen gestaltet, produziert, verkauft und getragen, ist sie unveränderlich an den Faktor Zeit gebunden. Erst die bildliche Darstellung in Zeichnungen, Drucken, Collagen, Gemälden, Fotografien oder Film verleiht ihr eine gewisse Dauerhaftigkeit. Im gesamten Lebenszyklus der Mode spielen Bilder eine fundamentale Rolle: Am Beginn der kreativen Arbeit dienen sie der Inspiration, in ersten Skizzen hält der Modeschöpfer Ideen fest, technische Zeichnungen vermitteln die Details der Fertigung, interne Kollektionsbilder dokumentieren die fertigen Modelle. Erst dann kommt die Modeillustration ins Spiel: Der Illustrator ist – ähnlich dem Fotografen – der erste Interpret des fertigen Kleidungsstücks. Er setzt es für seine Bildidee in Szene, betont die Besonderheiten, akzentuiert Proportionen und Farben, verändert Details und ergänzt bisweilen Neues.

„Zeichnungen sind frei wie die Phantasie", formulierte es René Gruau treffend.[5] Der Modeillustrator ist – anders als der Fotograf – nicht zwingend an das Modell gebunden. Auch wenn erste Skizzen im Modeatelier, während einer Modenschau oder auf der Basis von veröffentlichten Fotografien gezeichnet werden, stehen dem Illustrator alle Möglichkeiten der Interpretation offen. Die Umsetzung des Gesehenen in die eigene Bildsprache, mit neuer Farbgebung und in gewollter Reduktion, realisiert der Illustrator oft ganz unabhängig.

Als im Dezember 1955 in der illustrierten Zeitschrift *Kristall* (1948–1966) fünf der damals bekanntesten deutschen Modegrafiker vorgestellt wurden, erklärte man die Vorzüge der künstlerischen Modegrafik so: „Sie zeigt neue modische Umrisse in übersteigerter Form. Sie drückt künstlerisch die Idee, den Geist der Mode aus. Sie hebt die neue Linie hervor; die Einzelheiten des Modells treten zurück. An einer solchen Zeichnung lernt man, den modischen Stil zu begreifen."[6]

Wie groß die kreative Bandbreite der Modegrafik ist, zeigt überzeugend die Auswahl dieses Buches. Manche Illustratoren bevorzugen bestimmte künstlerische Techniken: Molly Bartling die klassische Zeichnung, Fredrik Tjernström die Silhouettenkunst, Cem Bora die Collage, Minni Havas die Fotografie oder José Luis Merino die Druckgrafik. Modeillustrationen können erzählerische Komponenten enthalten, die sie mit dem Comic und der Bildgeschichte teilen, etwa jene von Jean-Philippe Delhomme. Sie können satirisch und humorvoll auftreten. Manche Modeillustratoren greifen historische Vorbilder auf, etwa Anja Kröncke mit Rückbezügen auf den Jugendstil oder Tanya Ling mit expressionistischen Anleihen.

Laird Borrelli hat in ihrem im Jahr 2000 erschienenen Buch zu zeitgenössischen Modezeichnern drei Stilrichtungen definiert: „Sensualisten", „Freche Gören" und „Technokraten". In der Gruppe der „Sensualisten" ist man beeindruckt von „den weichen, geschmeidigen Silhouetten und Bewegungen bei Alterio, dem Minimalismus eines Mats Gustafson, von den klaren Holzschnittkonturen

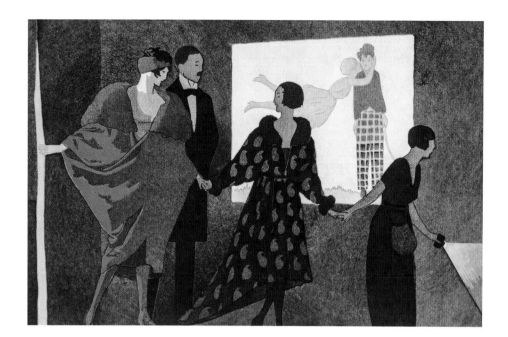

André Marty, 1919
Le Ciné

→ Georges Barbier, 1914
L'Oiseau volage

bis zur ‚concept art' eines Berthoud (S. 2) und den unverkenn-
baren Charakteren von Mattotti (S. 25).“[7] In der vorliegenden
Auswahl lassen sich unter anderem die Illustrationen von Ann
Field dieser Richtung zuordnen. Die Künstler der Stilrichtung
der „Frechen Gören“ nutzen den Stilisierungseffekt der karikatur-
artigen, charmanten Überzeichnung, wie es zum Beispiel bei
Ruben Toledo der Fall ist. Die „Technokraten“ schaffen Cyber-
Girls und Pop-Art-Figuren, sie bieten surreale und hyperrealistische
Kompositionen wie beispielsweise Autumn Whitehurst.

Weitere stilistische Tendenzen der Modeillustration sind in
der Individualisierung und Psychologisierung der Bildinhalte zu
finden, zu sehen etwa bei Sandra Suy. Festzustellen ist in jüngerer
Zeit auch ein erstarktes Interesse an der realistischen Figuren-
zeichnung, wie etwa am Beispiel von Elisa Mazzone erkennbar.

Das nachfolgende Panorama zeitgenössischer internationaler
Modeillustrationen zeigt eindrucksvoll die Lebendigkeit und
Breite des Genres. Der Horizont reicht von Realismus bis Abstraktion, vom Individuellen zum Globalen, von der Produktinszenie-
rung bis zur Fantasiewelt. Modeillustrationen wecken Emotionen,
sie sprechen den Betrachter mit vielschichtigen kulturellen
Bezügen an und erzählen ihm Geschichten von schönen Dingen
und interessanten Menschen. Folgen wir dieser Einladung in
die Welt der Mode!

Die Kunst- und Modehistorikerin Dr. Adelheid Rasche,
geboren in Salzburg (Österreich), leitet seit 1990 die Sammlung
Modebild – Lipperheidesche Kostümbibliothek (Kunstbibliothek,
Staatliche Museen zu Berlin). Sie ist Kuratorin zahlreicher
Ausstellungen, Herausgeberin und Autorin von Fachbüchern,
Mitglied in Fachjurys, Expertin für Modebilder und Beraterin
für historisches Kulturerbe im Modesektor.

1. Bereits in der zweiten Hälfte des 16. Jahrhundert war in den sogenannten
„Trachtenbüchern“ der Fokus auf die Kleidung aller Nationen und Stände
gerichtet worden. In diesen weit verbreiteten Grafikfolgen stand allerdings
die Aktualität der Kleidung an zweiter Stelle, vielmehr konzentrierten sich
die Zeichner auf die regionalen Unterschiede.
2. Weiterhin zu nennen sind Paul Gavarni, der für *La Mode* (1829–1862)
zeichnete, sowie die Schwestern Laure Noël, Anaïs Toudouze und
Héloïse Colin, die zahlreiche Illustrationen für *Le Follet* (1829–1892) und
andere Journale entwarfen.
3. Die Grafiker Paul Iribe, Georges Lepape, Charles Martin, Georges Barbier,
André Marty sowie Umberto Brunelleschi, Étienne Drian und Pierre Brissaud
veröffentlichten ihre Illustrationen in kostspieligem Pochoirdruck auch im
Journal des Dames et des Modes (1912–1914) und in der einflussreichen *Gazette
du Bon Ton* (1912–1925).
4. „[...] modern rococo extravagance through line, form and color“ in: Roger u.
Mauricio Padilha: *Antonio Lopez – Fashion, Art, Sex & Disco*. New York 2012, S. 9.
5. René Gruau in einem Interview zu seinem 90. Geburtstag, in: *Süddeutsche
Zeitung Magazin*, 5.2.1999, S. 33.
6. Kristall, Dezember 1955, S. 39f. Vorgestellt wurden Antonia Hilke, Elisabeth
Charlotte von der Horst, Walter Voigt, Regina May und Gerd Hartung.
7. Ingrid Loschek: Essay. In: *Laird Borrelli: Illustrationen der Mode. Internationale
Modezeichner und ihre Arbeiten*. München 2000, S. 9.

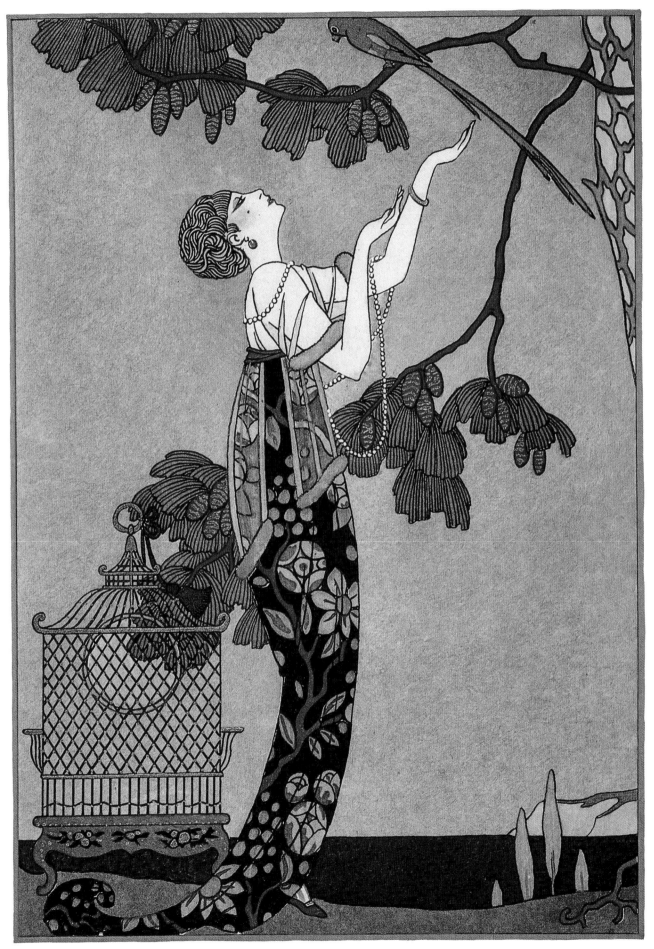

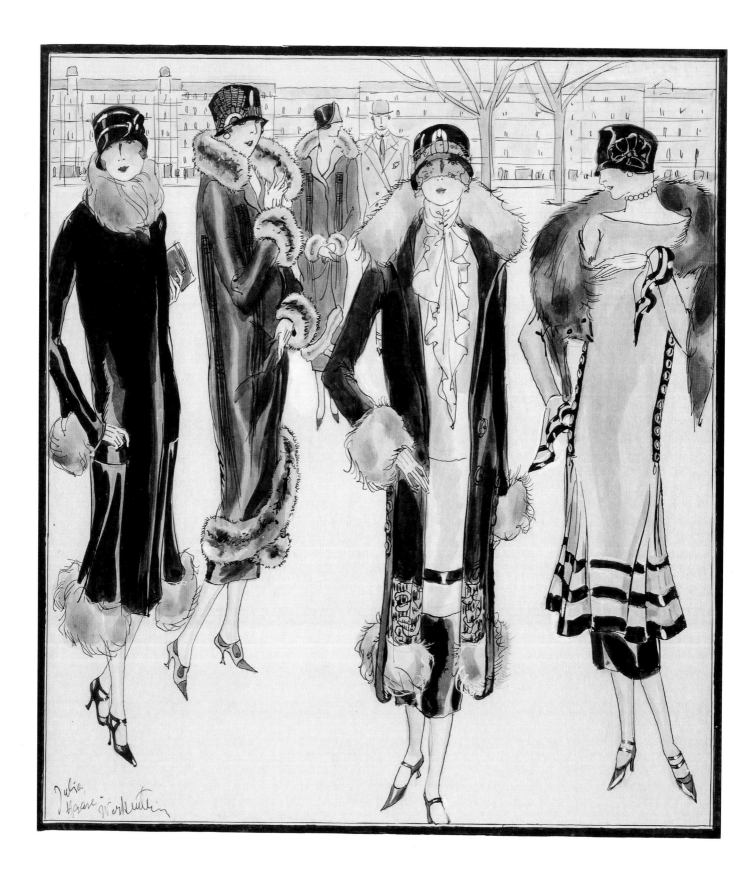

Julie Haase-Werkenthin, 1924
Frauen in Mänteln

Images de style

Une histoire de l'illustration de mode

par Adelheid Rasche

La mode, comprise comme un phénomène social, se nourrit de notre fascination pour la nouveauté. Elle est le fruit d'une relation interactive entre des acteurs, une scène et un public. Les faiseurs de tendances s'affichent avec leurs nouvelles tenues dans des endroits en vue, où les observateurs intéressés les prennent comme modèles.

Ce n'est qu'au début du XVIIe siècle que les tendances de la mode commencèrent à se répandre à l'échelle internationale. À cause de la suprématie commerciale et culturelle de la France, la noblesse et les classes moyenne de toute l'Europe essayaient de suivre le rythme de la cour royale française. Ceux qui avaient visité la France parlaient des soies chatoyantes de Lyon, de la dentelle délicate des provinces du nord, et des coupes élégantes des tailleurs et modistes de Paris. Des corporations bien organisées et un système commercial qui assurait une protection spéciale aux biens fabriqués sur son territoire placèrent la France en tête de l'Europe dans la production de biens de luxe, ainsi que dans le secteur de la mode.

Banquets, bals, sorties au théâtre ou même promenades étaient autant d'occasions pour ceux qui fréquentaient la cour de faire étalage de leurs tenues et accessoires à la dernière mode. À l'époque, tout cela était fait exclusivement à la main, en exemplaires uniques ou en très petites séries. Ceux qui ne pouvaient se rendre à Paris, le centre du monde de la mode, devaient pour s'informer compter sur les nouvelles rapportées par d'autres, mais surtout sur les images. Les illustrations de mode devinrent donc rapidement très recherchées dans toutes les cours d'Europe.

Dans les années 1620, deux séries d'images artistiques apparurent à Paris, que l'on peut considérer comme les premières illustrations de mode. Ces gravures à l'eau-forte et sur cuivre de Jacques Callot et Abraham Bosse connurent une grande diffusion (p. 12). On pouvait y voir des portraits en pied d'hommes et femmes de la noblesse qui semblaient se tenir sur une scène. L'attention se concentrait sur leurs atours et leur posture, et toute représentation d'eux-mêmes en tant qu'individus était purement secondaire[1].

Pendant le règne de Louis XIV apparurent de nombreuses gravures de personnages distingués portant des costumes somptueux et reflétant le prestige de la cour royale. Il y avait parmi elles des gravures basées sur des dessins de Nicolas Arnoult, Robert Bonnart et Antoine Trouvain qui devinrent célèbres dans toute l'Europe (p. 10). Elles représentent des personnages en pied dans une pose statique, avec des arrière-plans d'intérieurs, de parcs ou de paysages urbains. De ces images, il ressort clairement que les illustrations de mode ont toujours reflété les tendances contemporaines de l'art – il suffit de penser aux portraits en pied d'Antoine van Dyck ou de Diego Velázquez.

Autre ancêtre direct et influent des illustrations de mode actuelles, la série intitulée *Galerie des Modes* (1778–1787), publiée à Paris à peine un siècle plus tard. Avec plus de 340 gravures colorées à la main, c'est le document de mode le plus important sur l'époque rococo française. D'un style qui évoque les tableaux de François Boucher et Nicolas Lancret, cette série a bénéficié des contributions distinguées et très variées d'artistes de l'envergure de François Watteau et de Claude-Louis Desrais (p. 13). Elle comprend des scènes de genre en plein air à la composition élégante, des personnages isolés sculpturaux vus de devant ou de derrière, des études finement détaillées de chapeaux ou de coiffures, ainsi que de charmantes natures mortes d'accessoires de mode. Nombre des compositions de la *Galerie des Modes* trouvent encore un écho dans les illustrations de mode du XXIe siècle.

Dans les années 1780, les premiers magazines de mode firent de l'illustration une facette incontournable du métier de la mode. À cette époque, deux styles prédominaient. Parallèlement au luxe de la mode de cour parisienne, que certains considéraient comme raffinée, mais d'autres comme surchargée, les goûts simples et rationnels de la bourgeoisie britannique étaient un modèle que beaucoup préféraient suivre. Les deux styles sont représentés dans des dessins élégants colorés à la main dans le *Cabinet des Modes* (1785–1793) (p. 14).

Autour de 1800, les bouleversements de la Révolution française provoquèrent une transformation radicale des silhouettes, aussi bien chez les femmes que chez les hommes, par exemple avec des

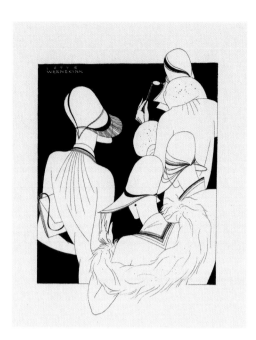

Lotte Wernekink, c. 1928
Frauen mit Hutmodellen

→ Lorenzo Mattotti, 1986
Issey Miyake

robes-chemises semi-transparentes de style grec pour les femmes, et des pantalons moulants pour les jeunes dandys. Nous voyons ici pour la première fois une nette corrélation entre changement notable dans la mode et innovation dans l'art de l'illustrateur de mode : les dessins de Philibert-Louis Debucourt dans *Modes et Manières du Jour* (1798–1808) et la série *Incroyables et Merveilleuses* (1810–1818) d'Horace Vernet peuvent être considérés comme des sommets de l'illustration de mode française de l'époque (p. 15). Dans leur travail, les deux artistes mêlent élégance et information, vivacité et comique de situation, légèreté et monumentalité. Leurs gravures sont aujourd'hui des pièces de collection très recherchées.

Les illustrateurs du nombre croissant de magazines de mode qui apparurent à travers l'Europe au cours des années suivantes, et dont certains survécurent pendant des décennies, travaillèrent avec beaucoup plus de simplicité. Leurs illustrations s'inspiraient plus des grandes revues de mode parisiennes que des vêtements originaux. Si la pratique plus ou moins légale de la copie mena irrésistiblement au déclin de l'illustration de mode véritablement artistique, le travail de certains illustrateurs français talentueux réussit néanmoins à se démarquer de l'abondance d'images produites en masse. Il y avait parmi eux Jules David (p. 15), qui fournit des illustrations au *Moniteur de la Mode* (1843–1913) pendant des décennies[2]. Ses planches minutieuses, évocatrices et denses en détails représentaient parfaitement les tendances, et reflétaient les valeurs de la bourgeoisie. Les références à l'art contemporain – des portraits de Jean-Auguste-Dominique Ingres jusqu'aux portraits en pied des impressionnistes, en passant par les tableaux de groupe des maisons royales européennes de Franz Xaver Winterhalter – sont évidentes.

Avec la photographie, et son intégration technique à l'imprimerie à la fin du XIXᵉ siècle, l'illustration de mode vit arriver une concurrence sérieuse. Tout d'abord, d'intéressants métissages apparurent, par exemple, des illustrations dessinées d'après photographie, ou bien des photographies retouchées à la peinture (p. 16). La majorité des illustrations de mode de la Belle Époque restèrent cependant fidèles aux concepts artistiques du XIXᵉ siècle.

Ce n'est qu'en 1908, lorsque l'ingénieux couturier parisien Paul Poiret collabora avec le jeune artiste Paul Iribe pour publier l'album *Les Robes de Paul Poiret racontées par Paul Iribe*, que l'illustration de mode entra soudainement dans l'âge moderne (p. 18). Comme cela allait être le cas dans le deuxième album de Poiret, publié en 1911 avec des dessins de Georges Lepape (p. 19), Iribe mélangea les styles avec un grand raffinement. Les deux artistes empruntèrent des éléments du répertoire classique et de l'Empire, et s'inspirèrent également de l'orientalisme et des Ballets Russes, qui à l'époque avaient pris Paris d'assaut. Dans le même temps, ils assimilèrent certaines idées du mouvement Arts and Crafts ainsi que de l'excellente illustration de livres pour enfants britannique.

L'énorme succès des deux albums de Poiret assura à la génération de dessinateurs suivante des carnets de commandes bien remplis. Les illustrations d'André Marty et Georges Barbier pour l'album parisien annuel *Modes et Manières du Jour* (1912–1921) figurent aujourd'hui encore parmi les meilleurs exemples de l'illustration de mode artistique (p. 20 et 21)[3]. Le travail des illustrateurs allemands de cette décennie était du même niveau. Berlin possédait une industrie de la mode florissante et leur offrait du travail dans de grands magazines de mode tels que *Die Dame* (1912–1942), *Der Kleiderkasten* (1915), *Styl* (1922–1924) ou *Die deutsche Elite* (1924–1930). Les illustratrices Lotte Wernekink (p. 24) et Julie Haase-Werkenthin (p. 22) reprirent des idées graphiques du mouvement expressionniste, s'inspirèrent du japonisme et de l'esthétique du cinéma des années 1920.

La concurrence internationale de magazines américains tels que *Harper's Bazaar*, né en 1867, et de *Vogue*, en 1892, eut un effet positif sur l'illustration de mode. Jamais à court de nouvelles idées, Erté prêta ses multiples talents à *Harper's Bazaar* pendant plus de 20 ans (p. 26). *Vogue* fournit du travail à de nombreux grands illustrateurs de mode tels que Georges Lepape, Eduardo García Benito et Christian Bérard, dont les dessins incisifs et évocateurs apparaissaient sur la couverture ou sous forme de séries de dessins dans les pages intérieures (p. 27), chacun portant la signature inimitable de l'artiste.

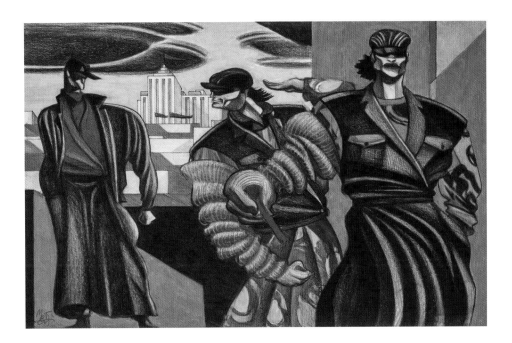

Depuis les années 1950, c'est la photographie qui a été le format prédominant pour illustrer la mode. Pourtant, l'illustration reste un moyen d'expression dynamique qui englobe un vaste éventail de styles artistiques. En France, Bernard Blossac, René Bouché et Eric (Carl Erikson) ont été les illustrateurs les plus fréquemment publiés, renommés pour l'élégance classique de leurs dessins. Les deux personnalités les plus remarquables dans ce domaine ont sans aucun doute été René Gruau (p. 4) et Antonio Lopez (p. 28). Le vocabulaire visuel de Gruau venait en grande partie d'Henri de Toulouse-Lautrec et de l'école du japonisme, et marqua profondément les générations suivantes d'artistes graphiques. «L'extravagance rococo moderne à travers la ligne, la forme et la couleur[4]» de Lopez mena à une modernisation radicale de l'illustration de mode à New York et Paris à partir du milieu des années 1960, et introduisit des éléments du Pop Art et de l'art psychédélique.

Lorsque le magazine parisien *La Mode en Peinture* (1982–1984) arriva sur le marché, le monde de la mode découvrit une nouvelle génération d'artistes qui, en plus de leurs projets personnels et de leur travail dans la publicité, étaient également actifs dans la mode.

En tant que produit matériel, la mode est éphémère. Dessinée, fabriquée, vendue et portée selon des cycles déterminés, elle est invariablement assujettie à un facteur temps. Ses représentations visuelles dans les dessins, gravures, collages, tableaux, photographies ou films lui donnent cependant une certaine mesure de longévité. Les images jouent un rôle fondamental tout au long du cycle de vie de la mode. Elles servent d'inspiration au début du processus créatif. Les premiers croquis fixent les idées du créateur. Les dessins techniques donnent des détails sur la production, tandis que les images internes documentent les produits finis. C'est alors que l'illustration de mode entre en jeu. Tout comme le photographe, l'illustrateur est le premier interprète du vêtement réalisé. Il met la tenue en scène dans son image, met en valeur ses particularités, accentue les proportions et les couleurs, analyse les différents détails, et parfois ajoute même quelque chose de nouveau.

«Les dessins sont aussi libres que l'imagination[5]» résuma un jour René Gruau. Contrairement au photographe, l'illustrateur ne doit pas nécessairement se concentrer uniquement sur le modèle. Même lorsqu'il travaille aux premiers croquis dans le studio, lors d'un défilé, ou à partir de photographies déjà publiées, l'illustrateur dispose d'une multitude de possibilités. Il peut traduire en toute indépendance ce qui est donné à voir dans son propre langage visuel. Il est libre de donner une nouvelle coloration, et de pratiquer une simplification délibérée.

Le numéro de décembre 1955 du magazine *Kristall* (1948–1966) présenta cinq des illustrateurs de mode les plus renommés d'Allemagne à l'époque, et résuma les avantages de l'illustration de mode artistique en ces termes: «Elle présente les grands traits des styles les plus récents sous une forme exagérée. Elle donne une expression artistique aux idées et à l'esprit de la mode. Elle met en valeur les nouvelles lignes et fait passer les particularités du modèle au second plan. Ce type de dessins aide les gens à comprendre la mode[6].»

La sélection présentée dans ce livre montre sans équivoque à quel point l'éventail créatif de l'illustration de mode est vaste. De nombreux illustrateurs ont leurs techniques artistiques de prédilection – Molly Bartling préfère le dessin classique, Fredrik Tjernström aime les silhouettes, Cem Bora le collage, Minni Havas la photographie, et José Luis Merino les gravures. Les illustrations de mode telles que celles de Jean-Philippe Delhomme peuvent raconter des histoires à la manière des bandes dessinées. Elles peuvent être satyriques et drôles. De nombreux illustrateurs de mode ont recours à des exemples historiques, comme Anja Kröncke et ses références à l'Art nouveau, ou Tanya Ling qui emprunte aux expressionnistes.

Dans son ouvrage publié en 2001, Laird Borrelli divise les illustrateurs de mode contemporains en trois catégories – les «sensualistes», les «gamins impertinents» et les «technocrates». «Les sensualistes nous impressionnent» avec les «silhouettes souples et délicates d'Alterio, le minimalisme de Mats Gustafson,

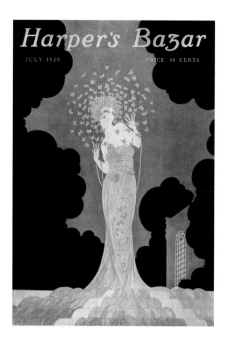

Erté, 1920
Harper's Bazaar, cover July, 1920

→   Eduardo García Benito, 1928
Vogue US, cover July 1, 1928,
Woman in print dress with shades

les contours nets de gravure sur bois et l'art conceptuel de Berthoud (p. 2), et les personnages inimitables de Mattotti (p. 25) [7] ». Ann Field est un autre nom que l'on peut ajouter à cette liste dressée par Borrelli. Les artistes classés sous la rubrique des gamins impertinents, comme Ruben Toledo, ont recours à la caricature et à l'exagération, tandis que les technocrates comme Autumn Whitehurst créent des cyber-girls et des personnages pop art dans des décors surréels et hyperréalistes.

On trouve aussi d'autres tendances de l'illustration de mode dans l'individualisation et la psychologisation du contenu visuel, notamment chez Sandra Suy. Récemment, certains illustrateurs, par exemple Elisa Mazzone, se sont fait remarquer par l'hyperréalisme de leur travail.

La vue d'ensemble de l'illustration de mode contemporaine internationale réunie dans ces pages démontre magistralement la vitalité et la diversité de ce genre. Il peut être réaliste ou abstrait, personnel ou universel. Sa finalité peut être de mettre en scène un produit, ou de créer un monde imaginaire. Les illustrations de mode éveillent les émotions, parlent à leur public à l'aide d'une multitude de références culturelles et lui racontent des histoires peuplées de belles choses et de personnages fascinants. Acceptons donc cette invitation dans le monde de la mode !

Née à Salzbourg (Autriche), Adelheid Rasche est historienne de l'art et de la mode. Depuis 1990, elle est conservateur en chef de la collection d'images de mode de la bibliothèque de costumes de Lipperheide, Musées Nationaux de Berlin. Elle a organisé de nombreuses expositions, a dirigé et rédigé de nombreux ouvrages spécialisés, et a fait partie de différents jurys. Elle est experte en illustration de mode, et consultante pour les entreprises du secteur de la mode concernant leur héritage culturel.

1. Dès la deuxième moitié du XVIᵉ siècle, des « livres de costumes » présentaient les vêtements portés dans tous les pays et pour les différents statuts sociaux. Ces publications très populaires s'intéressaient cependant bien davantage aux différences régionales qu'aux dernières tendances de la mode.
2. On peut également citer Paul Gavarni, qui dessina pour *La Mode* (1829–1862), ainsi que les sœurs Laure Noël, Anaïs Toudouze et Héloïse Colin, qui fournirent des illustrations pour *Le Follet* (1829–1892) et d'autres publications.
3. Les artistes Paul Iribe, Georges Lepape, Charles Martin, Georges Barbier et André Marty, ainsi que Umberto Brunelleschi, Étienne Drian et Pierre Brissaud ont tous publié leurs illustrations à l'aide du coûteux procédé d'impression au pochoir dans le *Journal des Dames et des Modes* (1912–1914) et dans l'influente *Gazette du Bon Ton* (1912–1925).
4. Voir Roger et Mauricio Padilha, *Antonio Lopez – Fashion, Art, Sex & Disco*. New York 2012, p. 9.
5. René Gruau dans un entretien marquant son 90ᵉ anniversaire dans le *Süddeutsche Zeitung Magazin*, 5 février 1999, p. 33.
6. *Kristall*, décembre 1955 p. 39f. Les artistes présentés étaient Antonia Hilke, Elisabeth Charlotte von der Horst, Walter Voigt, Regina May et Gerd Hartung.
7. Ingrid Loschek dans Laird Borrelli, *Illustrationen der Mode. Internationale Modezeichner und ihre Arbeiten*. Munich 2000, p. 9.

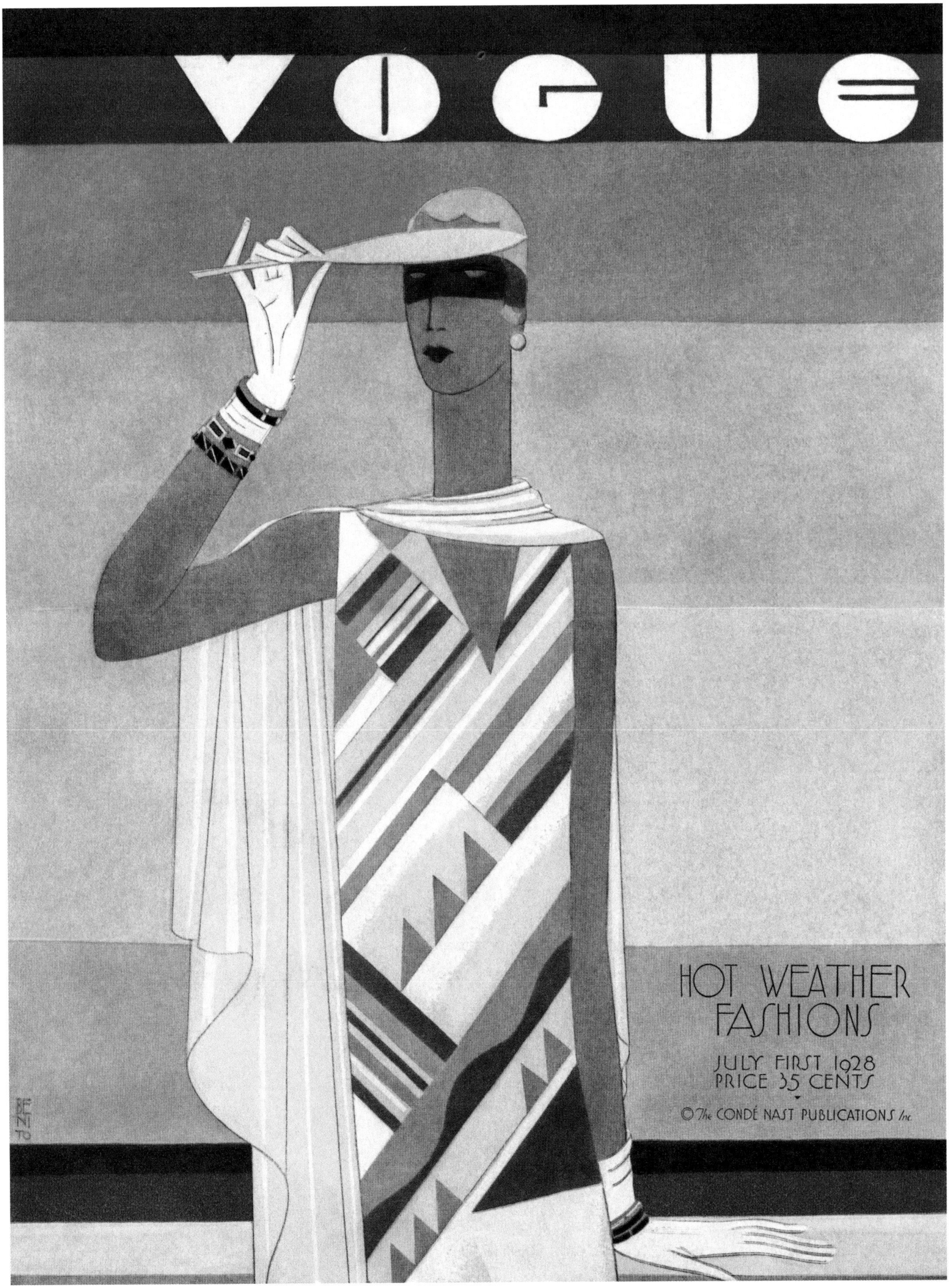

VOGUE

HOT WEATHER
FASHIONS

JULY FIRST 1928
PRICE 35 CENTS

© The CONDÉ NAST PUBLICATIONS Inc.

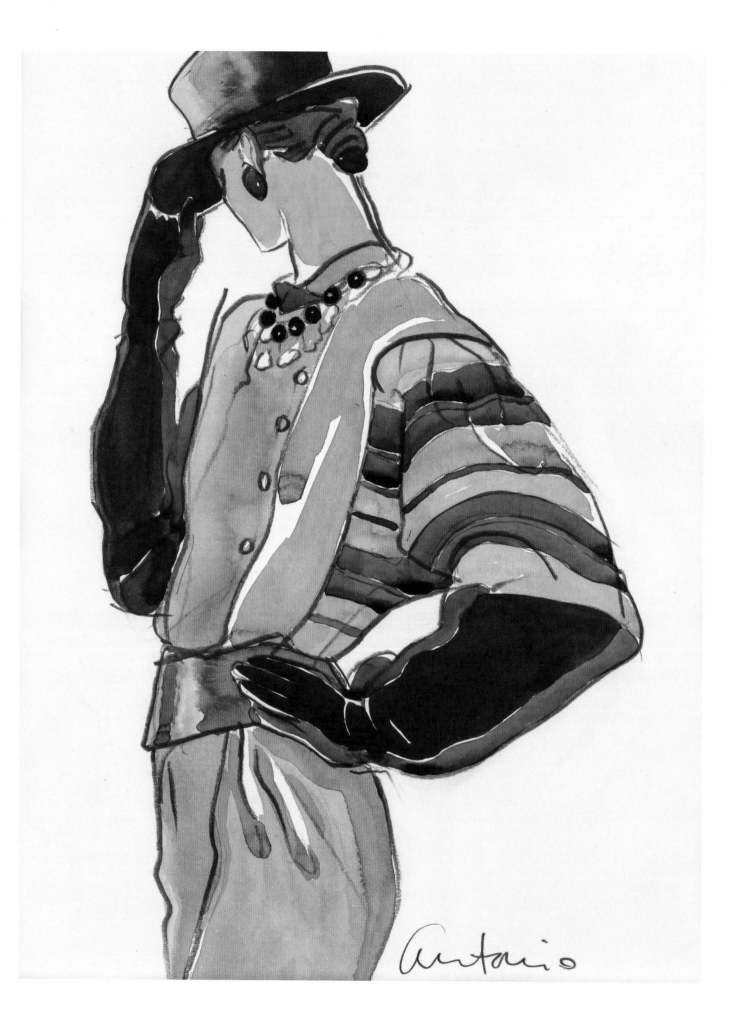

Fashion
ILLUSTRATORS
from A to Z

Henrik Abrahams

1972 born in Hanover | lives and works in Berlin
www.henrikabrahams.com

CLIENTS
Vogue, Tush magazine,
FHM Collections, Indie, Petra,
Berlin Fashion Week Photodiary

AGENT
V.O Valérie Oualid
France
valerieoualid.com

"Elegance and beauty are important and arise from a contemporary use of traditional techniques. 'Classic' is a big idea and my chief point of reference."

„Eleganz und Schönheit sind wichtig, sie entstehen durch zeitgemäßen Einsatz traditioneller Techniken. ,Klassik' ist als großes Konzept mein wesentlicher Referenzpunkt."

« L'élégance et la beauté sont importantes, et résultent d'une utilisation moderne de techniques traditionnelles. Ma référence est ‹ le classique ›.»

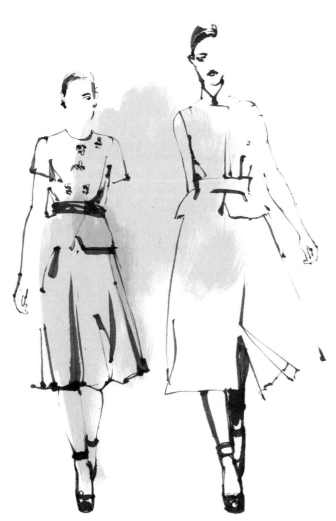

Dress #2, 2012
Personal work, interpretation of
Dior dresses Fall/Winter 2012–13;
ink and gouache

→   **Dress #1, 2012**
Personal work, interpretation of Dior
dress Fall/Winter 2012–13; silkscreen

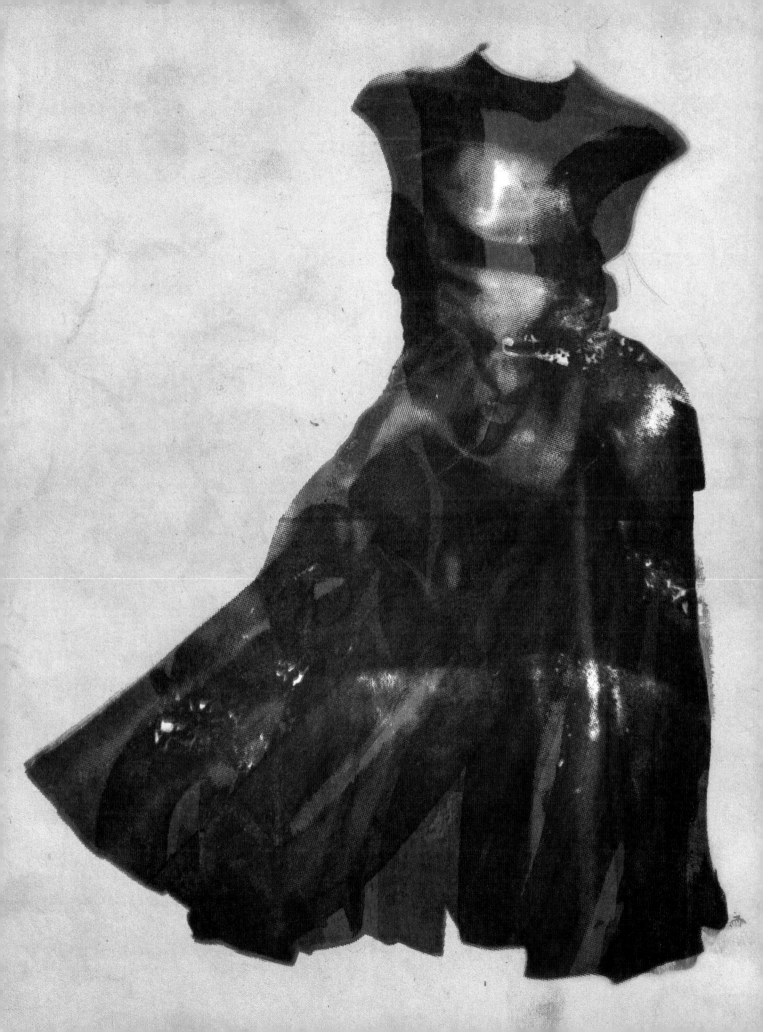

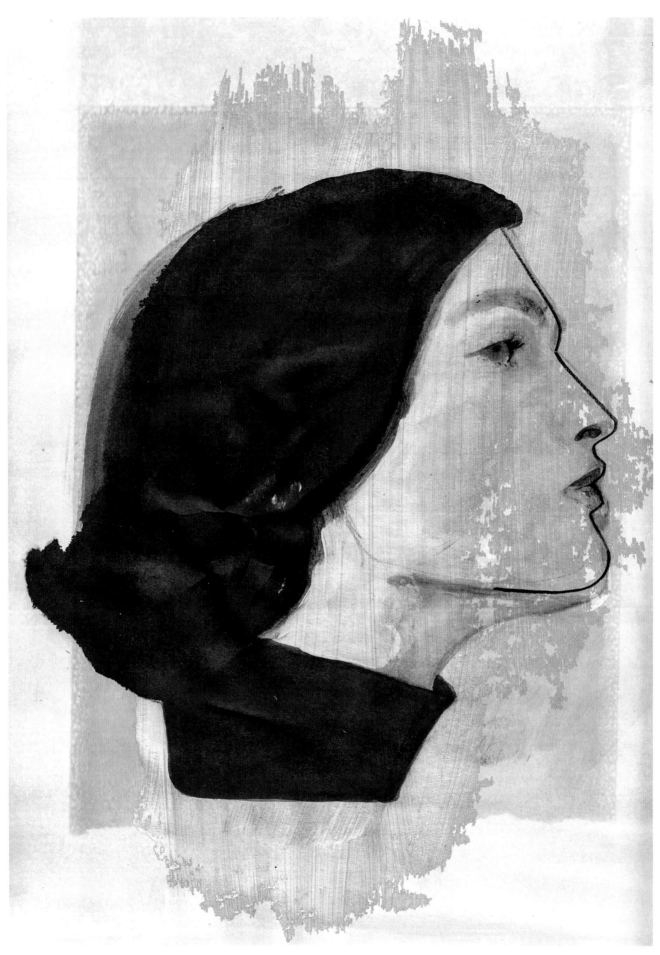

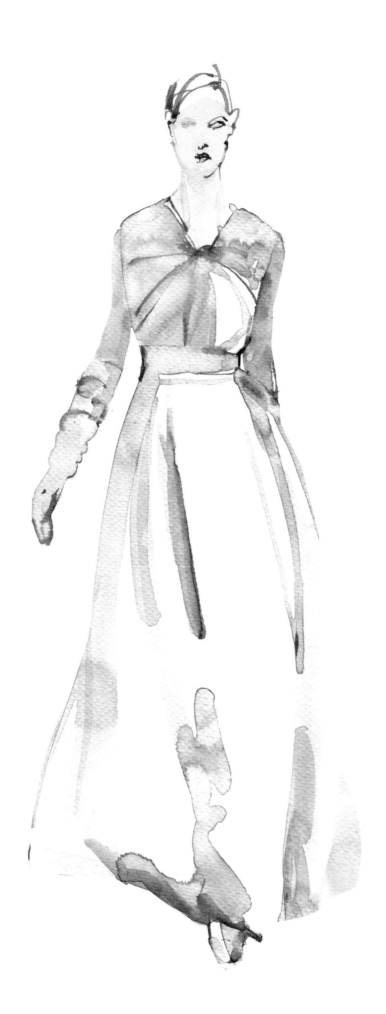

Dress #3, 2012
Personal work, interpretation of
Dior dress Fall/Winter 2012–13;
ink and gouache

← **Untitled, 2012**
Personal work; ink, gouache,
silkscreen and crayon

Lele Acquarone

1939 born in Turin | lives and works in Milan

CLIENTS
Vogue Italy, Vogue Germany,
Interview magazine

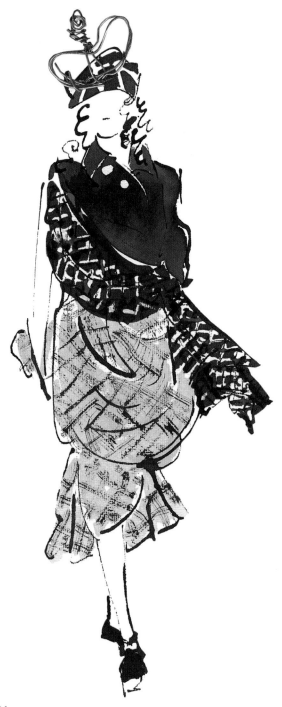

"As a traveler in Fashionland I have always found much to impress and amuse me. My sketches are like images from a non-iPhone travel journal."

„Als Reisende im Modeland finde ich immer viel Beeindruckendes und Unterhaltsames. Meine Skizzen sind wie Bilder aus iPhone freien Reisetagebüchern."

« Au pays de la mode, j'ai toujours trouvé de quoi m'émerveiller et m'amuser. Mes croquis sont comme des images tirées d'un carnet de voyage qui ne connaît pas l'iPhone. »

**Comme des Garçons,
Spring/Summer 2006**
Vogue Italy, editorial page
February 2006; china ink,
watercolor and wire

→   **Undercover,
Spring/Summer 2005**
Vogue Italy, editorial page
February 2005; watercolor

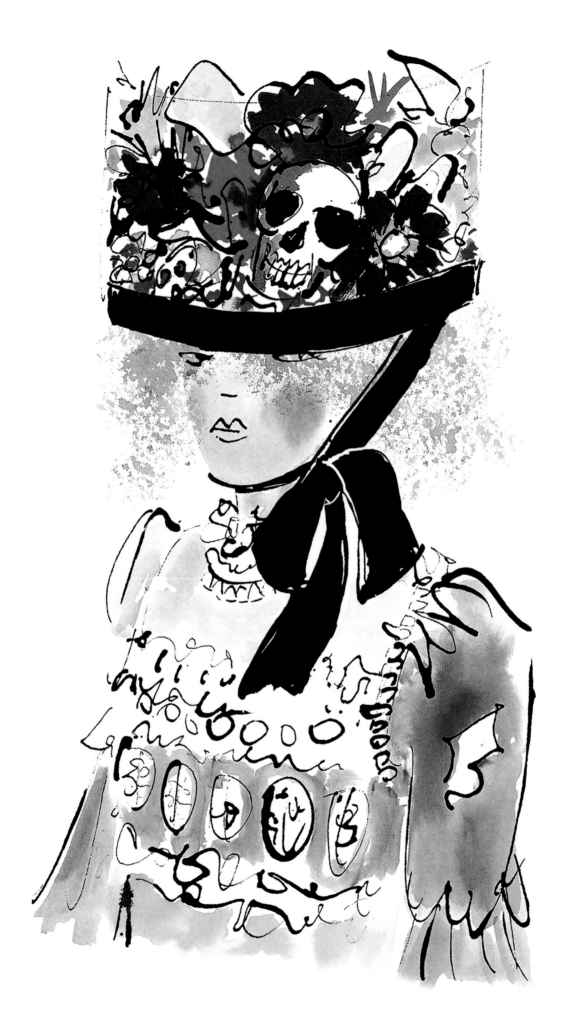

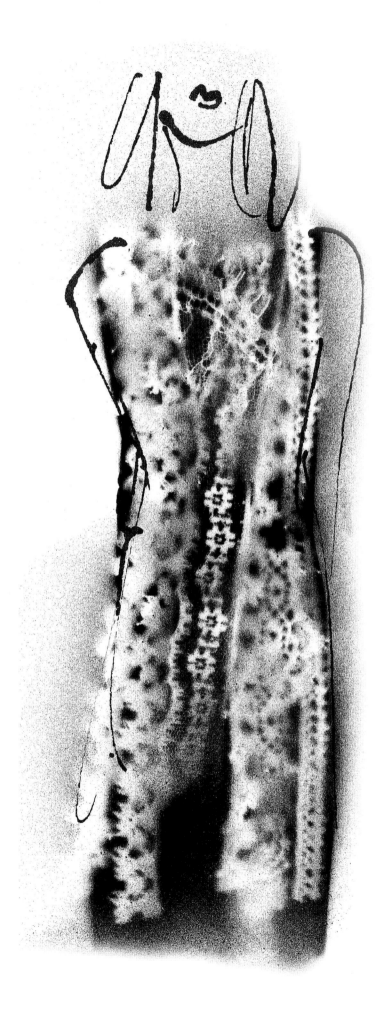

←   Dolce & Gabbana,
Spring/Summer 2006
Vogue Italy, editorial page March 2006;
china ink, spray paint on lace

→   Junya Watanabe, Fall 2009
Vogue Italy, editorial page October
2009; china ink and watercolor

↓   Tao, Spring/Summer 2010
Vogue Italy, editorial page March 2010;
china ink, watercolor and stamp

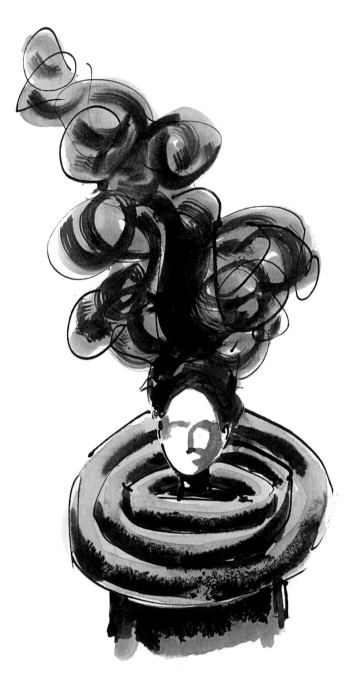

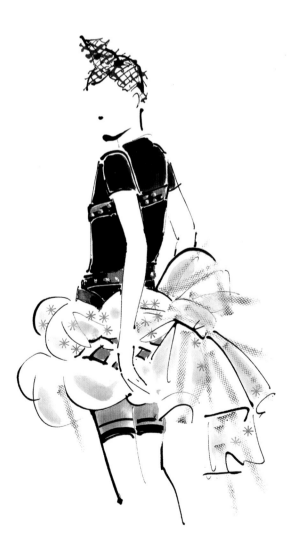

Leeay Aikawa

1983 born in Toronto | lives and works in Toronto and Toyama, Japan
www.leeayaikawa.com

CLIENTS
Amelia's Magazine

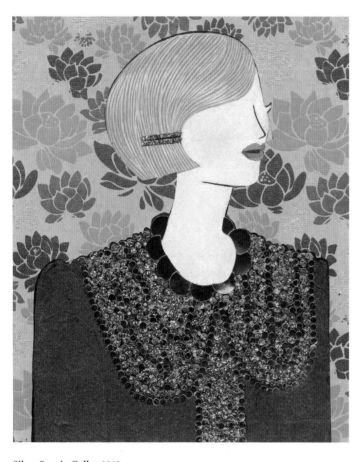

"I see fashion as collage.
I approach it with much more
of an emphasis on shape,
how shapes cover and sit around
the form of a woman's body."

„Ich betrachte Mode als Collage,
vor allem hinsichtlich der Figur,
wie also Formen den Körper der Frau
bedecken und darauf arrangiert werden."

« Pour moi, la mode est comme un
collage. Je mets l'accent sur la forme,
comment les formes couvrent le
corps d'une femme et l'épousent. »

Silver Sequin Collar, 2012
Mixed media

→   **Prada Sequin Dress, 2012**
Mixed media

→→ **Feather Dress, 2012**
Mixed media

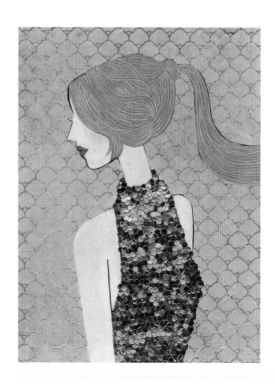

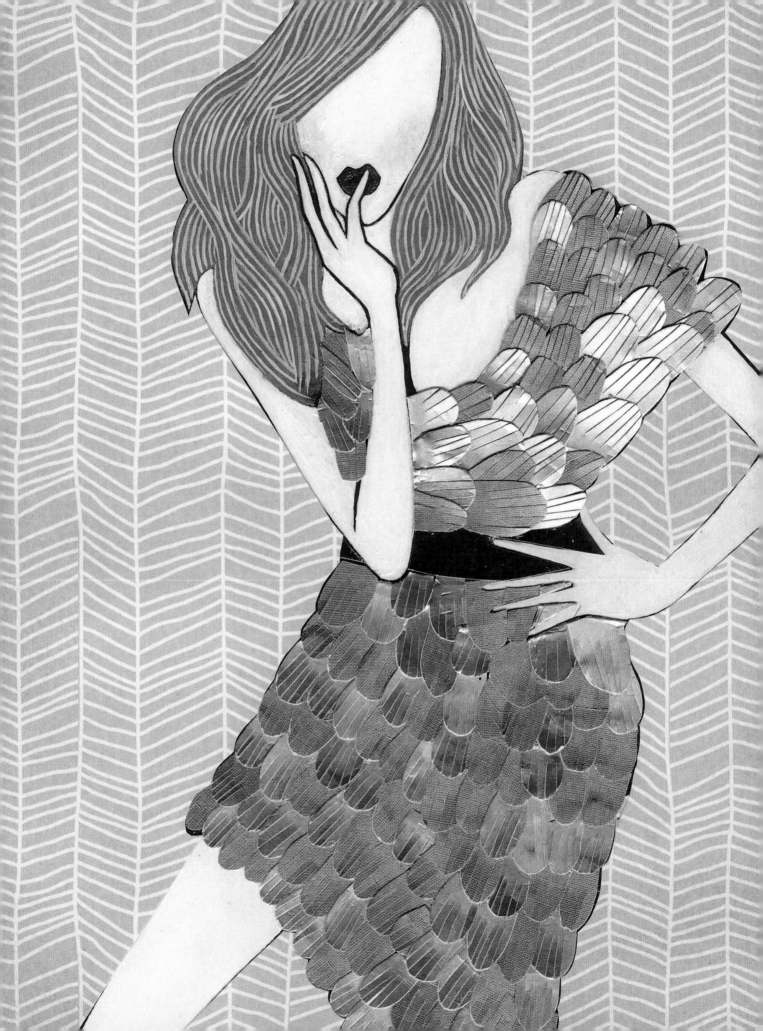

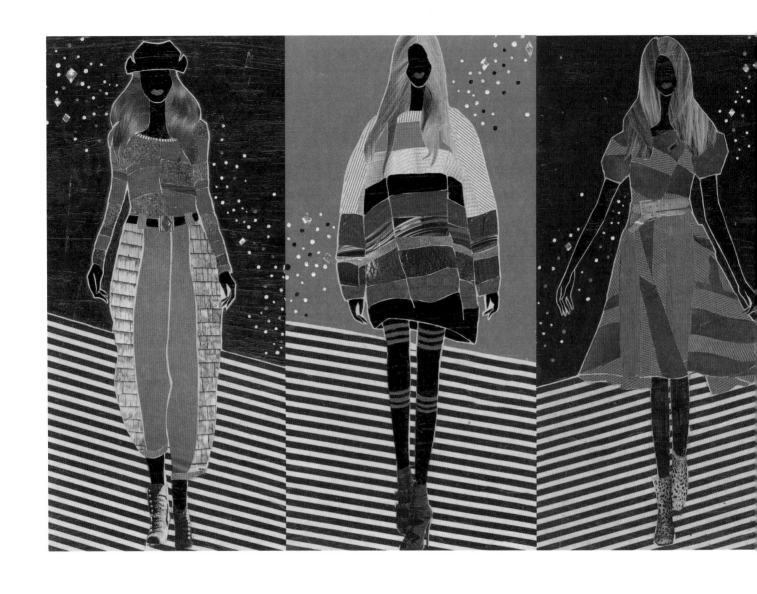

Study of Marc Jacobs
RTW 10, 2010
Mixed media

→ Vintage Vogue
Cover Inspired, 2012
Mixed media

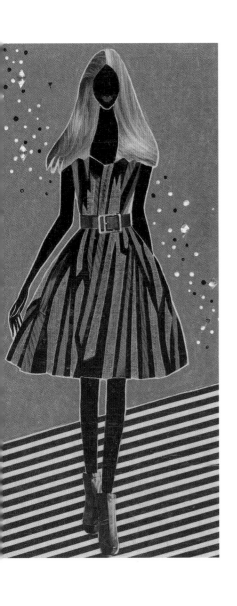

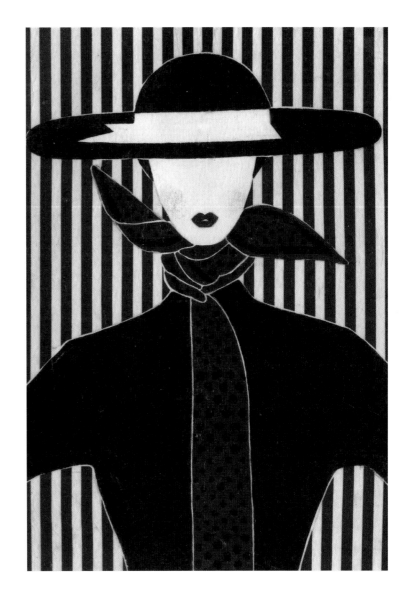

Sarah Arnett

1968 born in Harare, Zimbabwe | lives and works in Brighton
www.saraharnett.co.uk

CLIENTS
Dior Perfumes,
Modern Love

AGENT
Agency Rush
UK
agencyrush.com

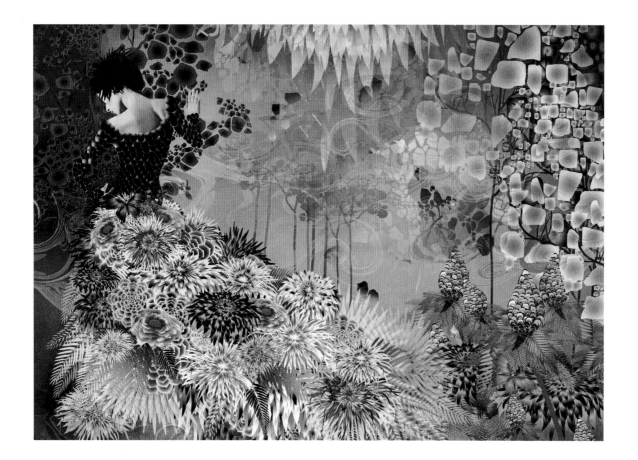

"I draw inspiration from nature, animals and landscape, mixing illustration and photography to add surreal elements in some of my work."

„Ich lasse mich von Tieren, Landschaften und Natur inspirieren. Um surreale Elemente in meine Arbeit einzubauen, kombiniere ich Illustration und Fotografie."

« Je m'inspire de la nature, des animaux et du paysage, je mélange l'illustration et la photographie pour ajouter des éléments surréels à mes œuvres. »

Flower Woman, 2010
Dior, part of the exhibition Dior
Illustrated: René Gruau and
the Line of Beauty, Somerset House;
photography and digital

→   Girl in the Garden, 2010
Dior, part of the exhibition Dior
Illustrated: René Gruau and
the Line of Beauty, Somerset House;
photography and digital

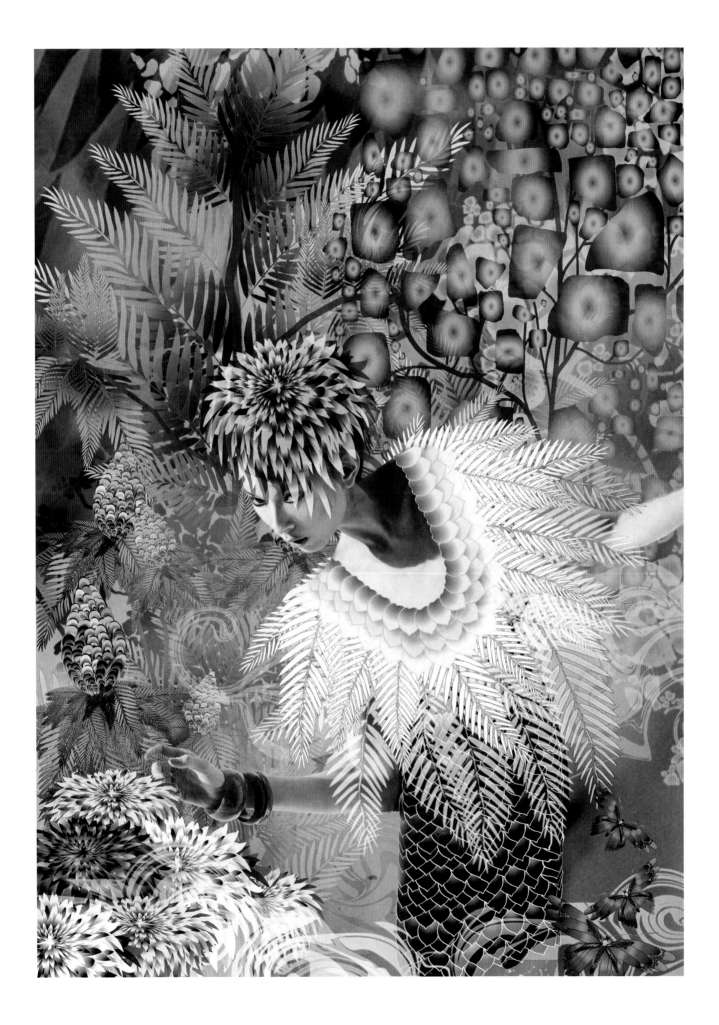

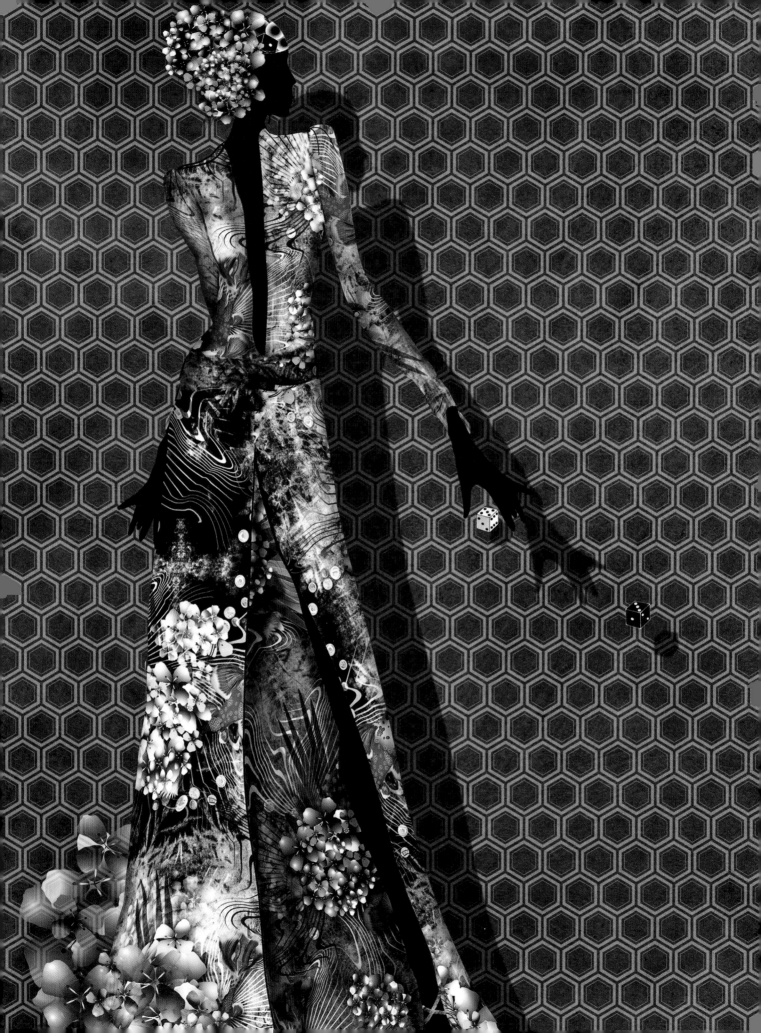

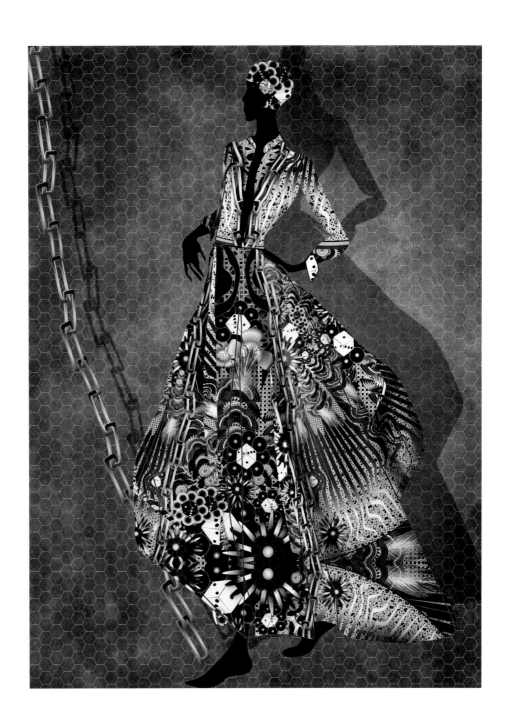

Chains, 2012
Modern Love, illustration
for collection; digital

← Hydrangea, 2012
Modern Love, illustration
for collection; digital

Molly Bartling

1971 born in Sweden | lives and works in Stockholm
www.mollybartling.com

CLIENTS
H&M, Swedish Fashion Council, Guldknappen,
Lars Wallin, Renck, Dagens Nyheter, Z-tv,
Alphabetical Order, PK-huset

AGENT
Building
Japan
bldg-jp.com

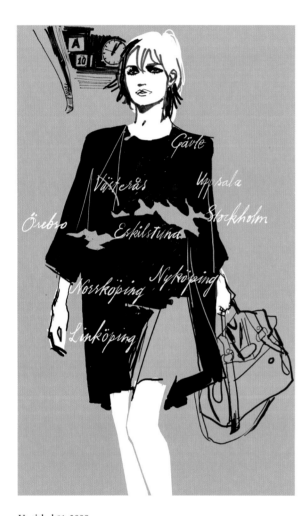

"I am fascinated by the way bodies
move and how this can be expressed
in different garments. It's this sense
of fun, whether elegant or a bit crazy,
that I try and catch in my drawings."

„Mich fasziniert die Bewegung des Körpers und wie
sich diese in Kleidungsstücken ausdrücken lässt.
Genau diesen Spaß, ob elegant oder etwas verrückt,
will ich in meinen Zeichnungen festhalten."

« Je suis fascinée par la façon dont les corps
bougent, et comment cela s'exprime dans les
vêtements. C'est cette élégance ou cette
folie que j'essaie de saisir dans mes dessins. »

Untitled #1, 2009
Tim, advertising; mixed media
and felt pen

→   Untitled #2 and #3, 2007
Swedish Fashion Council;
mixed media and felt pen

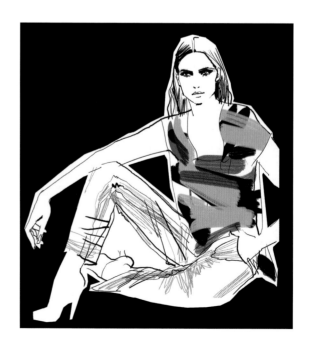

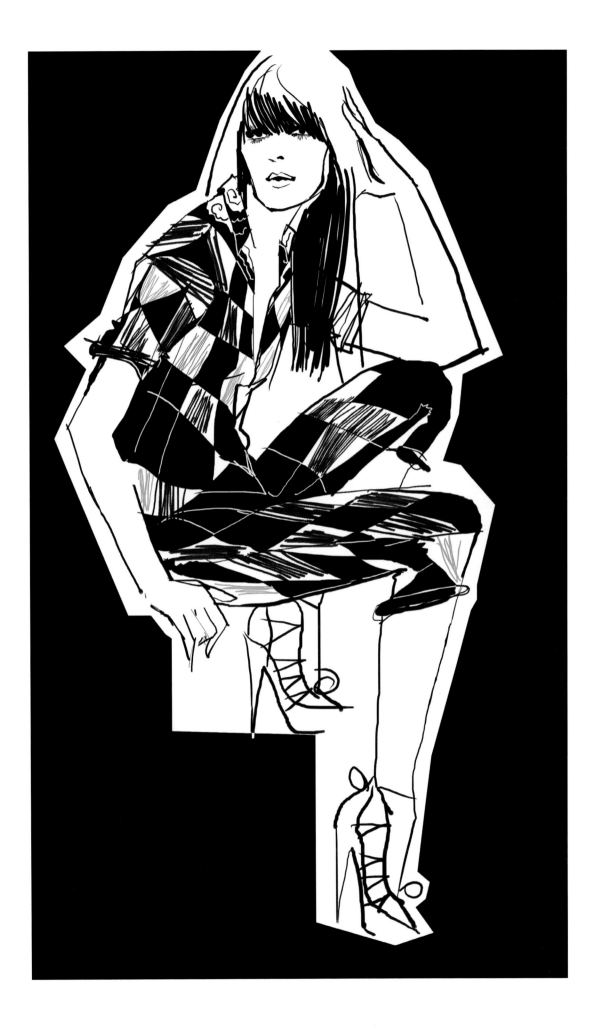

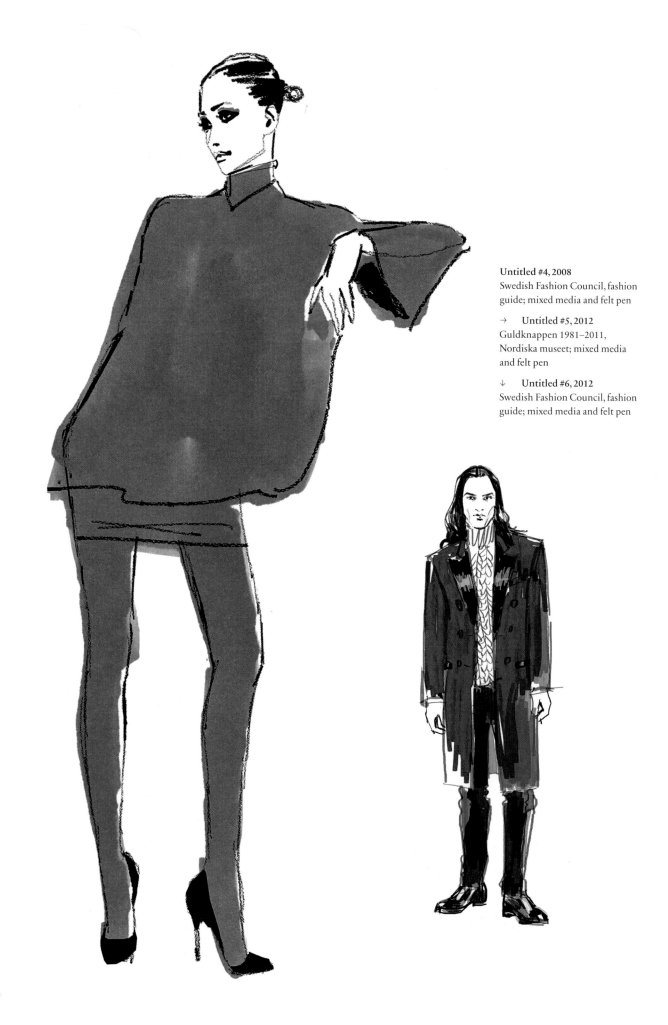

Untitled #4, 2008
Swedish Fashion Council, fashion
guide; mixed media and felt pen

→   Untitled #5, 2012
Guldknappen 1981–2011,
Nordiska museet; mixed media
and felt pen

↓   Untitled #6, 2012
Swedish Fashion Council, fashion
guide; mixed media and felt pen

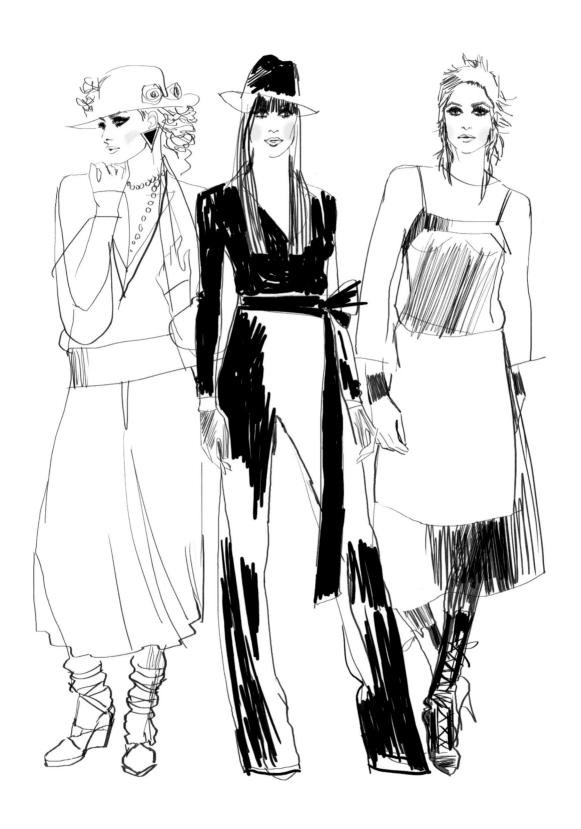

Sarah Beetson

1981 born in Manchester | lives and works in Wongawallan, Australia and London
www.sarahbeetson.com

CLIENTS
The British Fashion Council, Perth Fashion Week, More magazine, Fashion Monitor magazine, Stylesight NYC, Tank magazine, Clarks Shoes, American Eagle Outfitters

AGENTS
Illustration Ltd
UK
illustrationweb.com

i2i Art Inc
Canada
i2iart.com

19 Karen
Australia
19karen.com.au

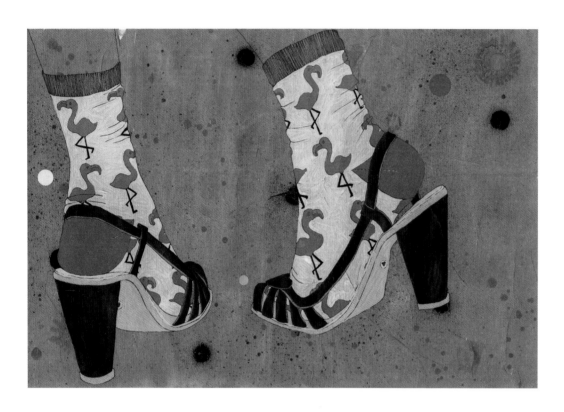

"I am fairly obsessed with patterns, rules and repetitions. Fashion illustration gives a way of retaining this structure within the chaos that is my painted world while as a stimulus it keeps me aware how my materials reflect fabric textures."

„Muster, Regeln und Wiederholungen sind meine Passion. Modeillustrationen bewahren diese Struktur innerhalb des Chaos meiner gemalten Welt, und dieser Reiz macht mir auch bewusst, wie meine Materialien Stoffstrukturen widerspiegeln."

« Je suis obsédée par les motifs et les répétitions. L'illustration de mode permet de conserver cette structure dans le chaos de ma peinture, et me stimule dans la façon de refléter les textures. »

Green Heart Heels
Flamingo Socks, 2010
Greeting card; acryl gouache, gel pen, fineliner, spray paint, tissue and collage elements on paper

→ Escha Ties Top, 2008
Fashion Monitor magazine, cover, Escha's Boutique; acryl gouache, gel pen, fineliner, spray paint, tissue and collage elements on wood

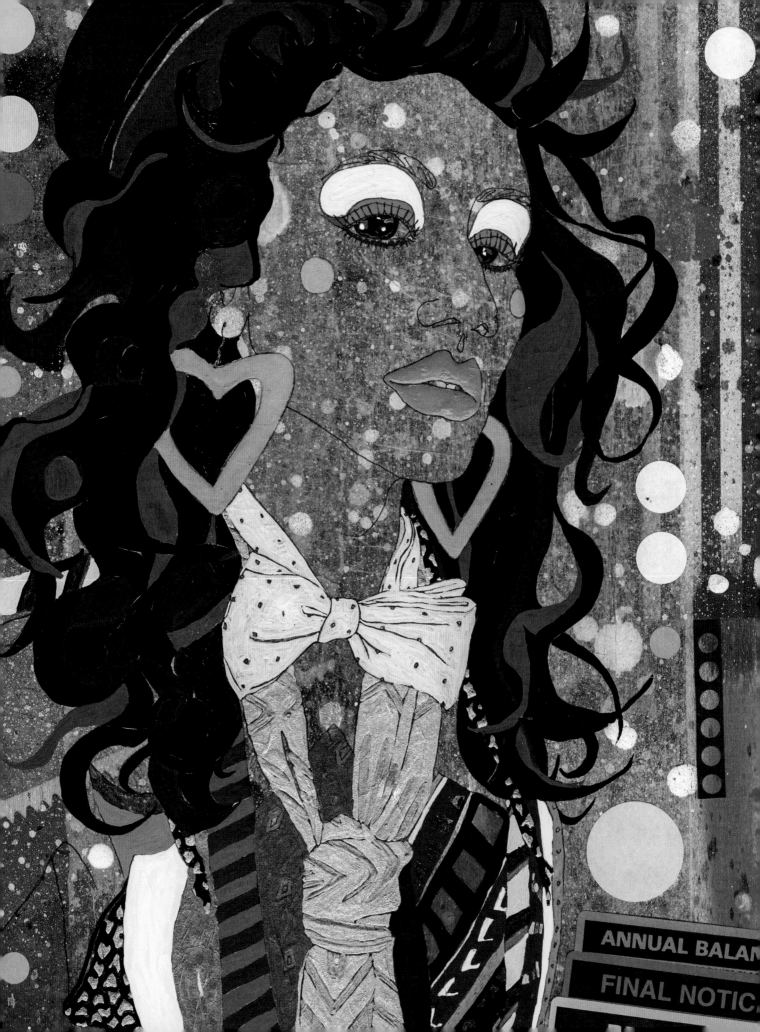

ANNUAL BALAN

FINAL NOTIC

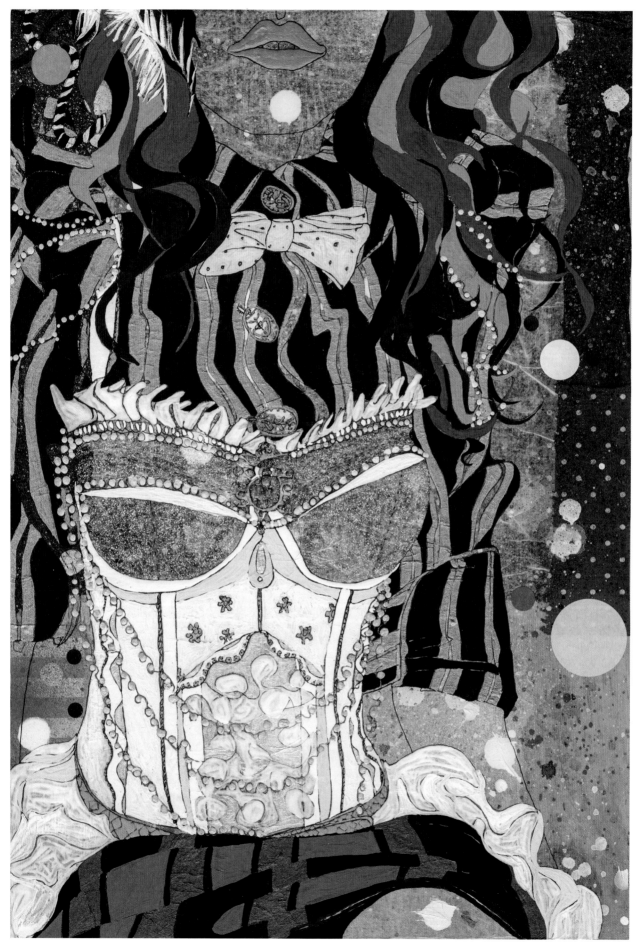

Exotically, 2011
AID International; acryl gouache,
gel pen, fineliner, spray paint and
collage elements on moleskine paper

← **Escha Striped Shirt + Corset, 2008**
Fashion Monitor magazine, cover,
Escha's Boutique; acryl gouache,
gel pen, fineliner, spray paint,
tissue and collage elements on wood

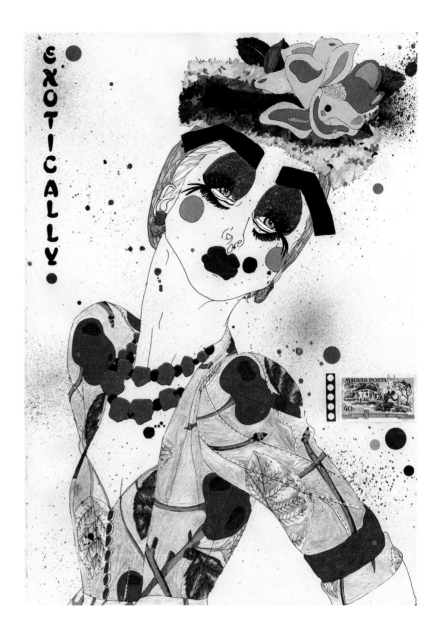

"Sarah Beetson is a walking version of one of her
designs, fully embodying her illustration style
in what she wears. With a colorful sense of humor
that often tackles sensitive subjects she generates
energetic images with youthful impact."

JONATHAN KYLE FARMER
Associate Professor of Fashion
Parsons The New School for Design

Montse Bernal

1976 born in Barcelona | lives and works in Turin
www.montsebernal.com

CLIENTS
The New Yorker, New York magazine, You magazine,
Nylon magazine, S magazine, Marie Claire, AD,
The Guardian, Nike, BMW, Phaidon

AGENTS
Kate Larkworthy
USA
larkworthy.com

Central Illustration Agency
UK
centralillustration.com

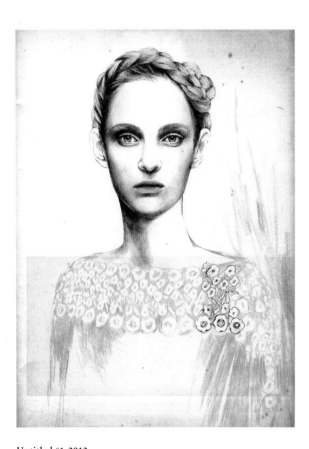

"When creating my fashion illustrations,
I often find the phrase coming to mind:
'beauty will save the world' (Dostoevsky)."

„Arbeite ich an meinen Modeillustrationen,
kommt mir oft dieses Zitat in den Sinn:
‚Die Schönheit wird die Welt retten.' (Dostojewskij)"

« Lorsque je crée mes illustrations de mode,
j'ai souvent en tête cette phrase :
‹ La beauté sauvera le monde › (Dostoïevski). »

Untitled #1, 2012
Iben Høj, Spring/Summer 13 lookbook;
graphite pencil and color pencil

→   Untitled #2 and #3, 2012
Iben Høj, Spring/Summer 13 lookbook;
graphite pencil, color pencil, collage,
embroidery, watercolor and digital

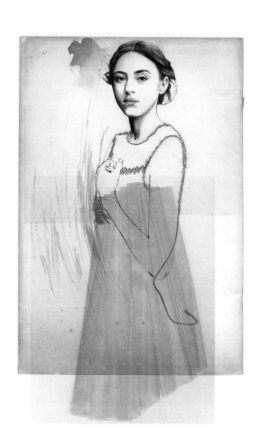

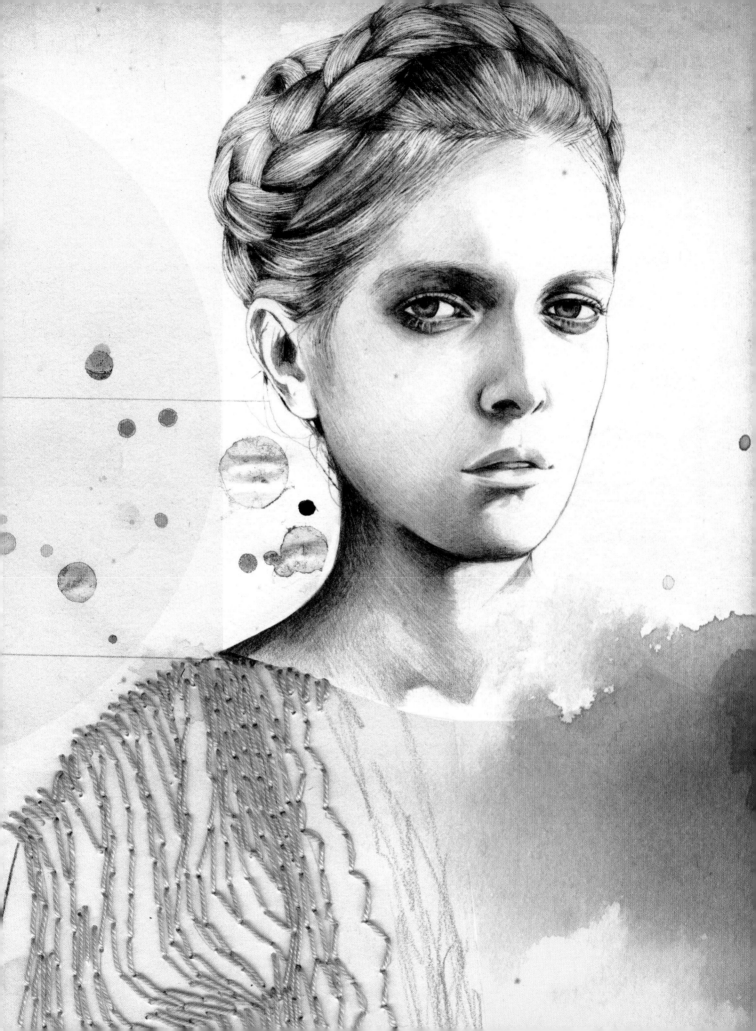

Tina Berning

1969 in Braunschweig | lives and works in Berlin
www.tinaberning.de

CLIENTS
The New York Times Magazine,
Vanity Fair, Cosmopolitan,
Vogue Japan, Mercedes-Benz

AGENTS
2agenten
Germany
2agenten.com

CWC International
USA
cwc-i.com

CWC Tokyo
Japan
cwctokyo.com

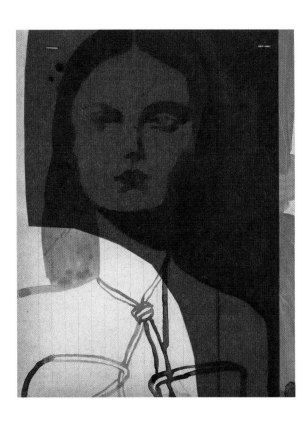
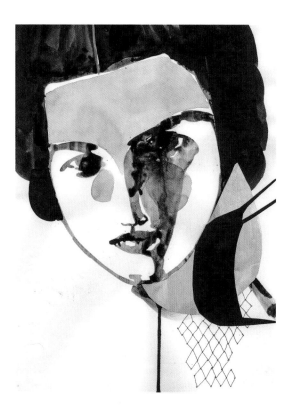

"When working on fashion I can deliberately expand
the way the figure is represented, add quotations or references,
or simply play with the continually recurring canon
of volume and line, silhouette and structure."

„Mich mit Mode zu beschäftigen ermöglicht es mir, bewusst den Ausdruck
der Figur zu erweitern, Zitate und Verweise anzubringen oder einfach mit dem immer
wiederkehrenden Kanon von Volumen und Linie sowie Silouette und Struktur zu spielen."

« Avec la mode, j'ai plus de liberté dans la représentation, je peux ajouter
des citations ou des références, ou jouer avec le canon récurrent du volume
et de la ligne, de la silhouette et de la structure. »

#05 Ali and #09 Mirte, 2010
Exhibition Face/Project, Camera Work,
in collaboration with Michelangelo
di Battista; mixed media collage

→ **Kristina Ti**, 2012
Visual for fashion label Kristina Ti;
watercolor and ink

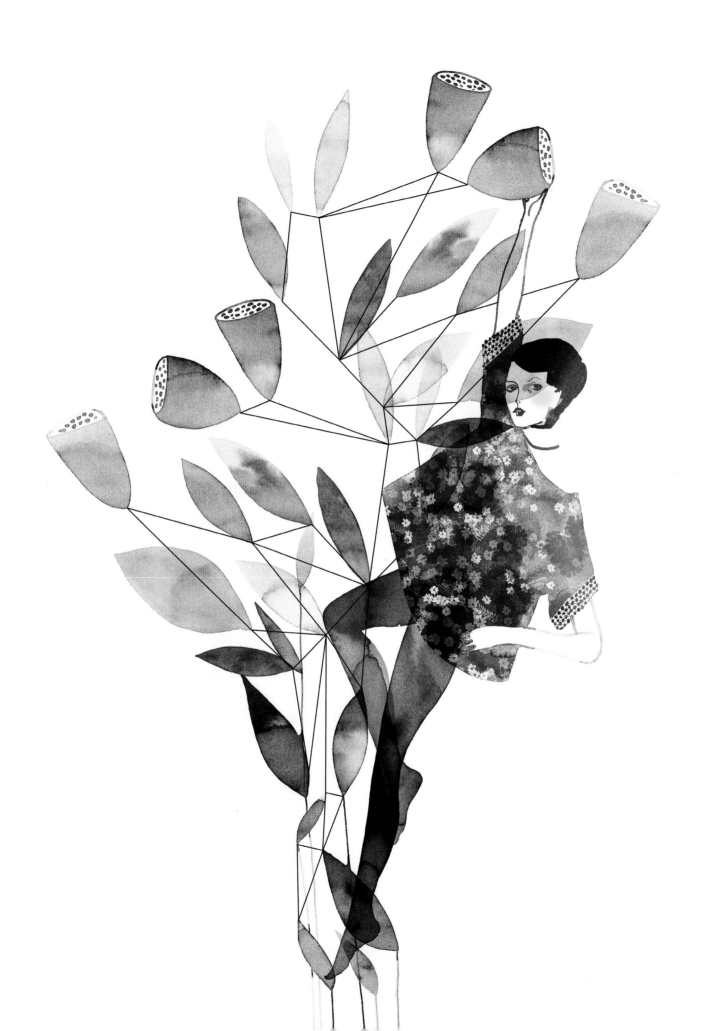

Maya Beus

1981 born in Split | lives and works in Zagreb and London
www.beus.com

CLIENTS
Fashion Fringe,
LVMH, Carlin,
Amelia's Magazine

AGENT
The Illustration Room
Australia
illustrationroom.com.au

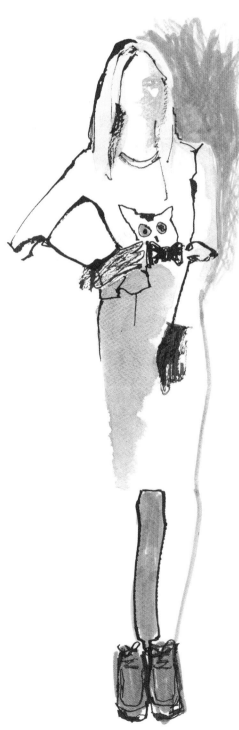

"I like to work in black ink and watercolor
to express the movement and transiency
of fashion and to mirror the glee that
looking at beauty creates in us."

„Ich arbeite bevorzugt mit schwarzer Tinte und Wasserfarben,
um die Bewegungen und das Transzendentale der
Mode auszudrücken und das Entzücken zu verdeutlichen,
das das Betrachten von Schönem in uns erweckt."

« J'utilise de l'encre noire et des aquarelles pour
exprimer le mouvement et l'éphémérité de la mode,
et la joie que la beauté crée en nous. »

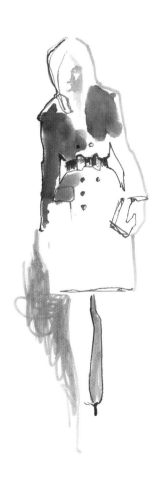

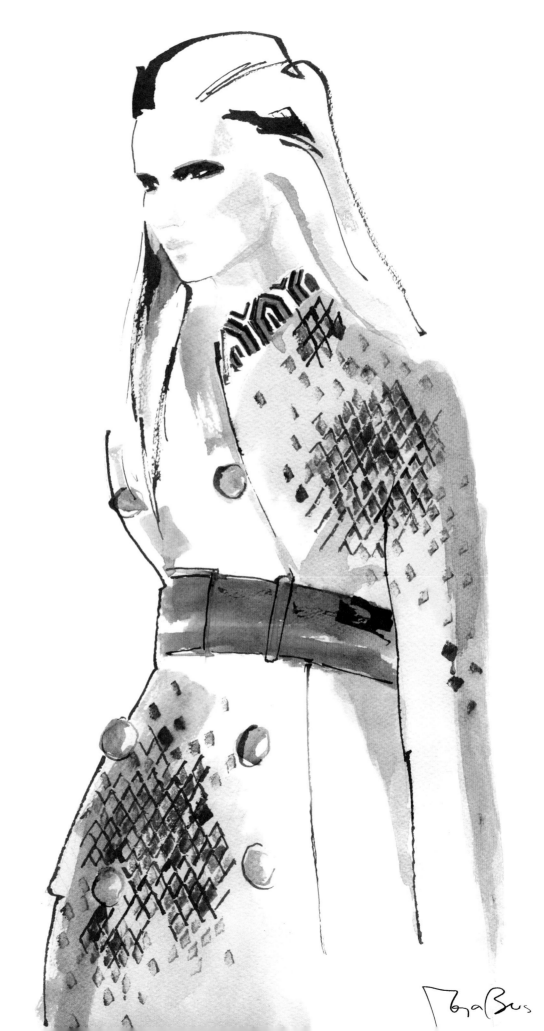

Print Trends, 2012
Fashion Fringe, illustration
competition (winner) by Sir Colin
McDowell; watercolor on paper

← **Burberry Pre-Fall 12, 2012**
Personal work; ink and
markers on paper

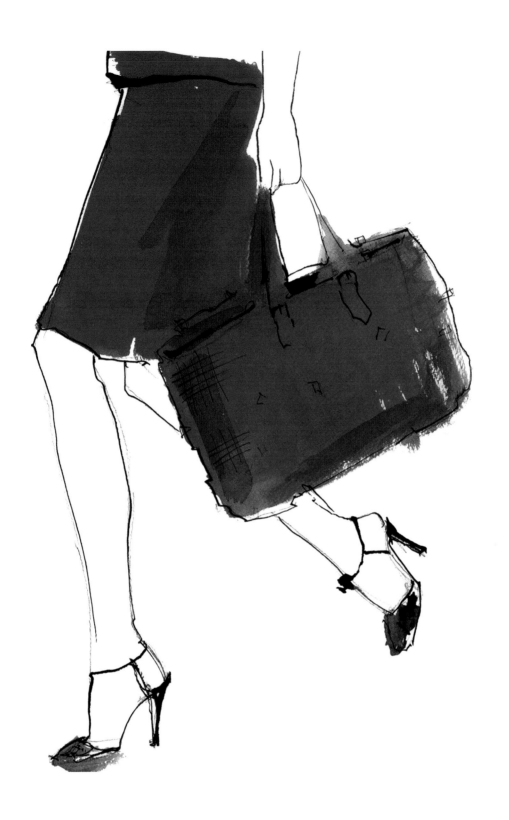

Bottega Veneta, Fall/Winter 2011
Personal work; watercolor
and ink on paper

→   Chill, 2012
Personal work; graphics tablet
and digital

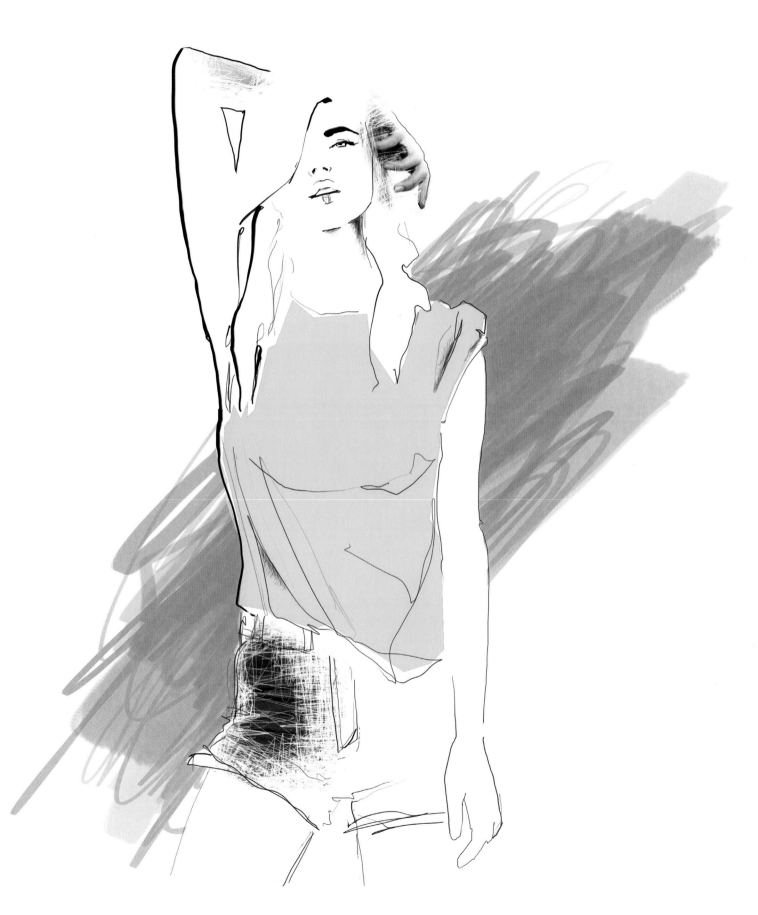

Lisa Billvik

1980 born in Arboga, Sweden | lives and works in Stockholm
www.lisabillvik.com

CLIENTS
Selfridges, Urban Outfitters, Part Two,
Habit magazine, Amelia's Magazine,
Nylon magazine,Catwalk Studio, Synk Casting

AGENTS
Peppercookies
UK
peppercookies.com

Snyder & the Swedes
USA
snyderandtheswedes.com

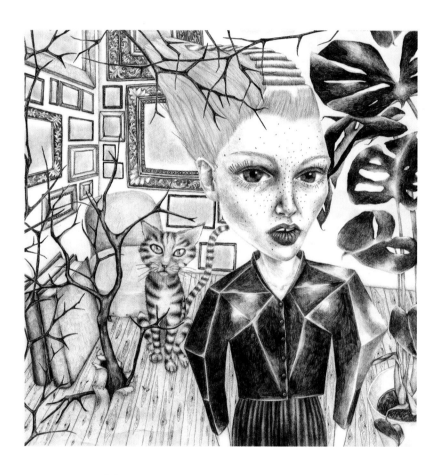

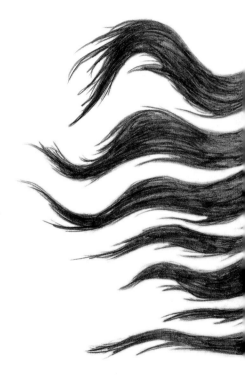

"I'm inspired by people and life stories from reality or fiction.
It's all about creativity. Everything is possible and there are no rules."

„Mich inspirieren Menschen und reale oder fiktive Lebensgeschichten.
Vor allem geht es um Kreativität. Alles ist möglich, keine Regeln!"

« Je m'inspire des gens et de vies réelles ou fictives. C'est une question
de créativité. Tout est possible et il n'y a pas de règles. »

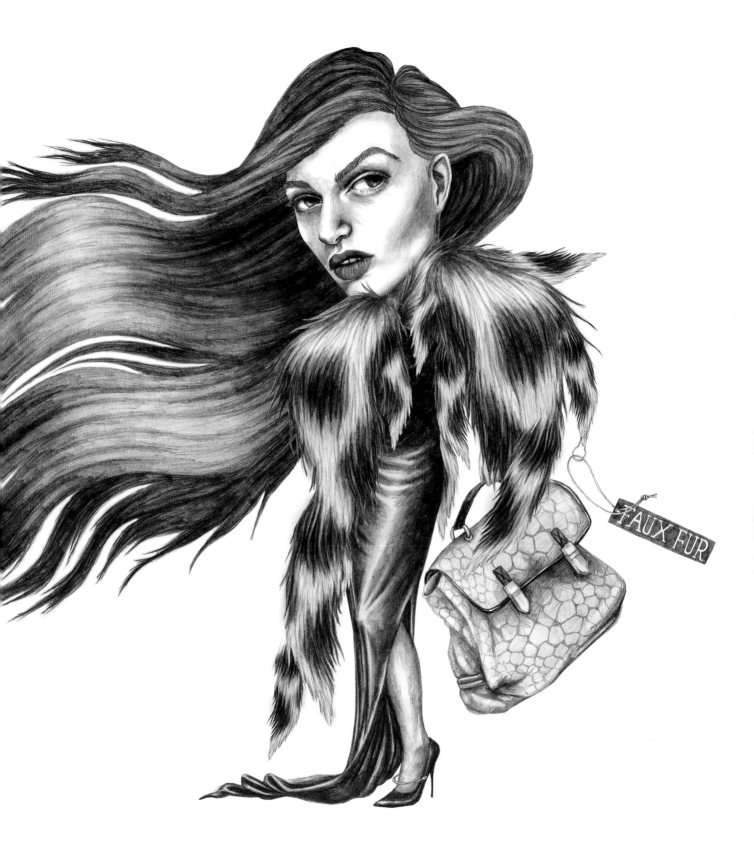

Untitled, 2011
Habit magazine, trend report
Fall/Winter 2012–13;
pencil and digital

←   Untitled, 2011
Part Two; textile print on scarf,
pencil and digital

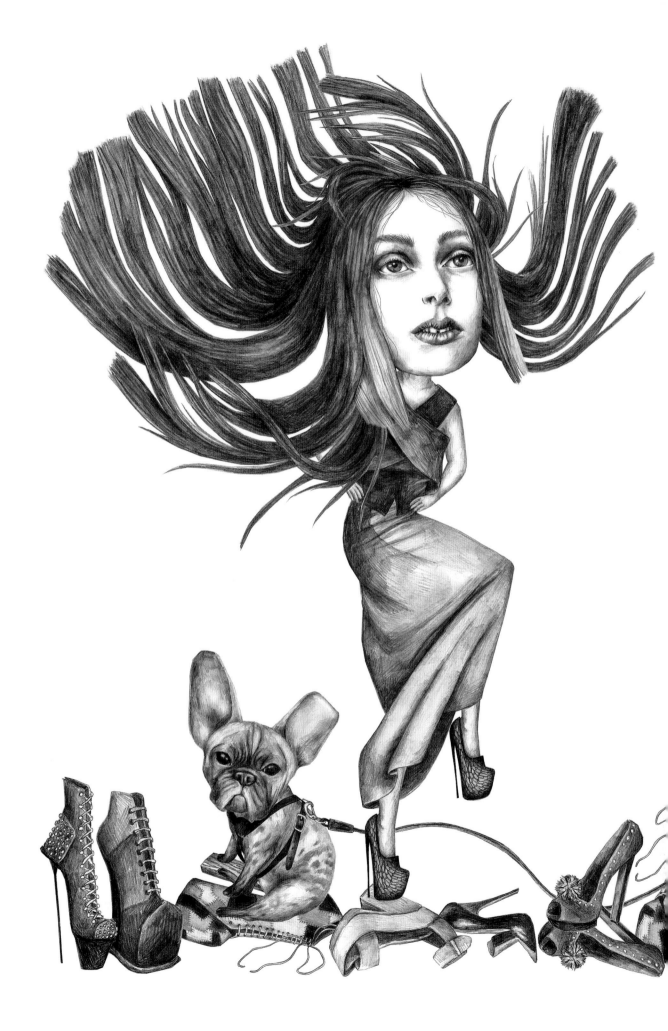

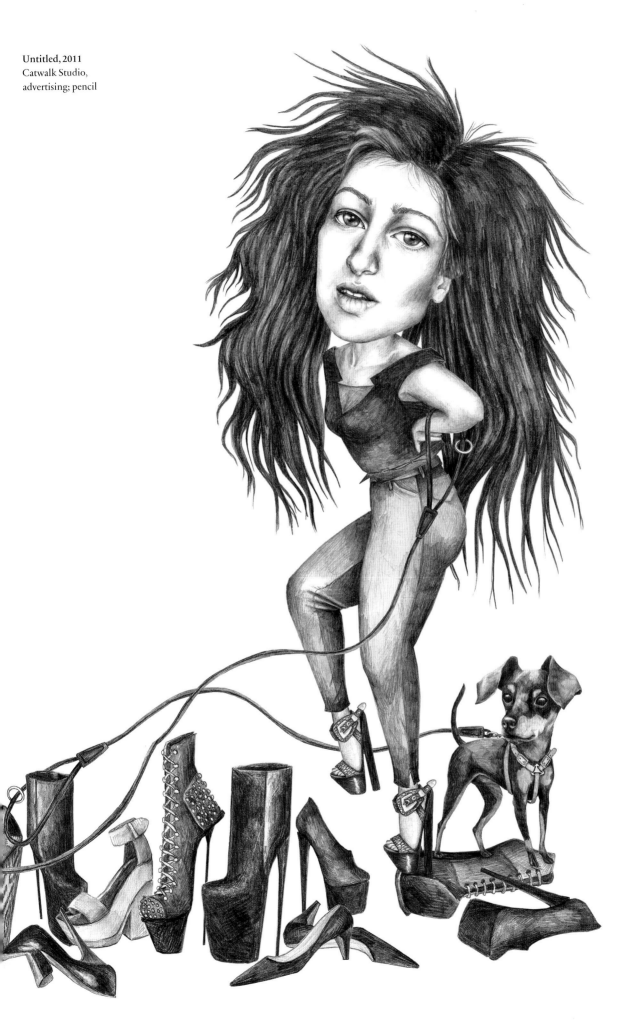

Untitled, 2011
Catwalk Studio,
advertising; pencil

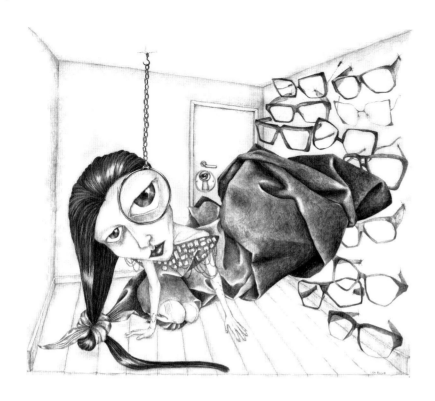

Untitled, 2009
Personal work; pencil

→   Untitled, 2011
Habit magazine, trend report
Fall/Winter 2012–13;
pencil and digital

↓   Untitled, 2011
Habit magazine, cover;
pencil and digital

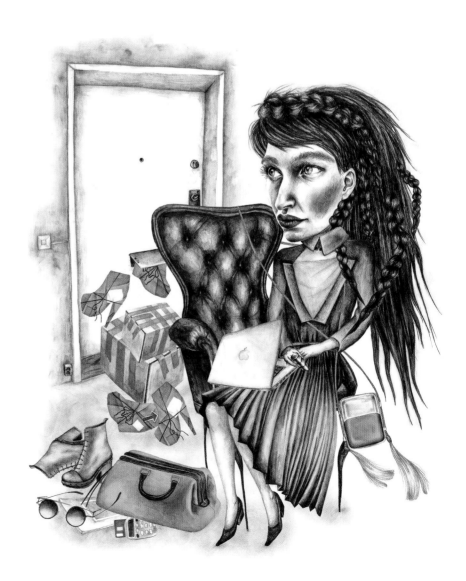

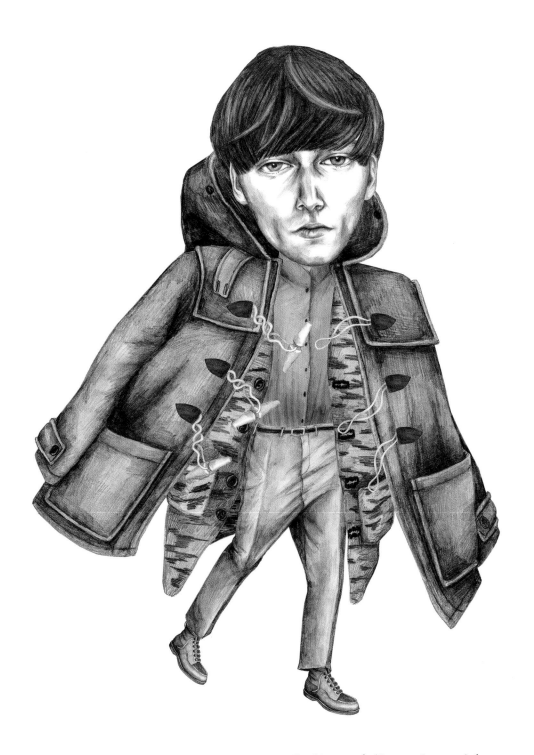

"By skillfully combining a feeling of discretion with a certain harshness, Lisa creates personal and, to an extent, surrealistic illustrations."

KRISTINA HOUMANN
Account Manager
Part Two/PRD Agency

Lina Bodén

born in Stockholm | lives and works in Stockholm
www.linaboden.se

CLIENTS
Whyred, Weekday, Monki, H&M,
Vogue Japan, Show Studio,
Way Out West, IKEA

AGENTS
Agent Molly & Co
Sweden
agentmolly.com

Peppercookies
UK
peppercookies.com

CWC Tokyo
Japan
cwctokyo.com

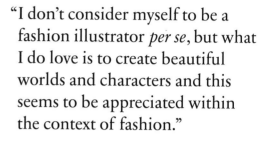

"I don't consider myself to be a
fashion illustrator *per se*, but what
I do love is to create beautiful
worlds and characters and this
seems to be appreciated within
the context of fashion."

„Ich verstehe mich nicht als Modeillustratorin
per se, aber ich kreiere gerne schöne Welten
und Charaktere. Im Modekontext wird das
offenbar sehr geschätzt."

« Je ne me considère pas comme une
illustratrice de mode, mais j'aime créer des
mondes et des personnages beaux,
et il semble que cela soit apprécié dans
le contexte de la mode. »

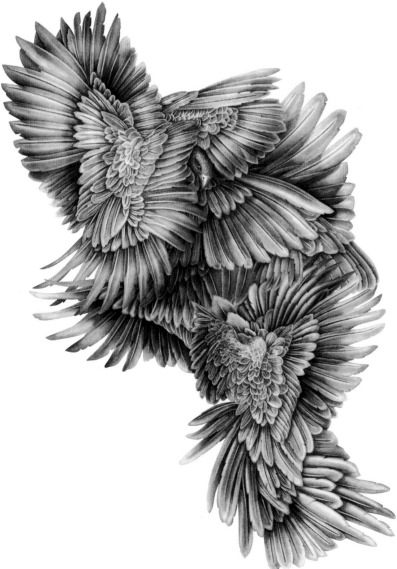

Untitled, 2011
Way Out West Festival, T-shirt print;
hand-drawn and digital

→   Untitled, 2012
IKEA, print/pattern; hand-drawn
and digital

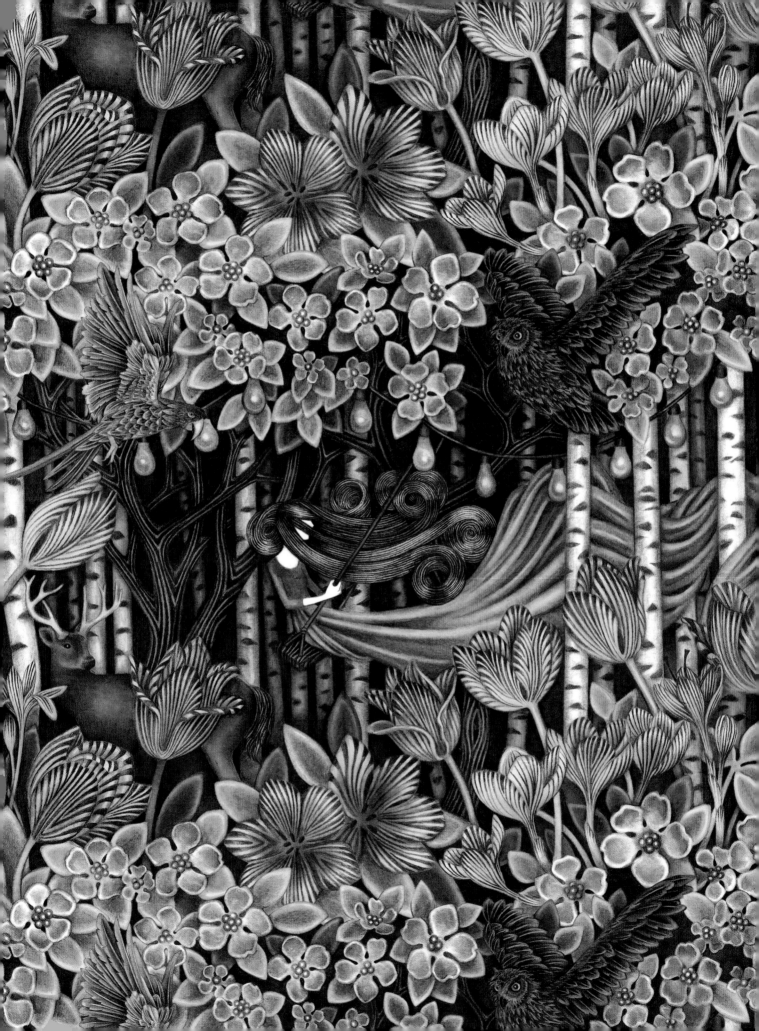

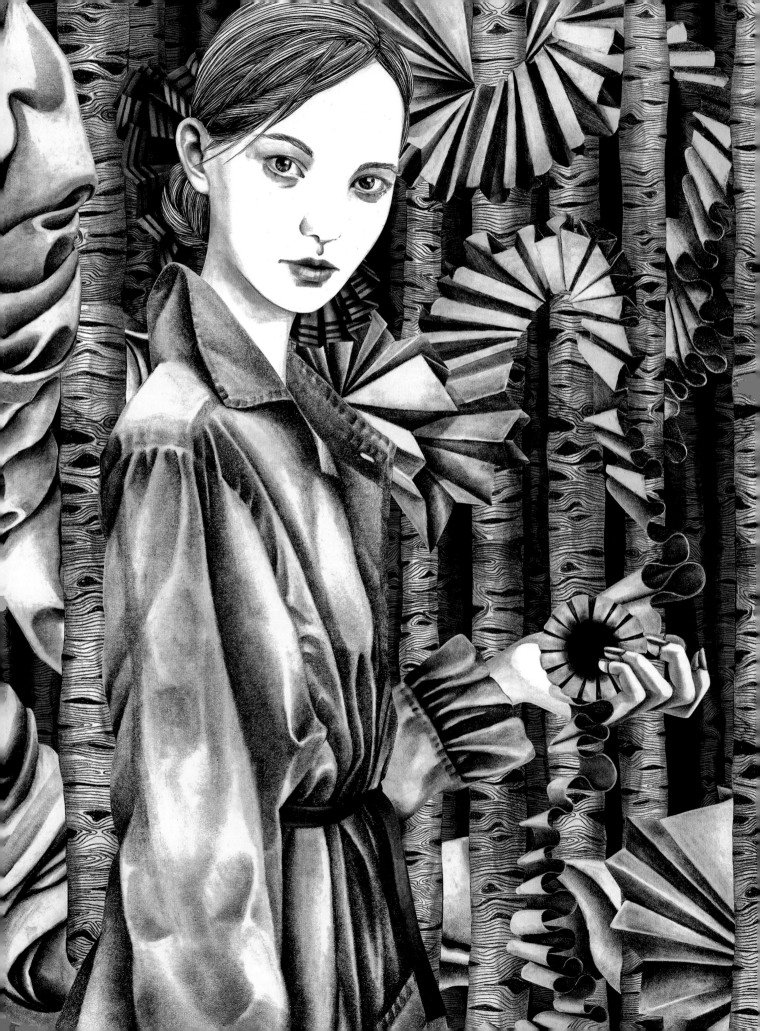

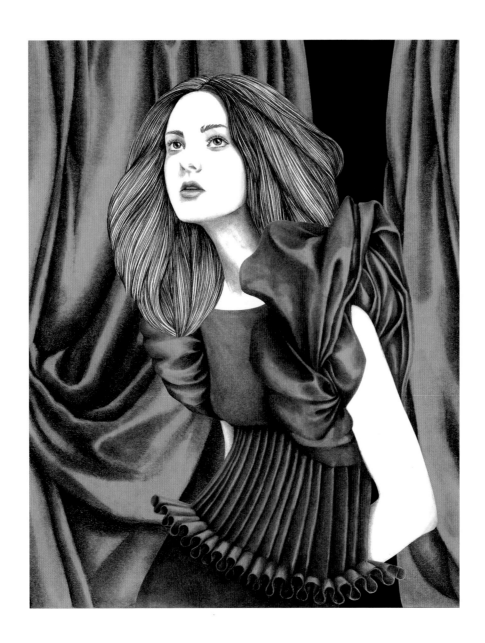

Untitled, 2008
Personal work; hand-drawn

←   Untitled, 2008
ODD Projects, exhibition
+46 Awards Fashion Fair, print;
hand-drawn and digital

Katarzyna Bogucka

1985 born in Łomza, Poland | lives and works in Warsaw
www.nioska.com

CLIENTS
Nenukko, Twój Styl, PanTuNieStal,
Dwie Siostry, Wytwórnia, Tatarak,
Ładne Halo

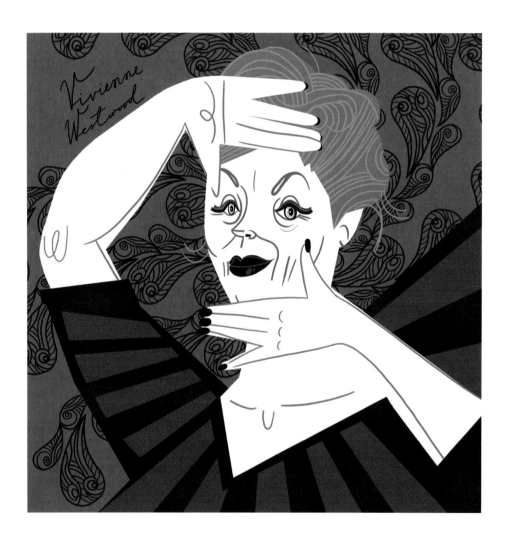

"Although I treat the subject in a humorous way, it all
makes me seriously interested in fashion illustration."

„Obwohl ich das Thema humorvoll behandle, bin ich doch ernsthaft
an Modeillustration interessiert."

« Bien que je traite le sujet avec humour, l'illustration
de mode m'intéresse très sérieusement. »

Untitled, 2011
Wydawnictwo Dwie Siostry,
book M.O.D.A., K. Świeżak; digital

→   Untitled, 2011
Wydawnictwo Dwie Siostry,
book M.O.D.A., K. Świeżak; digital

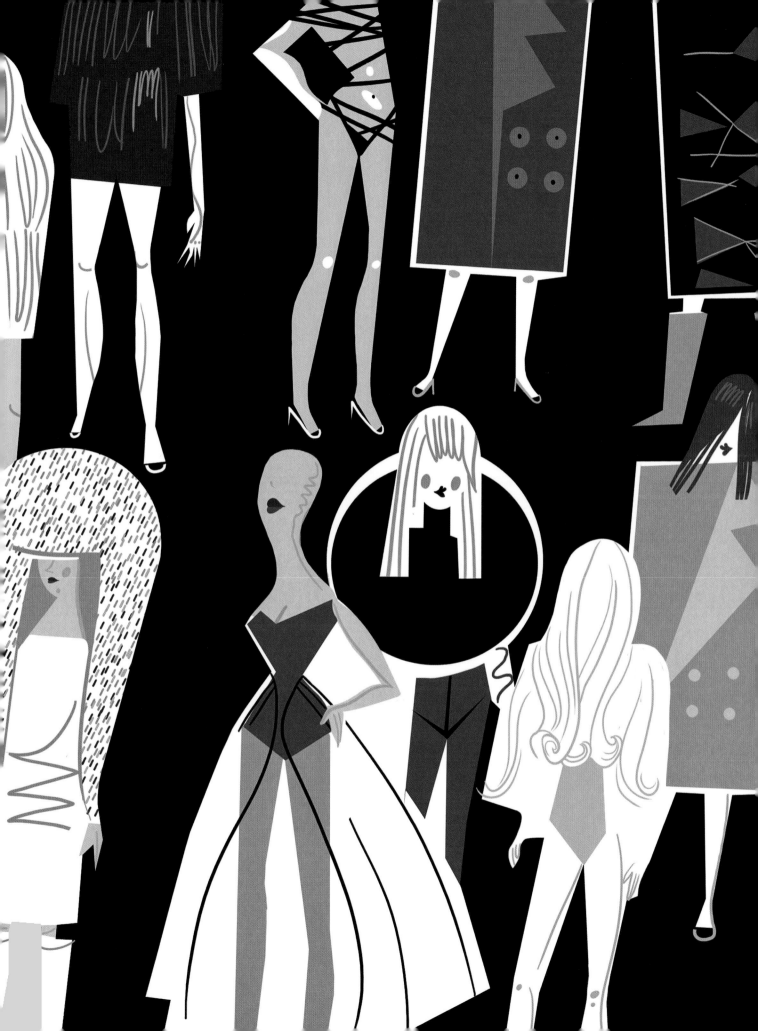

"Her style is very recognizable – vintage elements, combined with pure minimalism, retain a balance between portrait and geometric abstraction."

NENUKKO
Fashion Designer

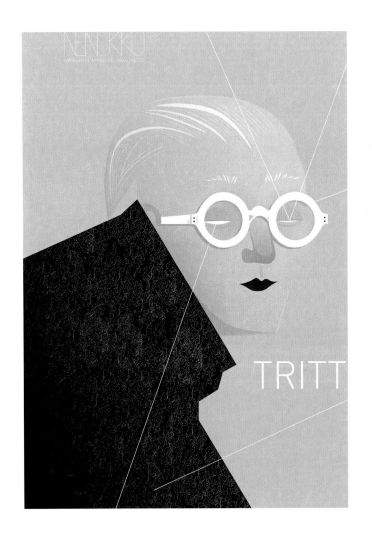

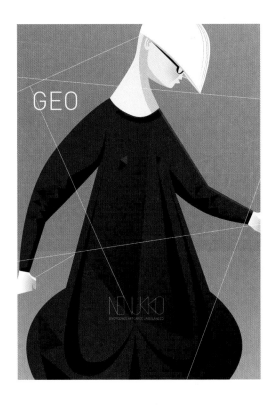

↑   **Geo, 2012**
Nenukko, poster; digital

←   **Tritto, 2012**
Nenukko, poster; digital

→   **Florence, 2012**
Personal work; digital

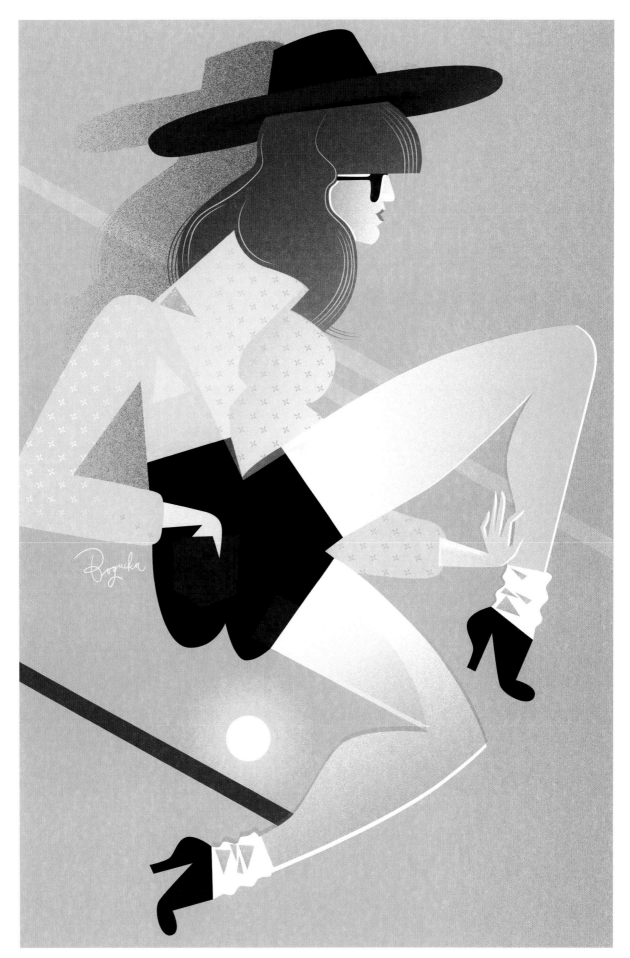

Cem Bora

1965 born in Istanbul | lives and works in Berlin
www.cem-bora.de

CLIENTS
Textile View, Comme des Garçons,
Colette, Messe Frankfurt, The Corner

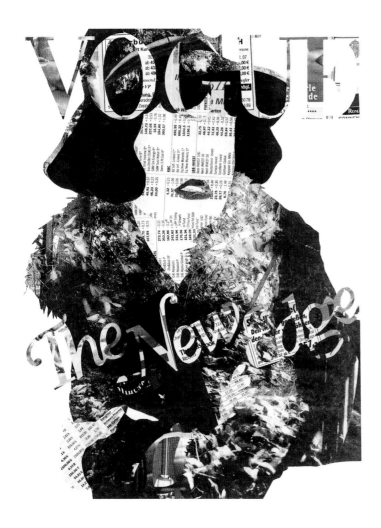

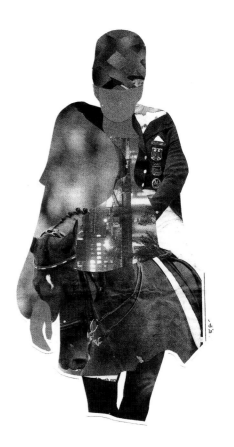

"For me, fashion illustration is the most
beautiful way to present fashion."

„Modeillustration ist für mich die schönste Art,
Mode in Szene zu setzen."

«Pour moi, l'illustration de mode est la plus
belle façon de présenter la mode.»

Balenciaga Fall 06, 2008
Personal work; collage

← **Vogue Italy, 2007**
Personal work; collage

→ **Yves Saint Laurent Fall 08, 2009**
Personal work; collage

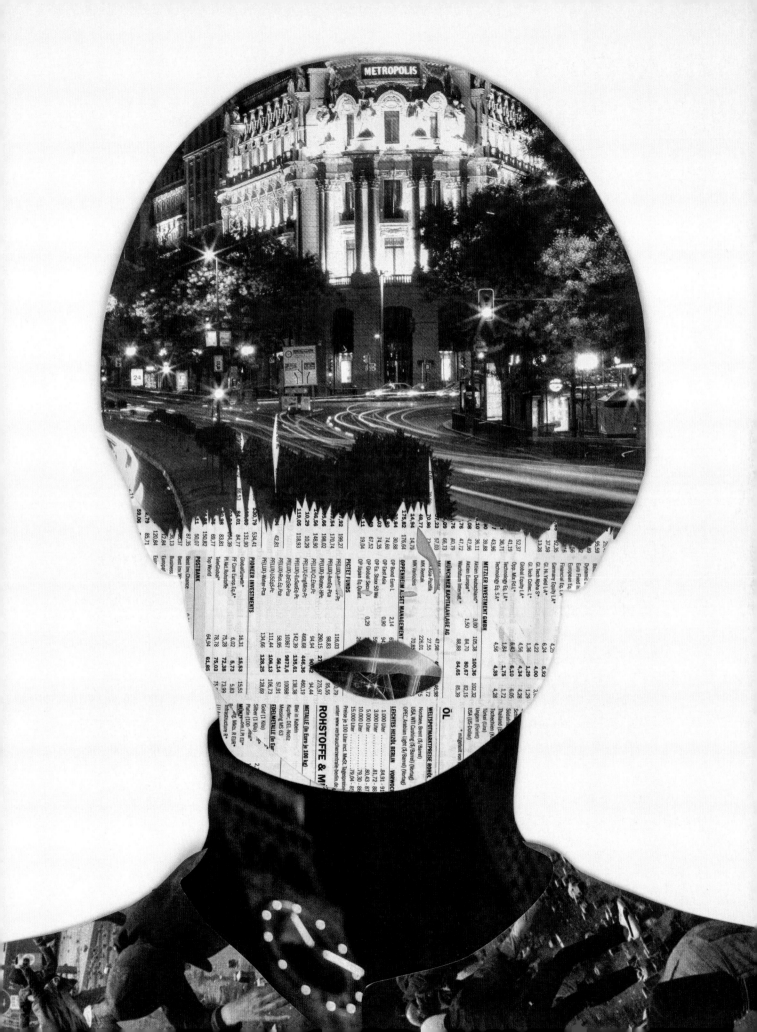

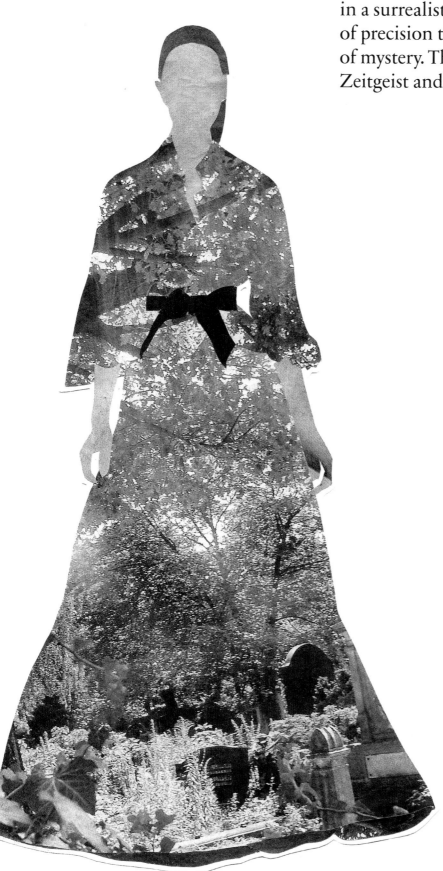

"Cem Bora's collages are concrete in a surrealistic way. With a clear sense of precision they still retain a touch of mystery. They vary between the Zeitgeist and timeless idealization."

ELKE GIESE
Fashion Journalist

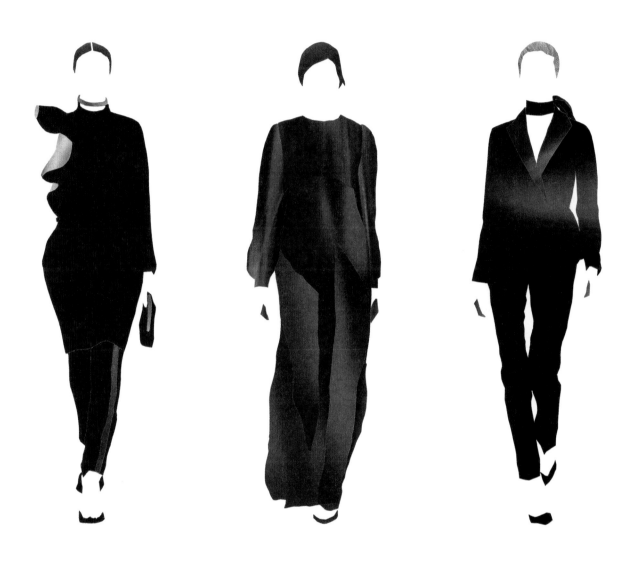

Givenchy, Valentino,
Jil Sander, Spring 13, 2012
Personal work; collage

←   Oscar de la Renta,
Spring 06, 2007
Personal work; collage

Annabel Briens

1982 born in Enghien-les-Bains, France | lives and works in Paris

CLIENTS
Le Mont St Michel,
Galeries Lafayette,
Grazia

AGENT
V.O Valérie Oualid
France
valerieoualid.com

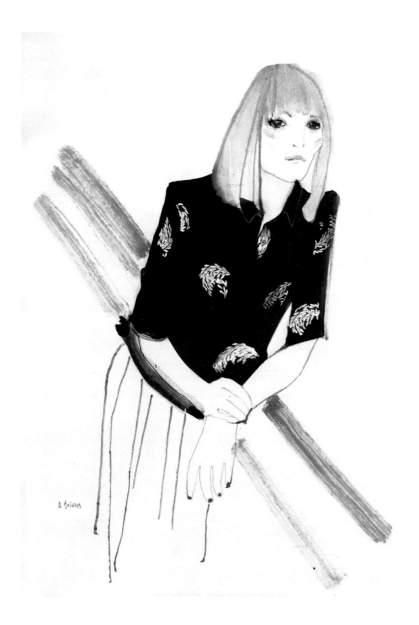

A. Briens

"I'm looking for what
the model is living,
inside and out."

„Ich suche danach, was
das Model lebt, im Inneren
und nach außen hin."

« Je cherche ce que le modèle vit,
à intérieur et à l'extérieur. »

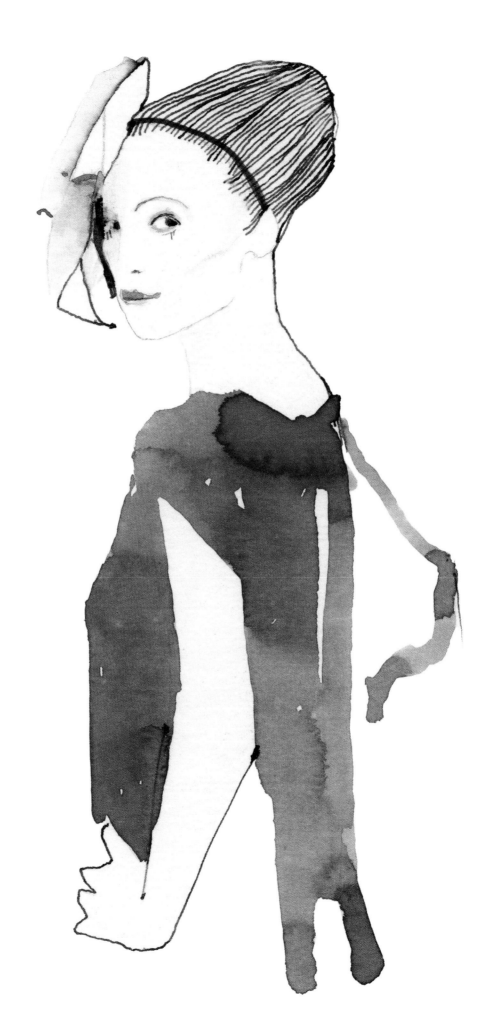

Issey, 2012
Backstage Issey Miyake;
ink and pencil on paper

← **Automne, 2012**
Le Mont St Michel, blog
Les Carnets du Mont St Michel;
oil and pencil on paper

Untitled, 2011
Personal work; oil and pencil on paper

→ **La Robe noire, 2012**
Le Mont St Michel, blog Les Carnets
du Mont St Michel; ink, oil and
pencil on paper

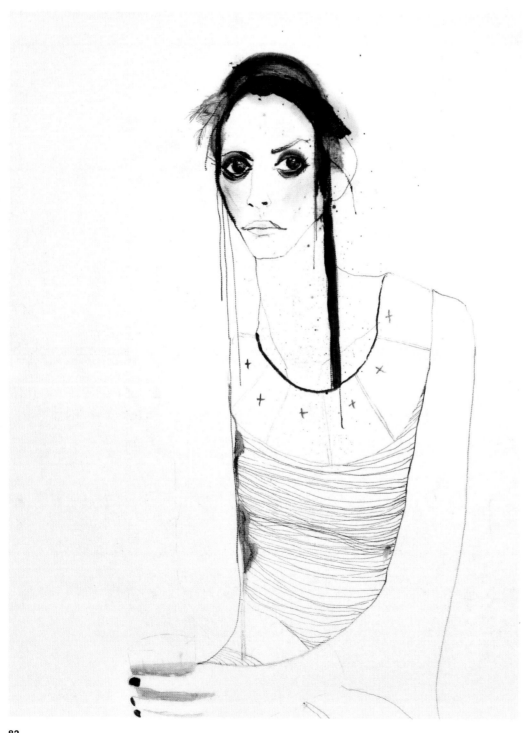

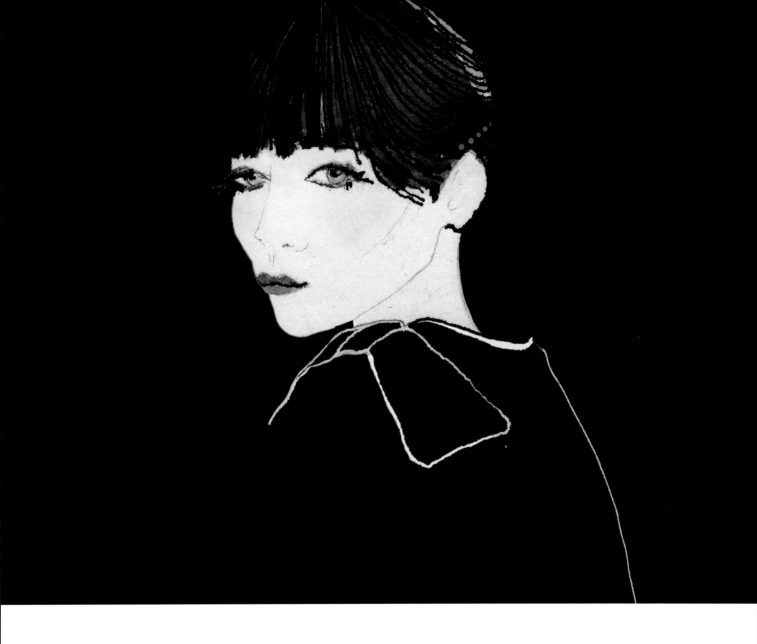

"Something happens to us when we see how Annabel sees people – something ineffable, unknowable and intriguing. Is it Paris that happens to us?"

NICHOLAS MIR CHAIKIN
Creative Director, Spill

Lovisa Burfitt

1973 born in Sydney | lives and works in Paris and Stockholm
www.lovisaburfitt.com

CLIENTS
H&M, Givenchy, Chanel, Guerlain, Kenzo, Liberty,
Franck & Fils, La Rinascente, Bloomingdale's,
Vogue, Elle, Fédération du Prêt-à-Porter Féminin

AGENT
Agent & Artists
France
agentandartists.com

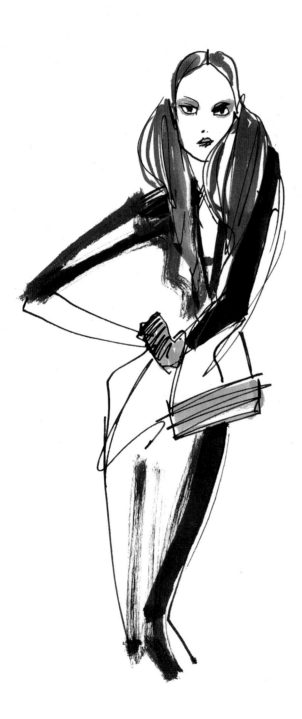

"With fashion illustration I can approach
the glamour and fantasy without actually
really having to take much part in the
fashion circus. I love it."

„Durch Modeillustration kann ich mich mit Glamour
und Fantasien beschäftigen, ohne wirklich in den
Modezirkus einzusteigen. Das liebe ich."

« Avec l'illustration de mode, je peux aborder
le glamour et la fantaisie sans devoir prendre
part au cirque de la mode. J'adore ça. »

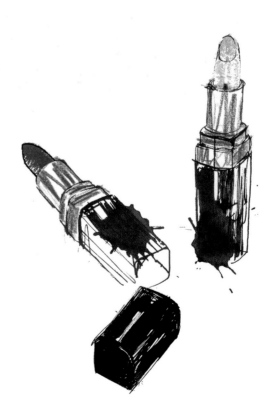

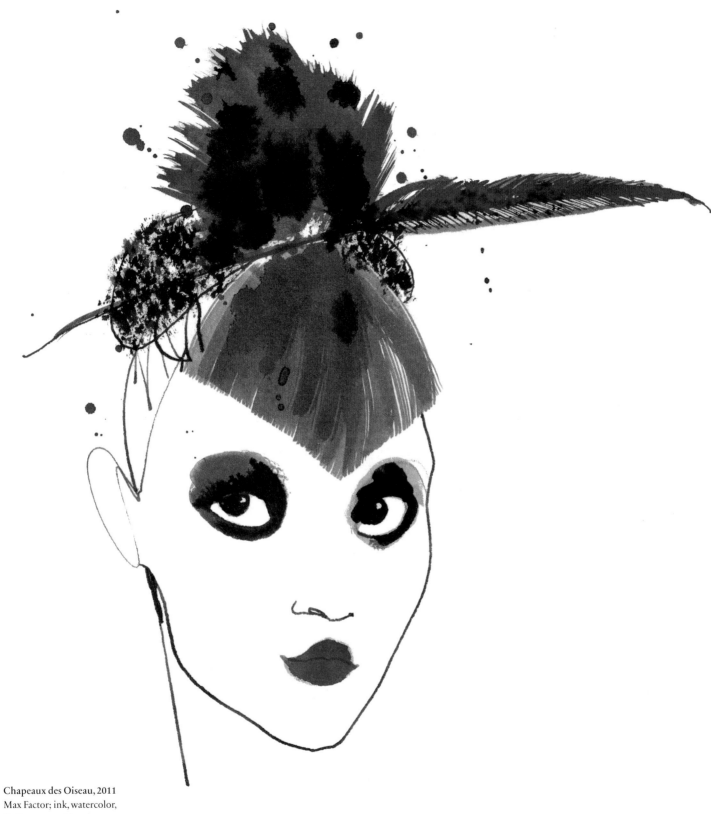

Chapeaux des Oiseau, 2011
Max Factor; ink, watercolor,
feather pen and brush

←   Rouge Coco, 2010
Chanel; ink, feather pen,
brush and lipstick

←← Femme en flames, 2011
Givenchy; ink, watercolor,
feather pen and brush

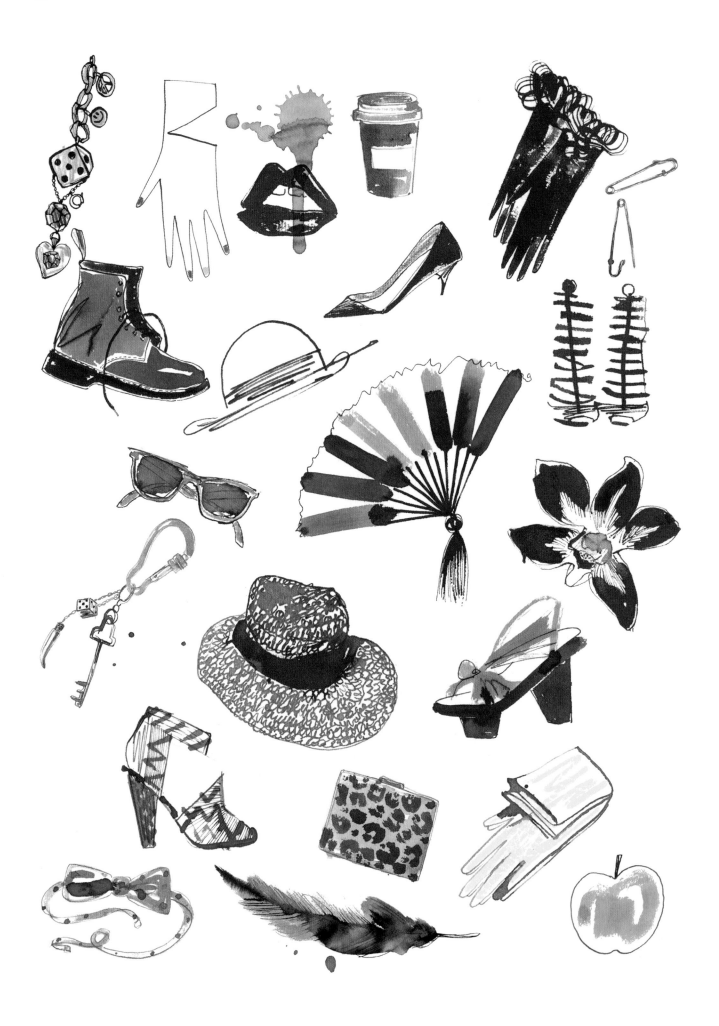

"Lovisa is a fantastic illustrator with a playful and elegant style. She started with me as an assistant ages ago and we love to work with her."

MARGARETA VAN DEN BOSCH
Creative Advisor, H&M

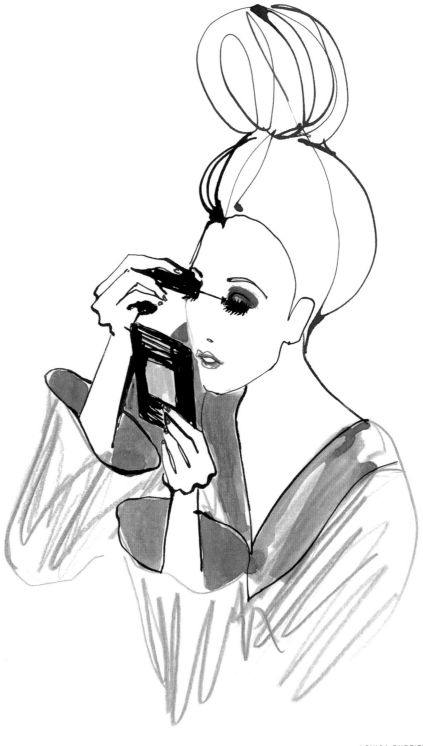

Maquillage green, 2008
H&M, wall decoration; ink,
feather pen, brush and color pencil

← **Accessories allover, 2012**
H&M, wall decoration; ink, watercolor,
feather pen, brush and color pencil

Jill Calder

1993 born in the UK | lives and works in the UK
www.jillcalder.com

CLIENTS
Billabong, Neiman Marcus,
Talbots, Elle, The Guardian,
Stella magazine

AGENTS
Friend + Johnson
USA
friendandjohnson.com

Central Illustration Agency
UK
centralillustration.com

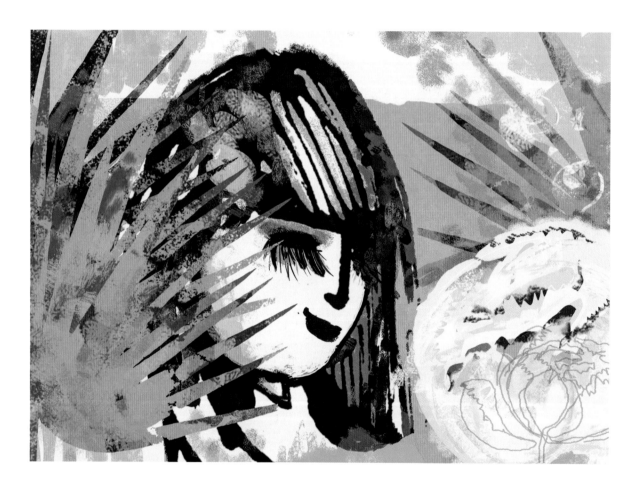

"I love drawing people – sometimes they are glamorous,
sometimes humorous, sometimes both!"

„Ich liebe es, Menschen zu zeichnen. Manchmal sind sie glamourös,
bisweilen humorvoll und mitunter beides!"

« J'adore dessiner les gens – ils sont parfois glamour,
parfois drôles, et parfois les deux ! »

Palmetto + Peony, 2008
The Guardian, Art Direction:
Sarah Habershon; ink and digital

→ **Bag Lady, 2009**
Personal work; ink and digital

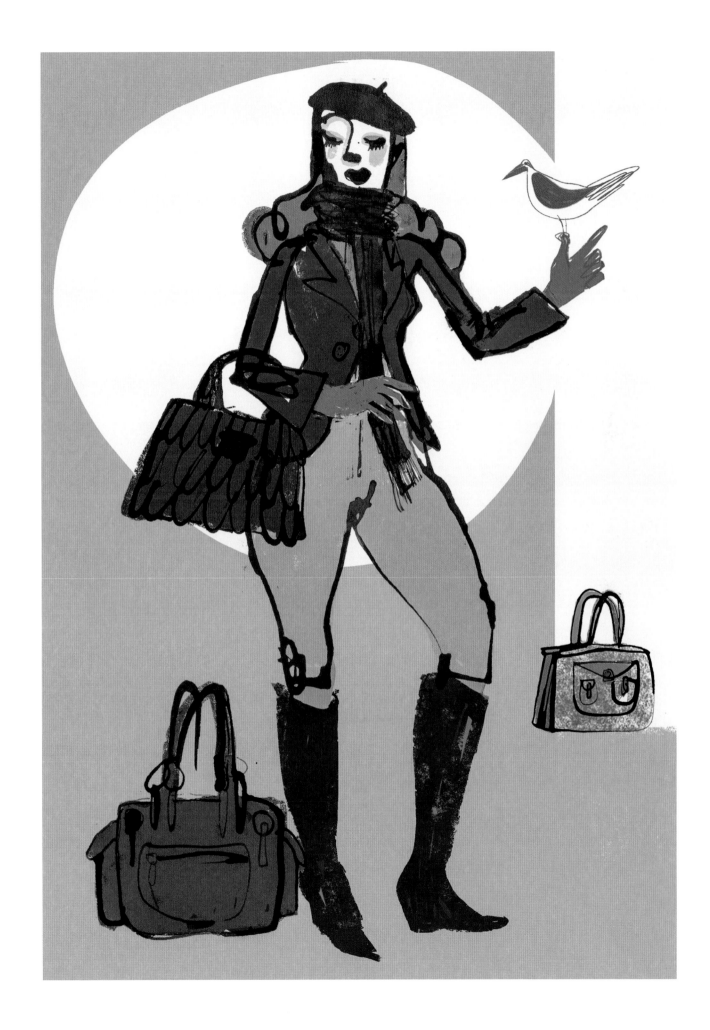

Kissy Kissy, 2007
The Sunday Herald; ink and acrylic

→ **USAville, 2007**
Personal work; ink and digital

↘ **Brassiere Boudoir, 2009**
Friend + Johnson, Art Direction:
Coco Connolly; pen and ink, digital

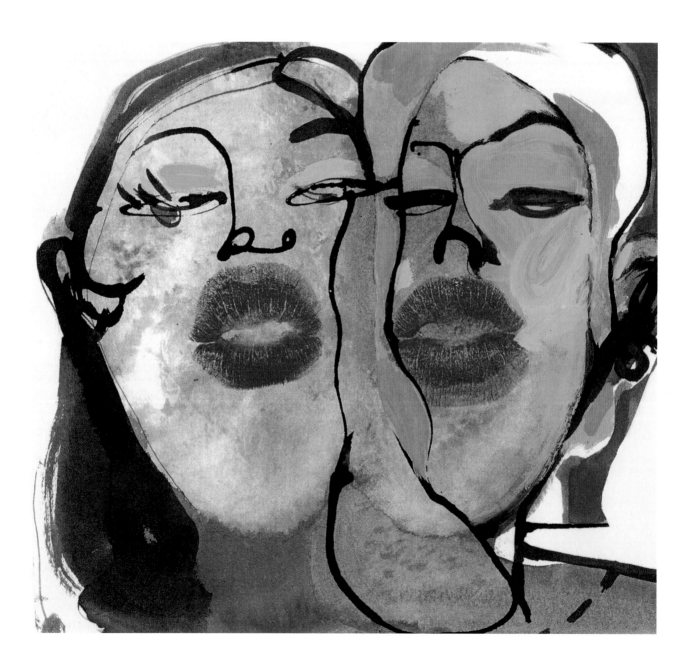

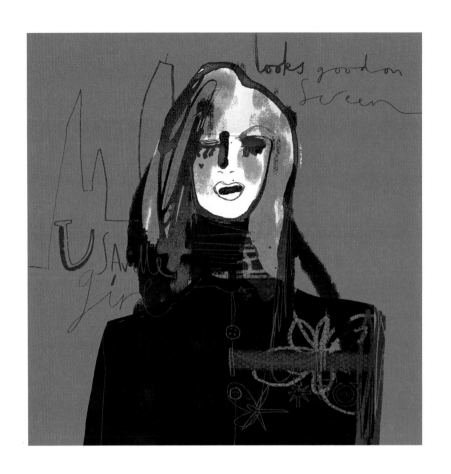

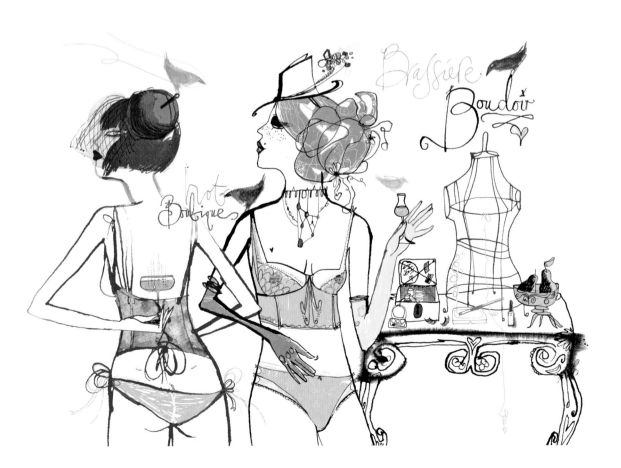

Carlotta

1959 born in Lyon | lives and works in Paris
www.carlotta.fr

CLIENTS
Grande Épicerie de Paris/
Bon Marché, Burberry, Elle,
Le Printemps, DIM

AGENTS
Philippe Arnaud
France
philippearnaud.com

Kramer+Kramer
USA
kramerkramer.com

Paumes
Japan
paumes.com

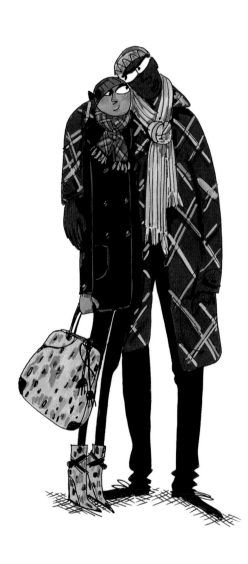

"My graphic style is economical
and I sketch elegant, mischievous girls.
Fashion is the reflection of life, and for
me an illustration can nail an era."

„Mein Grafikstil ist ökonomisch, ich skizziere elegante,
neckische Girls. Fashion spiegelt das Leben wider,
und für mich kann eine Illustration eine ganze
Ära auf den Punkt bringen."

« Mon style est économe, je dessine des filles
élégantes et malicieuses. La mode est le reflet
de la vie, et l'illustration fixe une époque. »

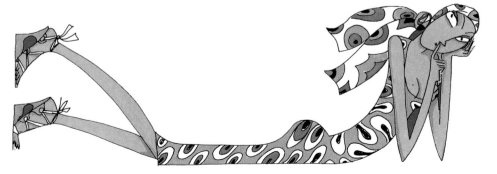

↑   **Winter, 2010**
Uomo magazine, Japan;
pen and gouache

←   **Vierge/Pucci, 2005**
Elle magazine, Art Direction:
Santiago Boutan; pen and gouache

→   **Vintage, 2007**
Elle magazine, Art Direction:
Santiago Boutan; pen, gouache
and digital

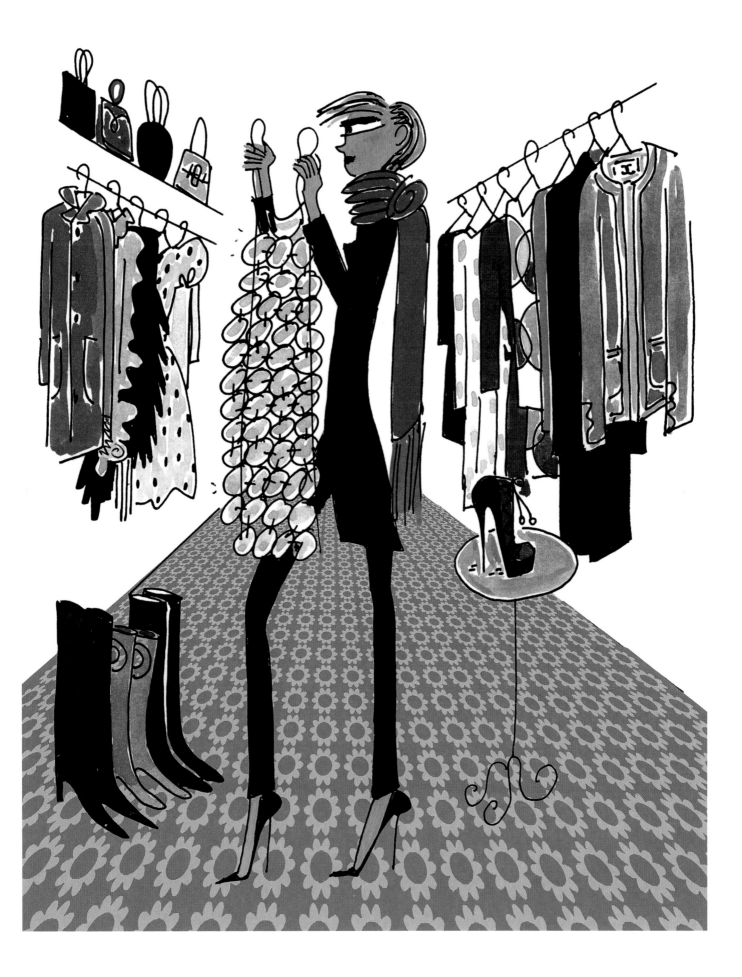

"Carlotta embodies Parisienne fashion. She captures its spirit, fantasy and impertinence. Her design-work is at once attentive and on edge; she is the archetype of the 'Made in France' product."

MARIE RUCKI
Director, Studio Berçot

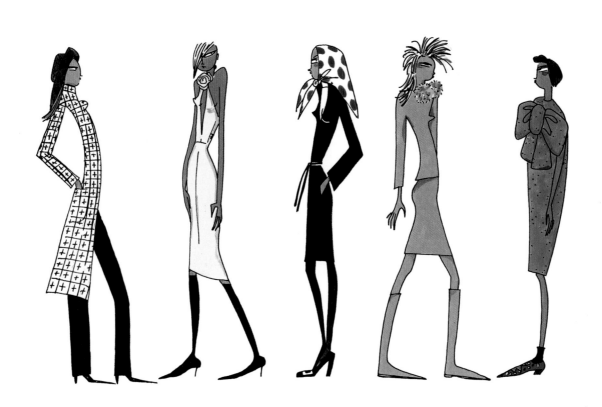

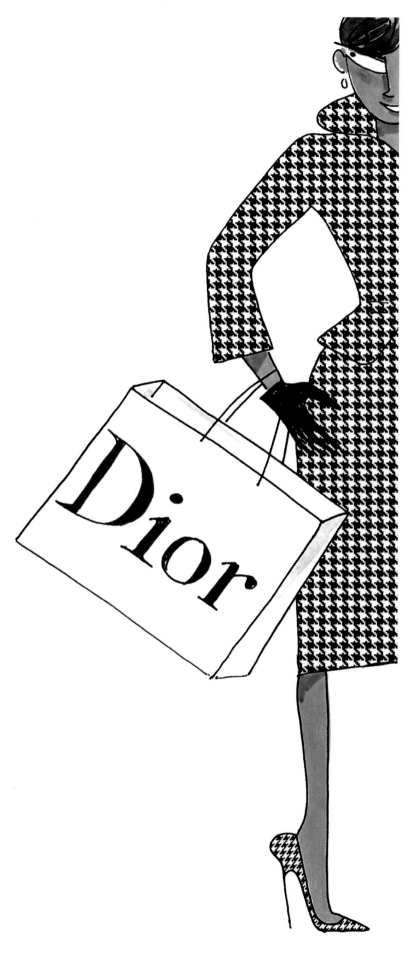

Dior Girl, 2011
Personal work, sketches for a book
cover; pen, gouache and digital

↖ **Ziggy Girl, 2010**
Maquia magazine; pen and gouache

← **Fashion Hits 2000, 2000**
Paumes editions, book Carlotta A to Z,
Art Direction: Hisashi Tokuyoshi;
pen and gouache

Cecilia Carlstedt

1977 in Stockholm | lives and works in Stockholm
www.ceciliacarlstedt.com

AGENTS

Illustration Division
USA
illustrationdivision.com

Agent Bauer
Sweden
agentbauer.com

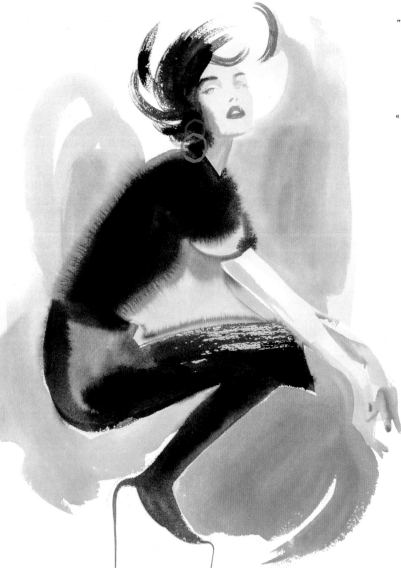

"What excites me when creating
a fashion illustration is the unlimited
scope for interpreting a design.
This combines with the satisfaction
of capturing, in an unexpected way,
what I aim to express."

„Bei Modeillustrationen finde ich besonders
spannend, dass ein Design praktisch unbegrenzt
interpretierbar wird. Dazu kommt die Genugtuung,
auf neuartige Weise das einzufangen,
was ich ausdrücken will."

« Ce qui m'intéresse dans l'illustration de mode,
c'est la marge illimitée d'interprétation d'un
vêtement, et la satisfaction de capturer de façon
inattendue ce que je veux exprimer. »

Untitled, 2011
H&M, interior wall design;
ink on paper and digital

→   Untitled, 2012
Swarovski; ink on paper and digital

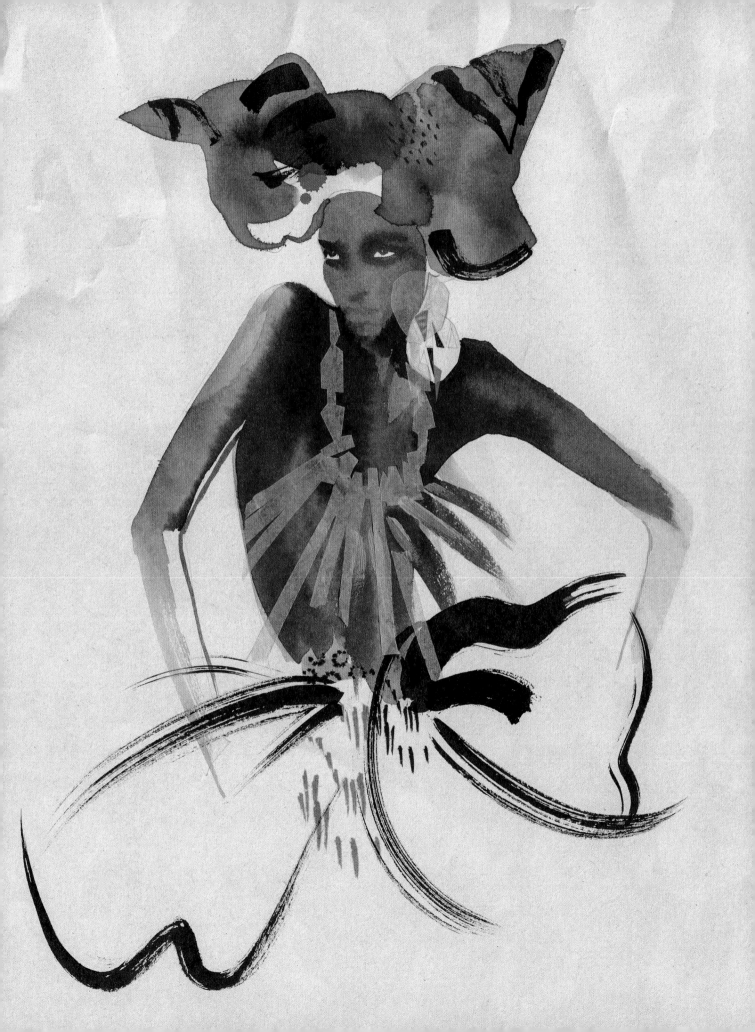

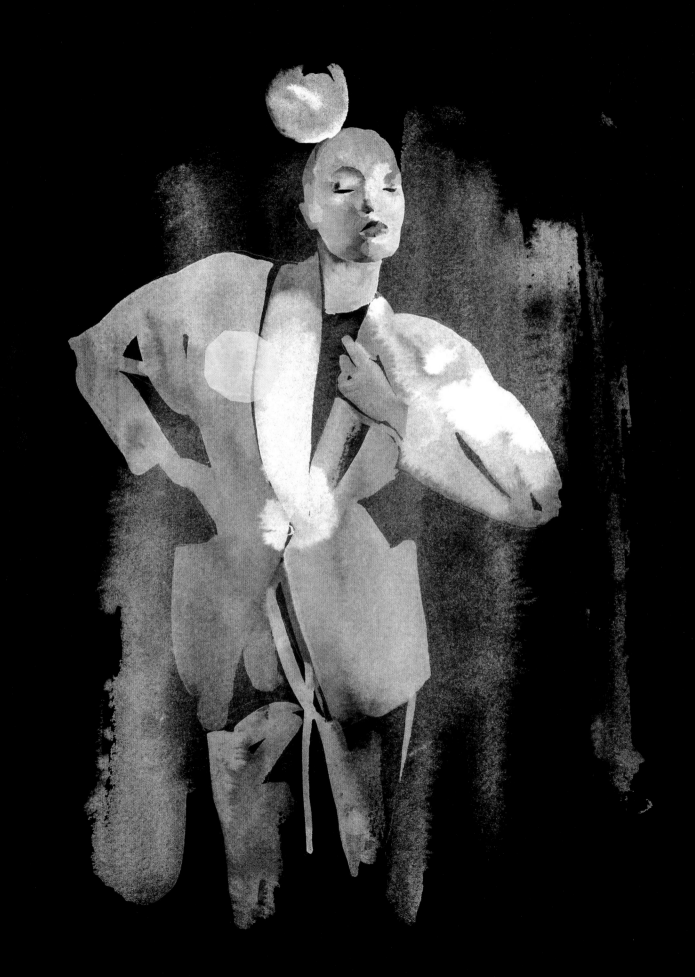

→   Untitled, 2012
Personal work; ink and collage
of screenprint on paper and digital

←   Untitled, 2011
Personal work; ink on paper
and digital inversion

↓   Gareth Pugh Design, 2012
Dash magazine; ink on paper
and digital

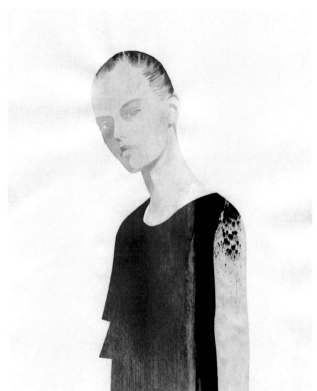

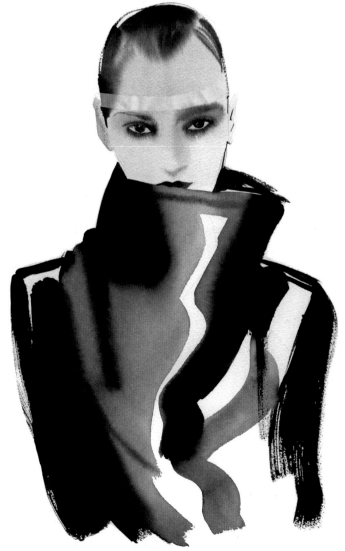

Annelie Carlström

1979 born in Stockholm | lives and works in Stockholm
www.anneliecarlstrom.se

CLIENTS
Monki, Minimarket, Fashion Tale magazine,
Elle Singapore, Elle Canada, Lamija Suljevic,
Nylon magazine, Bon magazine, H&M

AGENTS
Woo Agentur
Sweden
woo.se

Sticky Stuff
Netherlands
stickystuff.nl

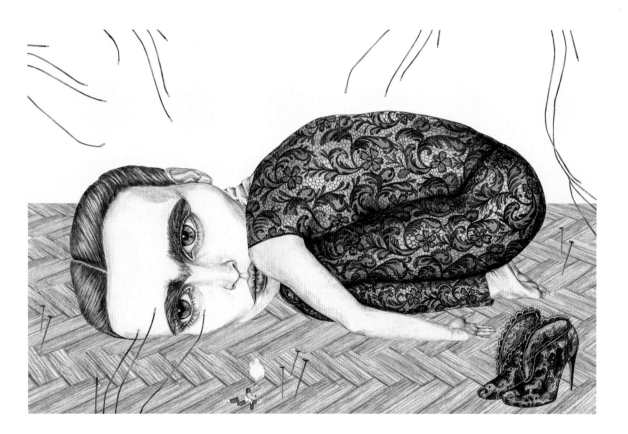

"I love working with fashion illustration. I find it truly interesting to play
with tone and expression. For me it's all about people, and our lives."

„Ich liebe die Arbeit mit Modeillustration. Vor allem interessiert es mich, mit Schattierung
und Ausdruck zu spielen. Dabei geht's für mich vor allem um Menschen und unser Leben."

« J'adore l'illustration de mode, et j'aime jouer avec le ton et l'expression.
Pour moi, c'est une affaire humaine, qui parle de nos vies. »

The Broken Column, 2008
Fashion Tale magazine; pencil
and digital

→　First-aid Kit Tee, 2012
First-aid Kit/Save the Children/Way out
West; T-shirt print, pencil and digital

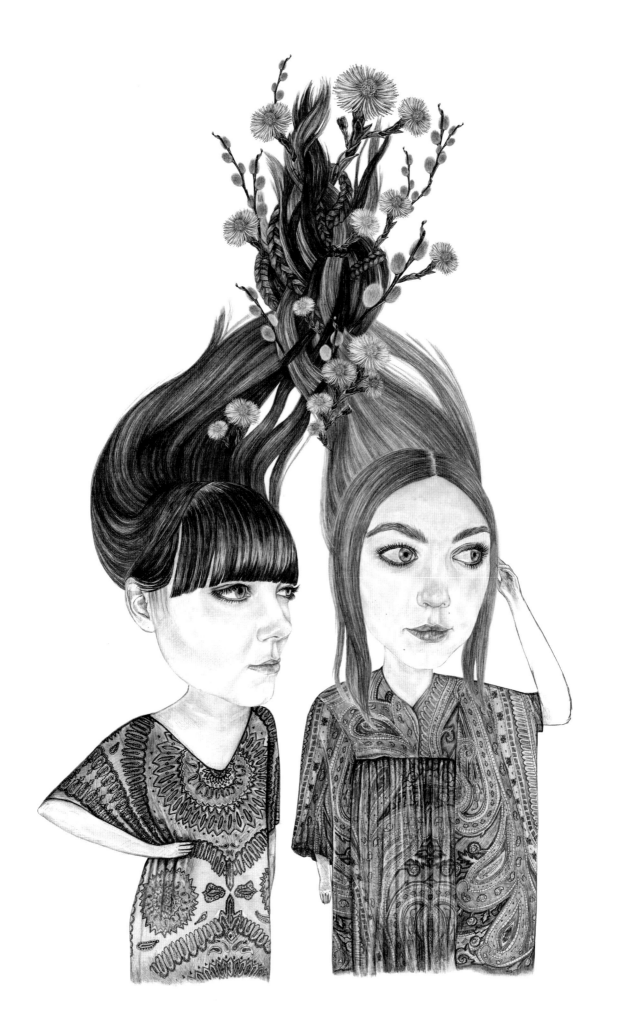

Shoes, 2010
Guldlådan, shoe bag; pencil and digital

→ **Home is Where I Stand, 2010**
Lamija Stuljevic, lookbook; pencil
and digital

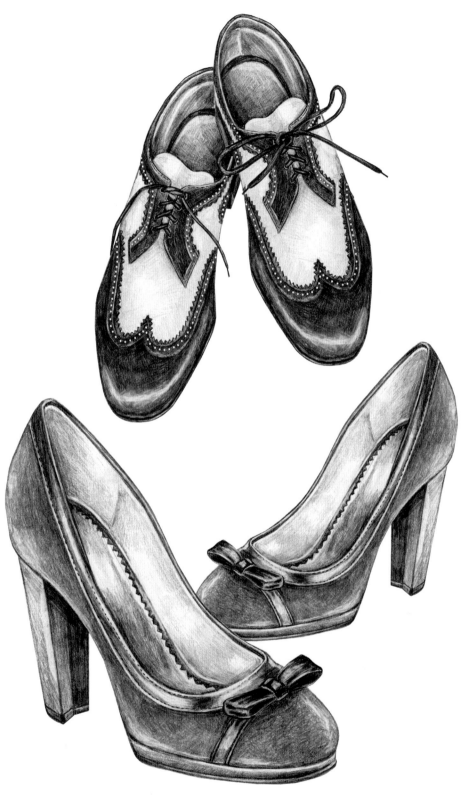

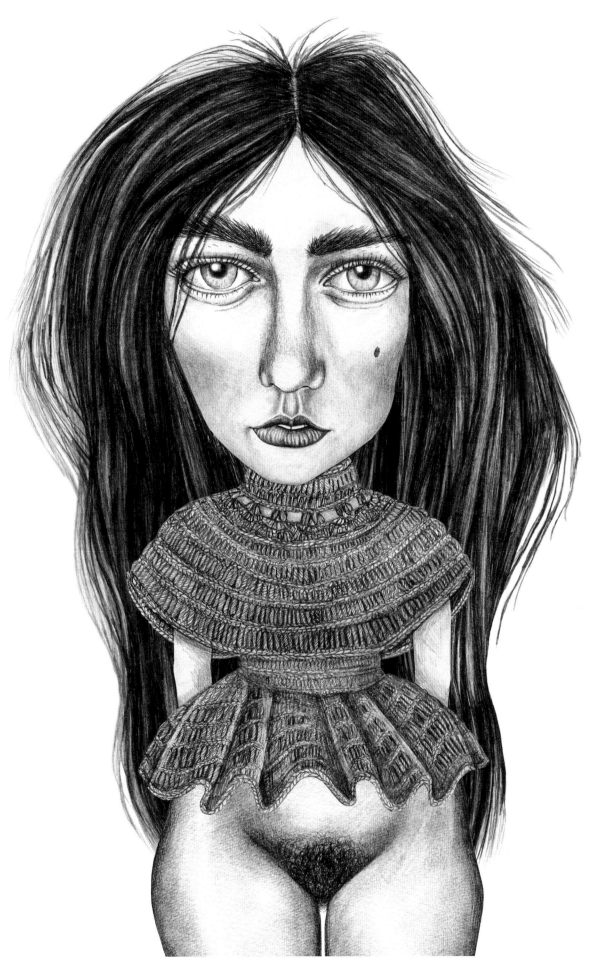

Alexandra Compain-Tissier

1971 born in Versailles | lives and works in Paris
www.alexandracompaintissier.com

CLIENTS
Saks Fifth Avenue, Moncler, American Express,
Total, GQ, Maison Martin Margiela, W magazine,
The New York Times Magazine, ZEITmagazin

AGENT
Illustration Division
USA
illustrationdivision.com

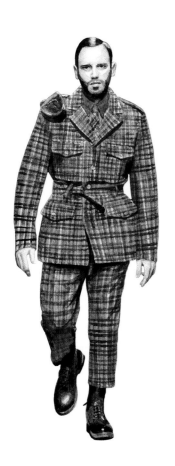
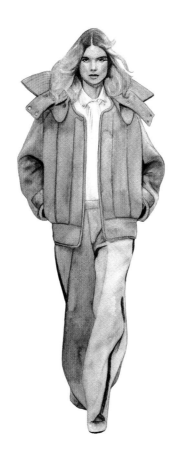
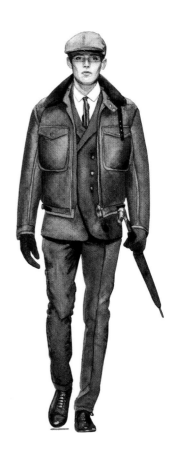

"In fashion illustration I can express my taste for color and pattern,
which give a thickness to the painting."

„In Modeillustrationen drücke ich meine Vorliebe für Farben und Muster aus.
Das verleiht der Zeichnung Substanz."

« Dans l'illustration de mode, je peux exprimer mon goût pour la couleur
et les motifs, qui donnent une épaisseur à la peinture. »

Catwalk Winter 2012
NZZ magazine; watercolor

→ **Madame Grès, 2011**
Les Inrocks magazine; watercolor

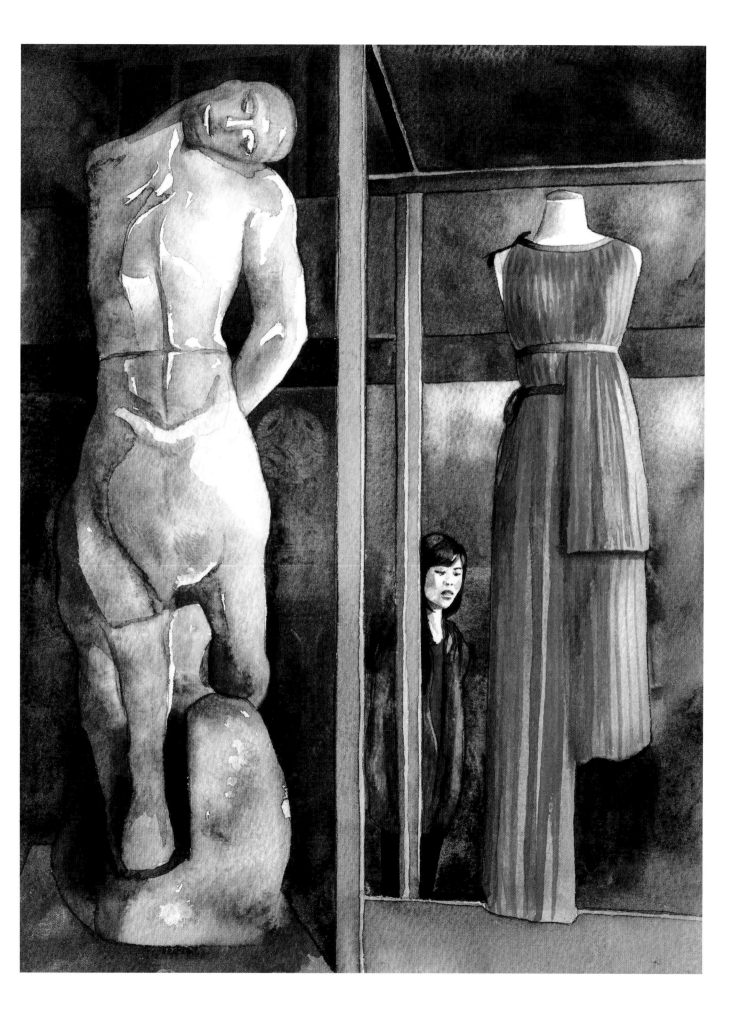

"With her incredibly skillful watercolor,
  Alexandra creates impressive images that are
  as moving as they are impeccable, capturing
  the viewer's attention and intelligently revealing
  the most sensitive sides of her subjects."

SOPHIE TOPORKOFF
Communications Art Director
Maison Martin Margiela

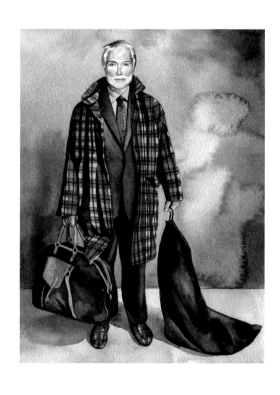

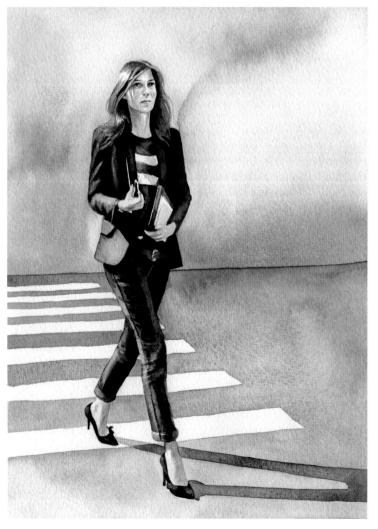

Glenn O'Brien, 2011
Les Inrocks magazine; watercolor

←   Emmanuelle Alt, 2011
Les Inrocks magazine; watercolor

→   Bill Cunningham, 2011
Les Inrocks magazine; watercolor

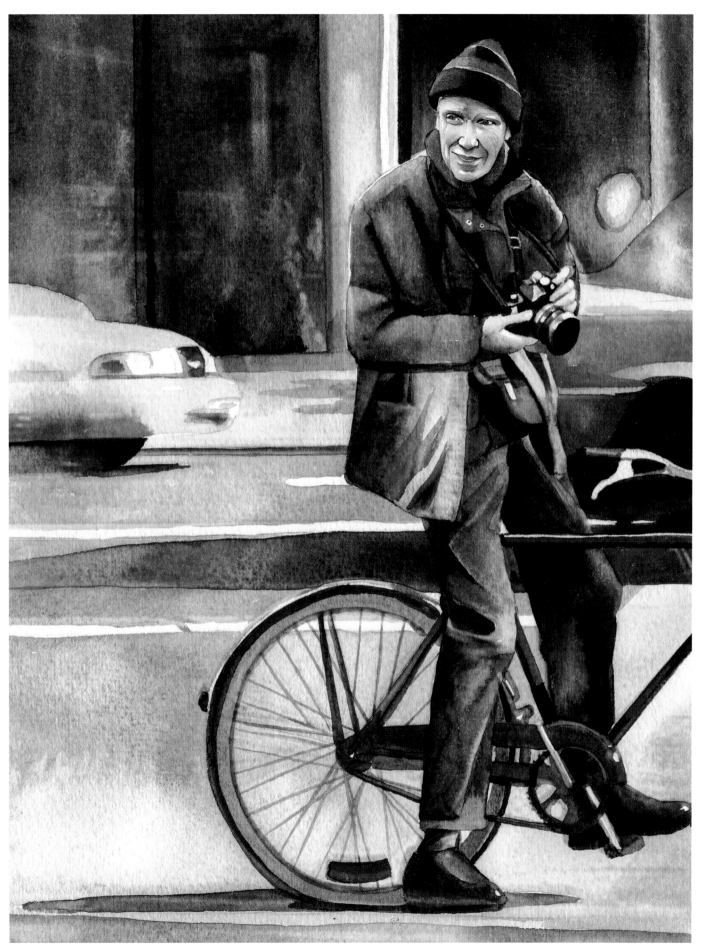

Jean-Philippe Delhomme

1959 born in Paris | lives and works in Paris
www.jphdelhomme.com

CLIENTS
Le Bon Marché Rive Gauche, Colette, Interview magazine,
Architectural Digest, Case da Abitare, Condé Nast Traveler,
The New Yorker, GQ, Stern, Barneys

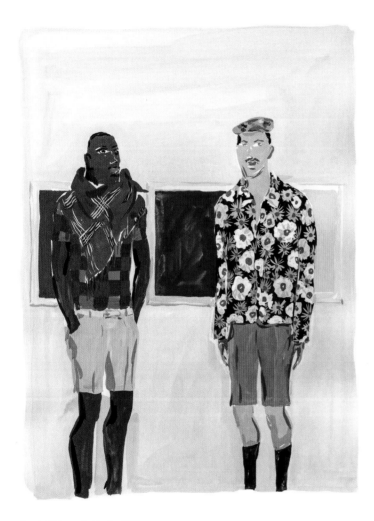

"Fashion offers an occasion to do some classical painting, just like when royal figures or a courtesan would have posed for a painting by Manet or Velázquez."

„Bei der Mode hat man die Chance, wie in der klassischen Malerei zu gestalten, ähnlich wie Angehörige des Hofes oder eine junge Prostituierte für ein Gemälde von Manet oder Velázquez posierten."

« La mode donne l'occasion de faire de la peinture classique, comme lorsque des têtes couronnées ou une jeune prostituée posaient pour Manet ou Velázquez. »

Louis Vuitton & Prada, 2012
Série limitée, France; gouache

→   **Yves Saint Laurent, 2012**
Série limitée, France; gouache

→→ **Lacoste, 2012**
Série limitée, France; gouache

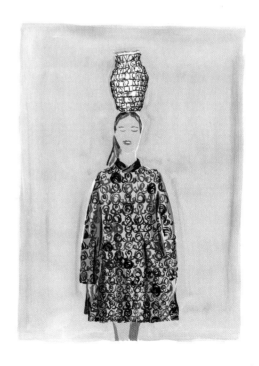

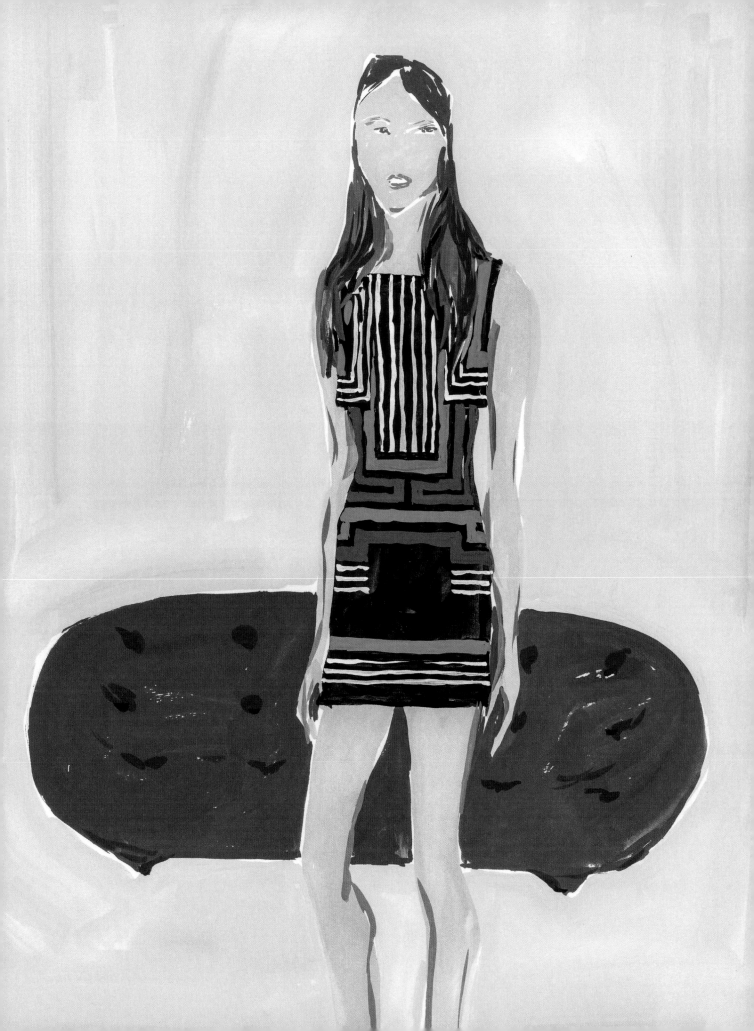

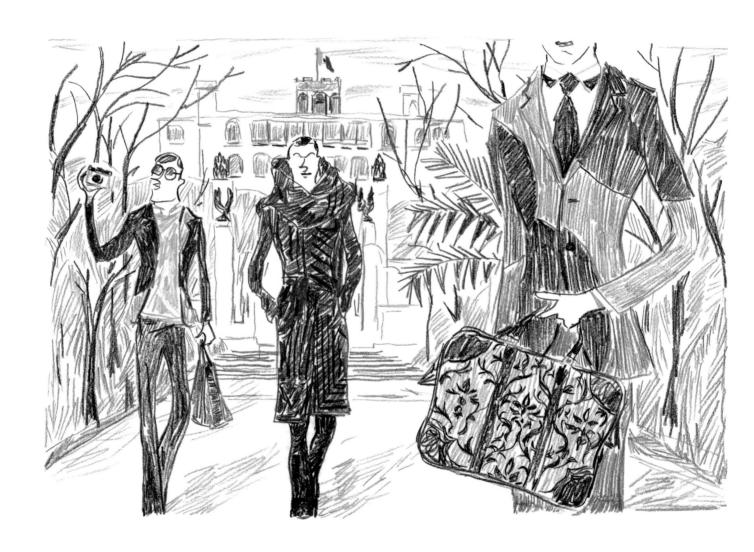

Men's Fashion, Fall/Winter 2012–13,
Gucci, Louis Vuitton, Bottega Veneta
El Palacio de Hierro, Mexico; color pencils

→　Men's Fashion, Fall/Winter
2012–13
El Palacio de Hierro, Mexico; color pencils

p.112　Women's Fashion, Fall/Winter
2012–13, DKNY, Etro, Burberry Prorsum
El Palacio de Hierro, Mexico; gouache

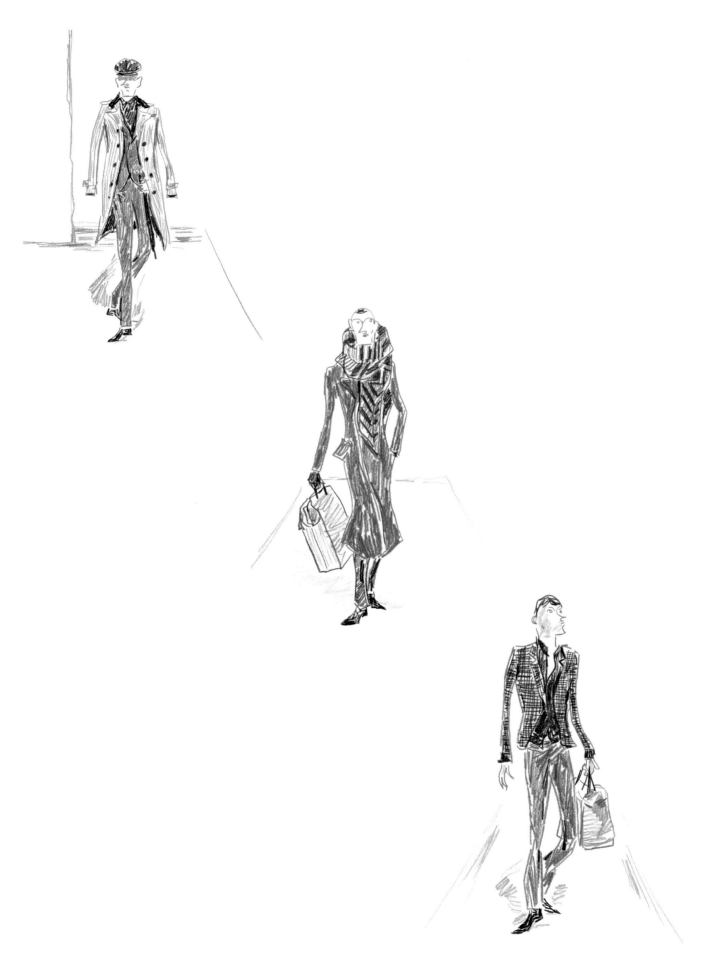

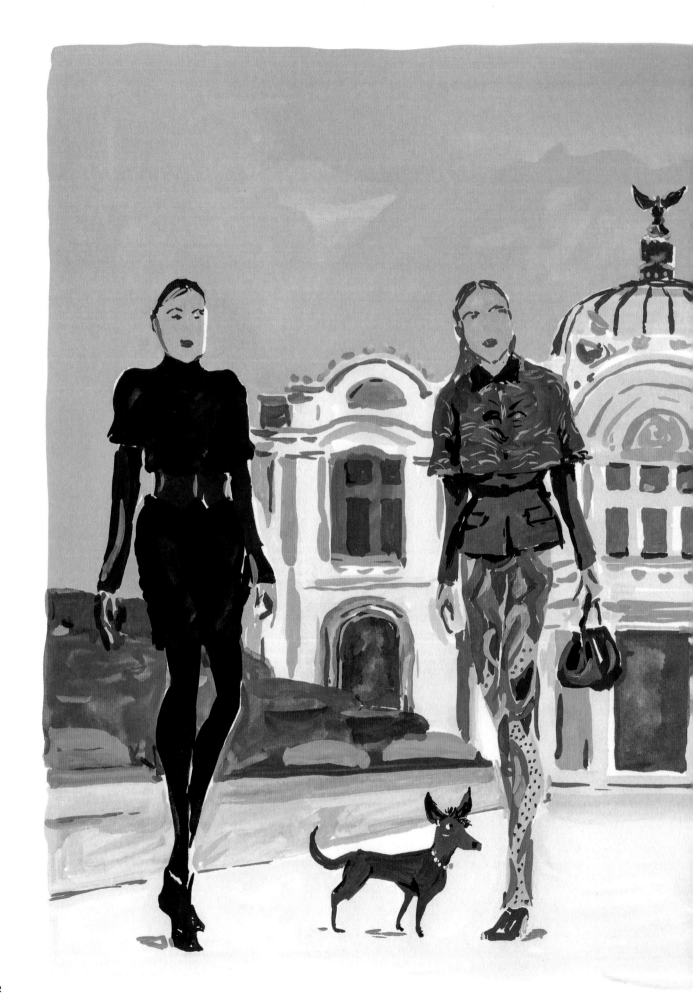

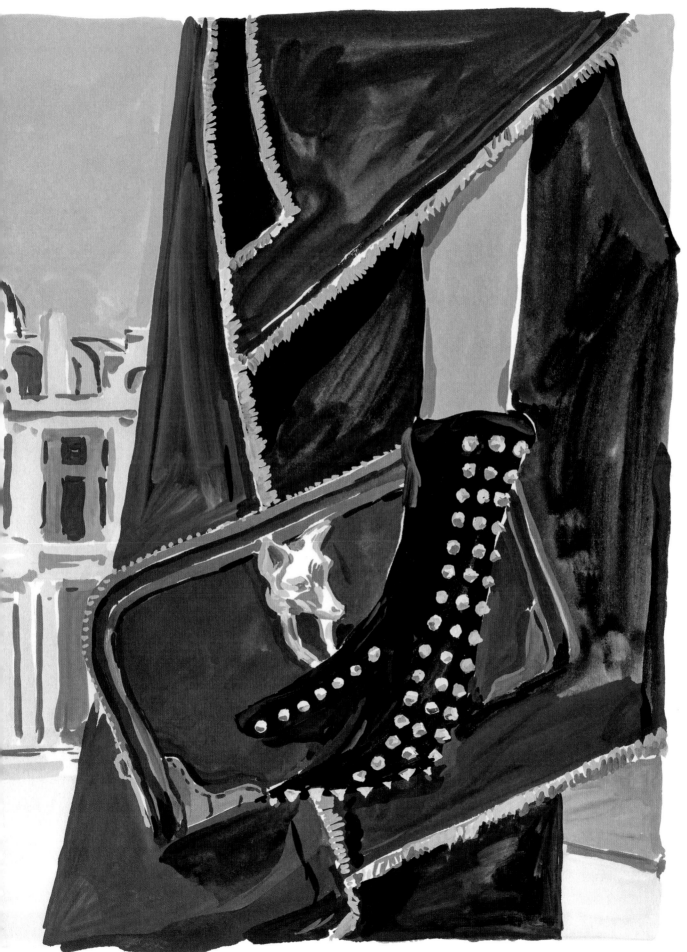

James Dignan

1964 born in Auckland | lives and works in Sydney and Hong Kong
www.jamesdignan.com

CLIENTS
Louis Vuitton, Katharine Hamnett, Hugo Boss,
Escada, Chloé, Jil Sander, Vogue Australia,
Vogue Japan, Vogue China, Vogue Pelle,
Visionaire, Moustache

AGENTS
Traffic Creative
Management
USA
trafficnyc.com

The Illustration Room
Australia
illustrationroom.com.au

Unit c.m.a.
Netherlands
unit.nl

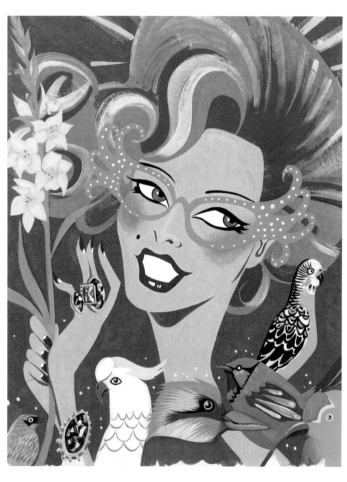

"Finding the essence, capturing a mood and injecting a touch of humour. I love to experiment and believe the element of play is supreme."

„Die Essenz finden, Stimmungen einfangen, eine Prise Humor ergänzen. Ich liebe es zu experimentieren und halte das spielerische Element für das Wichtigste."

« Trouver l'essence, capter une humeur et injecter une touche d'humour. J'aime expérimenter, et je pense que l'élément de jeu est suprême. »

Edna Everedge Updated, 2011
The Drawing Room, postcard series
celebrating Australiana; acrylic

→ **Warrior, 2011**
Glamour magazine, Germany,
awarded illustration in a readers
competition; gouache

→→ **Memphis, 2012**
Residence magazine; acrylic,
ink, gouache and digital

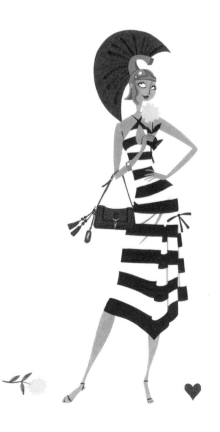

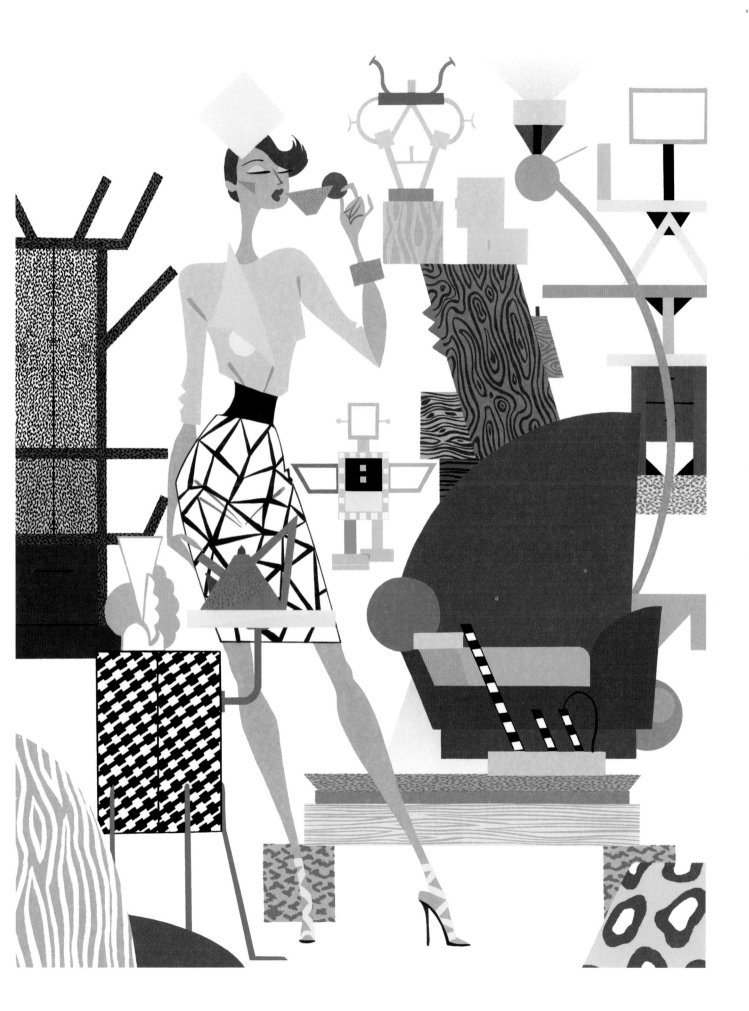

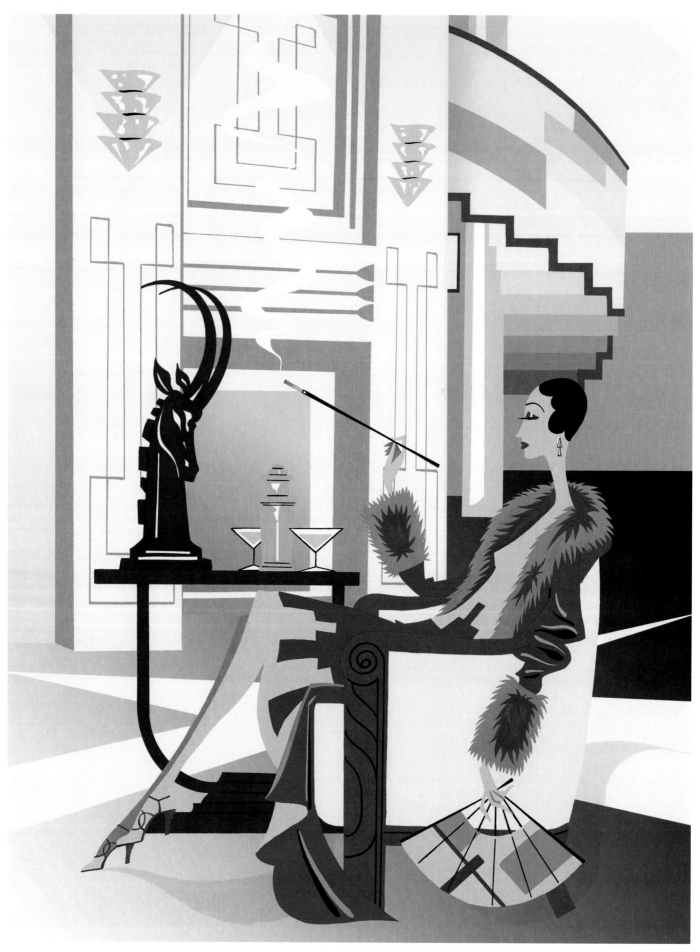

"Dignan's work is recognizable for its extremely assertive line. His drawings are authoritative, fashion-savvy, but always betray a sense of mischief."

STEPHEN TODD
Editor and Creative Director
Lumière magazine

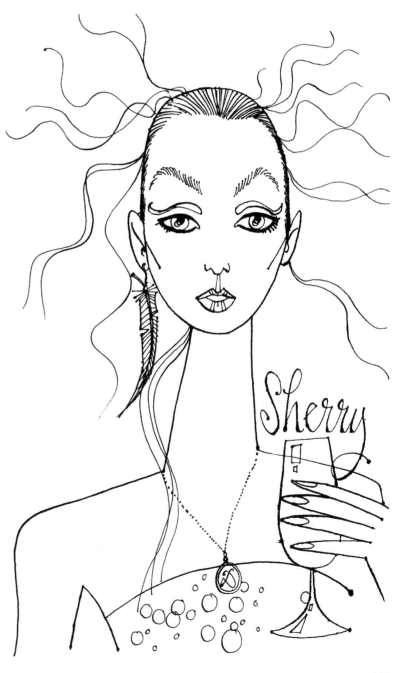

Sherry, 2013
Lumière, editorial for online magazine; ink

← **Deco,** 2012
Residence magazine; acrylic, ink, gouache and digital

Bil Donovan

1956 born in Philadelphia | lives and works in New York
www.bildonovan.com

CLIENTS
Christian Dior, Elle, Regis, Saks Fifth Avenue,
Neiman Marcus, Vogue, Marie Claire, Mercedes-Benz,
CFDA Estée Lauder, Harper Collins, Amazon.com

AGENT
Illustration Division
USA
illustrationdivision.com

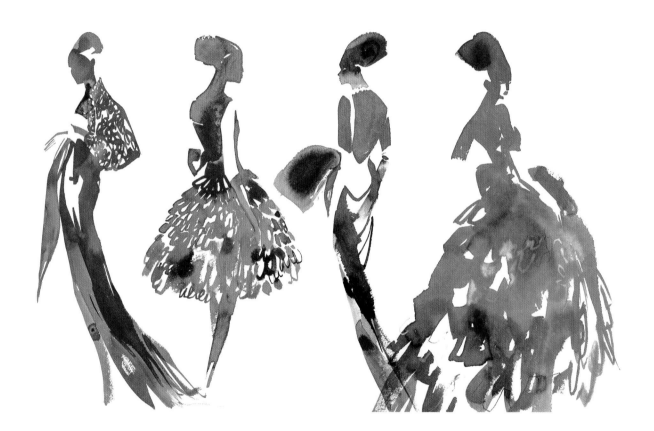

"I subscribe to a less-is-more aesthetic, through a minimal
amount of line and shape, and consider what is absent
to be as important as what is present."

„Durch minimalen Einsatz von Linie und Form widme ich mich einer Ästhetik
des ‚Weniger ist mehr'. Dabei ist Fehlendes genauso wichtig wie Vorhandenes."

«Mon esthétique est minimaliste, avec des lignes et des formes réduites,
et pour moi ce qui est absent est aussi important que ce qui est présent.»

Dior Timeline, 2012
St. Regis/Starwood Group,
Creative Direction: Bree Dahl;
ink on paper and digital

→ Dior Vintage, 2012
Christian Dior Beauty, Creative
Direction: Amanda Baldwin;
ink and gouache on paper and digital

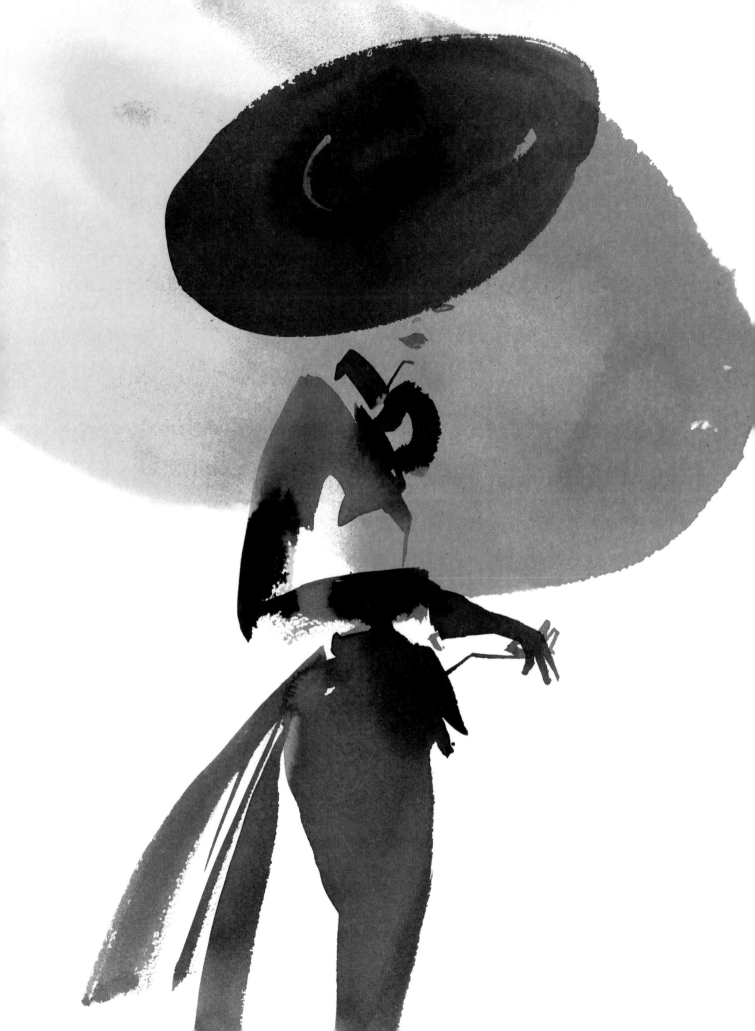

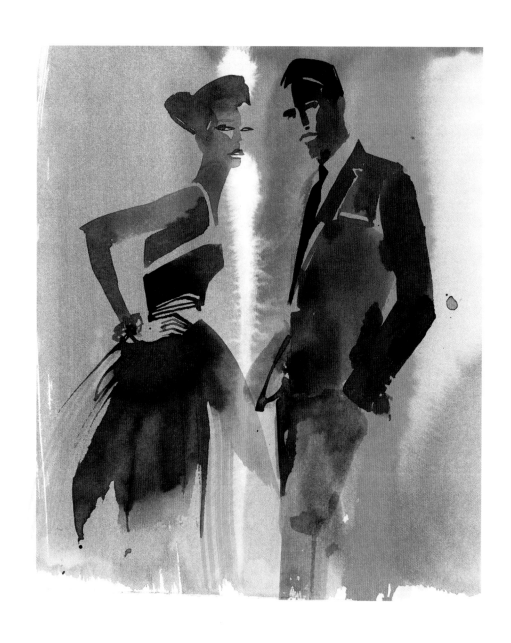

My Habit, 2012
Amazon.com, Creative Direction:
Tony Balquin; ink and gouache on paper

→ Glamourpuss, 2012
Personal work; ink and gouache on paper

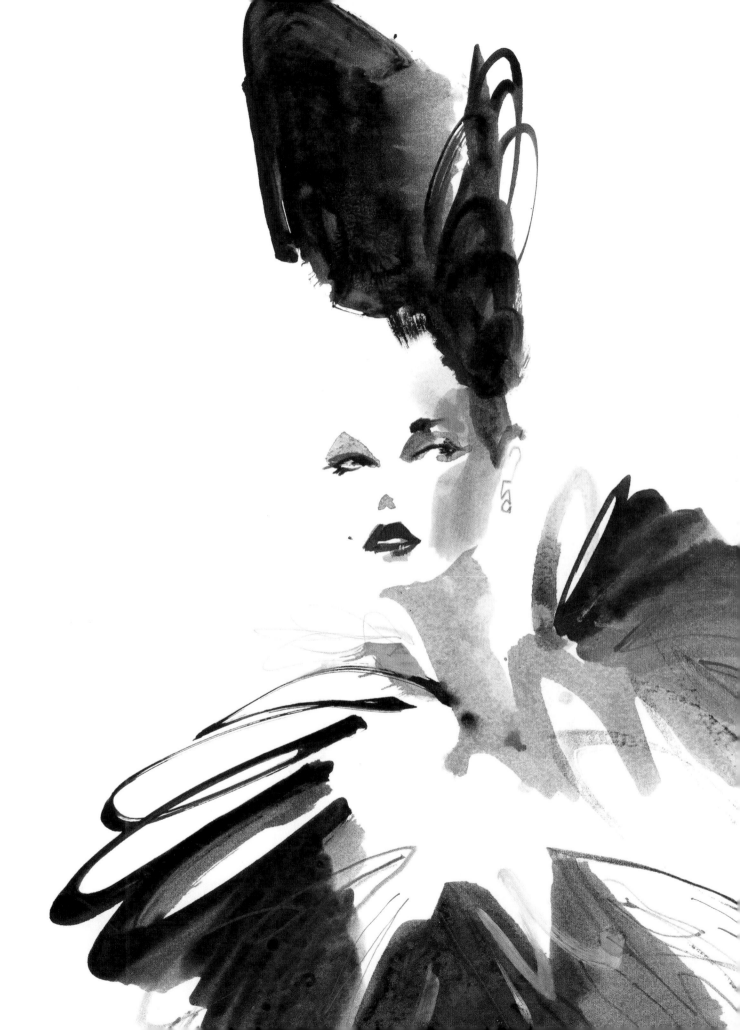

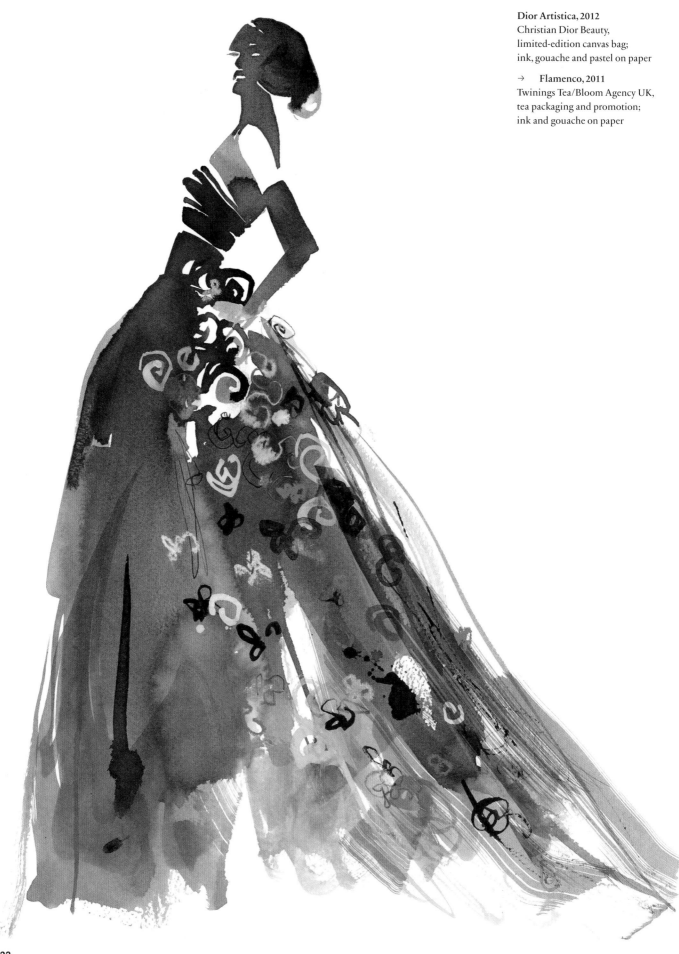

Dior Artistica, 2012
Christian Dior Beauty,
limited-edition canvas bag;
ink, gouache and pastel on paper

→   Flamenco, 2011
Twinings Tea/Bloom Agency UK,
tea packaging and promotion;
ink and gouache on paper

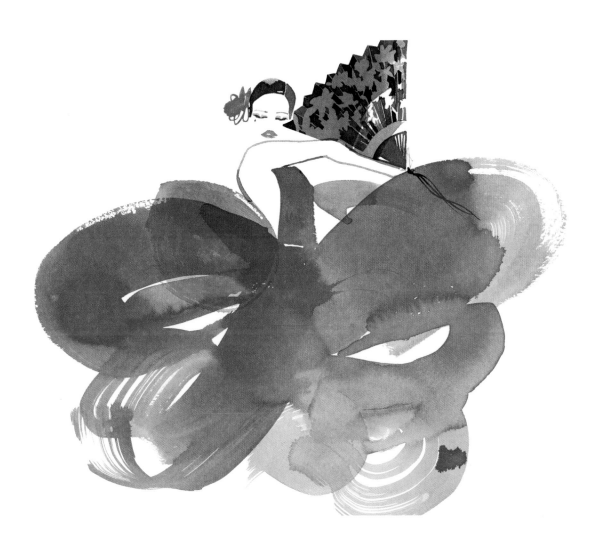

"Bil's work reflects his personality: it is elegant and effortless with an unmistakable element of charm and wit. He has a knack for capturing the essence of a garment and the woman wearing it in just a few strokes."

PAMELA BAXTER
President/CEO
Christian Dior Couture

Christina Drejenstam

1977 born in Gothenburg | lives and works in Stockholm
www.drejenstam.se

CLIENTS
Nike, H&M,
Lindex, Harrods

AGENTS
Peppercookies
UK
peppercookies.com

Molly & Co
Sweden
agentmolly.com

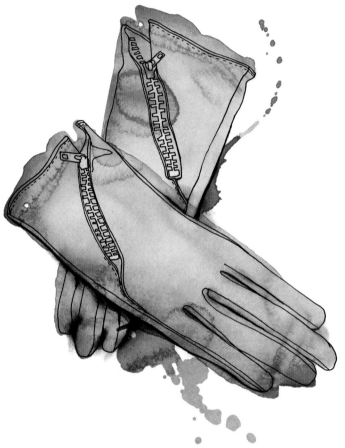

"When I work with fashion illustration I try to catch a certain movement, style, fluidity or shape but still leave enough for the viewer's imagination."

„Bei meiner Arbeit mit Modeillustration versuche ich eine bestimmte Bewegung oder Form, einen Stil oder ein gewisses Fließen einzufangen. Doch der Fantasie des Betrachters soll genug Raum bleiben."

«Avec l'illustration de mode, j'essaie de capter un certain mouvement, un style, la fluidité ou la forme, mais en laissant de la place à l'imagination.»

Gloves, 2012
Stella magazine; pen, watercolor

→   Parrot, 2012
Sophie by Sophie, lookbook;
pen, watercolor, photograph

→→ Portrait, 2011
Kicks magazine; pen, watercolor

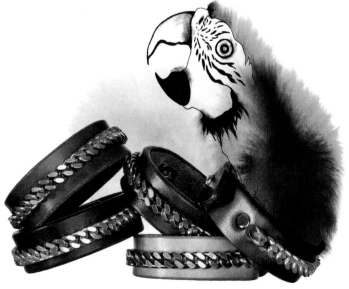

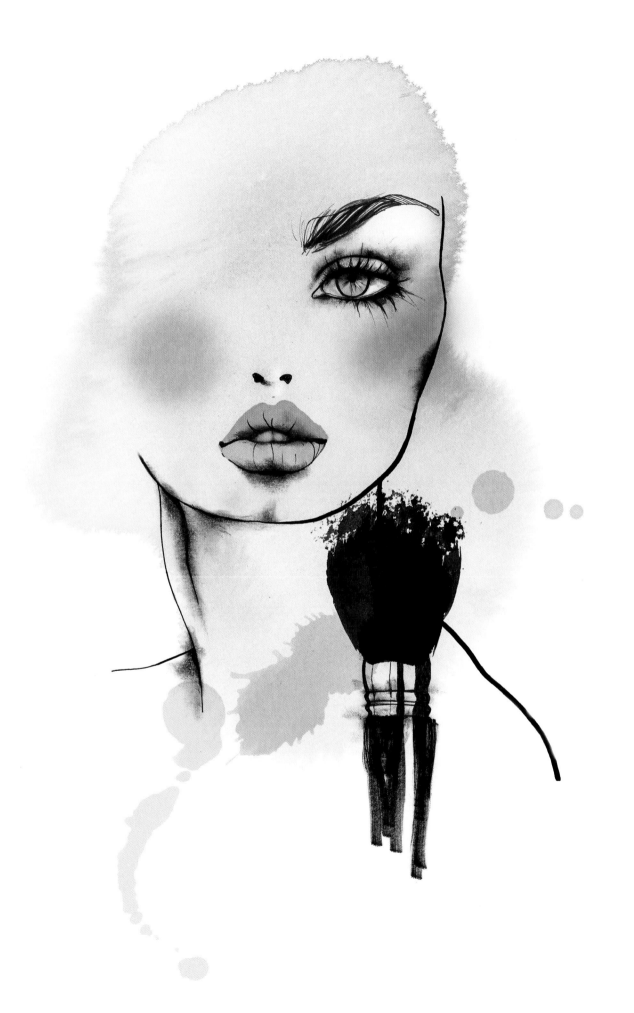

Daniel Egnéus

1972 born in Falköping, Sweden | lives and works in Athens
www.danielegneus.com

CLIENTS
Marie Claire, Velvet, Grey magazine,
Playboy, Berlin Fashion Week,
Nike, Adidas, H&M, Swarovski

AGENTS
Illustration Division
USA
illustrationdivision.com

Good Illustration Ltd
UK
goodillustration.com

2agenten
Germany
2agenten.com

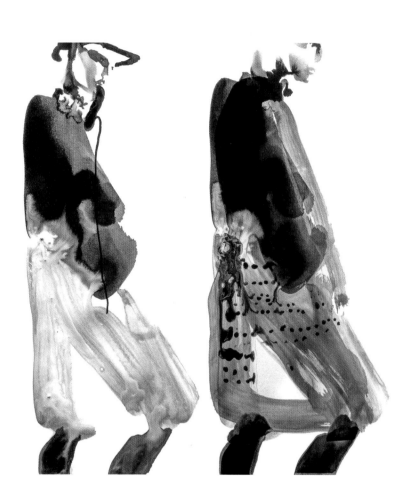

"It's not only the movement of the clothes that has to show in the image I'm painting but also that subtle story behind the person who wears them."

„Meine Bilder sollen nicht nur das Fließen der Kleidung zeigen, sondern auch dezent die Geschichte der Person, die sie trägt."

« Ce que l'image que je peins doit montrer, ce n'est pas seulement le mouvement des vêtements, mais aussi l'histoire subtile de la personne qui les porte. »

Two Women Walking, 2012
Personal work; watercolor and ink

→ **GeoGirl**, 2012
Personal work; watercolor and ink

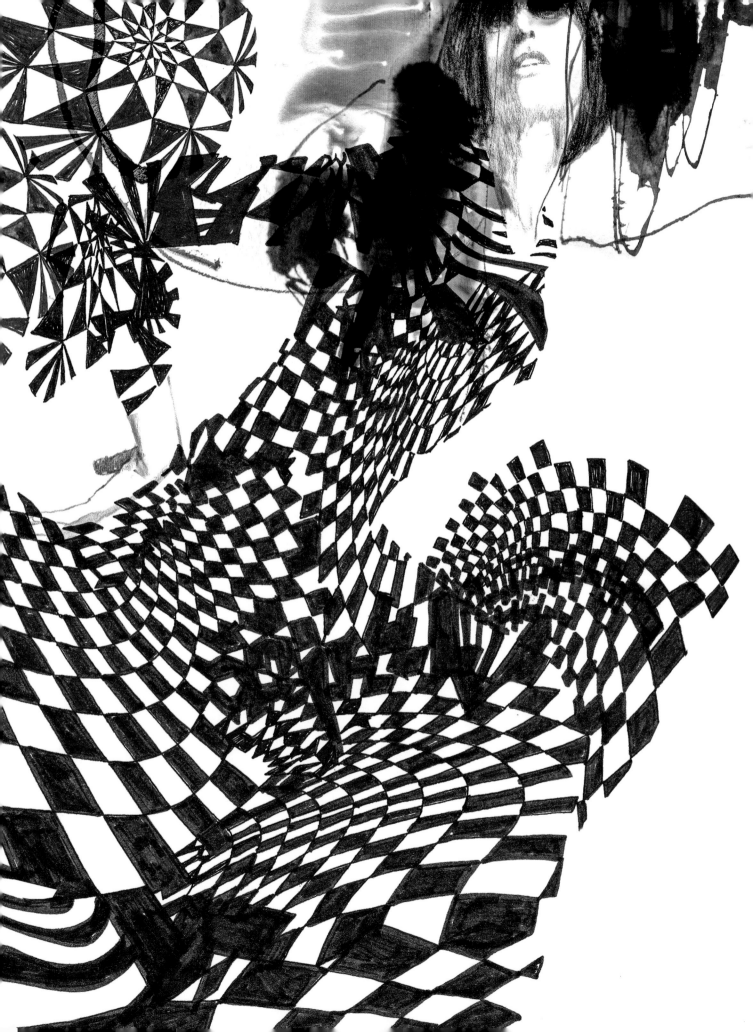

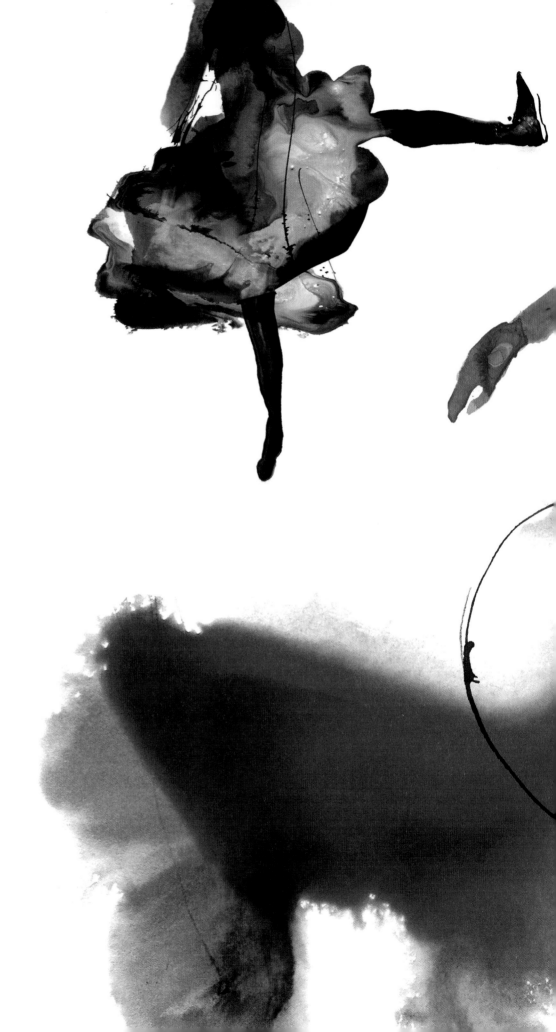

Dance, 2012
Personal work;
watercolor and ink

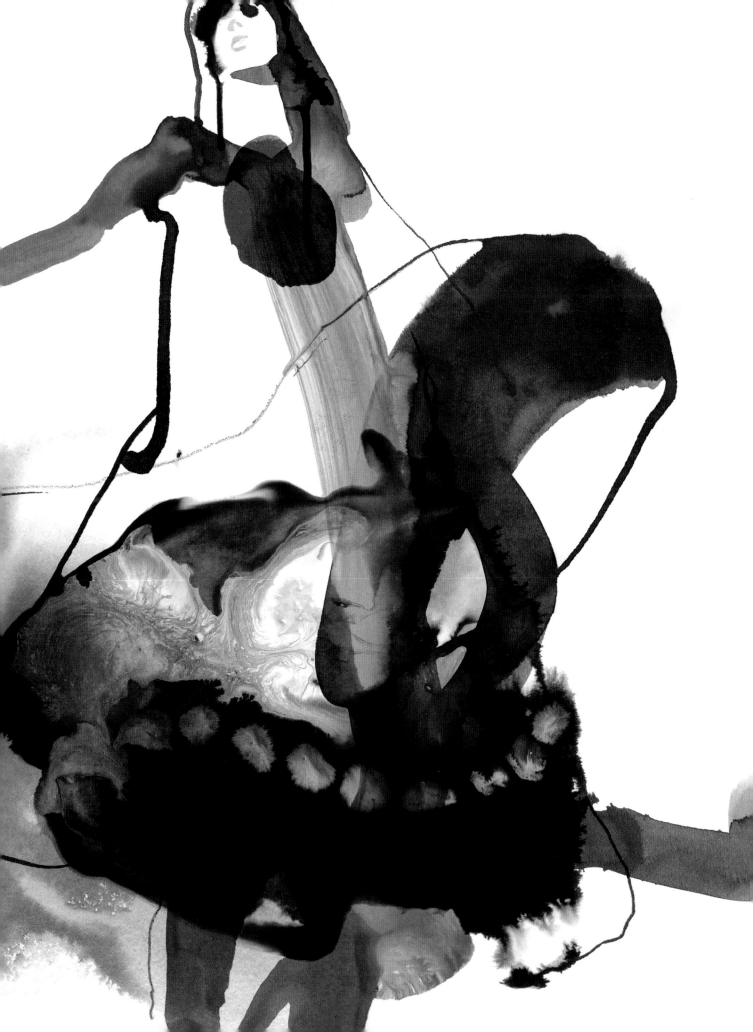

Sarah Egbert Eiersholt

1985 born in Copenhagen | lives and works in Copenhagen
www.sarahegberteiersholt.com

CLIENTS
The Independent on Sunday,
Miss magazine, Brand8, Die Presse,
Fleisch magazine

AGENTS
Peppercookies
UK
peppercookies.com

Caroline Seidler
Austria
carolineseidler.com

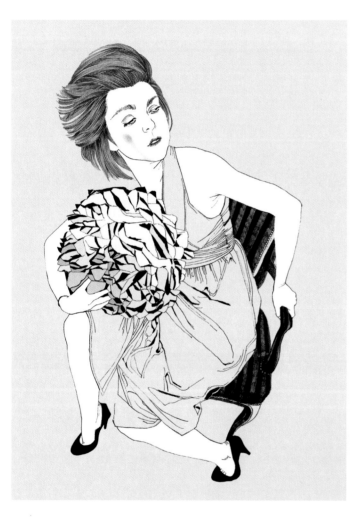

"The most interesting things for me are beauty and ugliness – finding a certain pattern, color or character in an environment where they do not belong."

„Am spannendsten finde ich Schönheit und Hässlichkeit – wenn ich bestimmte Muster, Farben oder Zeichen in einer Umgebung entdecke, in die sie nicht gehören."

« Ce qui m'intéresse le plus, c'est la beauté et la laideur – trouver un motif, une couleur ou un personnage dans un environnement où ils détonnent. »

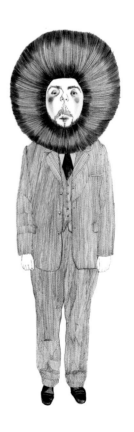

Posing, 2011
Personal work, poster; hand-drawn
and digital

→   **The Gentleman, 2011**
Brand8, T-shirt print; hand-drawn
and digital

→→ **Un homme et une femme, 2012**
Personal work, poster; hand-drawn
and digital

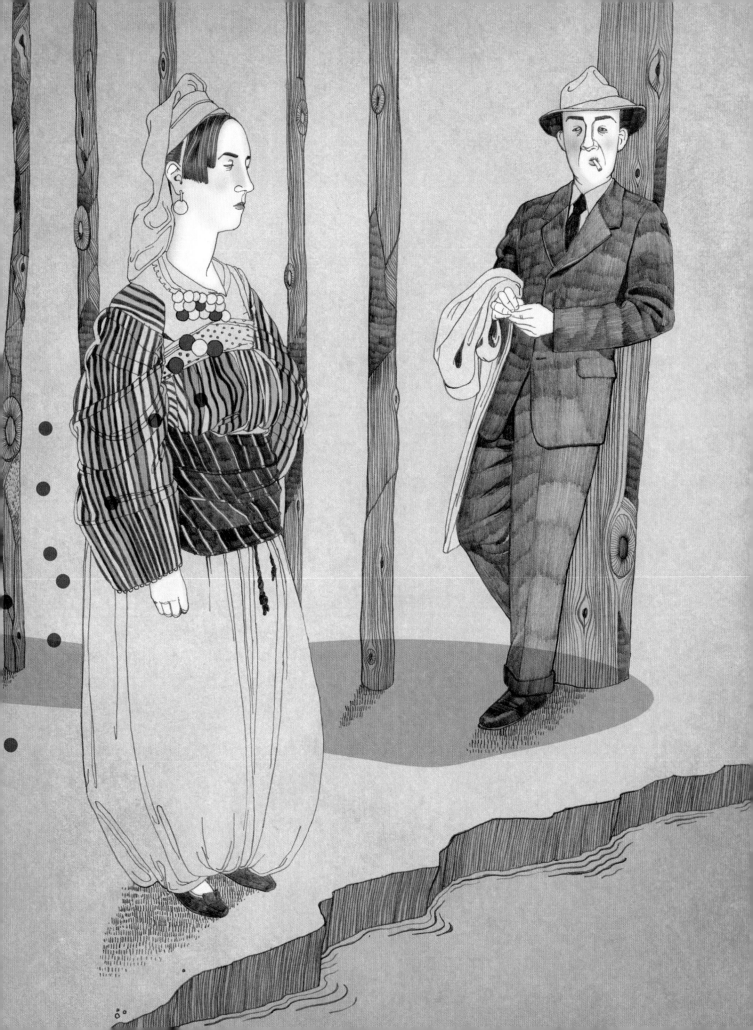

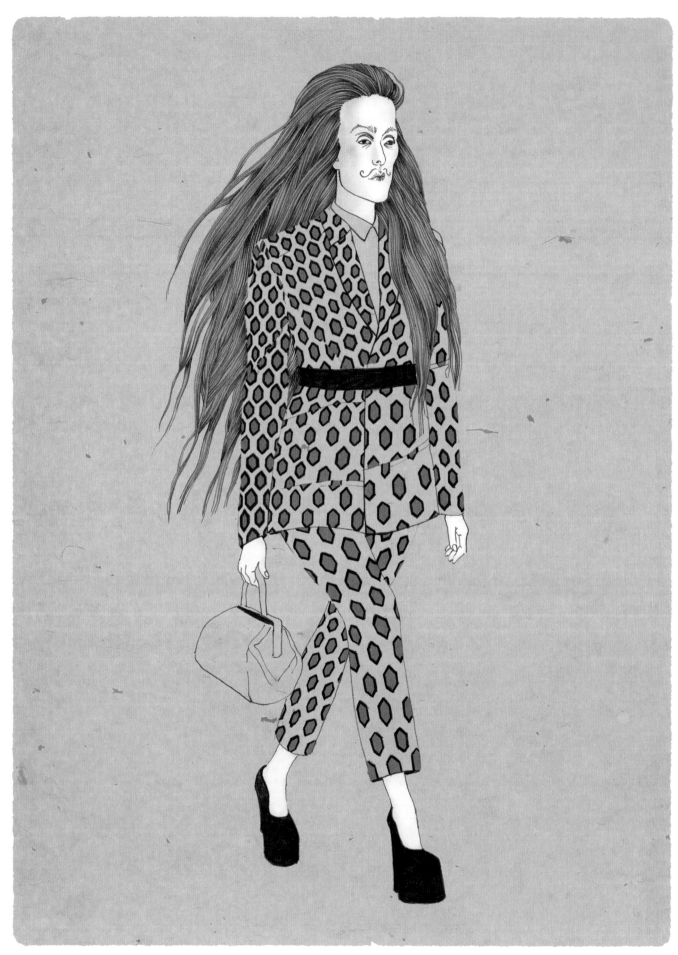

Catwalk #1, 2012
Personal work, poster;
hand-drawn and digital

←   Catwalk #2, 2012
Personal work, poster;
hand-drawn and digital

↓   Woman Smoking, 2012
Personal work, poster;
hand-drawn and digital

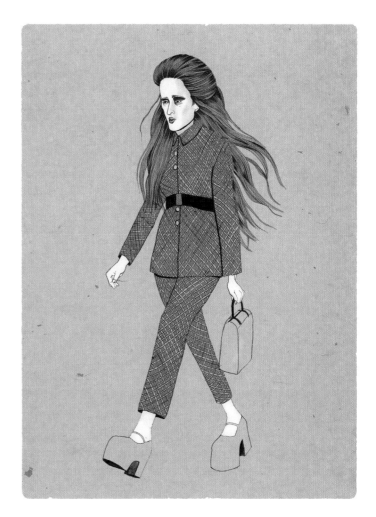

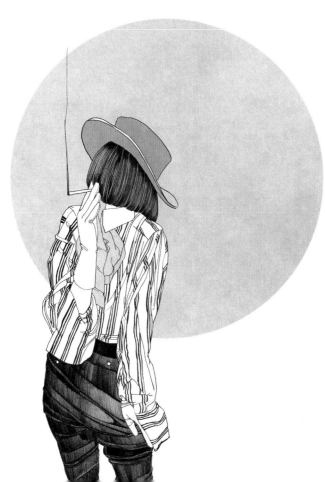

Ëlodie

1982 born in Royan, France | lives and works in Paris
www.elodie-illustrations.net

CLIENTS
Rochas, Rizzoli,
Target, Elle Quebec,
Glamour magazin
(Spain), Cosmopolitan

AGENTS
Colagene,
Illustration Clinic
Paris, Montreal, London
colagene.com

The Drawing Arm
Australia
thedrawingarm.com.au

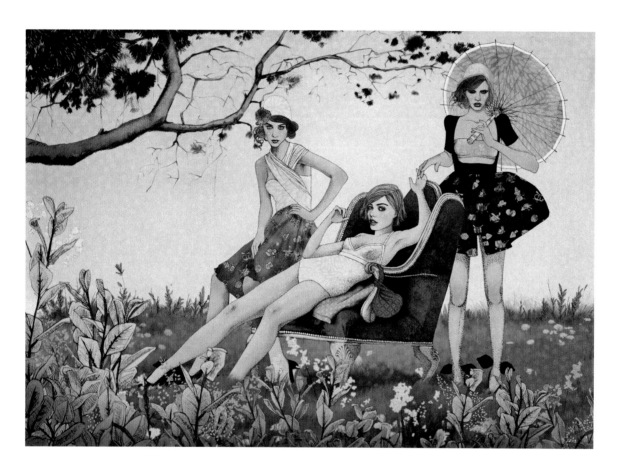

"Sometimes I'm just inspired by a color palette, or a pattern that stays in my mind for a few days until finally it comes out in a different form."

„Manchmal inspiriert mich schon eine Farbpalette oder ein Muster, das mir tagelang im Kopf herumgeht, bis es schließlich in anderer Form wieder auftaucht."

« Parfois je suis inspirée par des couleurs, ou un motif qui me reste à l'esprit quelques jours jusqu'à ce qu'il ressorte sous une forme différente. »

Untitled, 2012
La Marelle Éditions, shopping bag;
pigment liner, ink and digital

→ **Mysterious Girl, 2012**
Glamour magazine, Spain; pigment
liner and digital

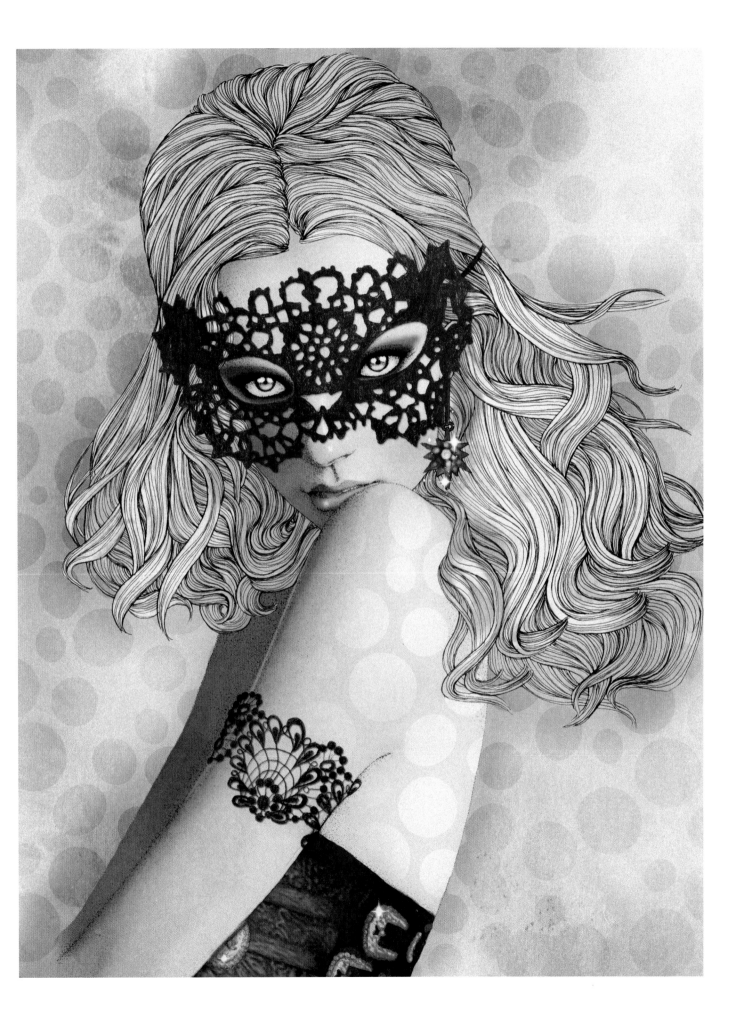

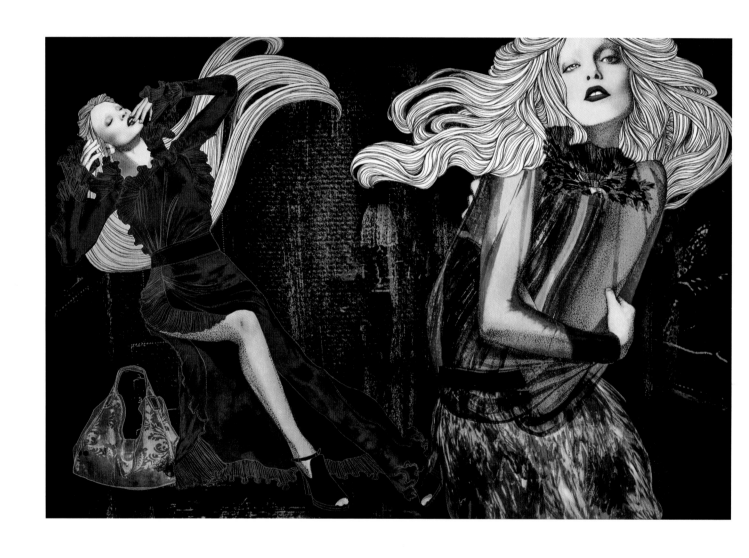

Untitled, 2012
Personal work; pigment liner,
ink and digital

→   Claudia, 2010
Personal work; pigment liner,
ink and digital

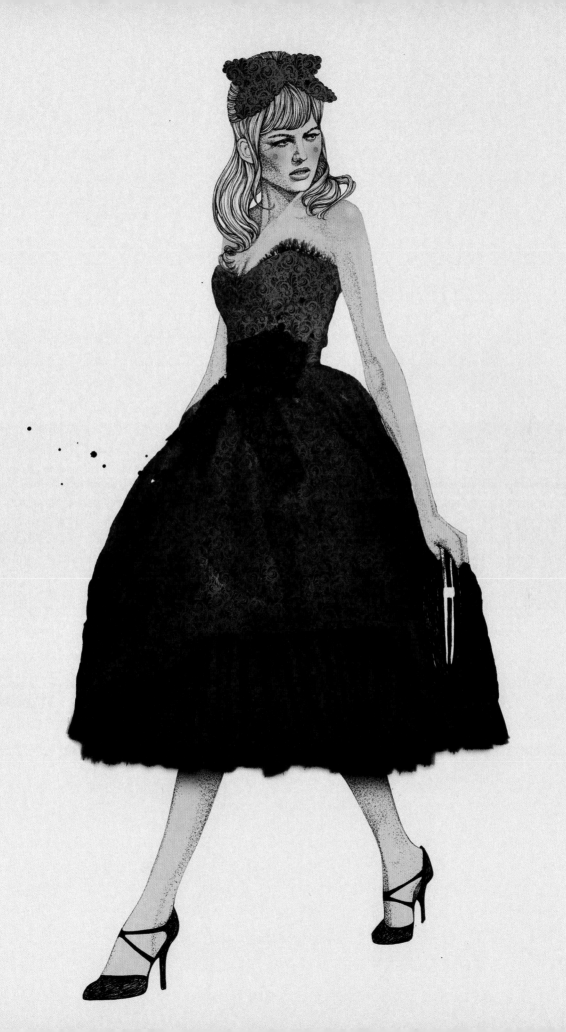

Maren Esdar

1972 born in Bielefeld | lives and works in Hamburg and Tel Aviv
www.marenesdar.com

CLIENTS

The New York Times, Vogue, Elle, GQ Style Italy,
Amica magazine Italy, Esquire, Tush magazine,
Surface magazine, W magazine, La Perla,
Mercedes-Benz, Neiman Marcus

AGENTS

Traffic Creative
Management
USA
trafficnyc.com

2agenten
Germany
2agenten.com

Unit c.m.a.
Netherlands
unit.nl

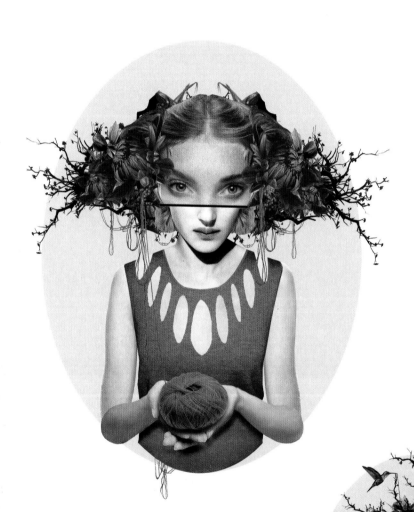

"I create poetic dream-worlds in
which sensual and spherical
individuals invite you to take
a closer look, to see a beauty
that lies beneath (the surface)."

„In meinen poetischen Traumwelten wird man
von sinnlich-sphärischen Wesen eingeladen,
näher hinzusehen und die Schönheit unter
der Oberfläche zu entdecken."

« Je créer des mondes oniriques et
poétiques où des personnages sensuels
et féériques vous invitent à chercher
la beauté sous la surface. »

Iben Høj #02 and #03, 2012
Iben Høj, lookbook Fall/Winter 2012;
collage and digital

→   **Black Dahlia, 2012**
Amica magazine, Italy;
collage and digital

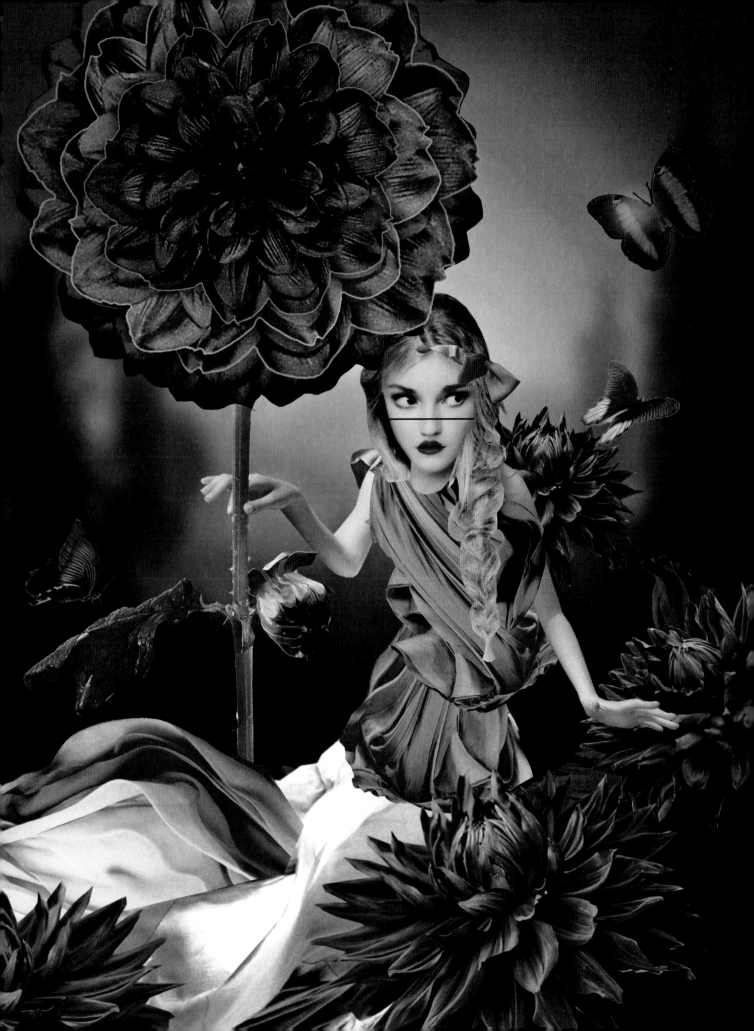

"I love Maren's uniquely surreal and stylish mixed-media collages. She transforms beautiful poetic ornaments into well-balanced and highly fashionable fairy-tales."

ANNEKE KRULL
Art Director and Blogger
iloveillustration.nl

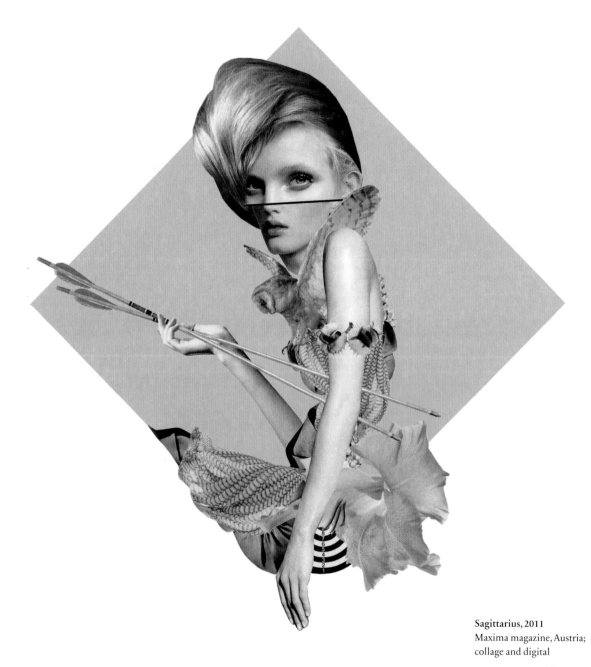

Sagittarius, 2011
Maxima magazine, Austria;
collage and digital

→ **Art Deco**, 2012
Dash magazine; collage and digital

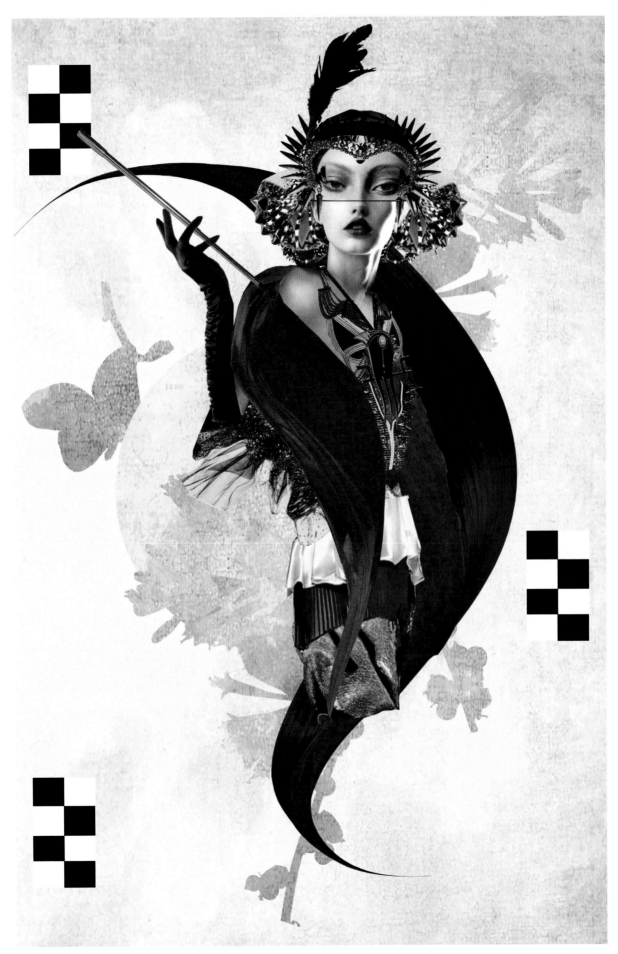

Ann Field

lives and works in London and Los Angeles
annfield.com

CLIENTS
Christian Dior, Barbara Barry,
Estée Lauder, Quiksilver/Roxy

AGENT
Friend+Johnson
USA
friendandjohnson.com

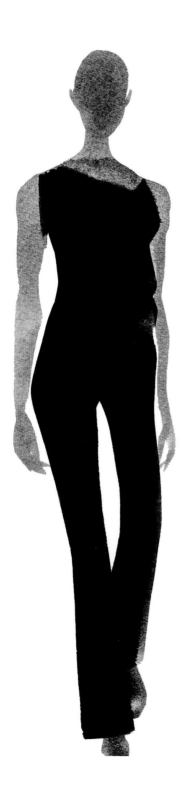

"I'm interested in the energy of the woman wearing the clothes and I always work to capture that."

„Ich interessiere mich für die Energie der Frau, die die Kleidung trägt, und arbeite stets daran, dies einzufangen."

« Je m'intéresse à l'énergie de la femme qui porte les vêtements, et j'essaie toujours de l'exprimer. »

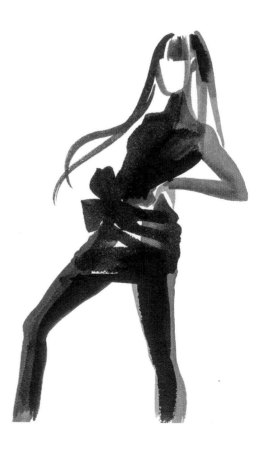

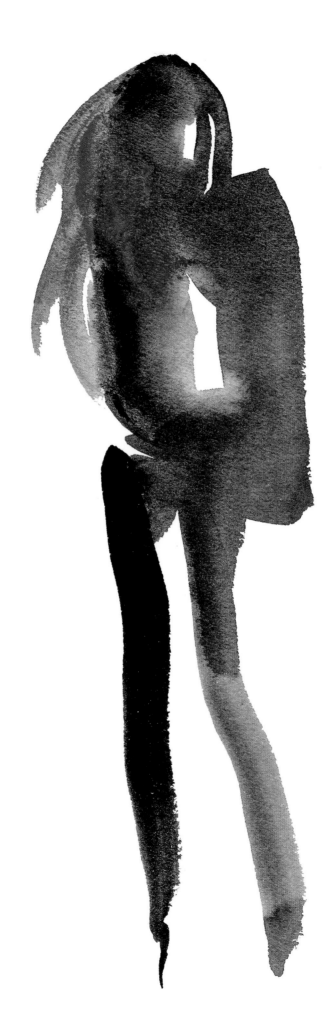

Blue, 2008
John Galliano/Dior;
watercolor and ink

←   Alexander McQueen, 2011
Portland magazine;
ink, watercolor and digital

←← Silhouette 2, 2004
The Limited; ink wash and digital

"I'm sure it will be brilliant!"

RIP GEORGES
Creative Director
Los Angeles Times Magazine

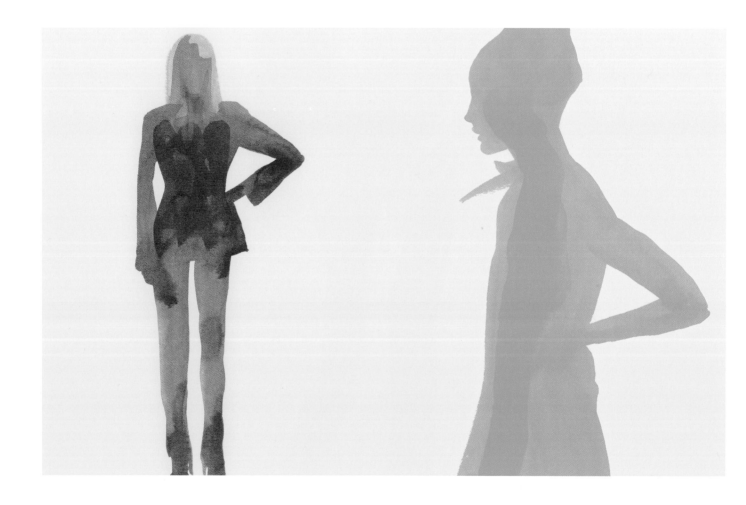

General, 2010
Personal work; brush and digital

→   **Silhouette 3, 2004**
The Limited; ink wash and digital

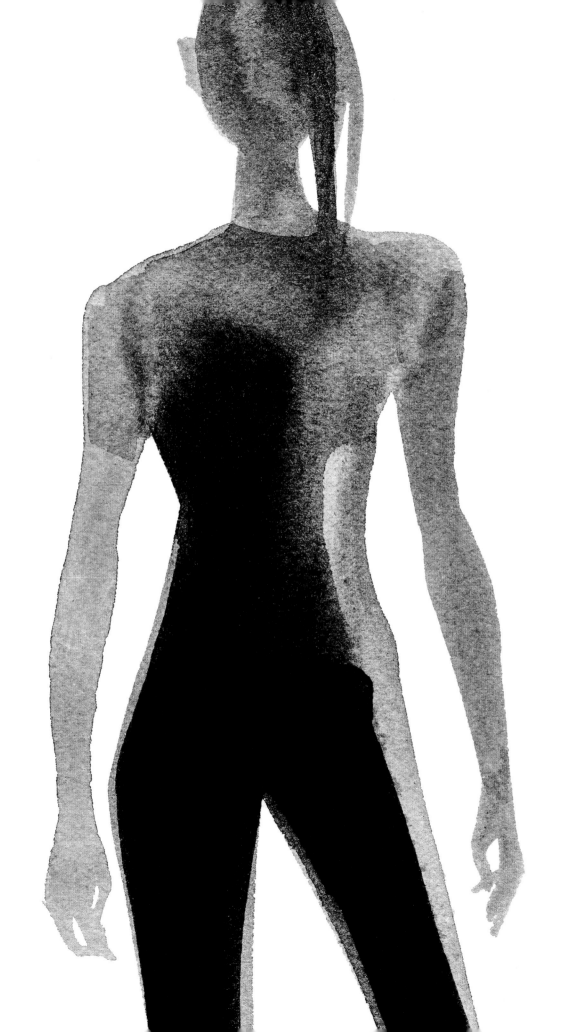

Furia

2004 founded in São Paulo | based in São Paulo
www.furia.com.br

CLIENTS
Vogue Brazil, Havaianas, Editora Abril,
Editora Globo, DMS Editora, Victor Hugo

AGENT
Jaime Mandelbaum
Czech Republic
jaime@furiaimages.com

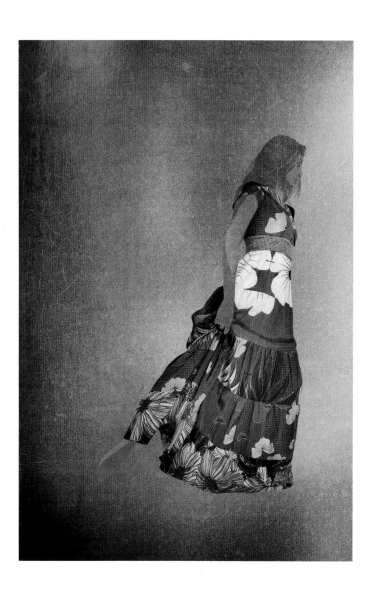

"We try to balance color, texture and movement in an emotional style so that we can see the human spirit beyond simply beautiful clothing."

„Wir versuchen Farbe, Textur und Bewegung in einem gefühlsbetonten Stil auszubalancieren, um hinter schöner Kleidung den menschlichen Geist zu erkennen."

« Nous essayons de trouver un équilibre entre couleur, texture et mouvement dans un style émotionnel afin que l'on puisse voir l'esprit humain. »

Adriana Barra, 2011
Quartier magazine, Art Direction: Douglas Marques, Ballet Dancer: Gabrielle Oliveira, Styling: Melissa Thomé, Fashion Design: Adriana Barra; photography, painting and digital

→ **Maríllia Pitta, 2011**
DMS Editora, Art Direction: Douglas Marques, Ballet Dancer: Gabrielle Oliveira, Styling: Melissa Thomé, Fashion Design: Maríllia Pitta; photography, painting and digital

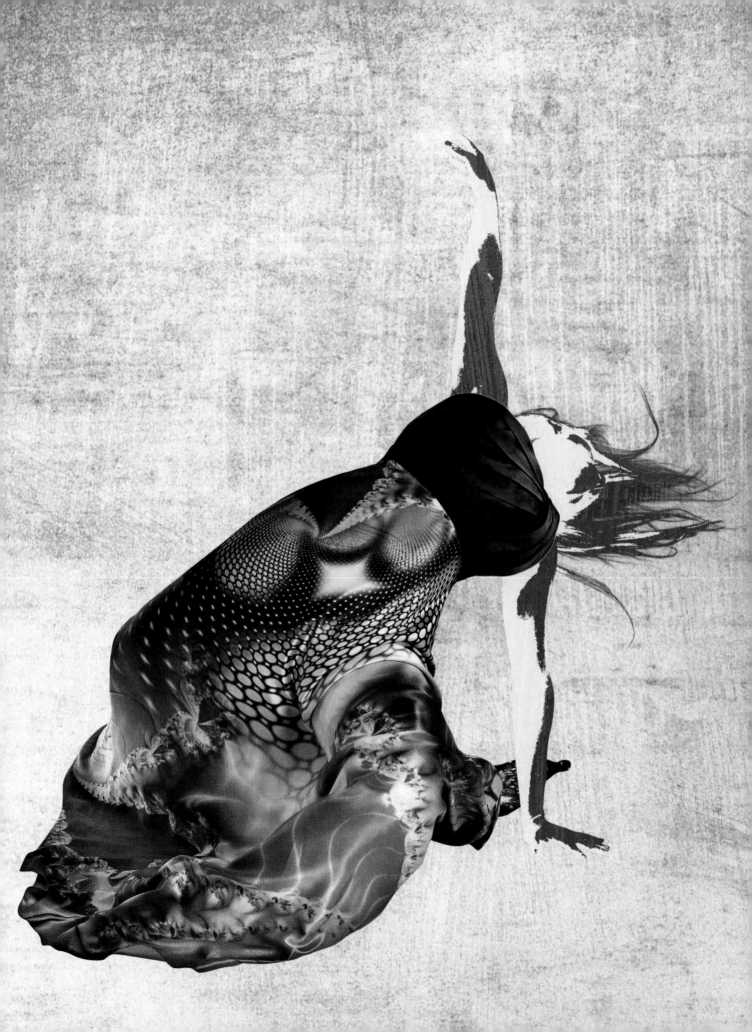

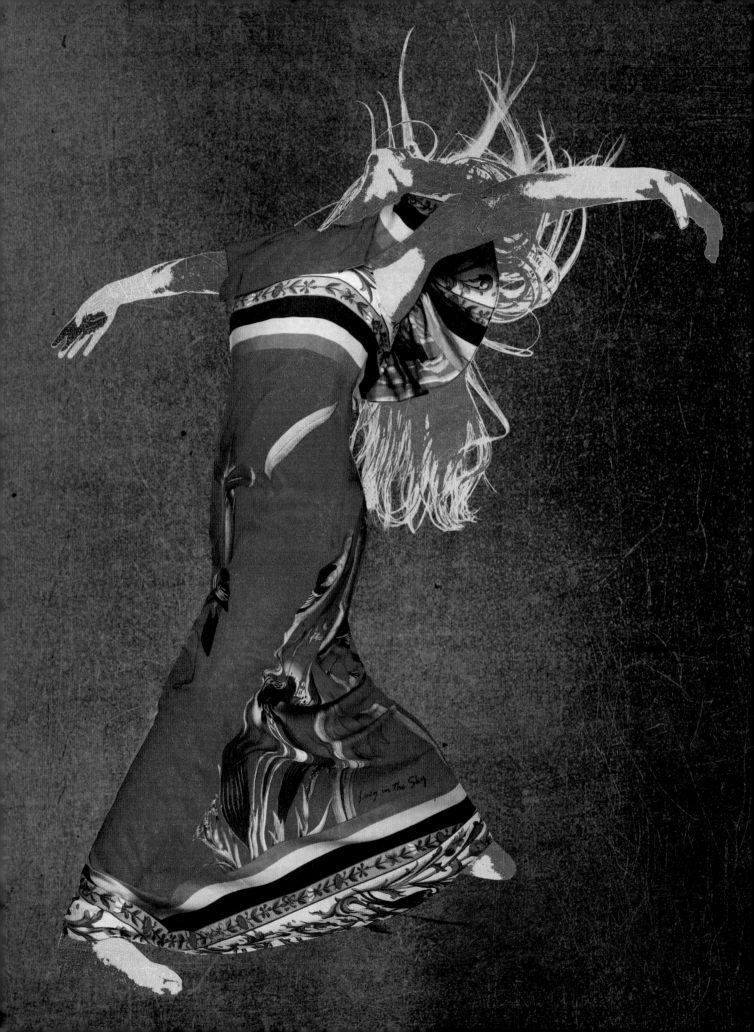

Neon-II, 2011
Quartier magazine, Art Direction:
Douglas Marques, Ballet Dancer:
Gabrielle Oliveira, Styling: Melissa
Thomé, Fashion Design: Neon;
photography, painting and digital

←   **Lucy in the Sky, 2011**
Quartier magazine, Art Direction:
Douglas Marques, Ballet Dancer:
Gabrielle Oliveira, Styling: Melissa
Thomé, Fashion Design: Lucy in the Sky;
photography, painting and digital

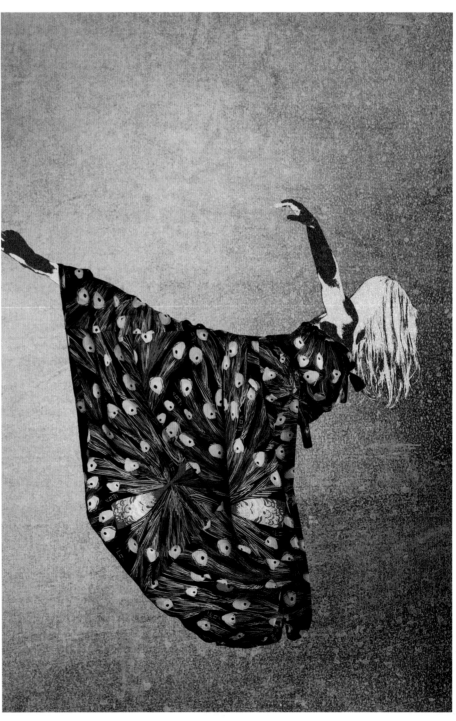

Carmen García Huerta

1975 born in Madrid | lives and works in Madrid
www.cghuerta.com

CLIENTS
Vogue Spain, L'Officiel Russia, Frau Japan, Viceroy,
Marie France, Glamour magazine, Morgan de Toi,
Eric Bompard, Hed Kandi, Custo Barcelona

AGENTS
Agent 002
France
agent002.com

Möve
Brazil
move.art.br

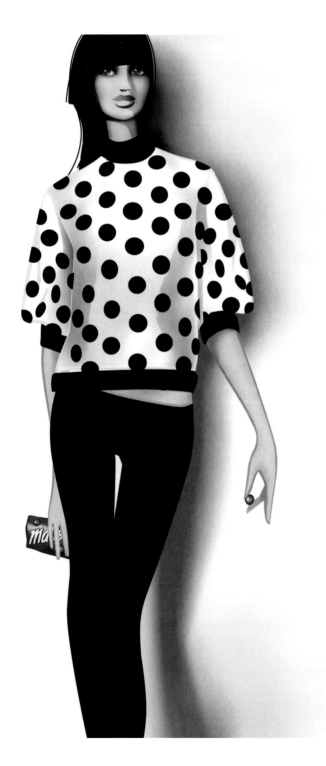

" At the shows for every new season
people want to wear what they
see, but I want to draw it instead.
I feel I own haute couture
when I draw it."

„Bei den Shows für jede neue Saison wollen
alle tragen, was sie sehen, aber ich will
es lieber zeichnen. Wenn ich Haute Couture
illustriere, habe ich das Gefühl, sie gehört mir."

« Les gens veulent porter ce qu'ils voient sur
les podiums, moi je préfère dessiner.
Dessiner de la haute couture, c'est aussi
me l'approprier. »

Maltesers, 2009
Vogue Spain, advertorial; digital

→   Roberto Verino, 2011
Roberto Verino fashion show,
press dossier Fall/Winter 2011,
Madrid Fashion Week; digital

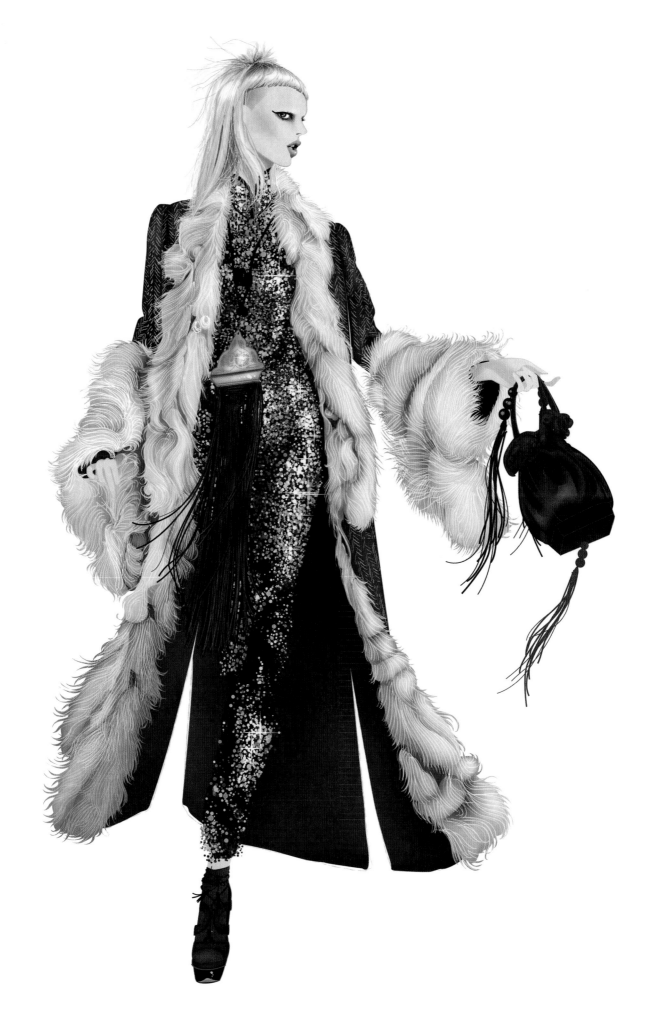

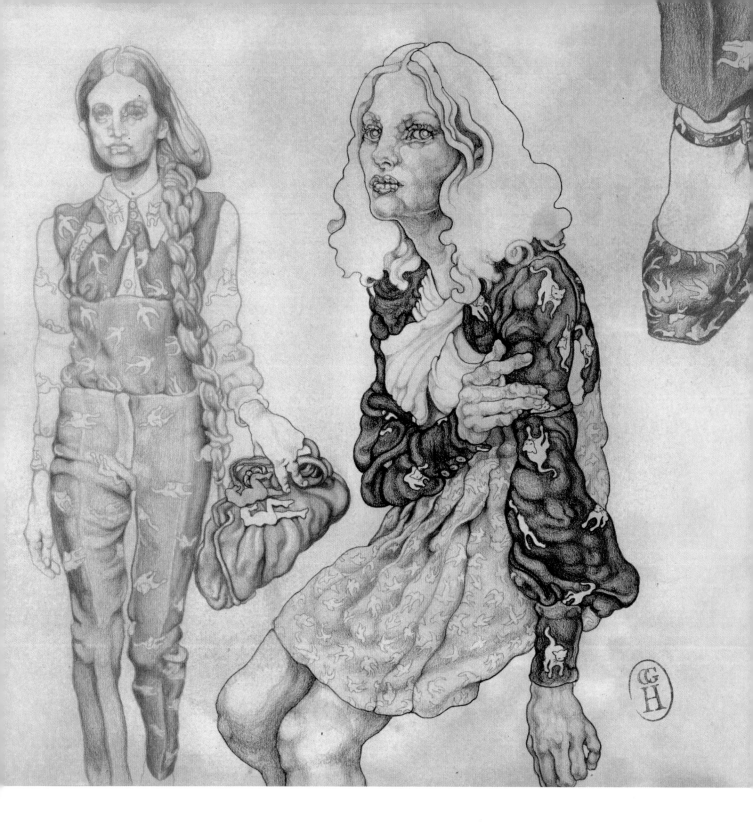

Miu Miu, 2010
Personal work; color pencil

→　Louboutin, 2010
Personal work; color pencil

"Whether subtle or brutal, perfectionist
or rough, clean or dirty, delicate or grotesque,
fashion is fully understood by Carmen and
she knows both sides."

BRENDA CHÁVEZ
Sub-Director, Cosmopolitan

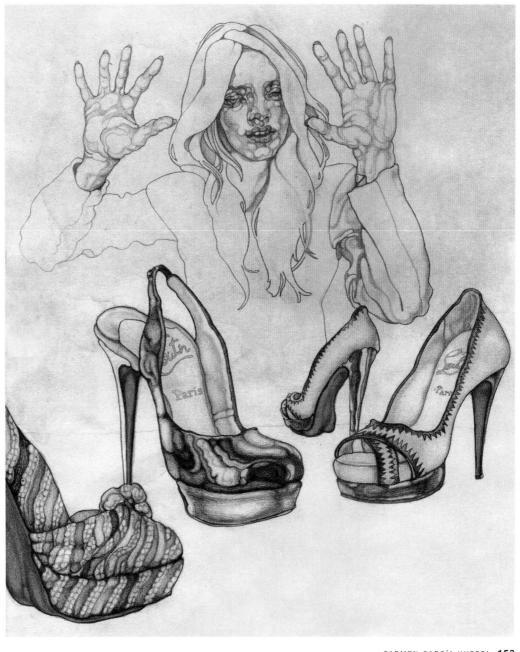

Jocelyn Gravot

1980 born in Nancy | lives and works in Paris and Nantes
www.jocelyngravot.com

CLIENTS
L'Essentiel Monsieur

AGENT
V.O Valérie Oualid
France
valerieoualid.com

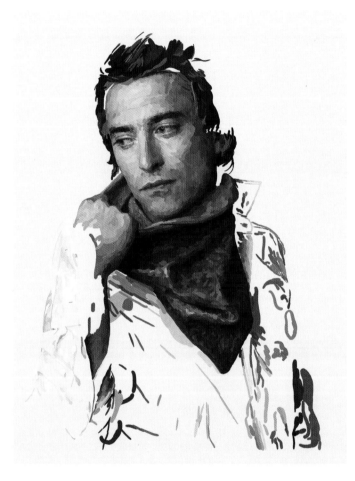

"I try to give an impressionist
dimension to the model
and the clothes that are worn
by playing with shapes and colors
and enhancing empty spaces."

„Indem ich mit Farben und Formen spiele
und freie Räume aufwerte, versuche ich
dem Model und seiner Kleidung impressionis-
tische Dimensionen zu verleihen."

« Au travers de touches impressionnistes
je tente de donner une autre dimension
au modèle et au vêtement par la mise en
valeur des vides et des couleurs. »

L'Essentiel Monsieur #8, #7 and #1, 2011
Lookbook, Photography: Samuel
Cornillet, Fashion Design: Simon
Mandin; digital mixed media

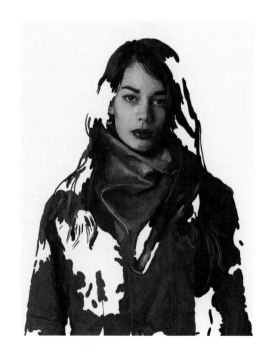

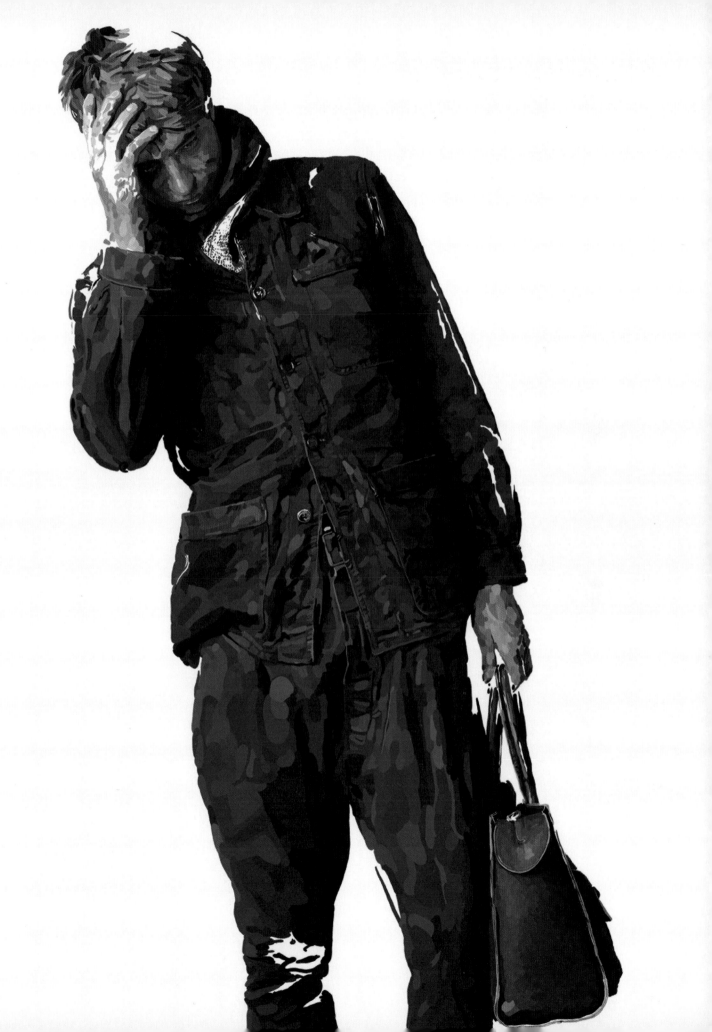

"Jocelyn Gravot's illustration style has a rare quality of modernity and elegance, a refreshing note in the world of fashion illustration."

MARIE DATHANAT
Art Buyer

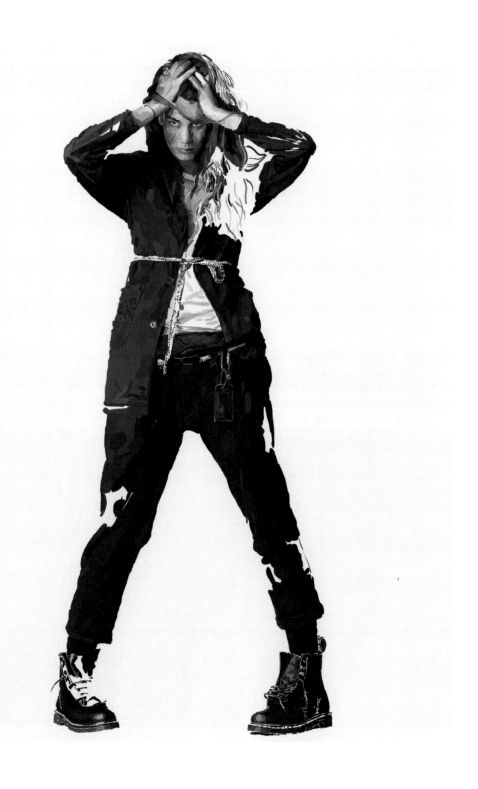

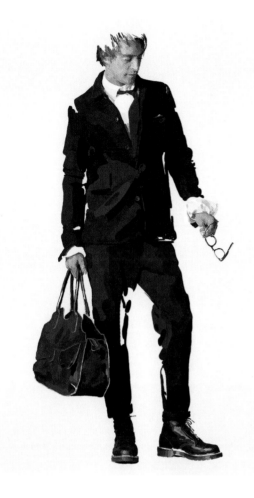

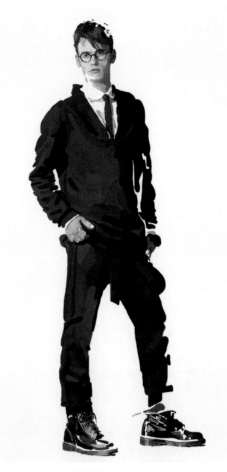

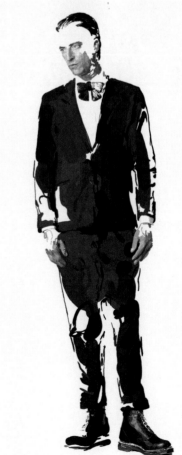

**L'Essentiel Monsieur #05, #04
and #03, 2011**
Lookbook, Photography: Samuel
Cornillet, Fashion Design: Simon
Mandin; digital mixed media

←   **L'Essentiel Monsieur #06, 2011**
Lookbook, Photography: Samuel
Cornillet, Fashion Design: Simon
Mandin; digital mixed media

Sophie Griotto

1975 born in Alès | lives and works in the South of France
www.sophiegriotto.com

CLIENTS
Swatch, Elle, Dior, Luiza Barcelos,
Jean Paul Gaultier, Givenchy,
Louis Vuitton, Vichy, Clarins

AGENT
Caroline Maréchal
France
caroline-marechal.fr

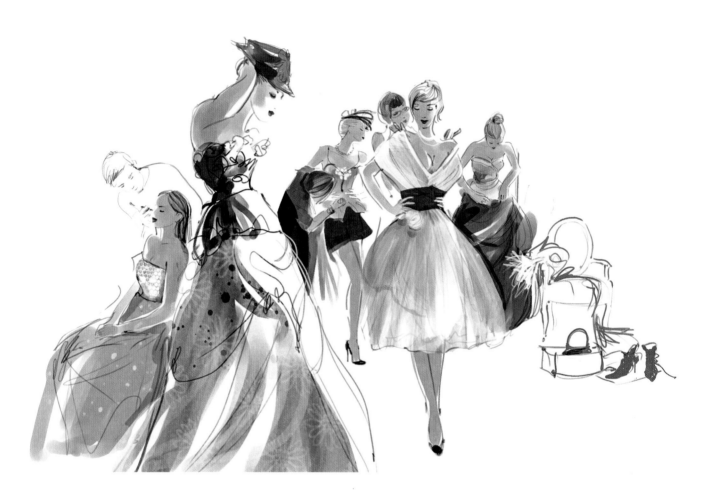

"I attach a great deal of importance to the folds of fabrics.
They reveal all the elegance and movement of the silhouette."

„Ich widme dem Wurf eines Stoffes sehr viel Aufmerksamkeit.
Darin enthüllen sich all die Eleganz und die Bewegungen der Silhouette."

« J'attache beaucoup d'importance aux plis des tissus.
Ils révèlent toute l'élégance et le mouvement de la silhouette. »

Backstage, 2011
Dior, storyboard for the film *Dior j'adore*,
Direction: Jean-Jacques Annaud;
ink and graphics tablet

→ Fashion Week, 2011
Fashion Week Illustrée, Paris;
ink and graphics tablet

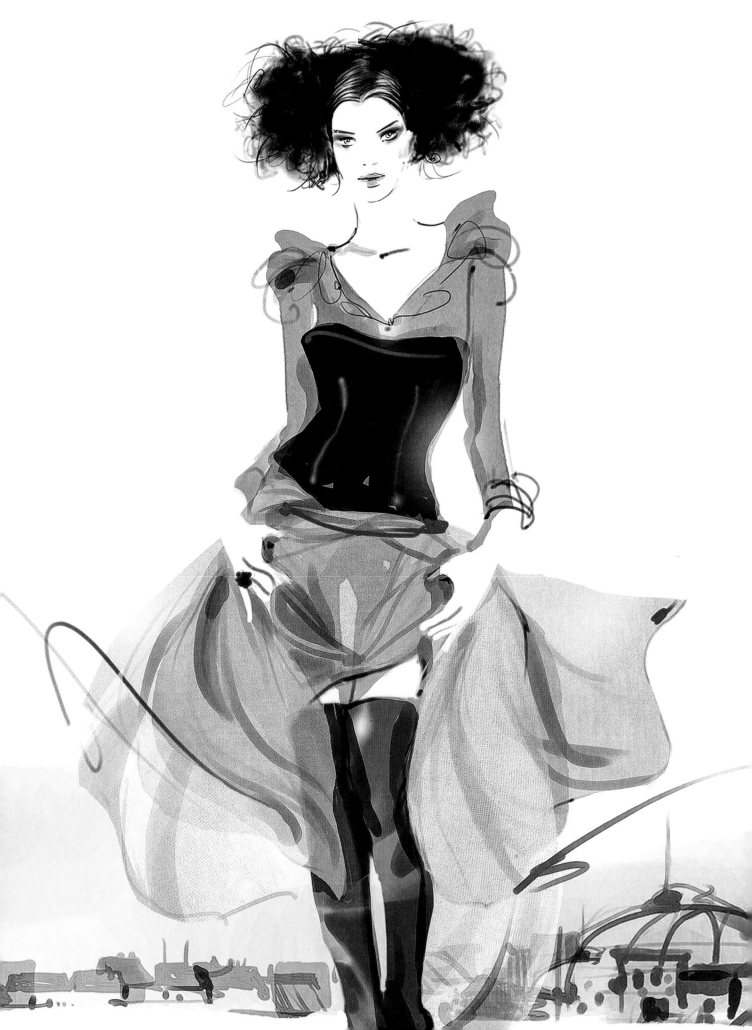

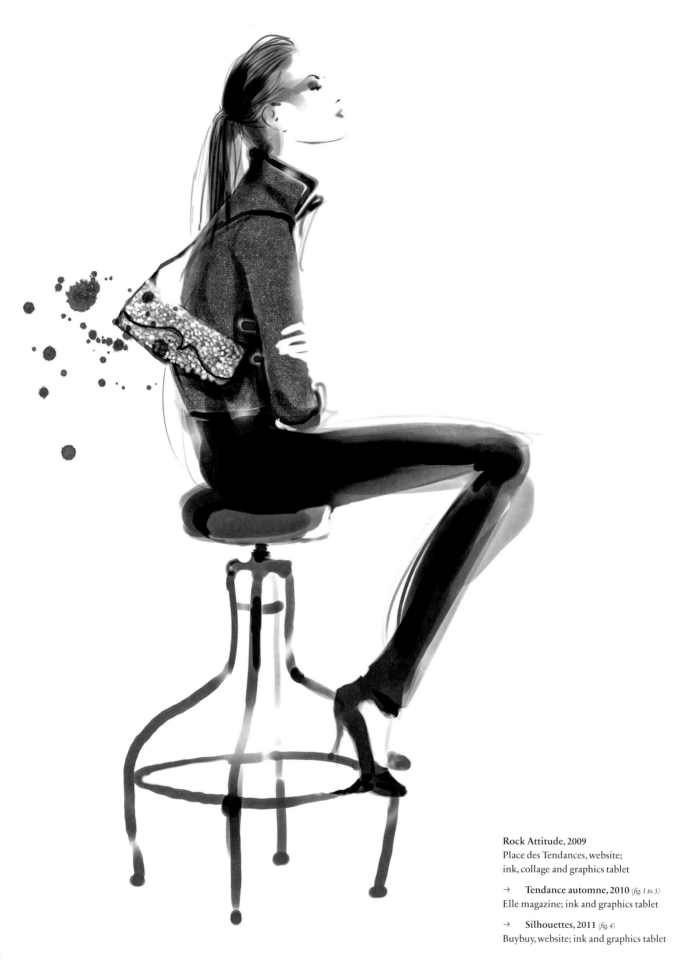

Rock Attitude, 2009
Place des Tendances, website;
ink, collage and graphics tablet

→ **Tendance automne, 2010** *(fig 1 to 3)*
Elle magazine; ink and graphics tablet

→ **Silhouettes, 2011** *(fig 4)*
Buybuy, website; ink and graphics tablet

"As in fashion, Sophie Griotto's characteristic trait is perpetual movement. I love the graceful hip movements and elegant nonchalance of her women."

MARION LAHORE
Journalist
Noticketforfashionshows.com

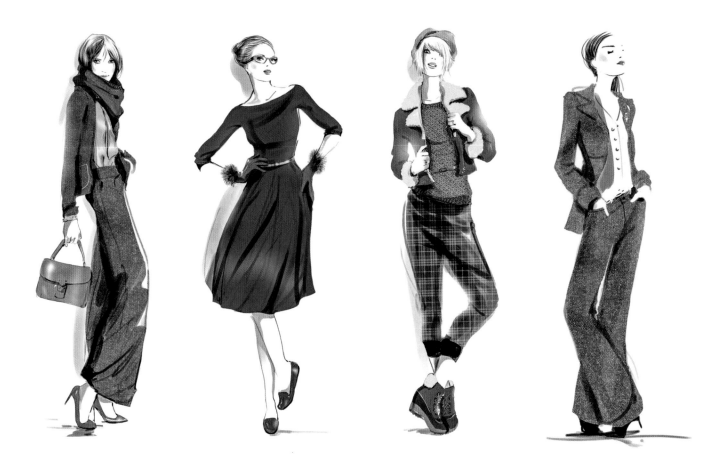

Catarina Gushiken

1981 born in São Paulo | lives and works in São Paulo
www.catarinagushiken.com.br

CLIENTS
Lola magazine, Decolar magazine, Claudia magazine,
Mood Life magazine, Folha magazine, Viand Co.
magazine, Joyce Pascowitch magazine

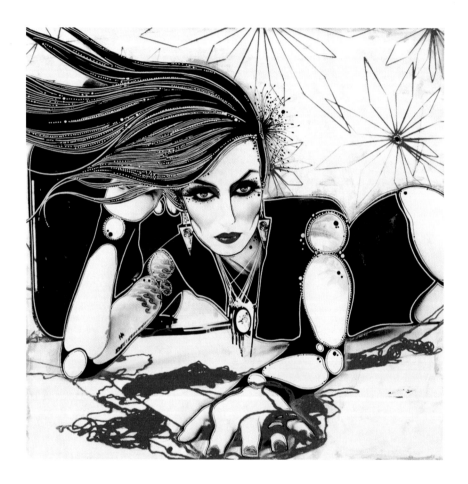

"I create whole worlds in each illustration. Passions and what moves the artist open up and are fulfilled; the work oozes imagination yet there is a sense of liberation."

„Mit jeder Illustration erschaffe ich Welten. Die Leidenschaften und was den Künstler bewegt, fließen mit ein und werden erfüllt. Die Arbeiten verströmen Fantasie, und doch gibt es eine Art Befreiungsgefühl."

« Chaque illustration est tout un monde. Les passions s'ouvrent et s'accomplissent ; le travail déborde d'imagination et pourtant il y a un sentiment de libération. »

Marina Dias #4 and #5, 2011
Model: Marina Dias, Photography:
Alexandre Wittboldt; ink, watercolor,
photography printed on fine art paper

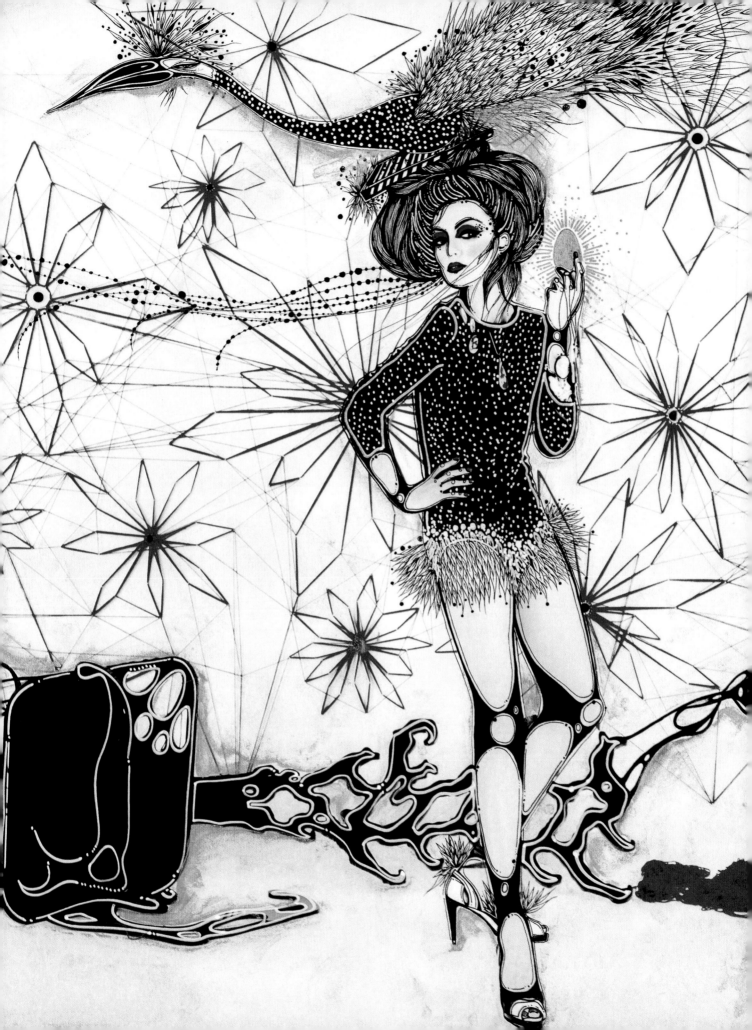

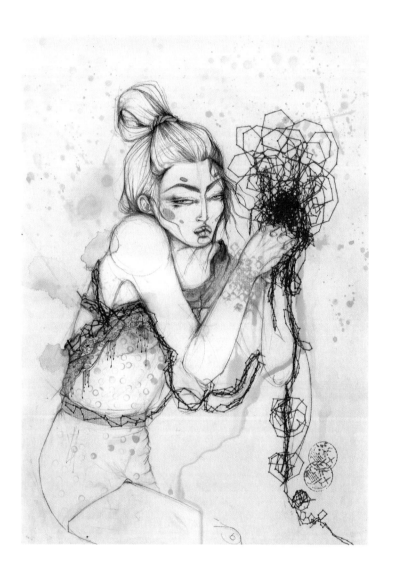

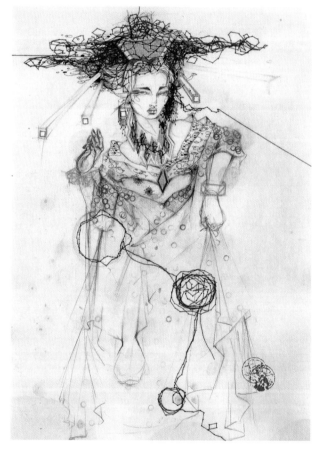

Akai Ito #1, #2 and #3, 2013
Personal work; pencil,
watercolor and embroidery

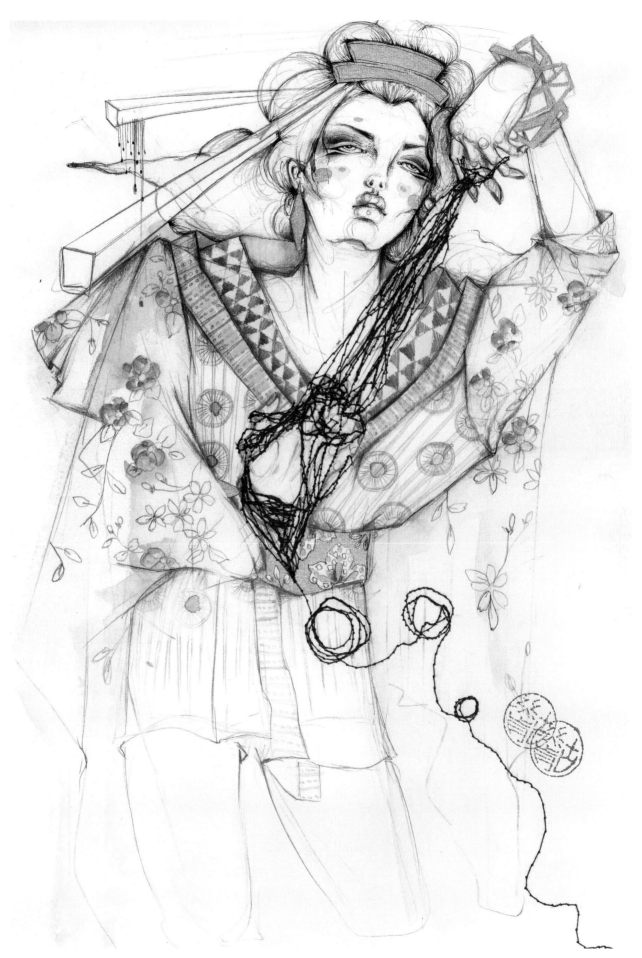

Samantha Hahn

1978 born in New York | lives and works in New York
www.samanthahahn.com

CLIENTS
New York magazine/The Cut, Marc Jacobs, J.Crew,
Epoca Japan, Thursday Friday, Elle, DailyCandy,
Hatch Collection, Refinery 29

AGENTS
CWC International
USA
cwc-i.com

CWC Tokyo
Japan
cwctokyo.com

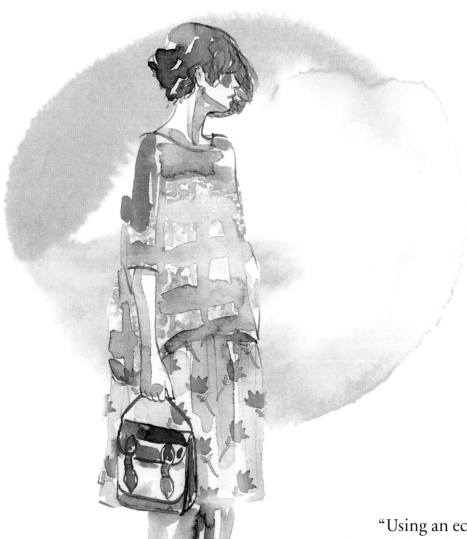

Chris Benz, New York
Fashion Week, Fall 2012
New York magazine/The Cut;
concentrated inks applied with
quill and brush

→   Hervé Léger Bodice, New York
Fashion Week, Fall 2012
New York magazine/The Cut;
concentrated inks applied with
quill and brush

"Using an economy of expressive and
delicate lines I create decidedly feminine
watercolors imbued with emotion."

„Mit sparsam gesetzten ausdrucksstarken wie auch
filigranen Linien schaffe ich ausgesprochen feminine
Aquarelle, durchdrungen von Emotionen."

« Je crée des aquarelles résolument féminines imprégnées
d'émotion à l'aide de traits expressifs mais parcimonieux. »

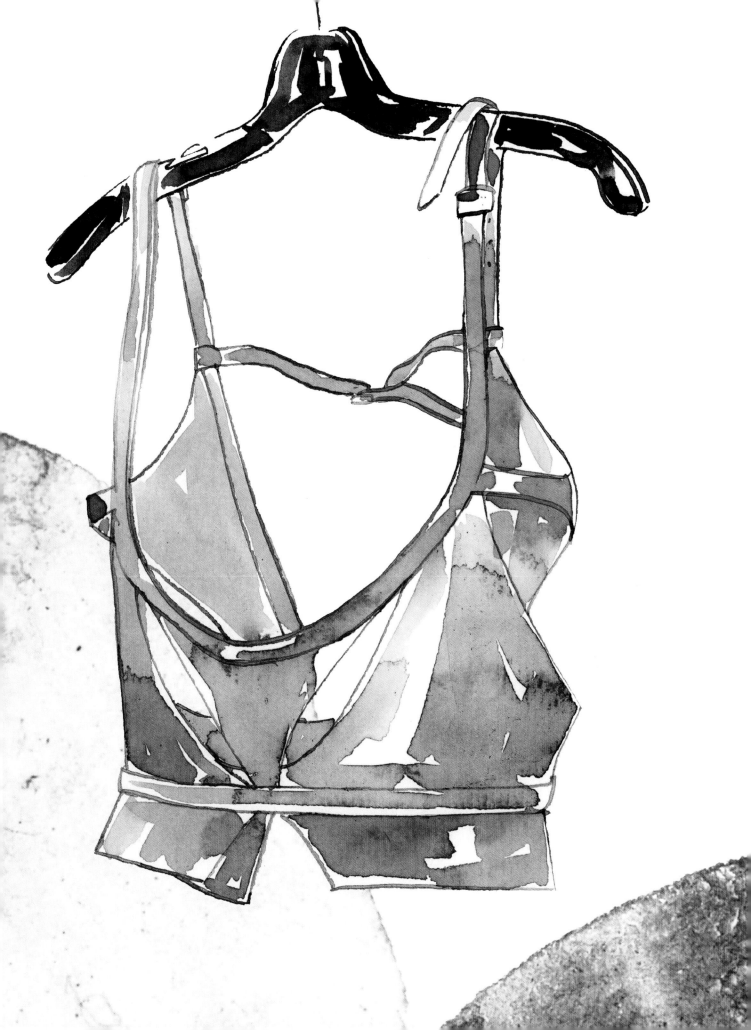

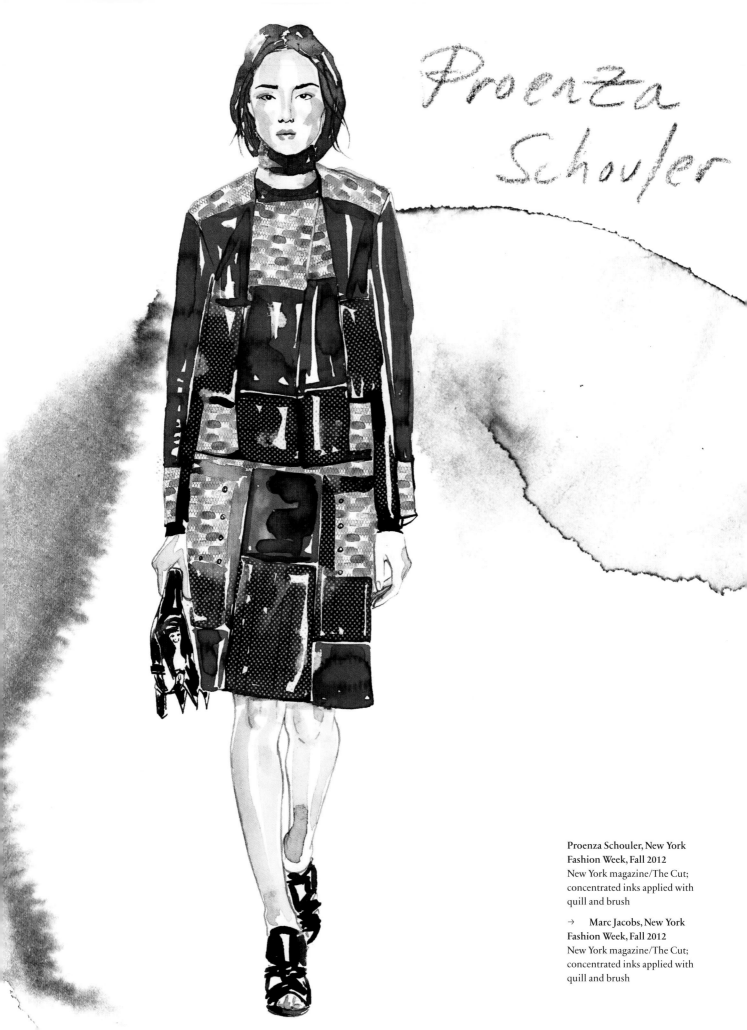

Proenza Schouler

Proenza Schouler, New York
Fashion Week, Fall 2012
New York magazine/The Cut;
concentrated inks applied with
quill and brush

→   Marc Jacobs, New York
Fashion Week, Fall 2012
New York magazine/The Cut;
concentrated inks applied with
quill and brush

"A good illustration adds a bit of magic to its subject and Samantha's accomplish this with both style and warmth – a difficult balance in fashion. In her hands a gown's folds invite desire, her portraits charm with lightness and delicacy."

STELLA BUGBEE
Editor in Chief
New York magazine/The Cut

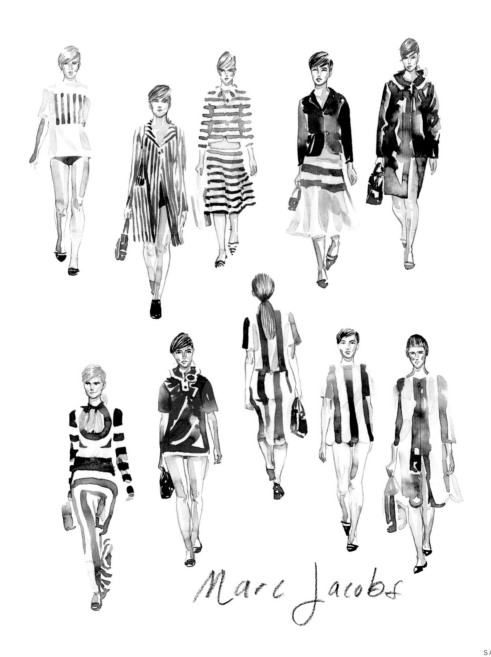

Marc Jacobs

Richard Haines

1951 born in Balboa, Panama | lives and works in New York
www.designerman-whatisawtoday.blogspot.com

CLIENTS
Prada, The New York Times, J. Crew, Barneys,
Calvin Klein, W magazine, Unionmade Goods,
GQ Italy, Pitti Uomo, Paper magazine, Grazia

AGENT
Jed Root Inc
USA
jedroot.com

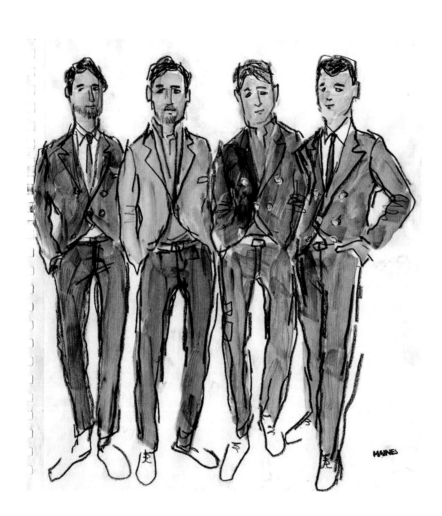

"I believe in the beauty of the line, and capturing the immediacy of the moment.
Drawing is a primary means of expression, made modern via technology."

„Ich glaube an die Schönheit der Linie und daran, den Moment direkt einzufangen.
Zeichnen ist – technologisch modernisiert – ein primäres Ausdrucksmittel."

« Je crois à la beauté du trait, et à capter l'immédiateté du moment.
Dessiner est un moyen d'expression primaire, que la technologie a modernisé. »

Bruno Cucinelli, Pitti Uomo, 2011
The New York Times, T Magazine blog;
hand-drawn

→ Seated Dude, 2012
Unionmade Goods, online catalog
and visual display; hand-drawn

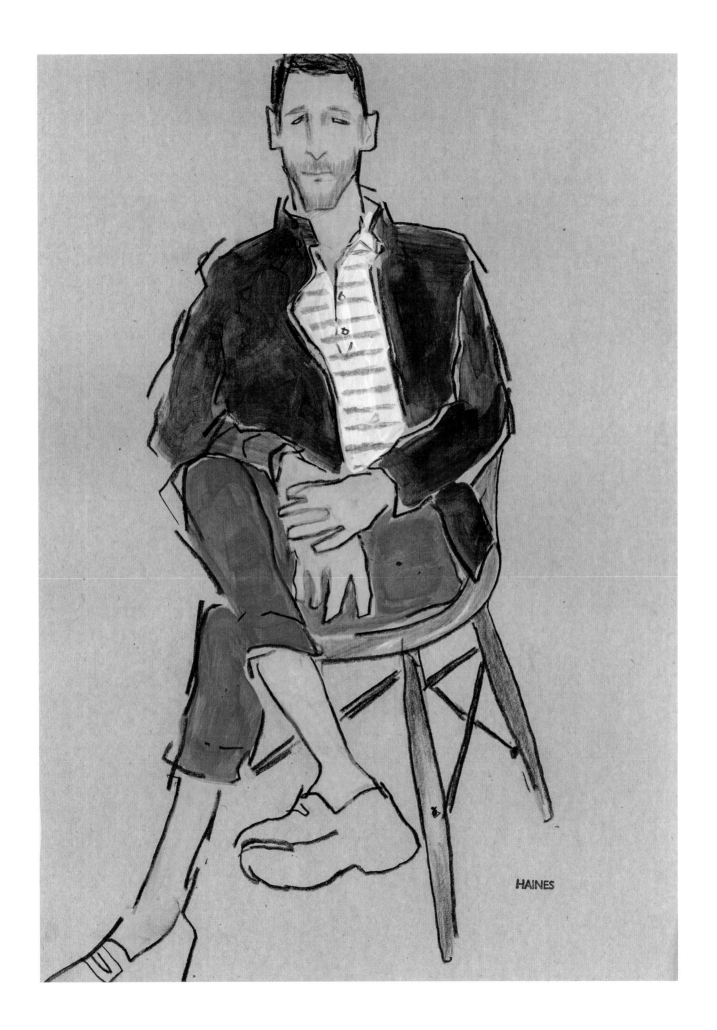

HAINES

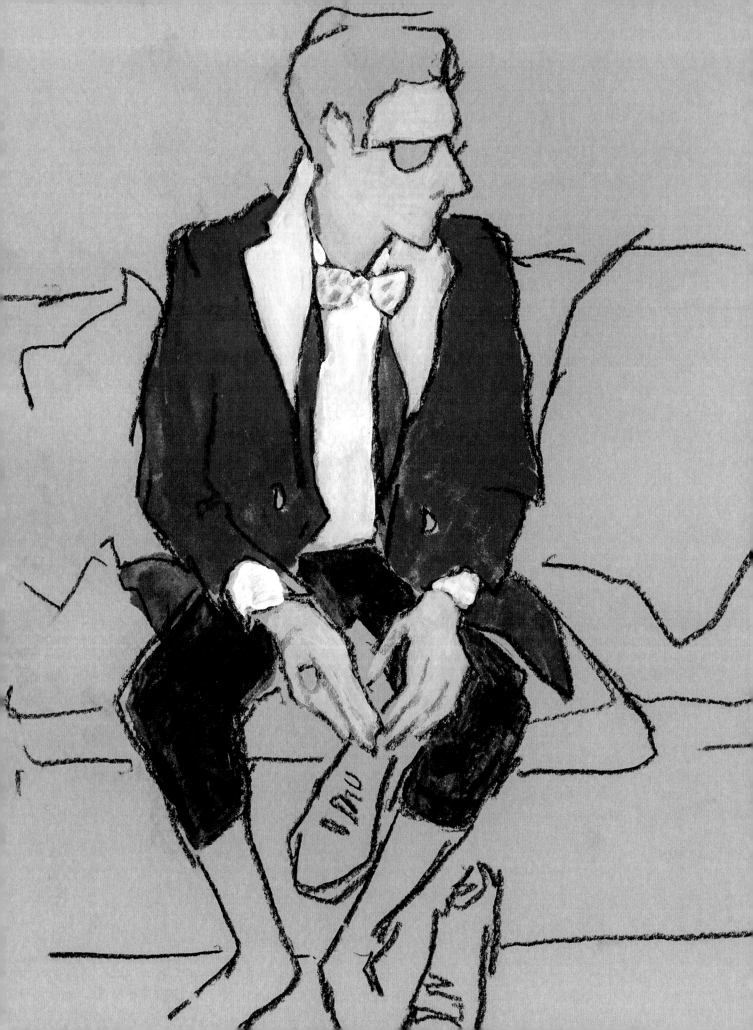

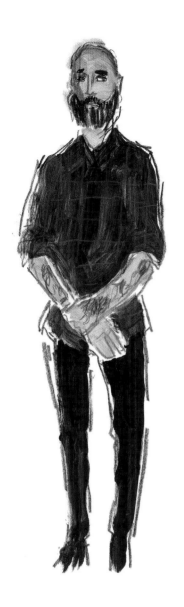

"With a certain hand and sensibility from a bygone era, Richard puts his own spin on modern-day subjects – cool and casual, never overdone. He translates what others see into something spectacular."

TODD BARKET
Retailer/Store Owner
Unionmade Goods

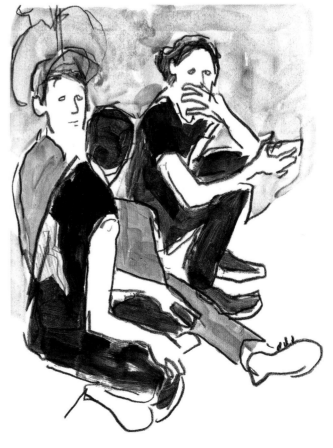

At Smile…, 2012
Personal work, online blog;
hand-drawn

→　**Block Party, 2012**
Personal work, online blog;
hand-drawn

←　**Luigi Tadini Seated, 2011**
Paper magazine; hand-drawn

Spiros Halaris

1989 born in London | lives and works in London
www.spiroshalaris.com

CLIENTS
Harrods, Revlon, Dolce & Gabbana, Printemps,
Christian Louboutin, London Fashion Week, Elle,
Marie Claire, V magazine, Maria Luisa Paris, Diesel

AGENT
Machas
UK
itsmachas.com

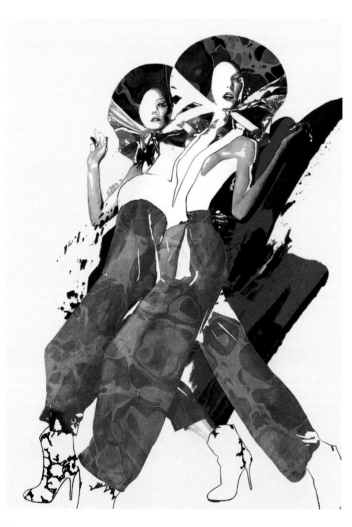

"My approach is a minimalist
play of deconstructive elements
that together construct a dramatic
pop aesthetic with vibrant
colours and graphics."

„Ich spiele minimalistisch mit dekonstruktiven
Elementen und konstruiere daraus eine
dramatische Popästhetik mit leuchtenden
Farben und Bildern."

« Mon approche est un jeu minimaliste
d'éléments déconstructifs qui forment une
esthétique pop spectaculaire avec des
couleurs vives et du graphisme. »

Runaways, 2012
Personal work, exhibition series;
hand-drawn, collage and digital

→ **The Look, 2012**
Personal work; hand-drawn
and digital

→→ **Crossover, 2011**
London Fashion Week, print
material; hand-drawn and digital

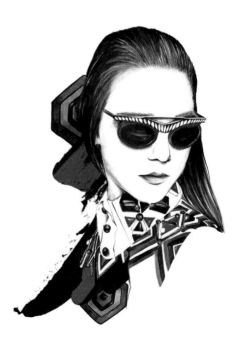

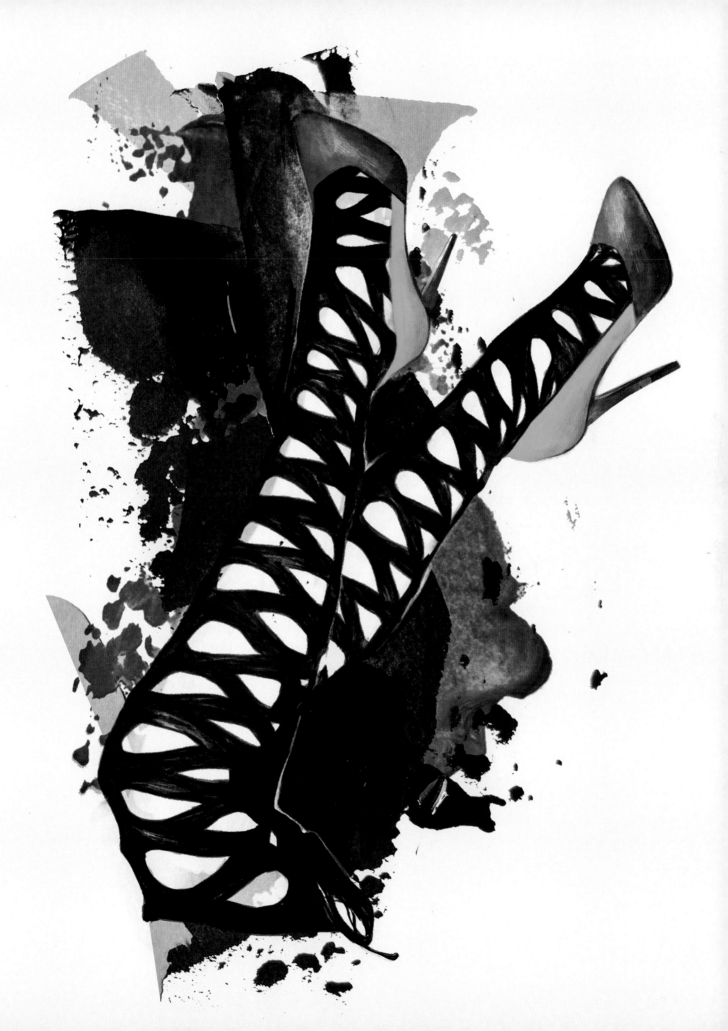

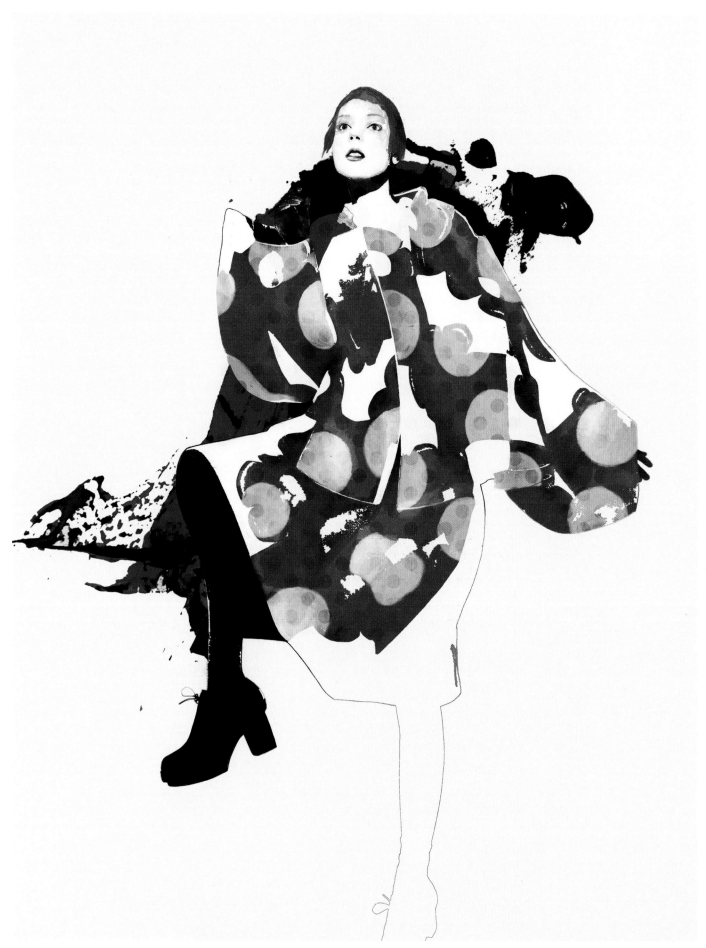

> "His characters and colors can endorse, trigger, as well as inspire other forms of creation and creativity."

FILEP MOTWARY
Fashion Designer and Photographer
Un Nouveau Ideal

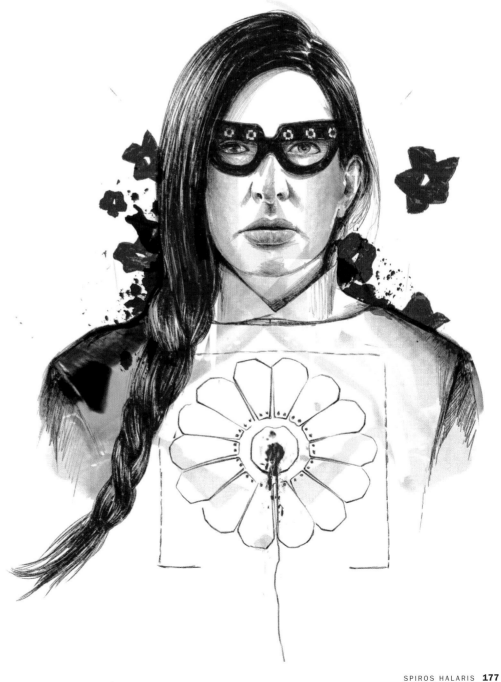

The Artist is Present – in Prada, 2012
Personal work, portrait of Marina
Abramović in Prada Spring/
Summer 2013; hand-drawn and digital

← **Comme des Garçons, 2012**
Personal work, exhibition series;
hand-drawn, collage and digital

Minni Havas

1983 born in Lahti | lives and works in Helsinki
www.minnihavas.fi

CLIENTS
Diesel, Monki, Wad magazine,
Revolution magazine,
Minni f. Ronya

AGENT
Agent Pekka
Finland
agentpekka.com

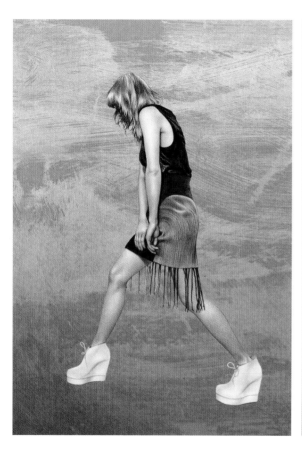 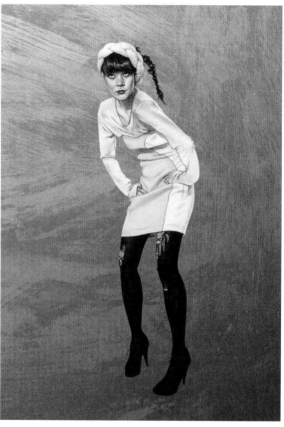

"With my background in fashion design and fine arts, I rely on intuition and my own views about fashion to illustrate it – it is a playground for the imagination, my designs like a story told in a picture."

„Mit Fashiondesign und Kunst als meinem Hintergrund verlasse ich mich bei der Illustration von Mode auf Intuition und meine eigene Sicht – ein Tummelplatz der Fantasie, bei dem meine Designs gleichsam zu bildhaft erzählten Geschichten werden."

« Avec mon expérience dans la création de mode et les beaux arts, je m'appuie sur mon intuition pour illustrer la mode – c'est un terrain de jeux pour l'imagination, je raconte une histoire en images. »

Helene #1 and #2, 2011
Anne Törnroos, trade show booth;
hand-drawn, acrylic and digital

→   Untitled, 2012
Monki; hand-drawn, watercolor
and digital

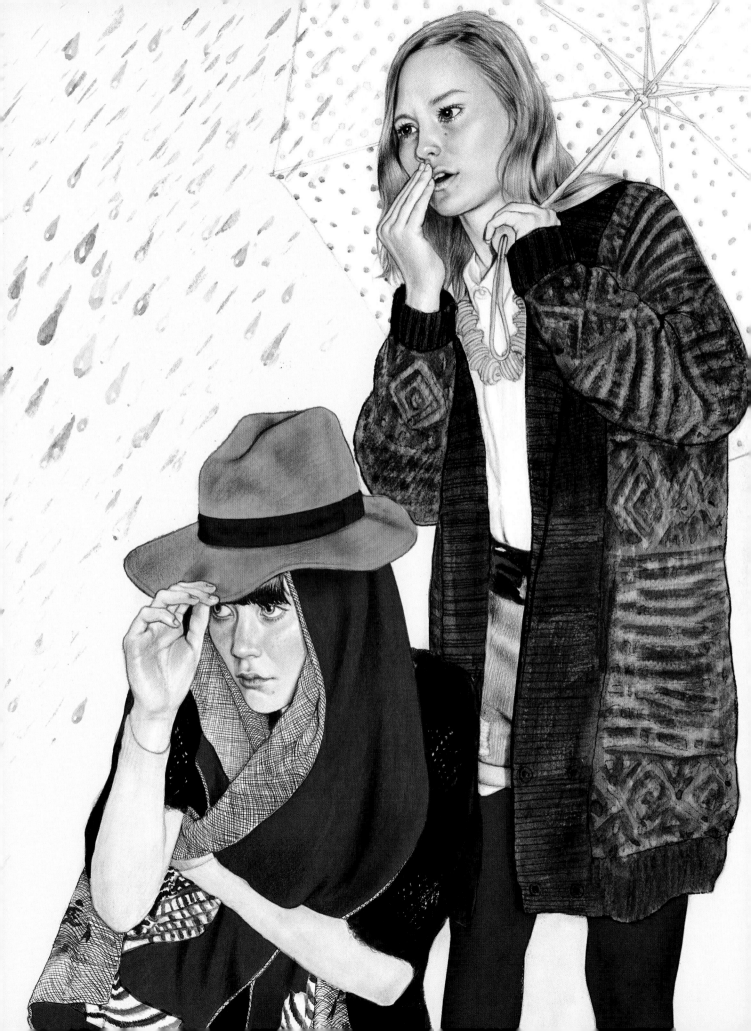

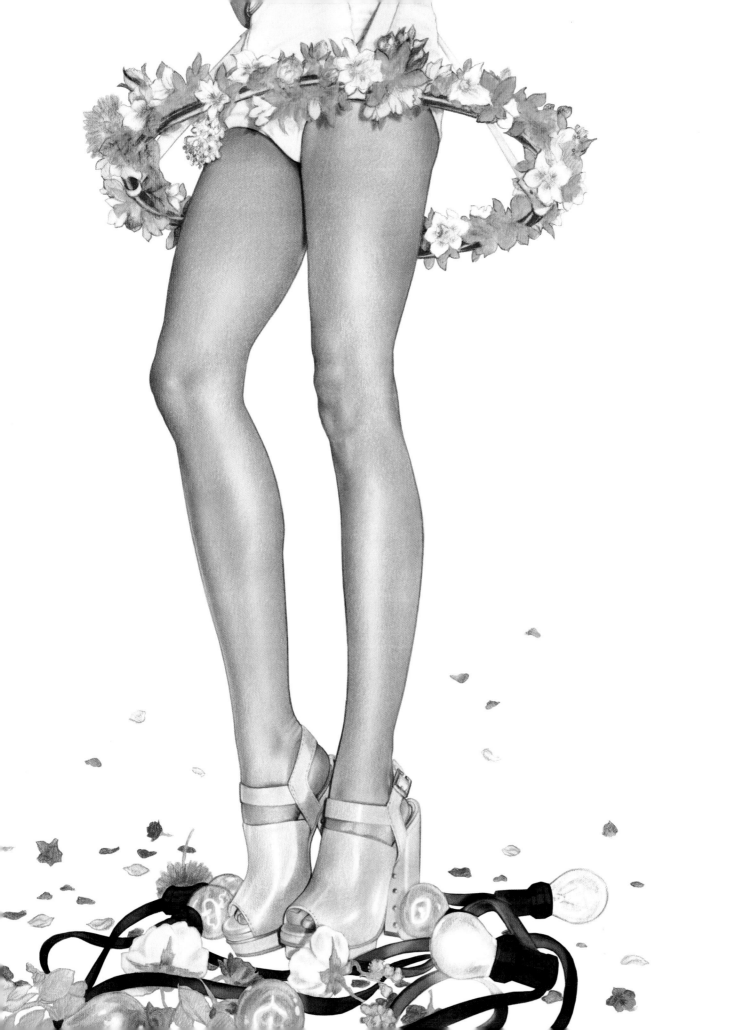

Untitled #1 and #2, 2011
New Nordic Fashion Illustration
Exhibition, Concept: Anne Törnroos;
hand-drawn, mixed media and digital

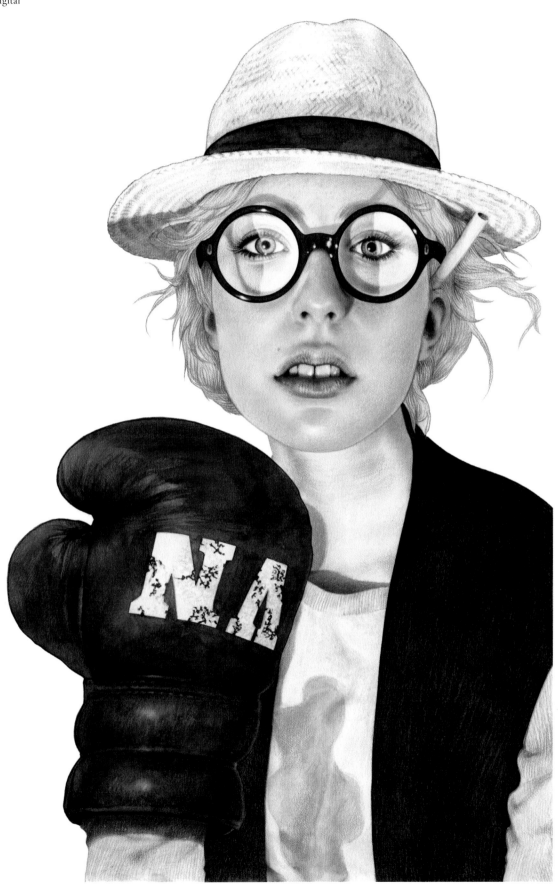

Anna Higgie

1985 born in Canberra | lives and works in Bristol
www.annahiggie.com

CLIENTS
Amelia's Magazine, Bloomingdale's, Nordstrom
department store, Nylon magazine, Sigerson
Morrison NYC, Net-a-Porter, Belle NYC

AGENT
Illustration Division
USA
illustrationdivision.com

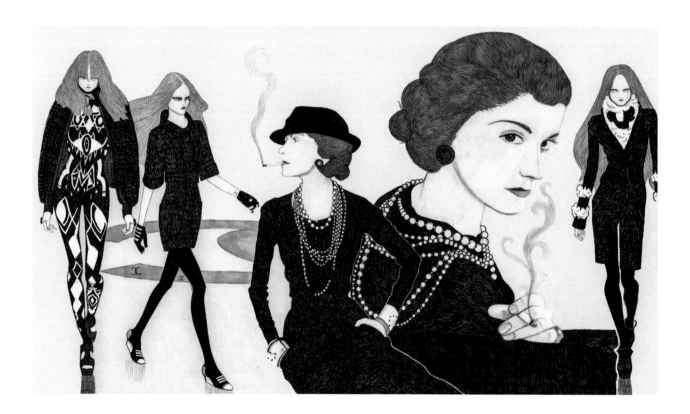

"I find creating and looking at high-fashion imagery very seductive, hypnotic.
I know it's not real, but maybe that escapism is part of the appeal."

„Die Bildsprache der Haute Couture umzusetzen und zu betrachten ist für mich
sehr verführerisch, hypnotisch. Natürlich weiß ich, dass es nicht real ist,
aber vielleicht birgt eben dieser Eskapismus auch seinen Reiz."

«Créer des images de haute couture et les regarder est très séduisant.
Je sais que ce n'est pas réel, mais c'est peut-être ça qui est attirant.»

Portrait of Coco Chanel, 2011
Kat Von D's Wonderland Gallery,
West Hollywood, group exhibition
I Want To Be First; ink and pencil on
paper and digital

→ **Girl Wearing Hat, 2012**
SHOP/Global Blue, illustration for
yearly Art Dept mailout; pencil and
watercolor on paper and digital

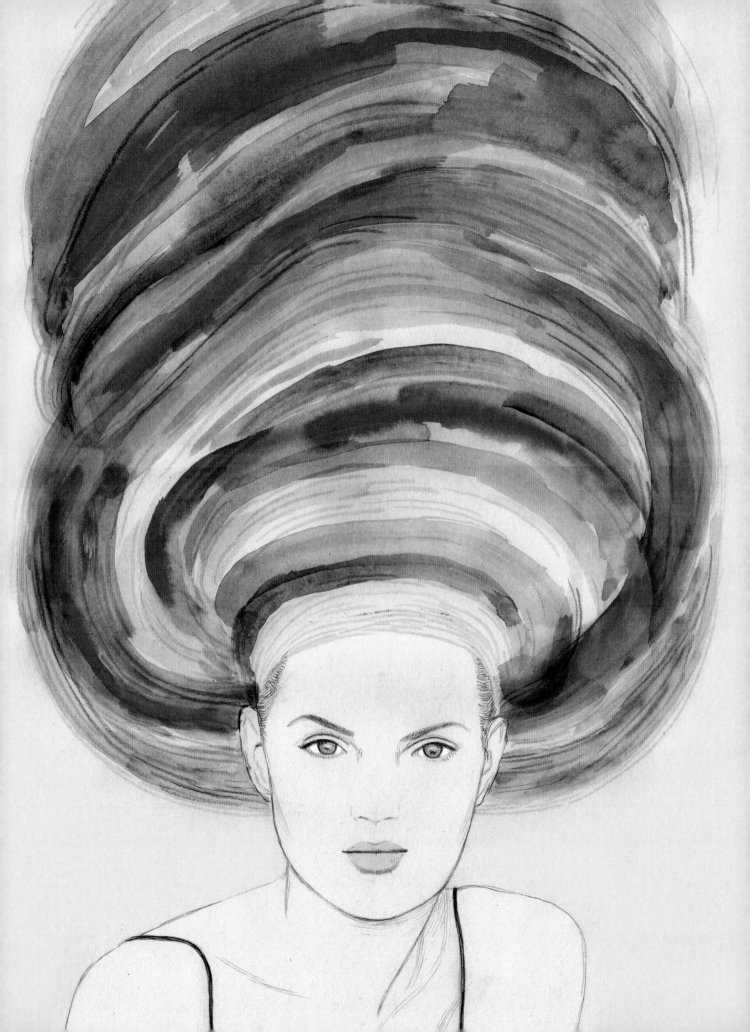

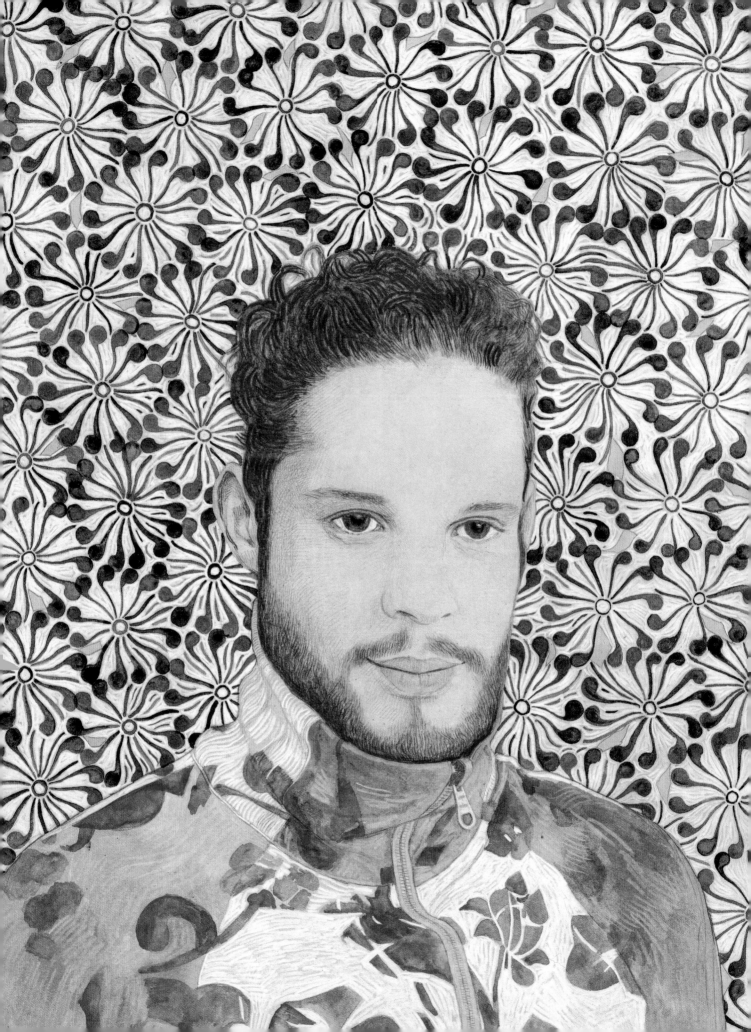

Mark Fast, London Fashion Week, 2012
Amelia's Magazine; ink and pencil
on paper and digital

← Portrait of Anthony Nuku, 2012
Alexander Wilson, Melbourne;
hand-drawn and watercolor on paper

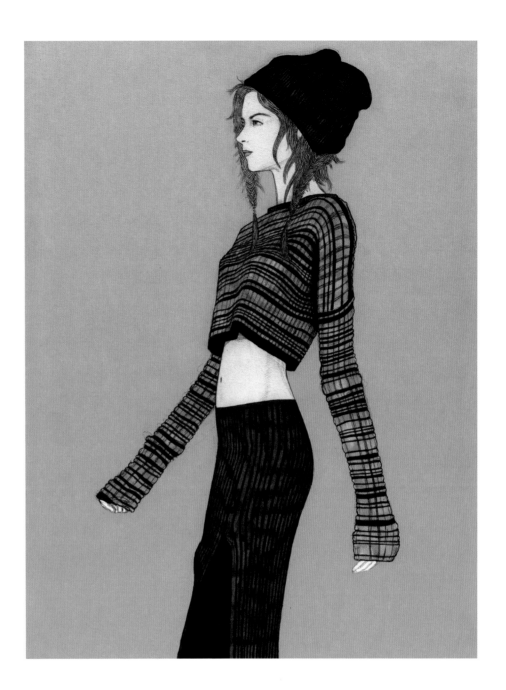

"On the fence between melancholic beauty and
optical illusion, close to 'optical art' and an atmosphere
some bloggers have defined as 'black cubism'."

LANCIA TREND VISIONS
lanciatrendvisions.com

Nicole Jarecz

1988 born in Mt. Clemens, USA | lives and works in Paris
www.nicolejarecz.ultra-book.com

CLIENTS
Glamour magazine (Germany), Company magazine,
Elle Girl Japan, Marie Claire China, Be magazine,
Madame Figaro, Undiz, commons&sense

AGENT
Colagene,
Illustration Clinic
Paris, Montreal, London
colagene.com

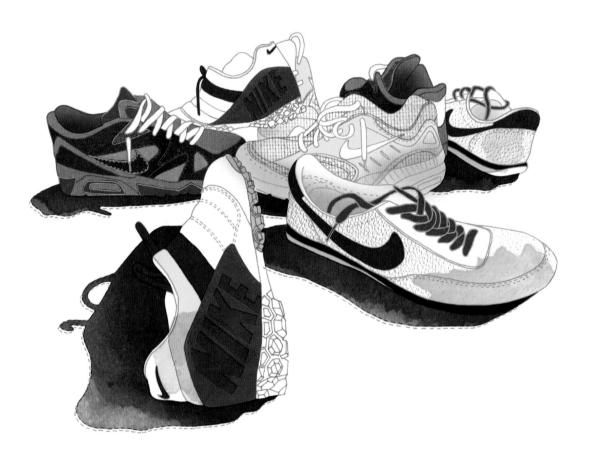

"With any fashion illustration I try to create an image that is soft
and feminine with the right amount of pop."

„Bei jeder Modeillustration versuche ich ein Bild zu schaffen, das weich und
feminin ist und die richtige Menge Pop enthält."

« Dans toutes mes illustrations de mode j'essaie de créer une image
douce et féminine avec la juste dose de pop. »

Nike, 2011
Personal work; pencil, watercolor,
found textures and digital

→   **Bubbles, 2012**
Personal work; pencil,
found textures and digital

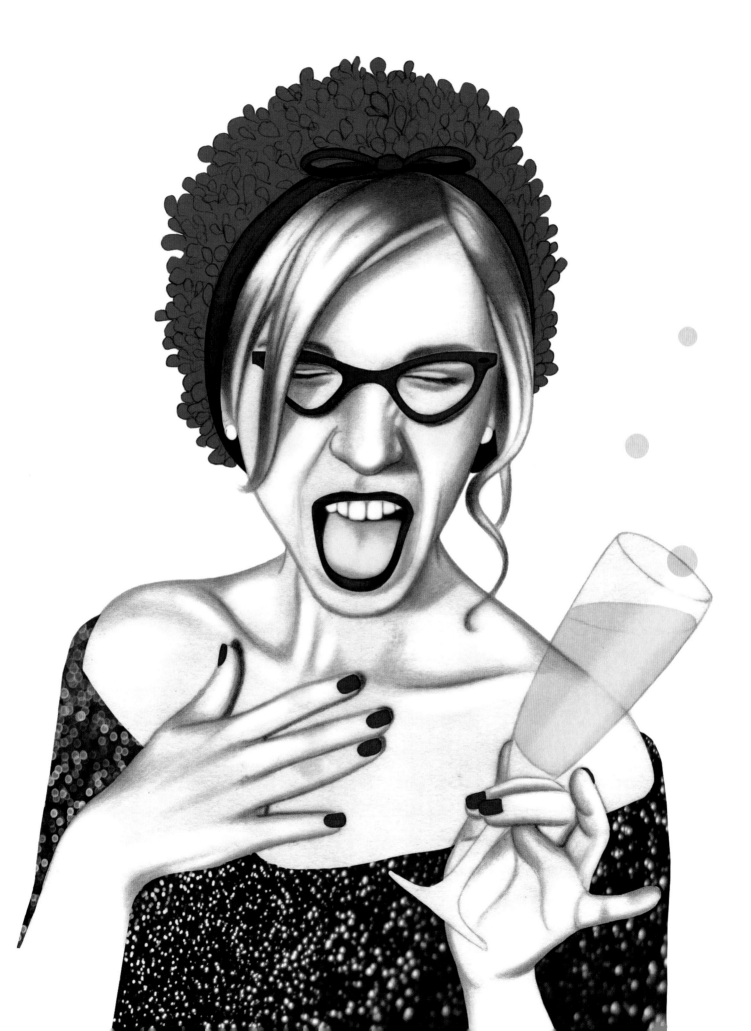

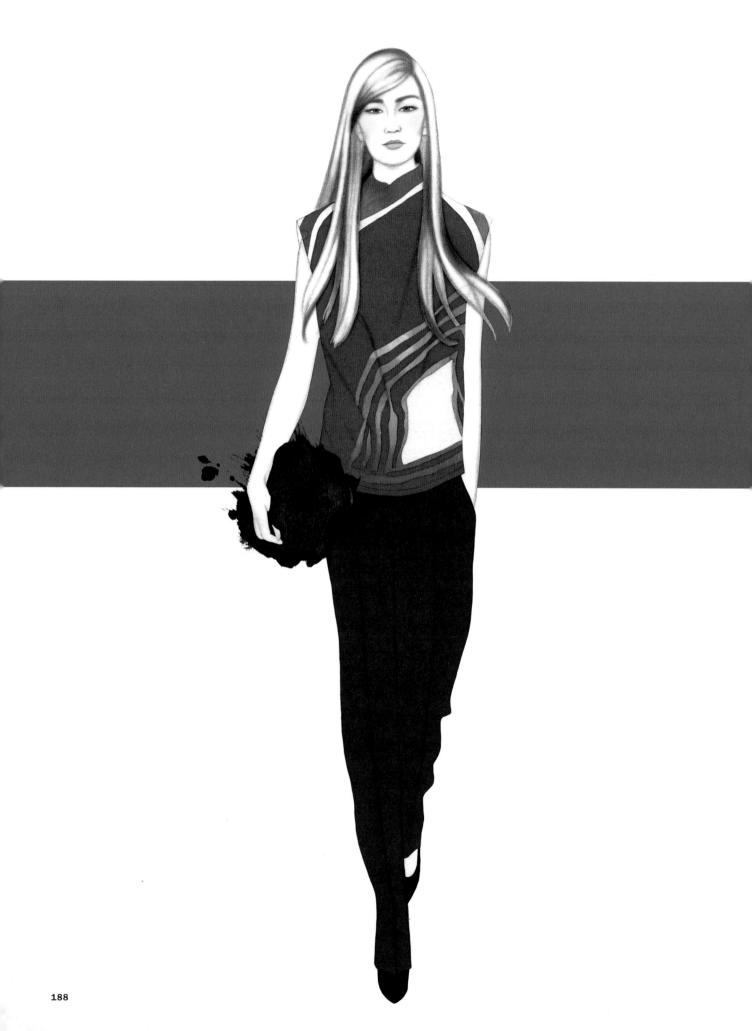

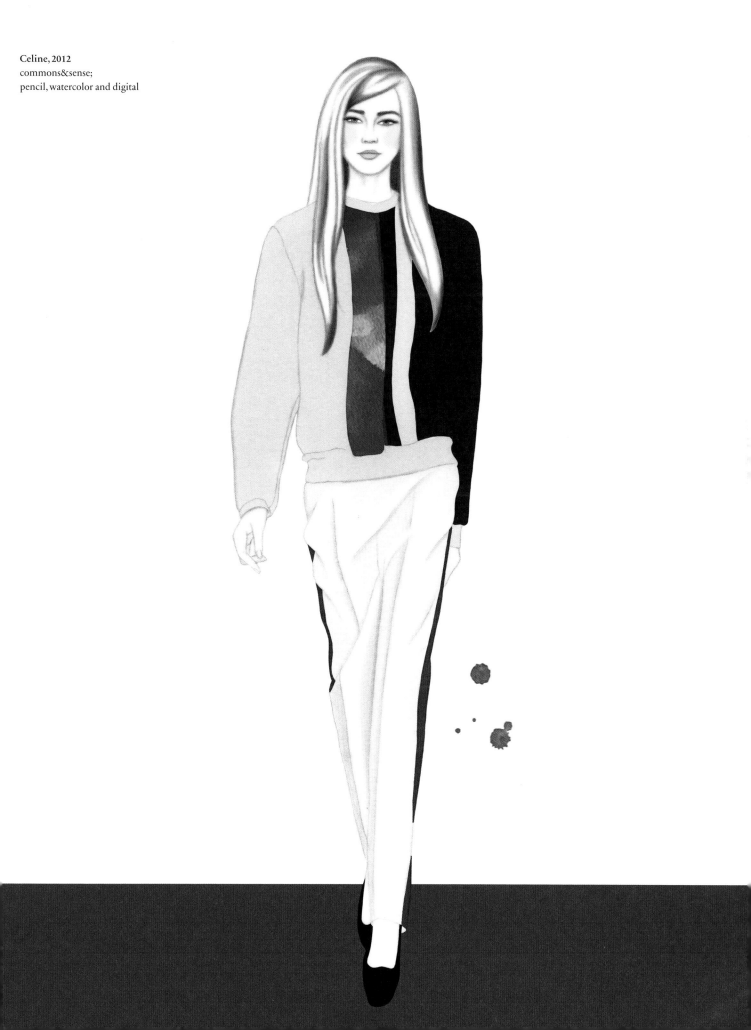

Celine, 2012
commons&sense;
pencil, watercolor and digital

Jules Julien

1975 born in Paris | lives and works in Paris
www.julesjulien.com

CLIENTS
Cartier, Citizen K, commons&sense,
Diesel Japan, Gyre Omotesando,
Keds, Soon magazine, Wad magazine

AGENTS
V.O Valérie Oualid
France
valerieoualid.com

Hugo & Marie
USA
hugoandmarie.com

MW Company
Japan
mw-company.com

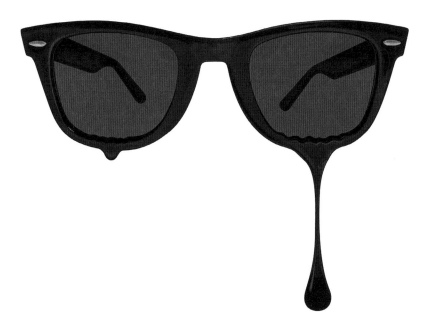

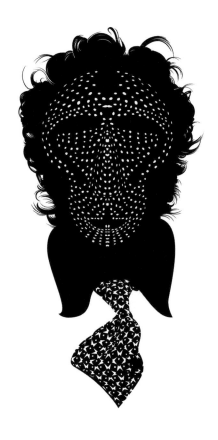

"A fashion illustration has to describe the outfit
and make it come to life – like a ghost trying
to tell us what it is and what has shaped it."

„Eine Modeillustration muss das Outfit beschreiben und
lebendig werden lassen – wie ein Gespenst, das uns
erzählen will, was es ist und wie es zu seiner Gestalt kam."

« Une illustration de mode doit décrire une tenue
et lui insuffler vie – comme un fantôme qui essaie
de nous dire qui il est et ce qui lui a donné forme. »

↑   **Mask #1, 2011**
It Post magazine; digital

↖   **Not Enough Fashionable, 2011**
Grazia magazine; digital

→   **Louis Vuitton Story, 2012**
commons&sense; mixed media

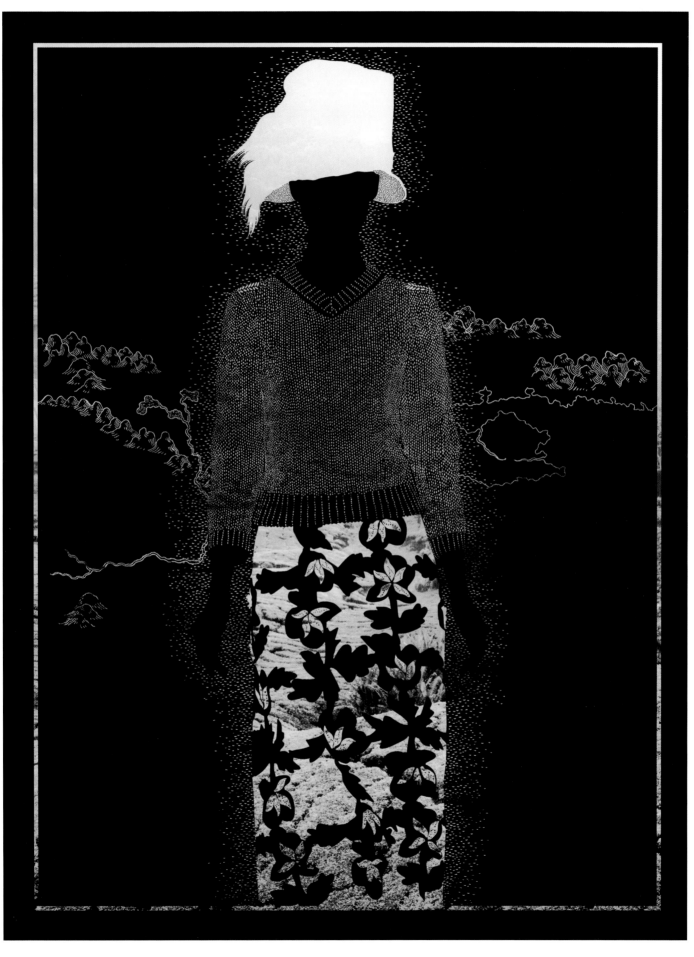

Anja Kröncke

1968 born in Vienna | lives and works in New York
www.anjakroencke.com

CLIENTS
Harvey Nichols, Isetan, Estée Lauder,
Mitsukoshi, Printemps, Vogue,
W magazine, Neiman Marcus,
Tiffany & Co, Victoria's Secret

AGENTS
Traffic Creative
Management
USA
trafficnyc.com

Eye Candy
Illustration Agency
UK
eyecandy.co.uk

2agenten
Germany
2agenten.com

Taiko & Associates
Japan
ua-net.com/taiko

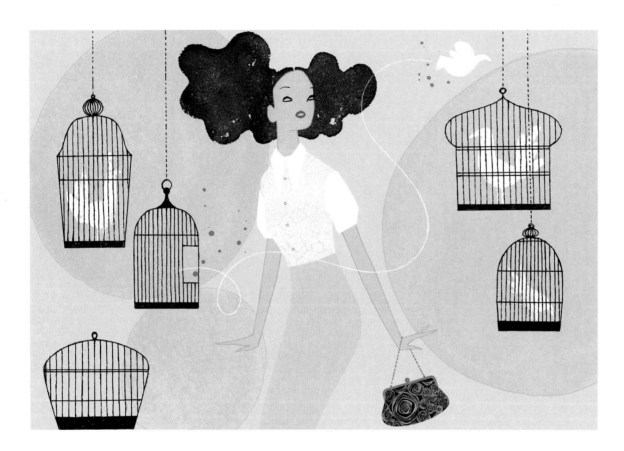

"I love being the author, stylist and set-designer of my own imagination,
inspired by fashion, art, music and the streets of NYC…"

„Ich liebe es, Autorin, Stylistin und Set-Designerin meiner eigenen Imagination zu sein.
Dabei lasse ich mich von Mode, Kunst, Musik und den Straßen von NYC inspirieren…"

« J'adore être l'auteure, la styliste et la décoratrice de ma propre imagination,
inspirée par la mode, l'art, la musique et les rues de New York…»

Dream a Little Dream…, 2010
Mitsukoshi, Japan, promotional cards;
mixed media

→   Cocktails, 2008
Vogue Japan, advertorial; mixed media

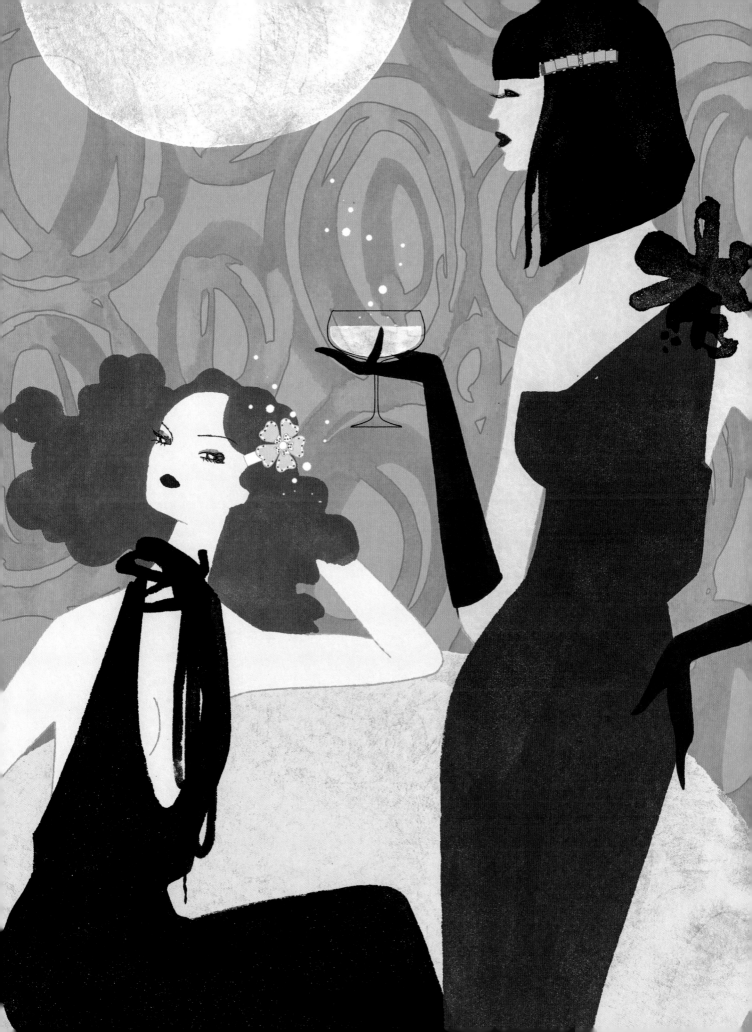

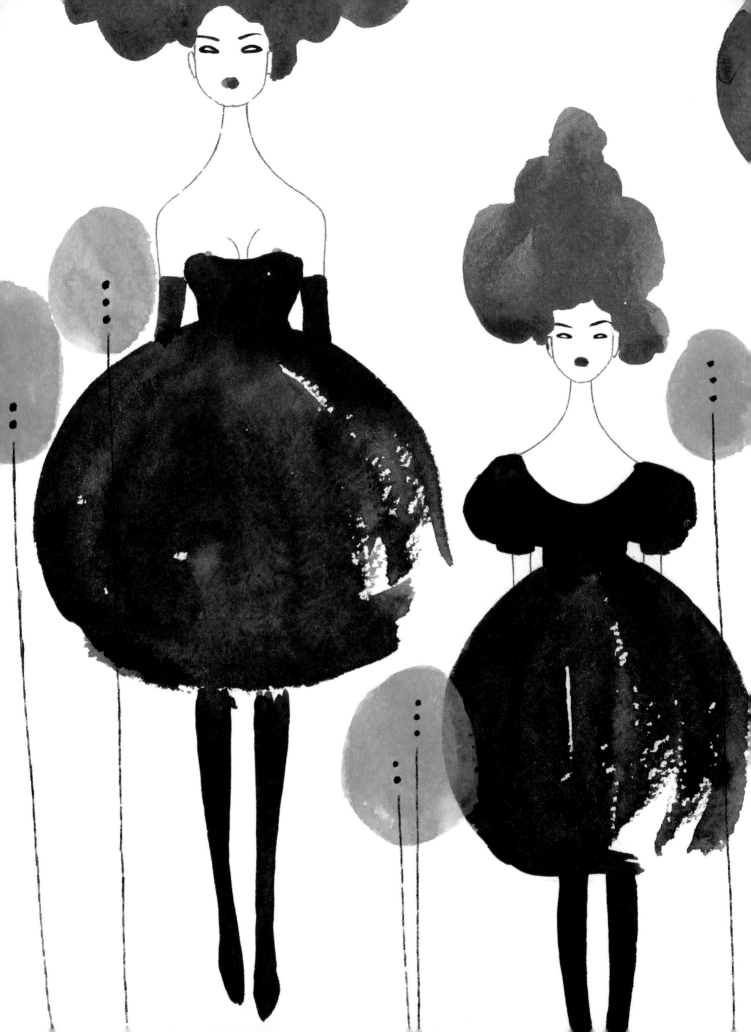

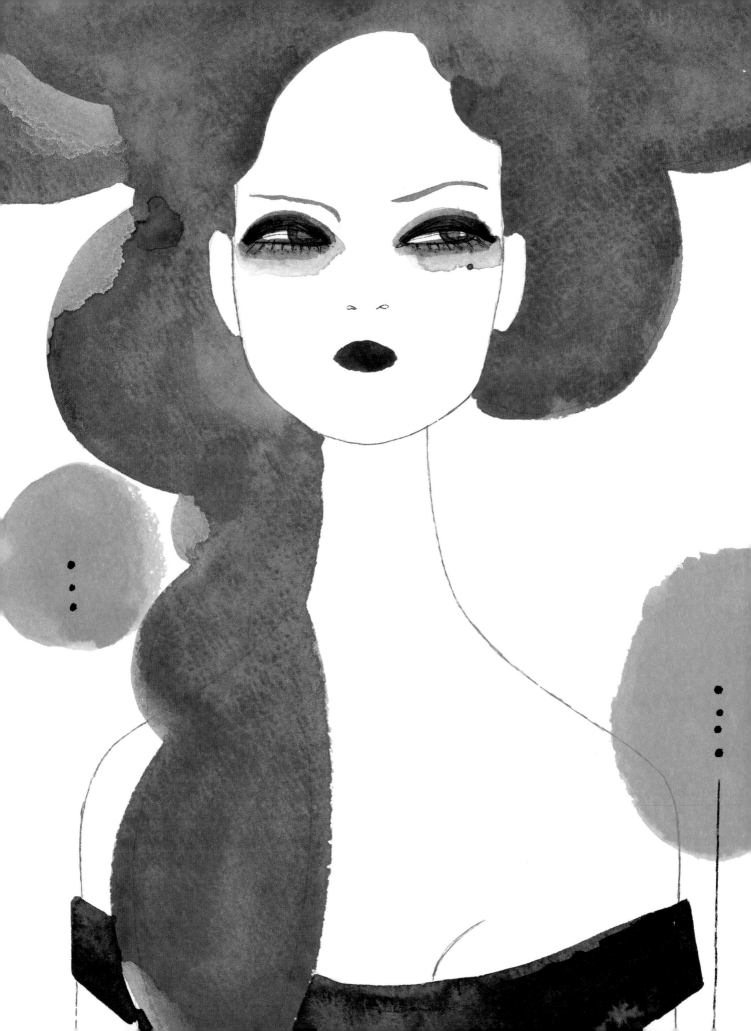

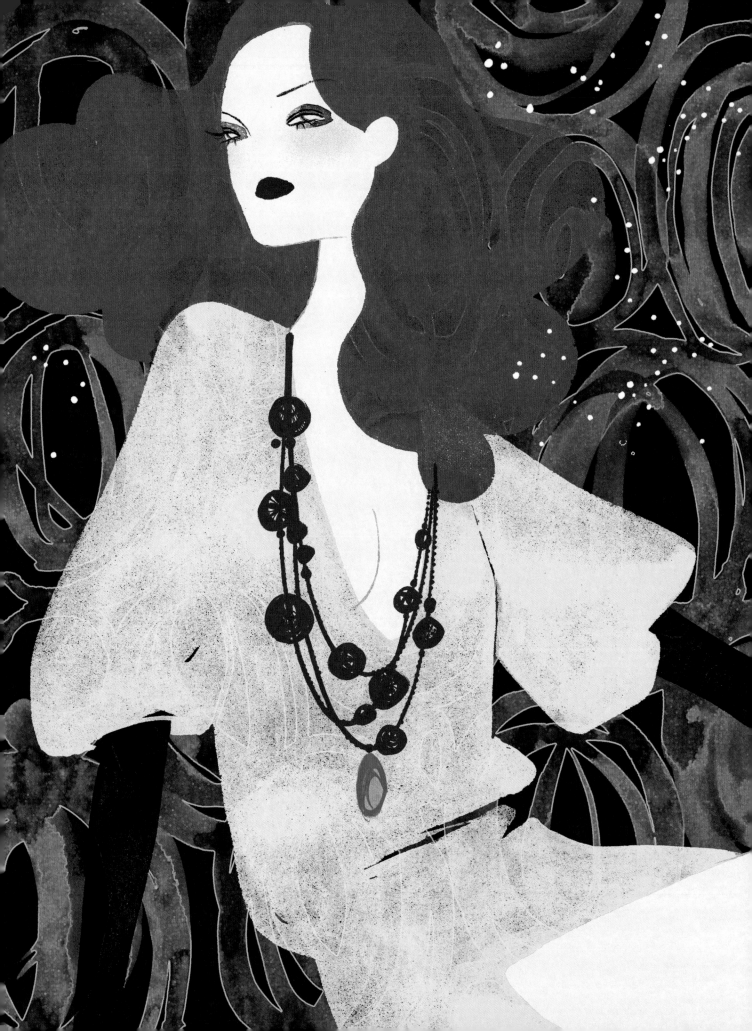

"Anja Kröncke's iconic fashion illustrations really take the pulse of society. Sleek explosions of form and texture, their movement and sass pop right off the page."

ANNE TELFORD
Editor-at-Large
Communication Arts magazine

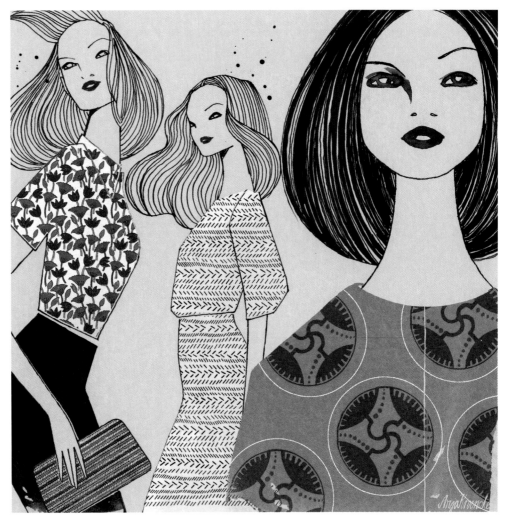

Charming Prints, 2012
The Wall Street Journal; mixed media

← **Lounging Girl/Cover, 2008**
Vogue Japan, advertorial; mixed media

p.194 **Emma & Her Sisters, 2007**
Squint magazine, Germany; watercolor

Aurore de La Morinerie

lives and works in Paris
www.auroredelamorinerie.com

AGENTS

Gallois Montbrun
& Fabiani
France
gmgf.fr

Galerie Bartsch
& Chariau
Germany
bartsch-chariau.de

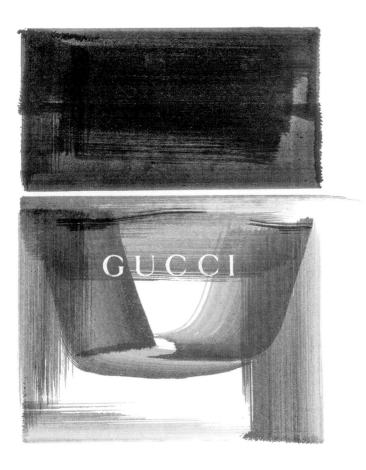

Gucci homme
Ink drawing on paper

→   Christian Lacroix
Haute Couture, 2008
Monotype on etching press
on japan paper

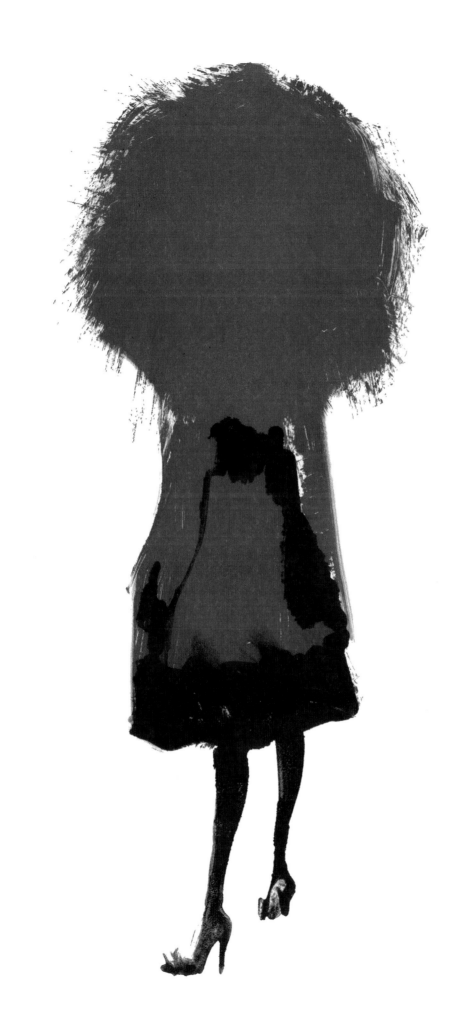

Chrissy Lau

1984 born in Hull, UK | lives and works in Sydney
www.chrissylau.com

CLIENTS
Mambo, Pocketto magazine,
Gary Pepper Vintage,
Women's Weekly

AGENT
The Illustration Room
Australia
illustrationroom.com.au

"Detailed patterns and flowing hair are often the key elements in my fashion illustrations. There is a simplicity to the colors but a complexity in the shapes."

„Detaillierte Muster und offene Haare sind in meinen Modezeichnungen meist zentrale Elemente. Die Farben sind eher schlicht, aber die Formen recht komplex."

« Les motifs détaillés et les cascades de cheveux ont souvent la vedette dans mes illustrations. Les couleurs sont simples, mais les formes complexes. »

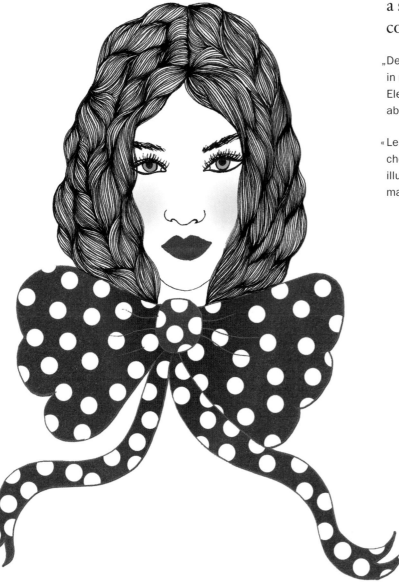

Bow Girl, 2012
Personal work;
hand-drawn and digital

→ Aquarius, 2012
Women's Weekly magazine;
hand-drawn and digital

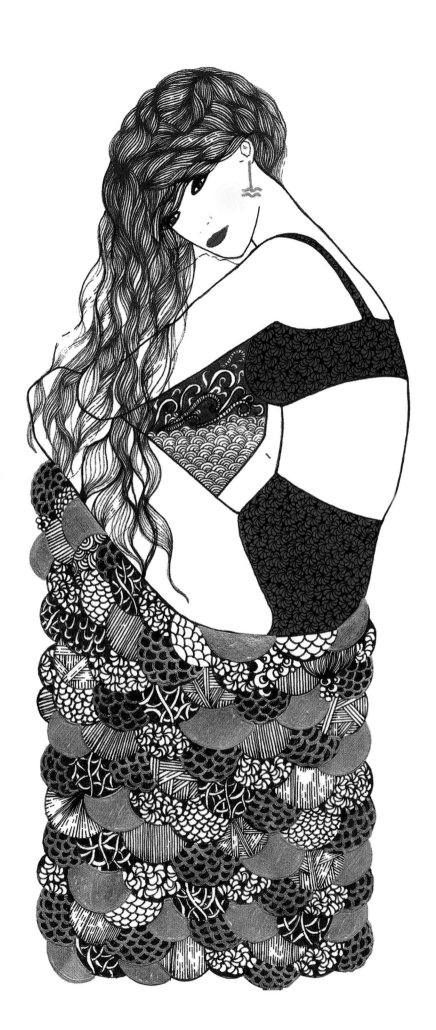

"Simply regurgitating a fashion-runway look is no option for Chrissy, especially when her pen wields such power in building a fantasy world around the clothes."

EMMA DO
Editor, Pocketto magazine

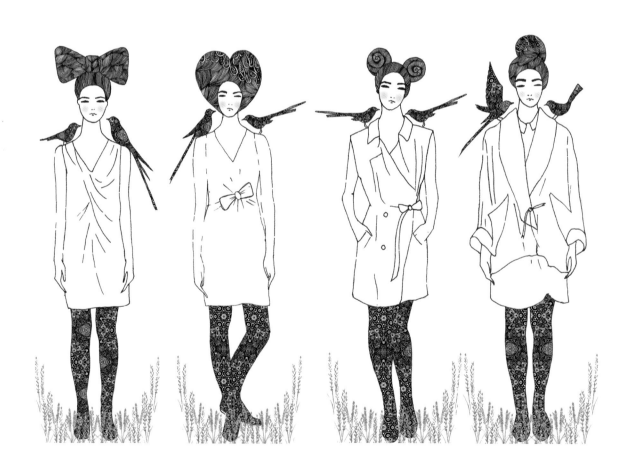

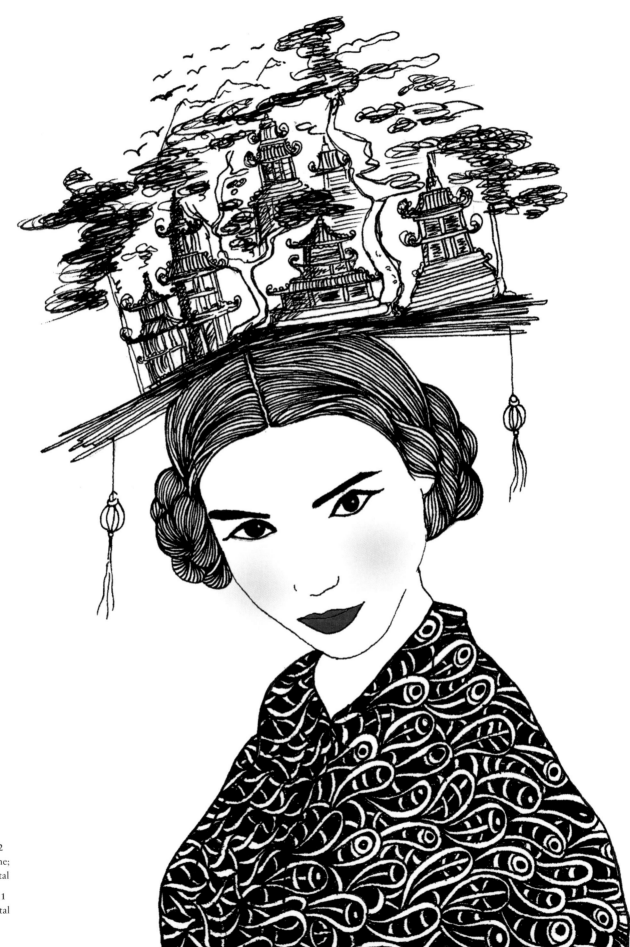

Beijing Girl, 2012
Pocketto magazine;
ink, pen and digital

←   Kuwaii, 2011
Ink, pen and digital

Tanya Ling

1966 born in Calcutta | lives and works in London
www.tanyaling.com

CLIENTS
Louis Vuitton, NARS, Selfridges,
Vogue, Harper's Bazaar

AGENT
Bipasha Ghosh Limited
UK
bgltd.co

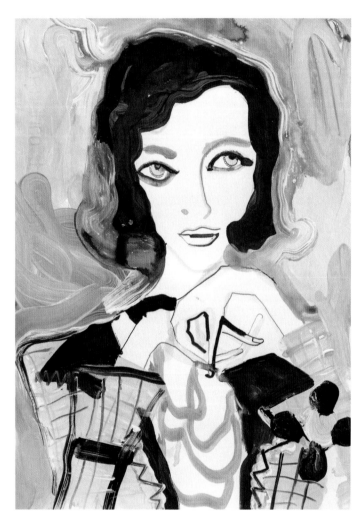

"I make drawings, paintings and sculptures and occasionally I'm asked to make fashion illustrations."

„Ich zeichne, male und mache Skulpturen, und gelegentlich fragt man mich nach Modeillustrationen."

« Je fais des dessins, des peintures et des sculptures, et parfois on me demande de faire des illustrations de mode. »

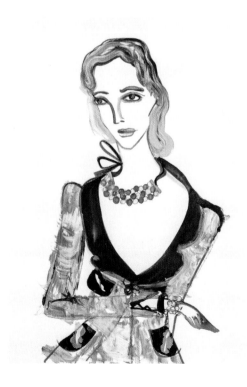

Chanel Fall Winter 2009
From Ling's series International
Ready-to-Wear; acrylic and ink on paper

→   Louis Vuitton Fashion Jewelry,
Fall/Winter 2012
Louis Vuitton, animated online film;
acrylic and ink on paper

→→ For Selfridges,
Prada Spring/Summer 2011
Acrylic and ink on paper

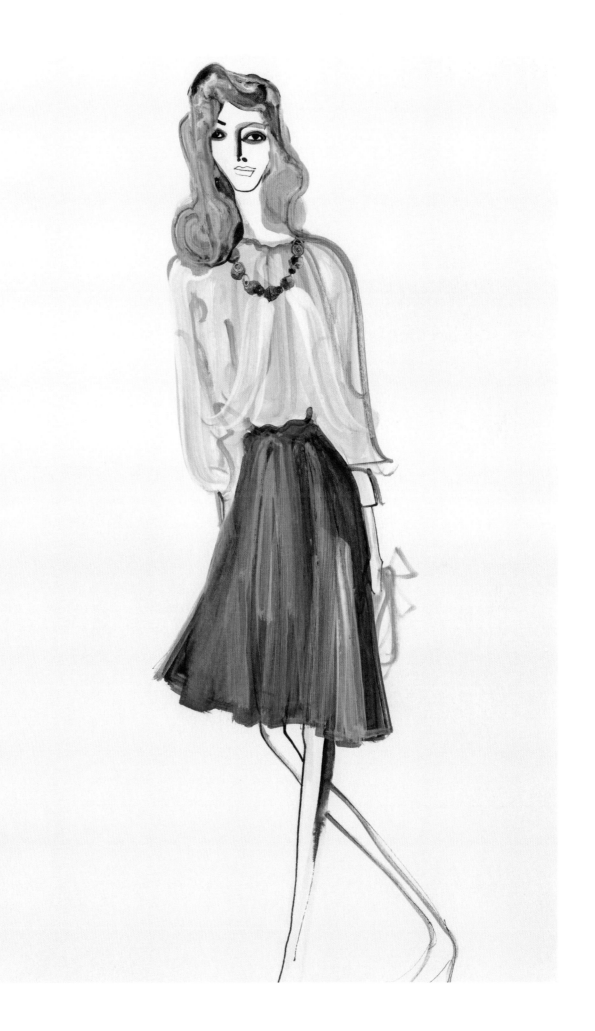

Idea Drawing #75, #116 and #94, 2012
From the series Idea Drawings;
ink and acrylic on paper

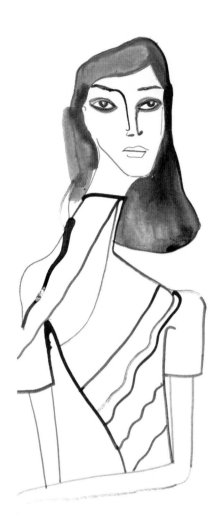

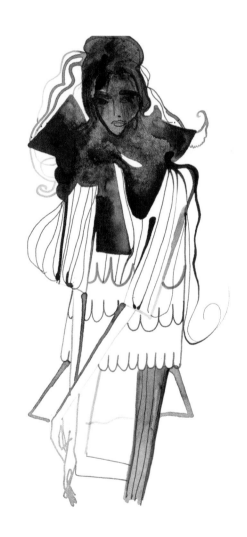

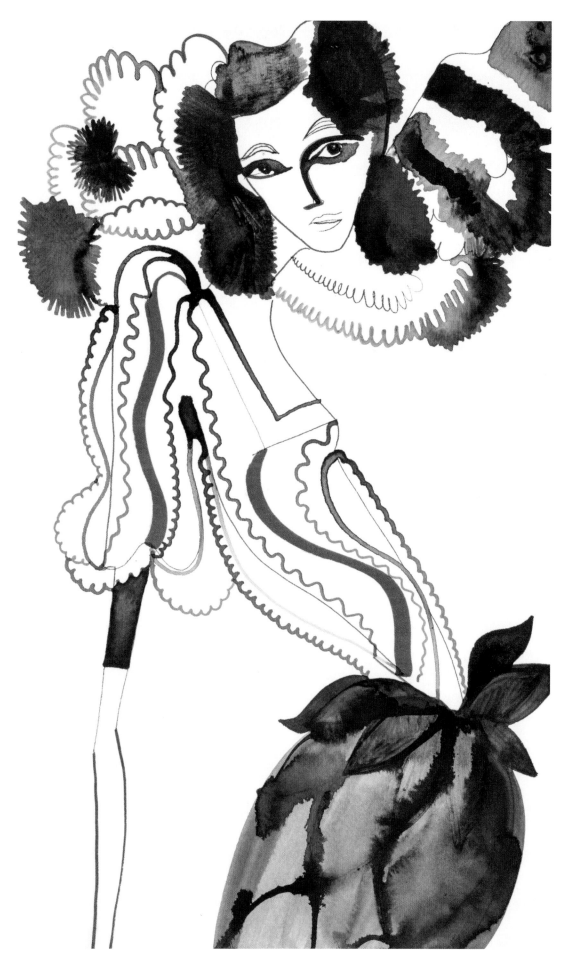

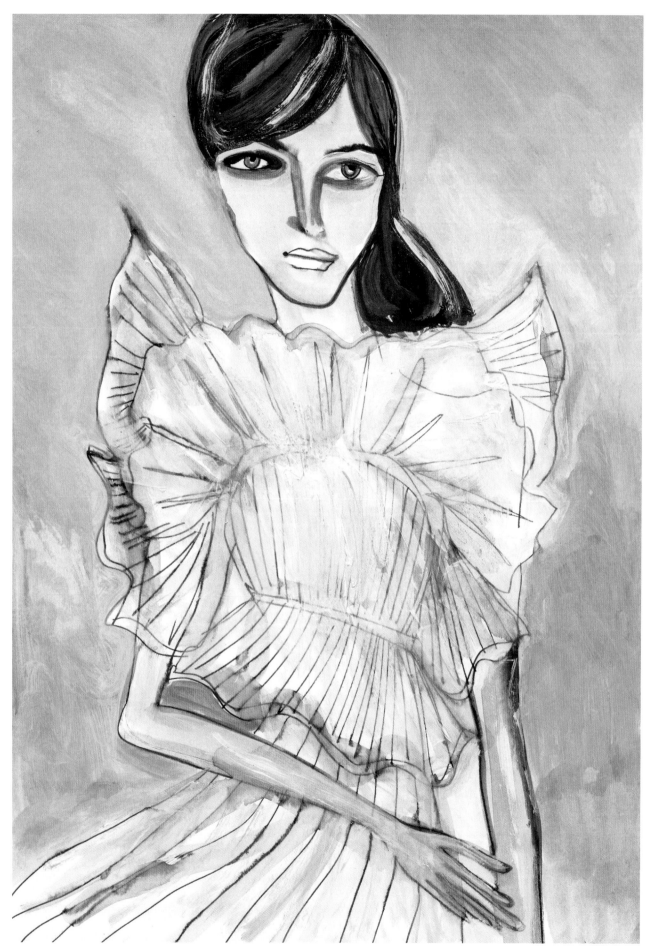

"Ling's work crosses the boundaries between fashion and art. She plays strength with fragility, a sense of melancholy against frivolity and defines contemporary. Her illustrations convey a sense of fashion that makes us dream."

PETER COPPING
Artistic Director, Nina Ricci

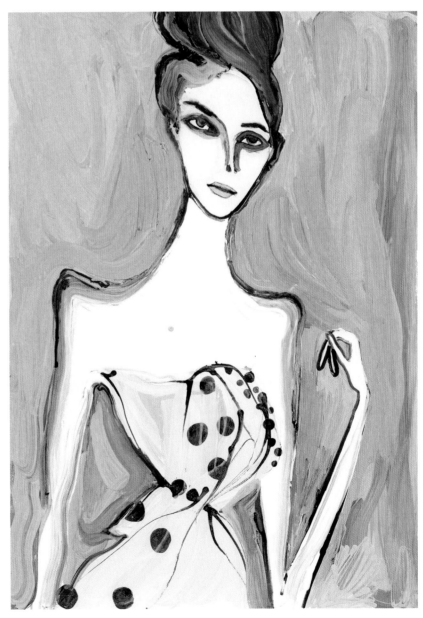

Nina Ricci Fall/Winter 2012
From Ling's series International
Ready-to-Wear; acrylic and ink on paper

← Chloe Spring/Summer 2012
From Ling's series International
Ready-to-Wear; acrylic and ink on paper

LULU*

1977 born in Solingen | lives and works in Berlin
www.plasticpirate.com

CLIENTS
Vogue Japan, Vogue Pelle, Adidas Originals,
Bloomingdale's, Tush magazine,
Elle Korea, Swarovski

AGENTS

CWC International
USA
cwc-i.com

CWC Tokyo
Japan
cwctokyo.com

Caroline Seidler
Austria
carolineseidler.com

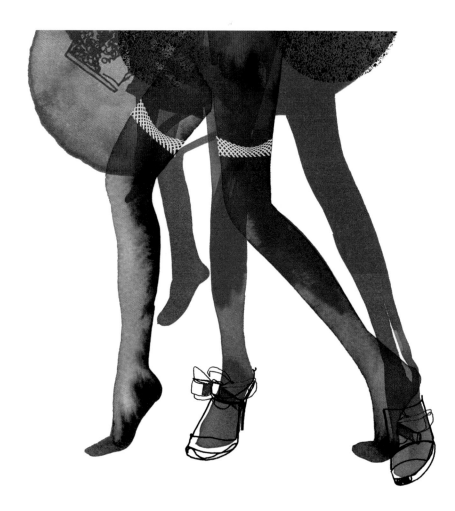

"The beauty of color, line and a touch of the '60s together inspire me
the most. I like to focus on the fabrics and emphasize good design."

„Die Schönheit von Farbe und Linie mit einer Prise Sixties inspirieren mich am stärksten.
Ich konzentriere mich gerne auf die Stoffe und betone gutes Design."

« Ce qui m'inspire le plus, c'est la beauté de la couleur, du trait, et une touche
d'années 1960. J'aime mettre en valeur les tissus et les coupes. »

Stockings, 2011
Flair Mondadori magazine, Vienna,
Art Direction: Karolina Stasiak;
hand-drawn, collage and digital

→   Nilla, 2012
Personal work; hand-drawn,
collage and digital

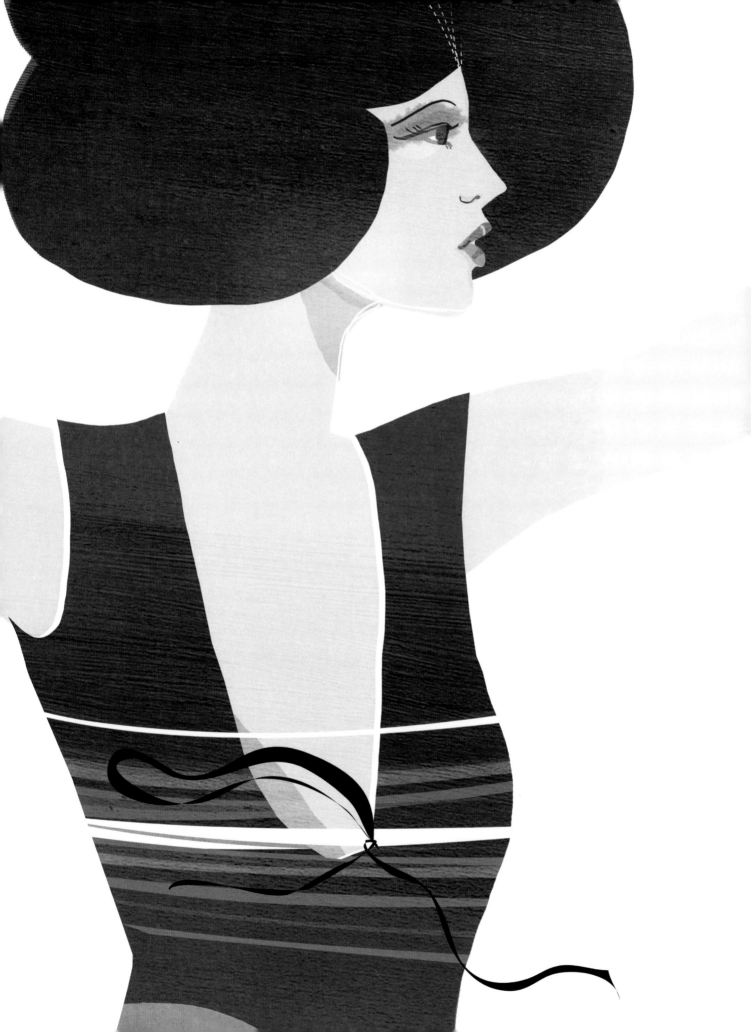

"LULU* is one of the greatest illustrators
of today – with a magic eye for color,
a virtuoso technique and the gift to
enrich beauty with depth."

MATEO KRIES
Director
Vitra Design Museum

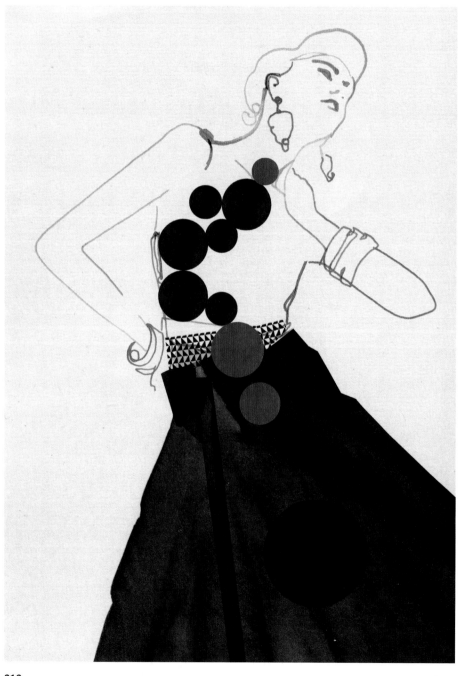

Untitled, 2012
Personal work; hand-drawn,
collage, ink and digital

→   Milla, 2012
Personal work; hand-drawn,
collage and digital

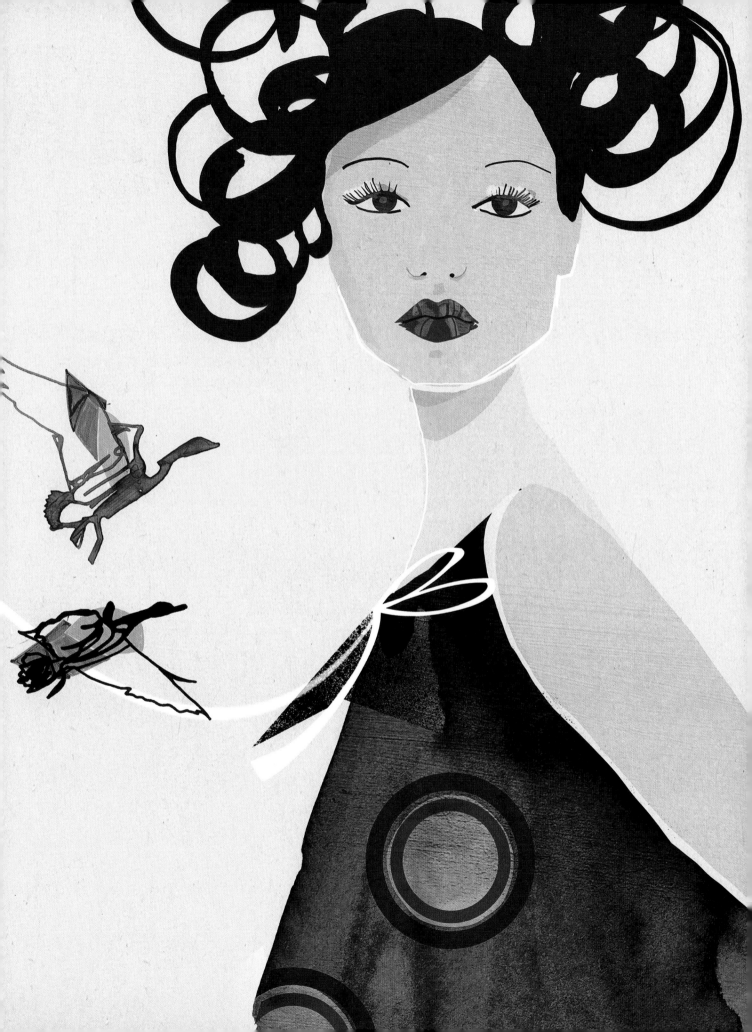

Cecilia Lundgren

1982 born in Halmstad, Sweden | lives and works in Helsingborg, Sweden
www.cecilialundgren.com

CLIENTS
Elle, Damernas Värld,
Femina magazine,
Metro, Costa Cruises

AGENT
Traffic Creative
Management
USA
trafficnyc.com

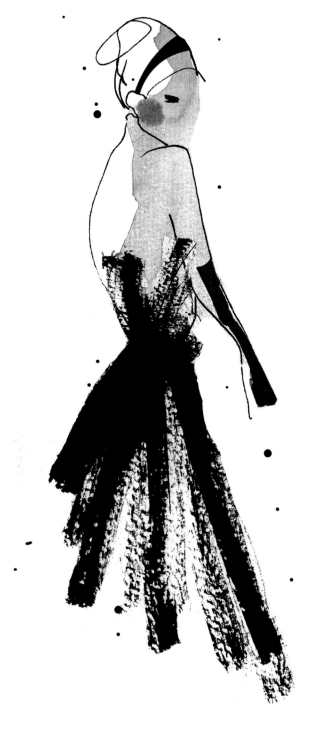

"I am inspired by life and dreams,
my ambition is to express identity
and feelings rather than beauty."

„Mich inspirieren das Leben und Träume.
Identität und Gefühle auszudrücken
ist mir wichtiger, als Schönheit zu zeigen."

« Je suis inspirée par la vie et les rêves,
mon ambition est d'exprimer une
identité et des sentiments plutôt que
de la beauté. »

Untitled, 2010
Personal work; watercolor,
pen, ink and digital

→ Untitled, 2010
Personal work; watercolor and ink

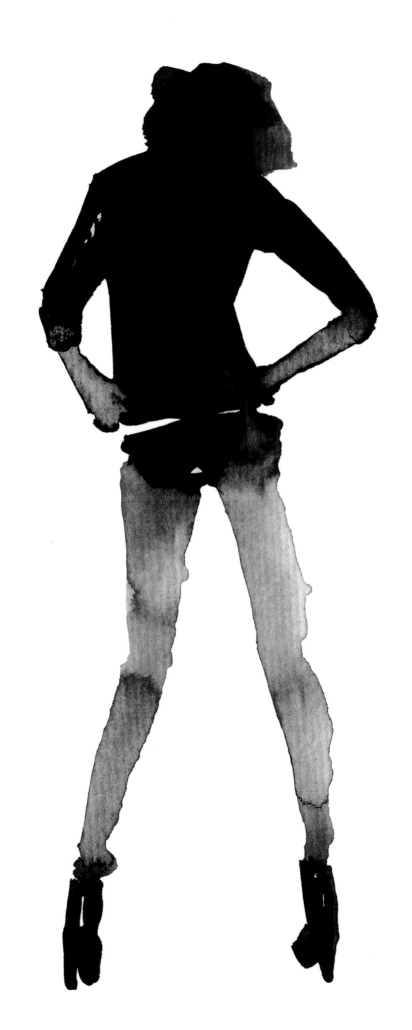

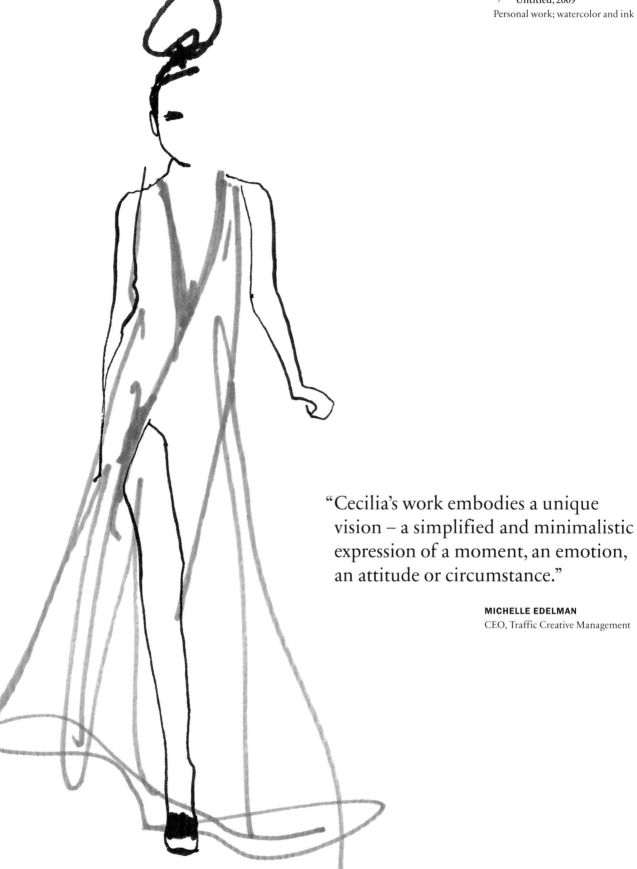

Untitled, 2009
Personal work; pen and pencil

→   Untitled, 2009
Personal work; watercolor and ink

"Cecilia's work embodies a unique vision – a simplified and minimalistic expression of a moment, an emotion, an attitude or circumstance."

MICHELLE EDELMAN
CEO, Traffic Creative Management

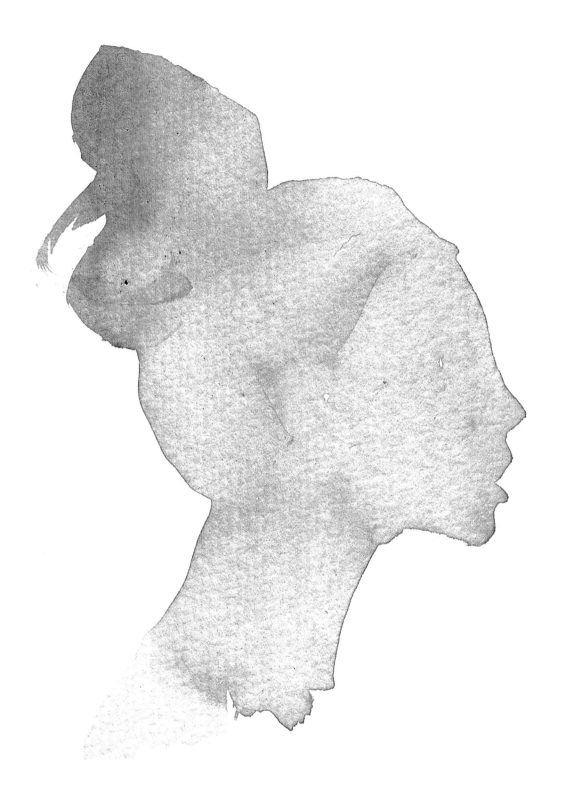

Margot Macé

1966 born in Venlo, Netherlands | lives and works in Barbizon, France
www.bookmargot.com

CLIENTS
Lancôme, Clarins, Escada, Vogue Pelle, Vogue Japan,
commons&sense, L'Officiel, Carrousel du Louvre,
Shanghai Exhibition Center

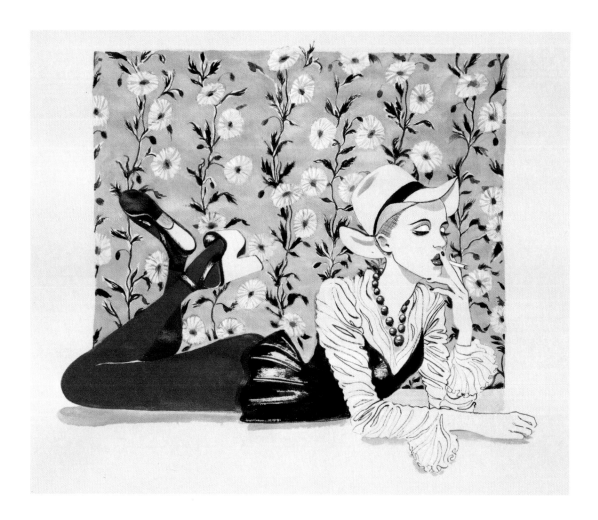

"Fashion is a playground for our personal desires; it's an excellent
setting for drawing and painting women in their best role."

„Mode ist der Tummelplatz für unsere persönlichen Wünsche: eine exzellente
Umgebung, um Frauen bildhaft in ihrer besten Rolle zu zeigen."

« La mode est un terrain de jeu pour nos désirs personnels ; c'est un décor
excellent pour dessiner et peindre les femmes dans leur meilleur rôle. »

Smoking, 2012
Personal work, exhibition in Shanghai
Exhibition Center; mixed media on
Japanese paper

→ Blackbird, 2012
Personal work, exhibition in Shanghai
Exhibition Center; mixed media on
Japanese paper

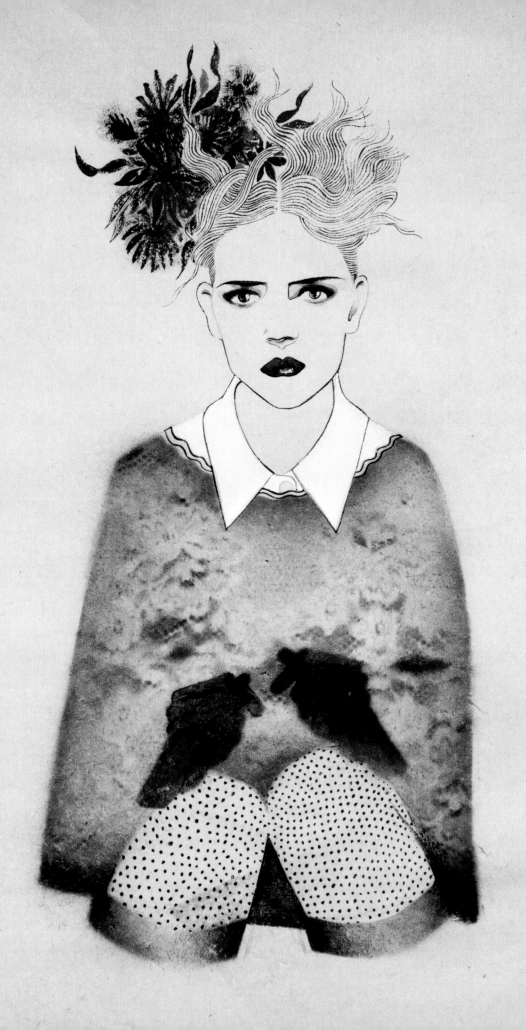

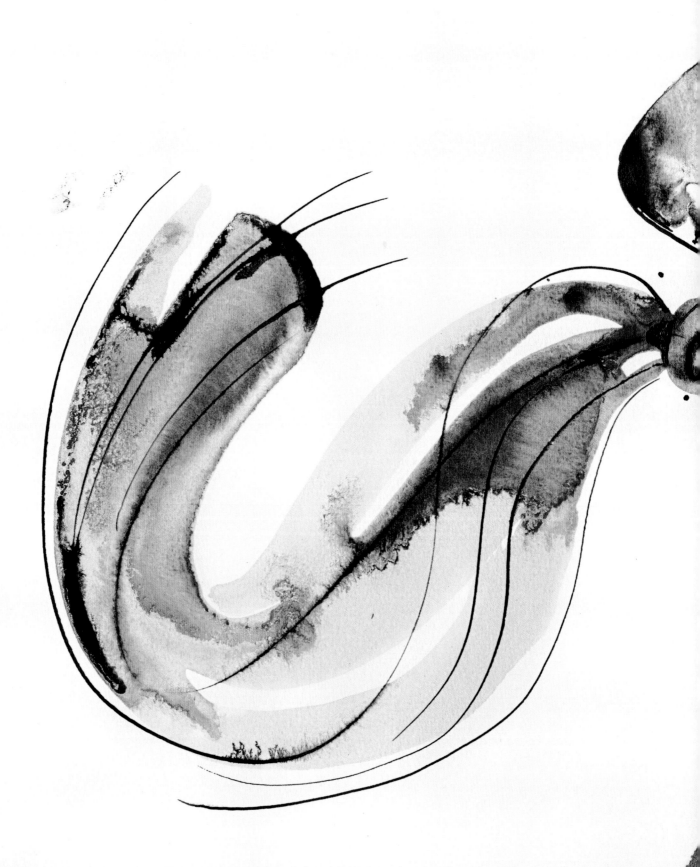

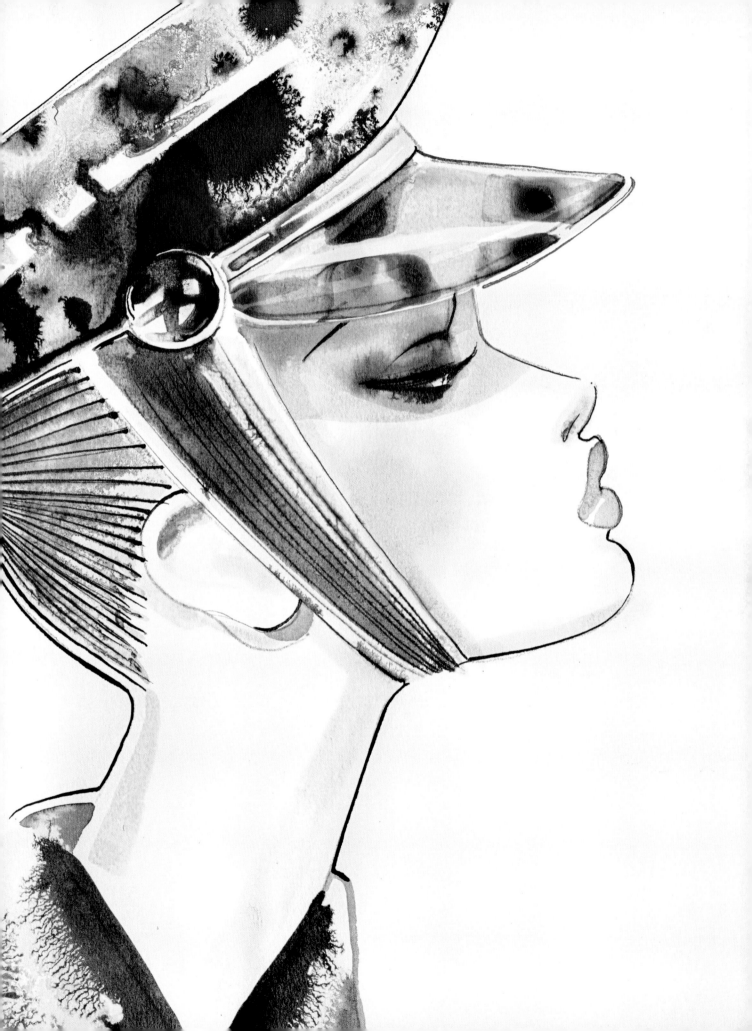

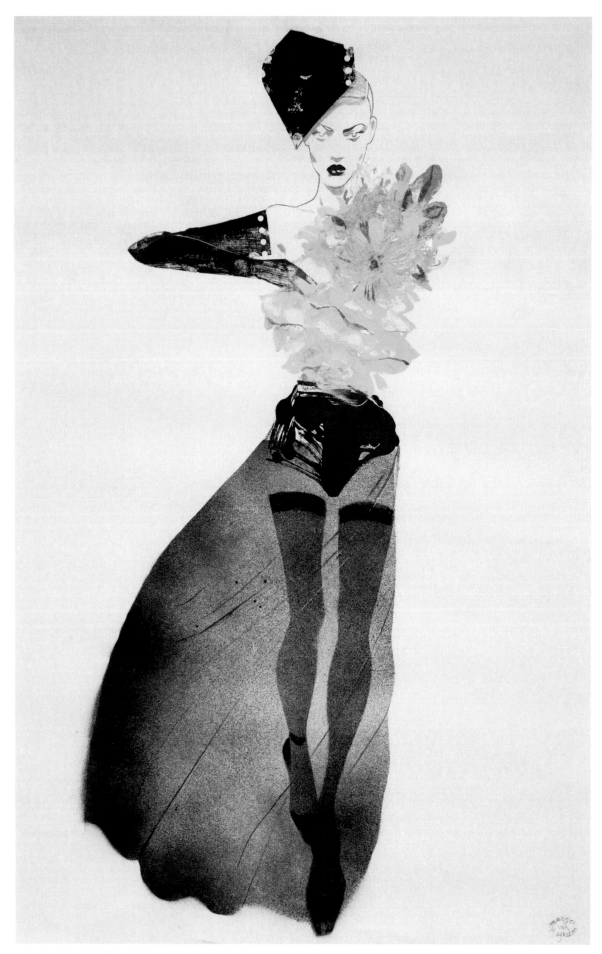

McQueen, 2012
Vogue Japan; mixed media
on Japanese paper

← **Sunflowers, 2012**
Vogue Japan; mixed media
on Japanese paper

p.220 **Pony Tail, 2012**
Vogue Japan; mixed media
on Japanese paper

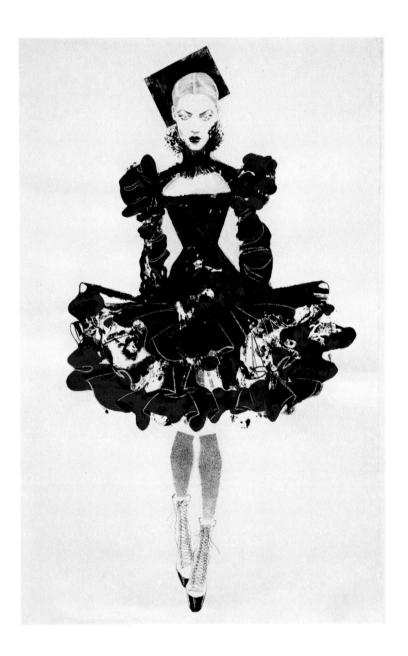

"Margot is the most talented illustrator I've worked with.
She is full of ideas and can always draw something I have
never imagined. Her work has a sensitive beauty."

SACHIKO IGARI
Contributing Beauty Editor
Vogue Japan

Anja Mathiesen

1970 born in Hamburg | lives and works in Hamburg
www.anjamathiesen.de

CLIENTS
Gruner+Jahr, Hubert Burda Media,
Globus Medien, Jahreszeiten Verlag,
Meth Media VerlagsgesmbH

AGENT
c/o Claudia Schönhals
Germany
schoenhals.de

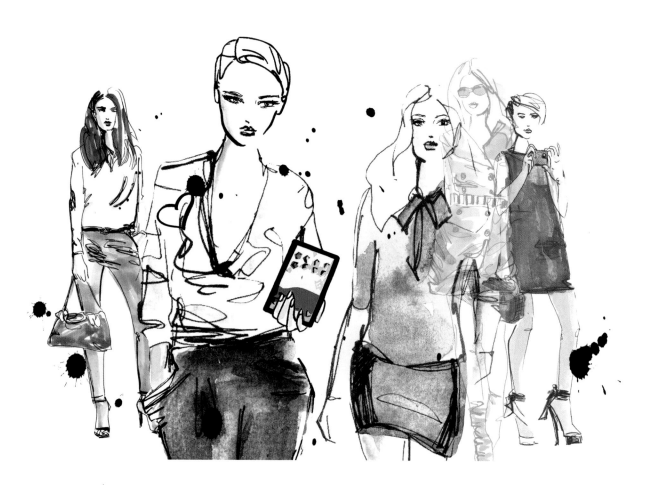

"I am inspired by the challenge of individually visualizing
and reinventing beauty by artistic means!"

„Mich inspiriert die Herausforderung, Schönheit durch künstlerische
Mittel individuell zu visualisieren und neu zu erfinden!"

« Je suis inspirée par l'envie de visualiser individuellement
et de réinventer la beauté grâce à l'art ! »

Runway, 2012,
Petra magazine; hand-drawn, collage

→   Zebra Style, 2012,
Personal work; hand-drawn

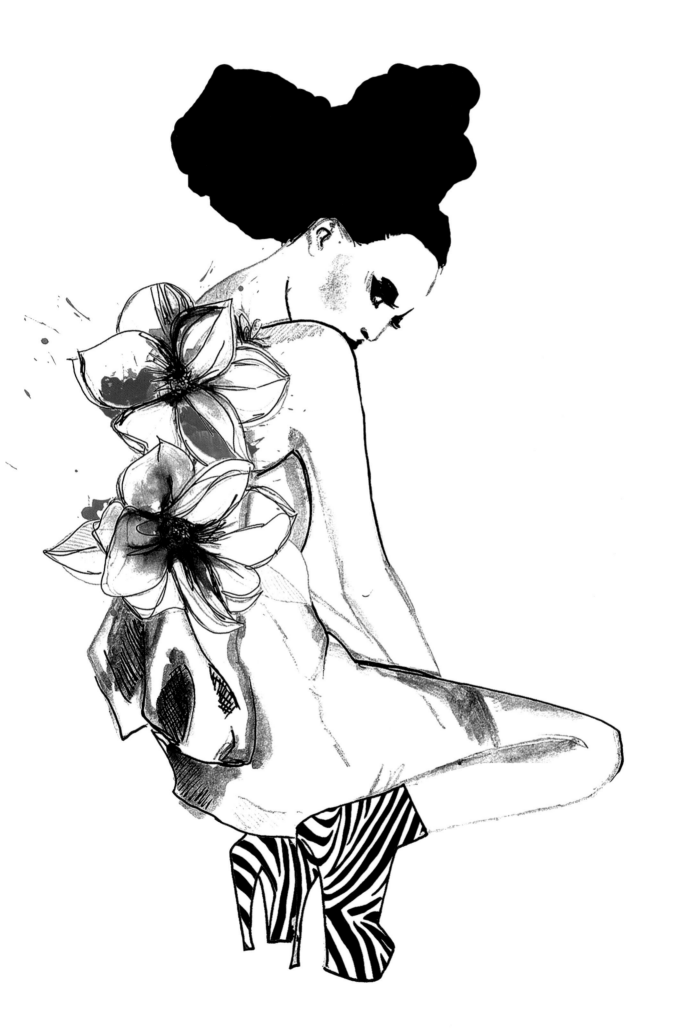

Elisa Mazzone

1981 born in Adelaide | lives and works in Paris
www.elisamazzone.com.au

CLIENTS
Mambo, Marks & Spencer, Madison, Style.com,
Hallmark, New Idea, The Strand Arcade, Companys
Original, Easy Living, Good Weekend Australia

AGENT
The Illustration Room
Australia
illustrationroom.com.au

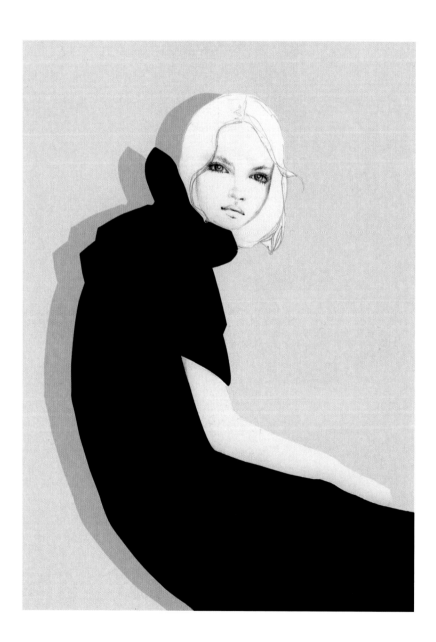

"It's about exploring where
a line can take you. A little
journey where the marks
become the main characters."

„Erforschen, wohin Linien dich bringen
können. Eine kleine Reise, bei der
Zeichen zu Hauptpersonen werden."

« Il s'agit d'aller là où le trait vous
emmène. C'est un petit voyage
où les lignes deviennent
les personnages principaux. »

Let It Be, 2010
Personal work, exhibition series;
hand-drawn

→   **Sixties Beauty, 2012**
Style.com/Print; hand-drawn
and digital

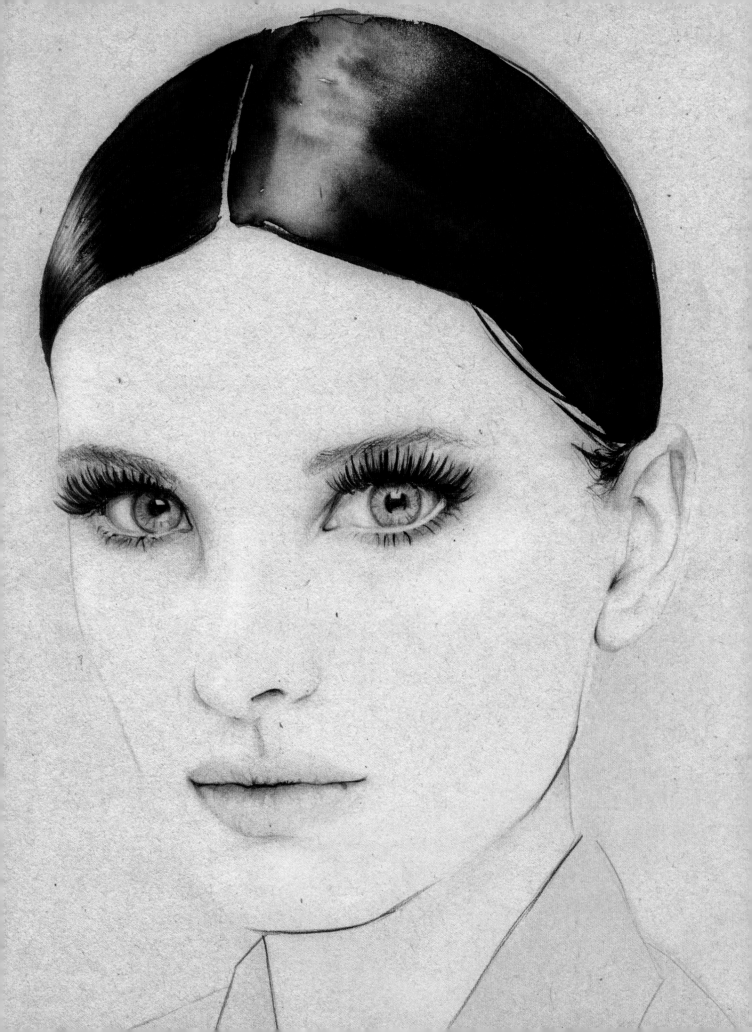

"Her watercolor and pencil fashion and beauty illustrations have a delicate vulnerability mixed with a feminine strength."

KATIE PERROTT
Agent, The Illustration Room

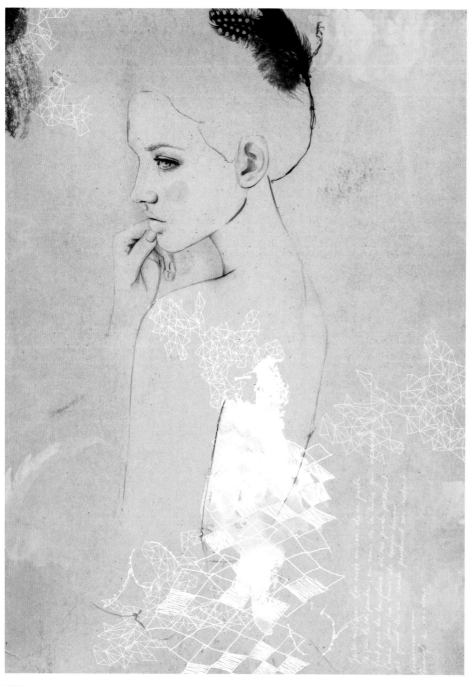

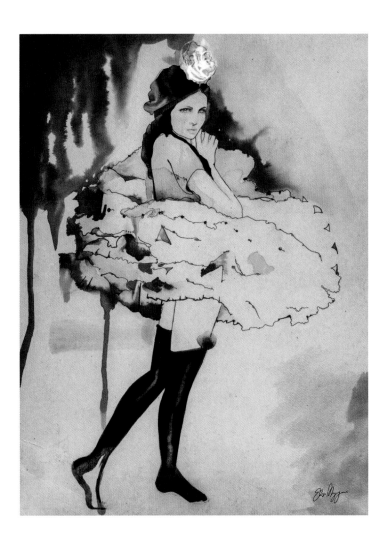

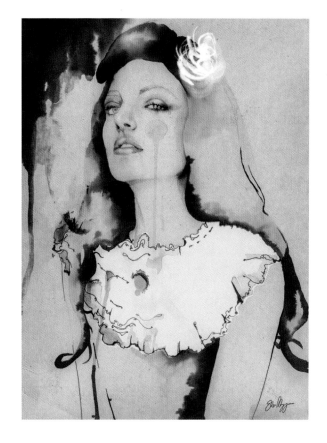

Folie #1 and #2, 2012
Personal work, exhibition series;
hand-drawn and digital

← **Winter, 2012**
Personal work, exhibition series;
hand-drawn and digital

Pippa McManus

1982 born in Perth | lives and works in Perth
www.pippasworkablefixative.blogspot.com.au

CLIENTS
Mary Katrantzou, Manning Cartell, 140 William,
Linneys, Aurelio Costarella, Claremont Quarter, Ellery,
Perth Fashion Festival, Dolce & Gabbana's Swide blog

AGENT
Melissa Lekias
Australia
magenta.net.au

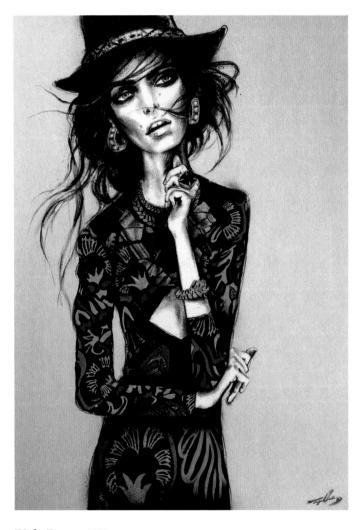

"Caught between a commercial
fashion-illustration life and a fine-art
life, I illustrate what I want to own
and who I want to be."

„Mein Leben bewegt sich zwischen kommerzieller
Modeillustration und Kunst – so illustriere ich,
was ich besitzen will und wer ich sein möchte."

« Entre l'illustration de mode commerciale
et les beaux arts, j'illustre ce que je veux
posséder et qui je veux être. »

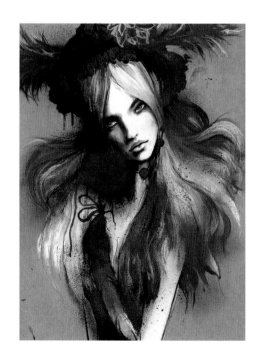

Z is for Zuzanna, 2012
Personal work, exhibition A is for
Arizona; acrylic, charcoal, spray paint
and paint-pens on canvas

→   Nicole in Red, 2012
Perth Fashion Festival, exhibition Best
Western; acrylic, charcoal, spray paint
and paint-pens on canvas paper

→ → X is for Xiao, 2012
Personal work, exhibition A is for
Arizona; acrylic, charcoal, spray paint
and paint-pens on canvas

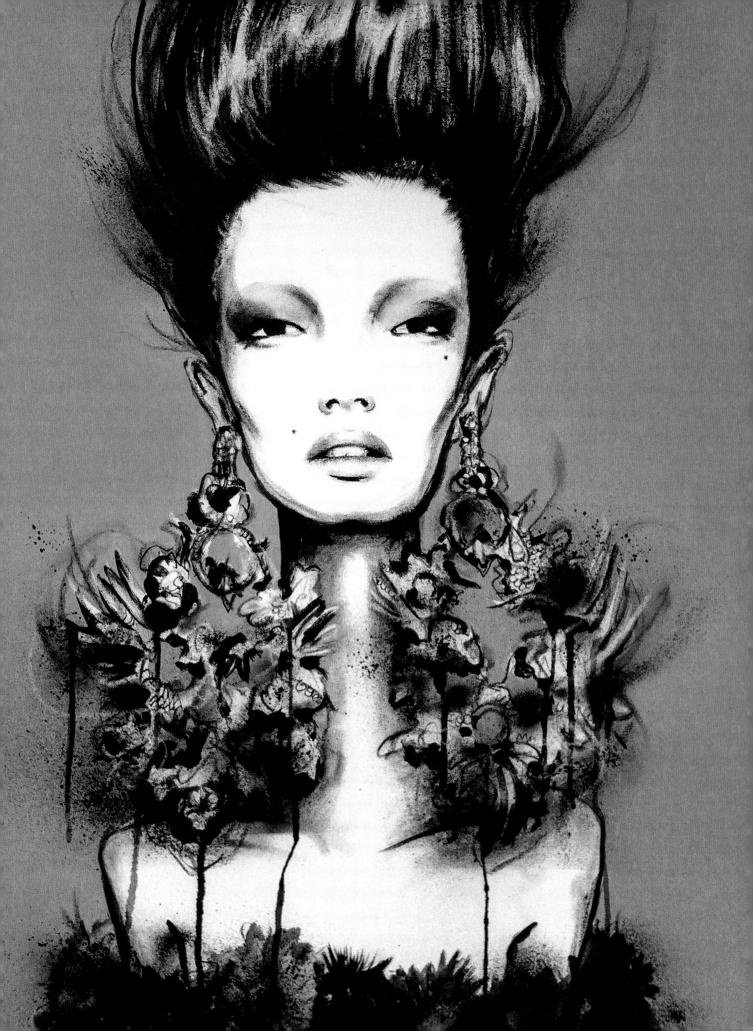

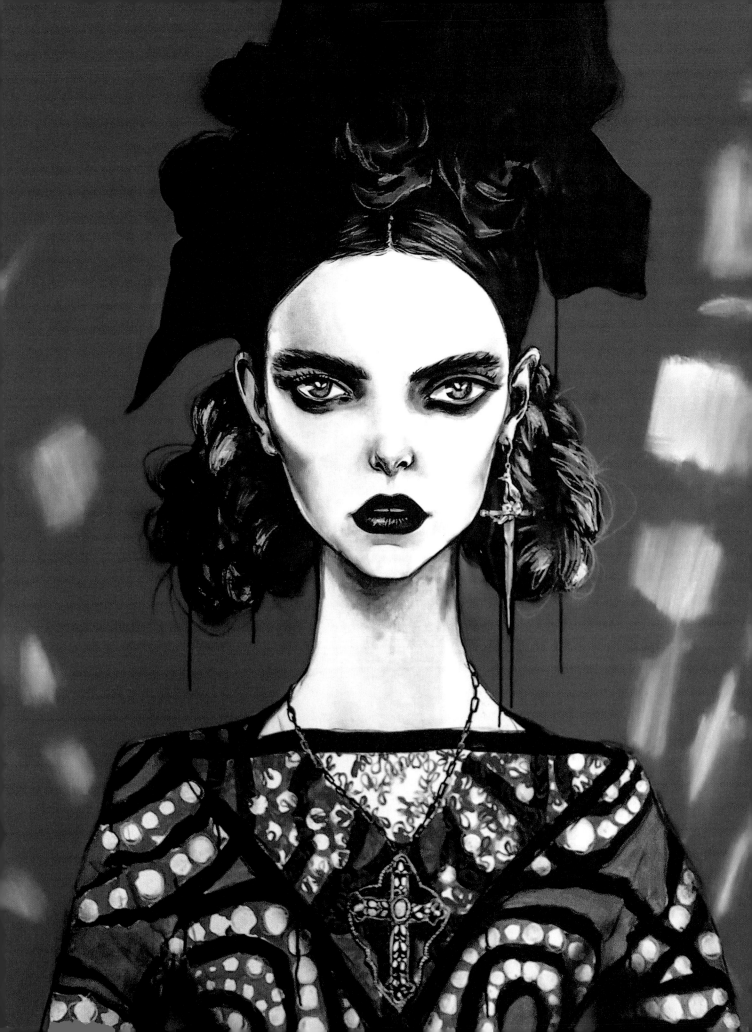

Mary Katrantzou, 2012
Competition entry; acrylic,
charcoal, spray paint and
paint-pens on canvas paper

←   **Imogen, 2012**
Personal work, exhibition
With Flowers in Their Hair…;
acrylic, charcoal, spray paint
and paint-pens on canvas

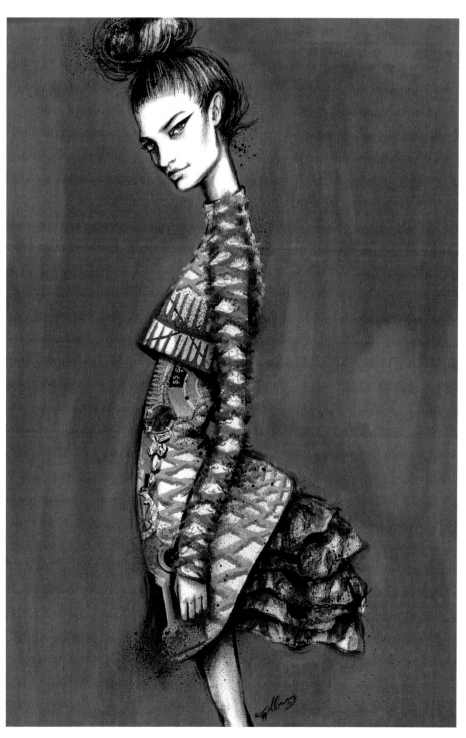

José Luis Merino

1962 born in Barcelona | lives and works in Barcelona
www.estudiomerino.com

CLIENTS
Elle Germany, GQ UK, Harper's Bazaar USA, Madame Figaro,
Neiman Marcus, Pedro García, Red magazine, The Guardian,
The Wall Street Journal, Town & Country

AGENT
Kate Larkworthy
Artist Representation
USA
larkworthy.com

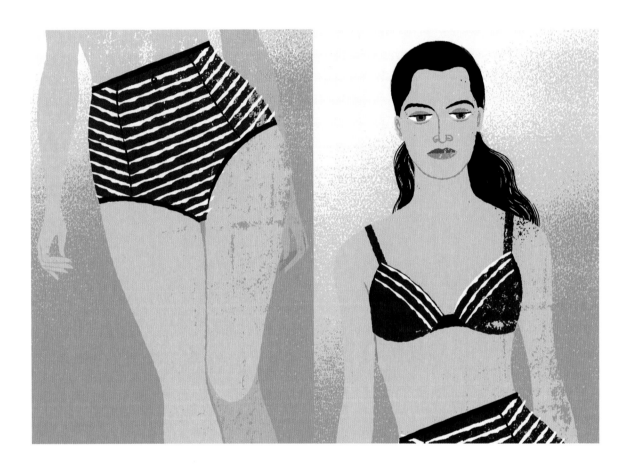

"Fashion illustration is not just about drawing nice clothes,
  sometimes it is closer to art than other types of simple illustration."

„Bei Modeillustration geht es nicht nur ums Zeichnen hübscher Kleidung,
  manchmal ist sie der Kunst näher als andere Arten einfacher Illustration."

« L'illustration de mode, ce n'est pas juste dessiner de beaux vêtements,
  parfois c'est plus proche de l'art que d'autres types d'illustration simple. »

Lingerie, 2010
Personal work; mixed media

→   **Maison Martin Margiela #1, 2010**
Personal work; mixed media

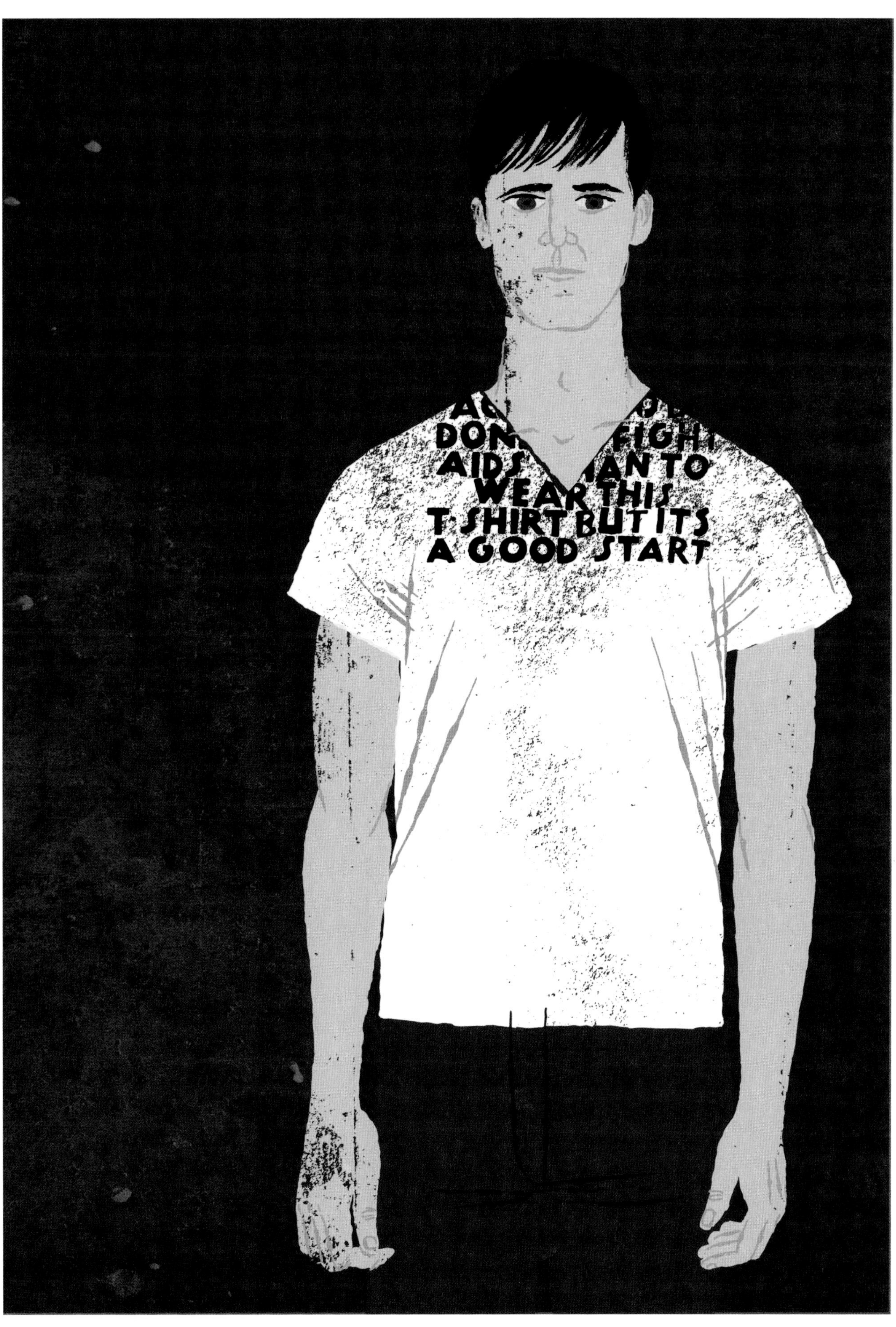
WEAR THIS
T-SHIRT BUT ITS
A GOOD START

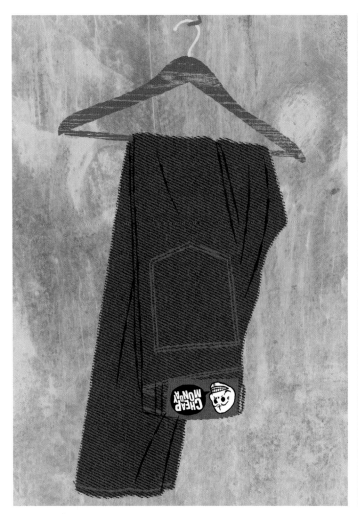

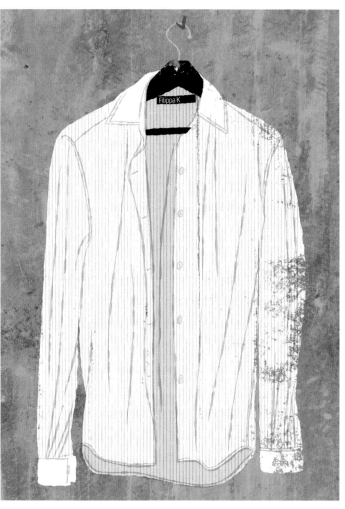

↑   Filippa K, 2010
Personal work; mixed media

←   Cheap Monday, 2010
Personal work; mixed media

→   Wooden Heels, 2010
Personal work; mixed media

↓   Maison Martin Margiela #2, 2010
Personal work; mixed media

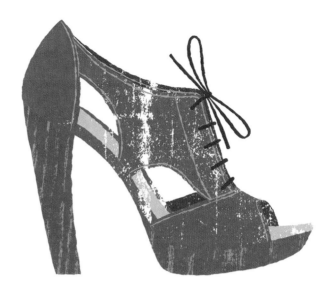

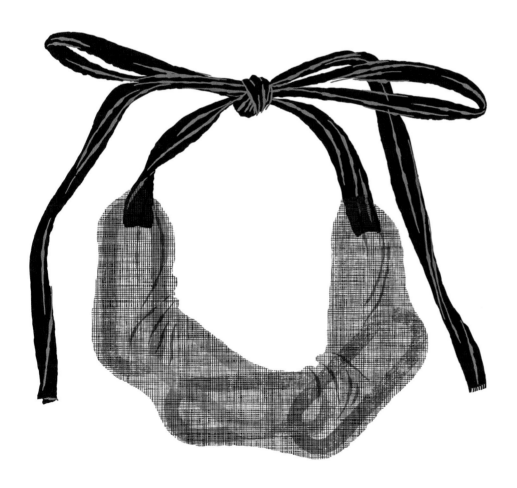

Tim Möller-Kaya

1971 born in Hamburg | lives and works in Hamburg
www.timmoeller.com

CLIENTS
Elle, Playboy,
Wiener magazine,
Architectural Digest

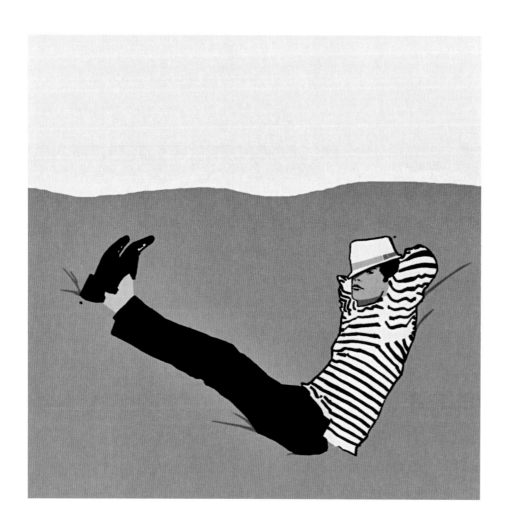

"In my illustrations I combine different techniques
(e.g. ink-wash + digital) so in a certain way they resemble
the combinations of different materials in fashion."

„Meine Illustrationen sind ein Mix aus verschiedenen Techniken (z.B. Tusche + Digital)
und ähneln somit in gewisser Weise den Materialkombinationen in der Mode."

« Je combine différentes techniques (par ex. lavis d'encre + numérique),
ce qui évoque les combinaisons de textures utilisées dans la mode. »

Relax, 2010
Jolie magazine; copic
marker, ink and digital

→ Grusskarte, 2010
Kuball & Kempe; copic
marker, ink and watercolor

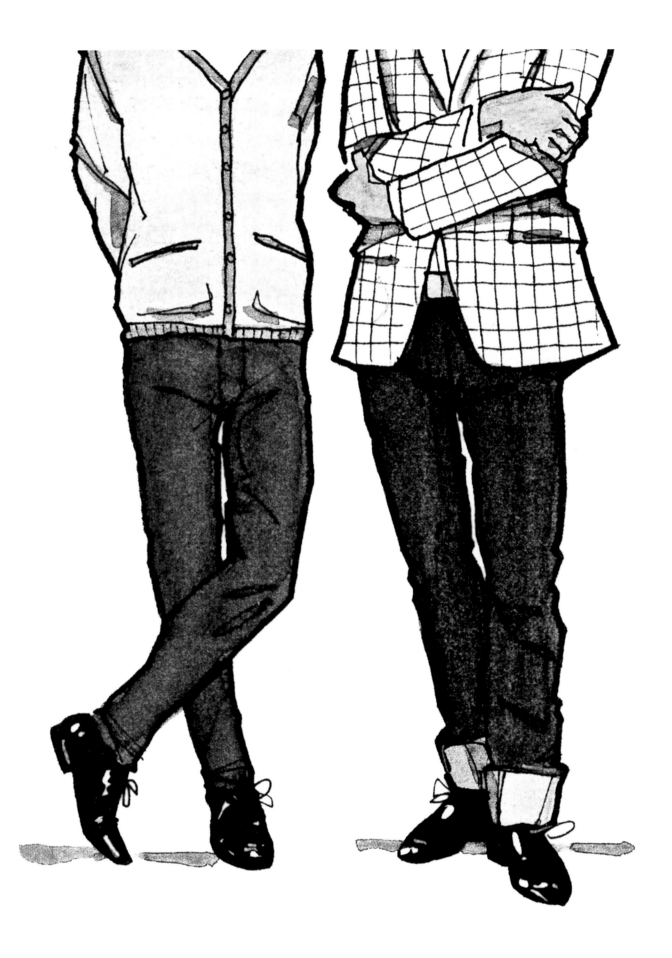

Monsieur Z

1965 born in Courrières, France | lives and works in Carqueiranne, France
www.monsieurz.com

CLIENTS
Guess, Redken (L'Orèal),
Salvatore Ferragamo,
Coccinelle, Saab

AGENTS
Agent 002
France
agent002.com

Traffic Creative
Management
USA
trafficnyc.com

Taiko & Associates
Japan
ua-net.com/taiko

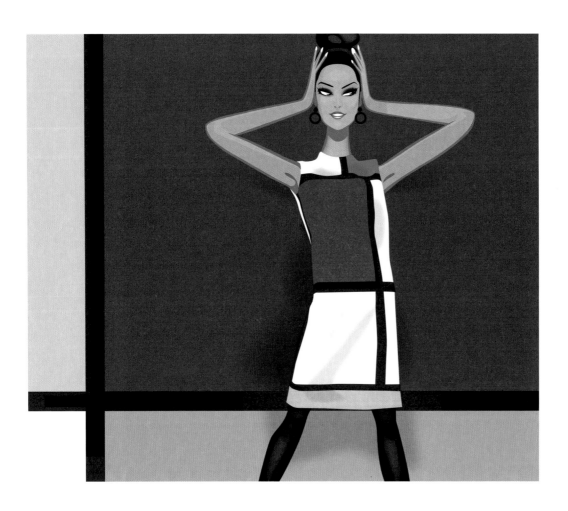

"Fashion, I love it…"

Mondrian Saint Laurent, 2011
Zut magazine; digital

→   **Bazaar Girl #02,** 2009
Personal work; digital

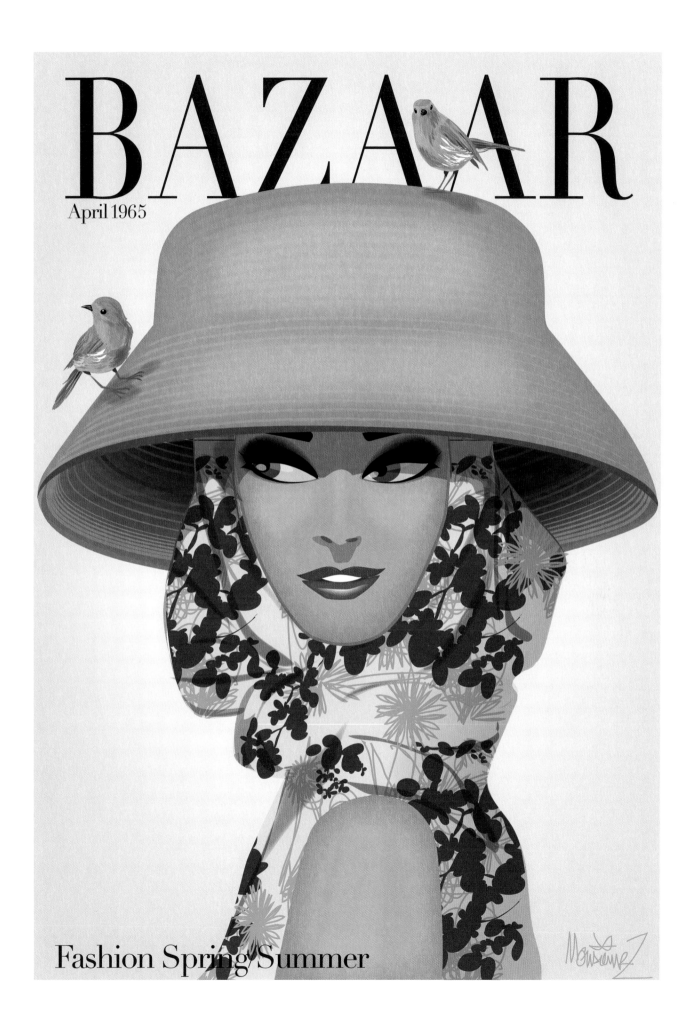

BAZAAR

April 1965

Fashion Spring Summer

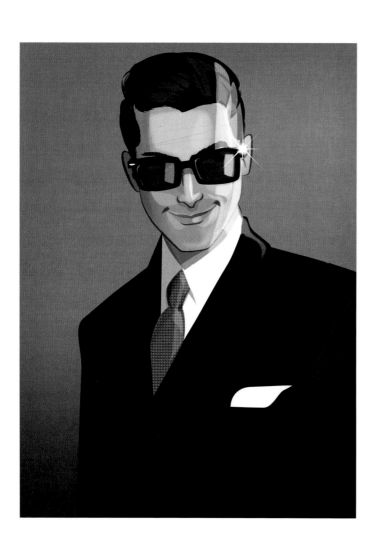

Homme au Ray-Ban, 2011
Amé Optique; digital

→   Femme en Ray-Ban, 2011
Amé Optique; digital

"Wallpaper* magazine,
Elle, Esquire, Vogue, Zoot…"

SANTIAGO BOUTAN
Creative Director
Elle France

→   Fifth Avenue, 2011
Traffic Creative Management; digital

→→ Robe à Pois, 2011
Traffic Creative Management; digital

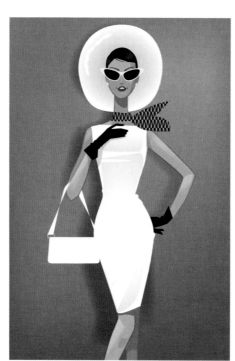

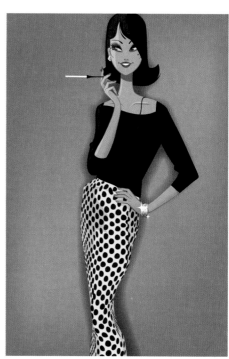

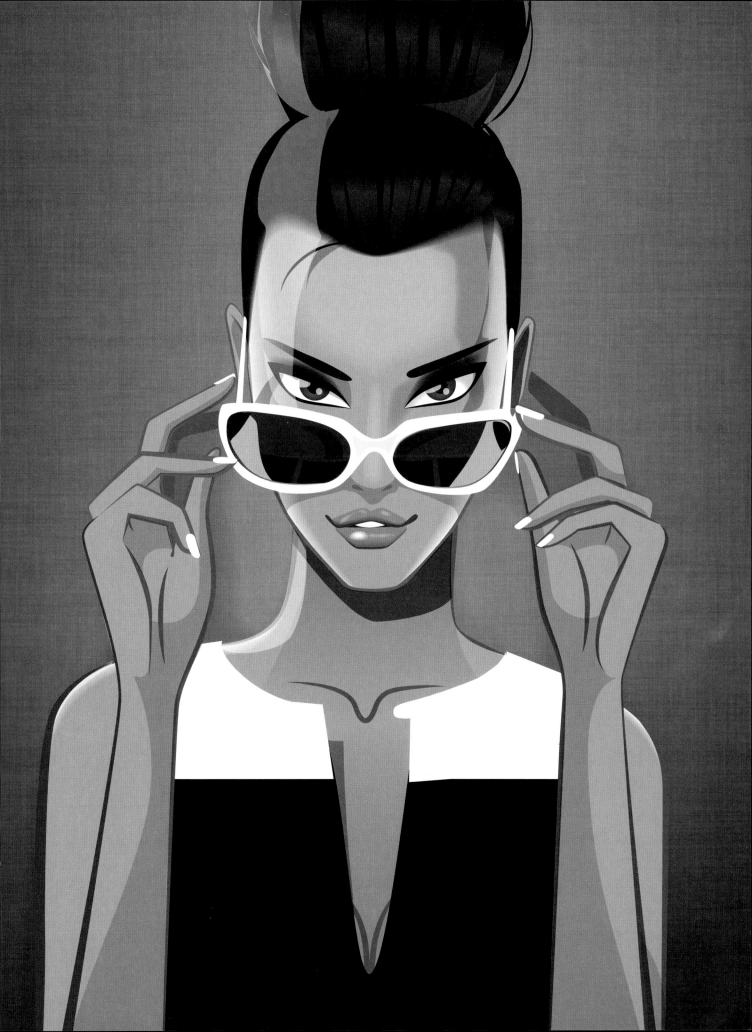

Keiko Morimoto

1976 born in Kobe | lives and works in Rossinière, Switzerland
www.morimoto.co.uk

CLIENTS
Madame Figaro Japan,
Femina magazine

AGENT
Kate Larkworthy
Artist Representation
USA
larkworthy.com

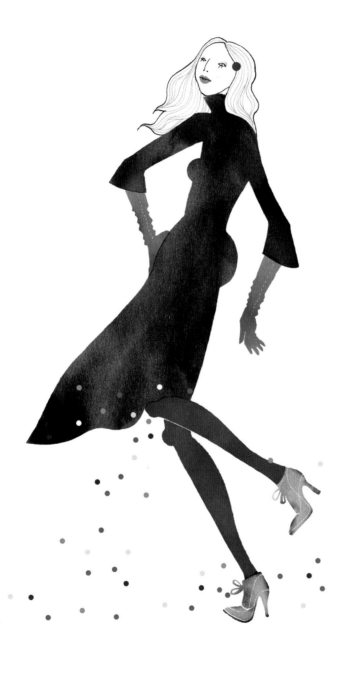

"Simple and colorful!"

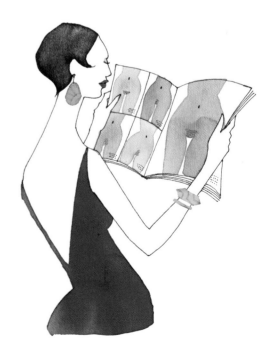

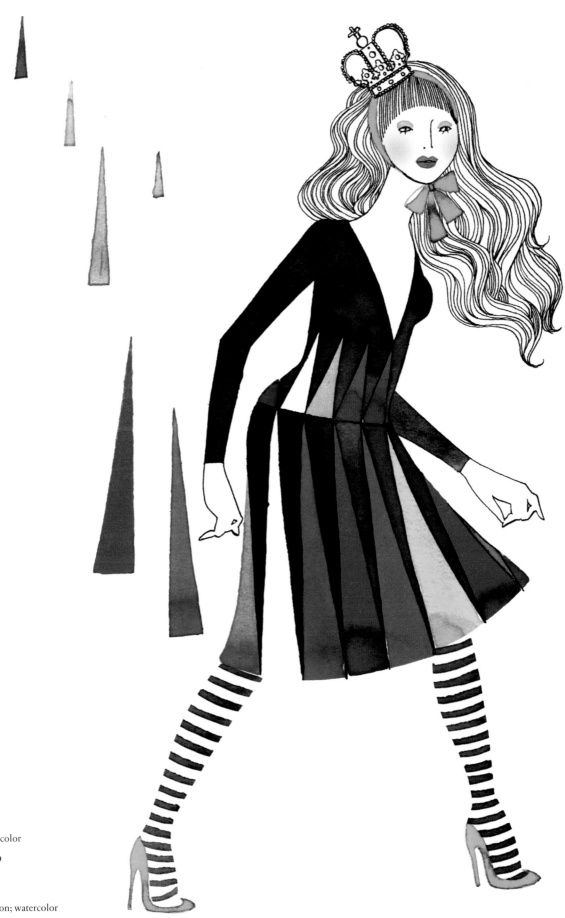

Untitled, 2011
Personal work; watercolor

←　　**Close Cut, 2009**
L'Hebdo; watercolor

←←　Untitled , 2009
The Telegraph, London; watercolor

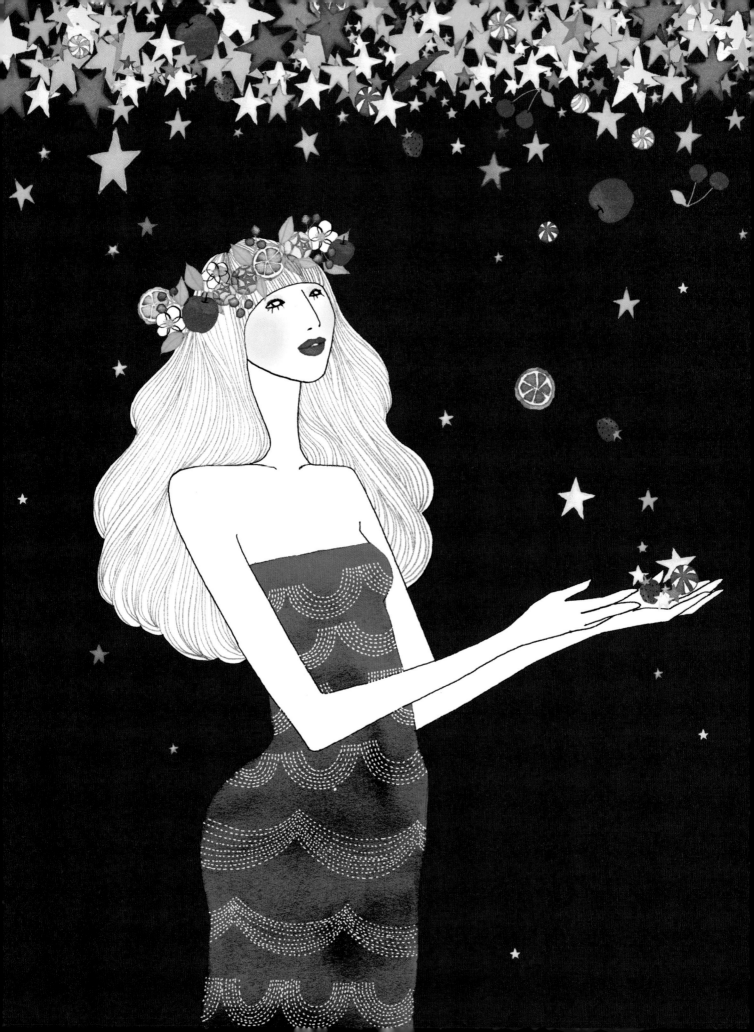

Friends?, 2011
Personal work; watercolor

←   Untitled #3, 2012
Femina magazine; watercolor

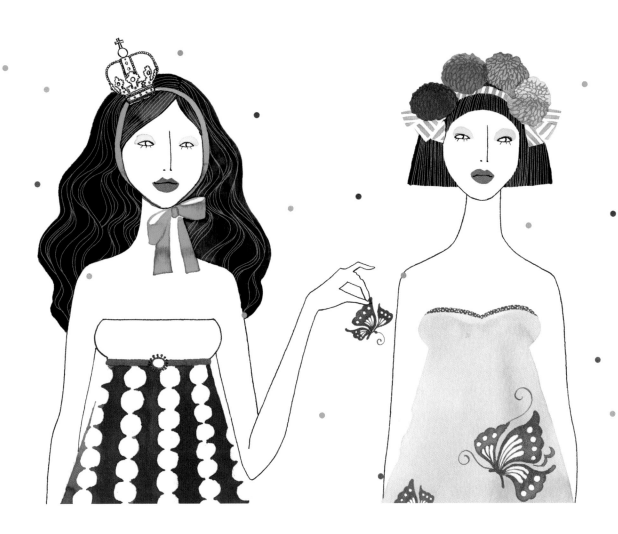

Bee Murphy

1960 born in Gisborne, New Zealand | lives and works in Los Angeles
www.supabee.blogspot.com

CLIENTS
Clinique, Evolu, Marie Claire USA,
Supabee USA, Qui est la? (Japan),
The Wall Street Journal

AGENT
Kate Larkworthy
Artist Representation
USA
larkworthy.com

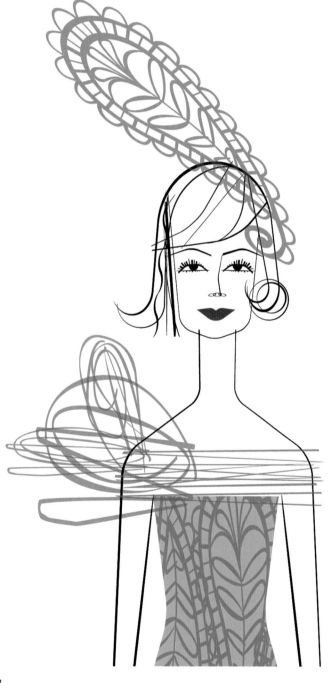

"I love the details, fantasy and romance of fashion. I love designing patterns. I enjoy watching people, what they wear, how they wear it."

„Ich liebe Details, Fantasie und Romantik der Mode. Ich liebe es Muster zu gestalten. Sehr gerne beobachte ich andere, was und wie sie etwas tragen."

« J'aime les détails, la fantaisie et le romantisme de la mode. J'aime créer des motifs et regarder les gens, ce qu'ils portent, comment ils le portent. »

Portrait, 2011
Evolu, advertising; digital

→ Boho, 2004
World, Tokyo, instore media for
Japanese boutique Qui est la?,
Creative Direction: Paul Westlake
(Evolu); digital

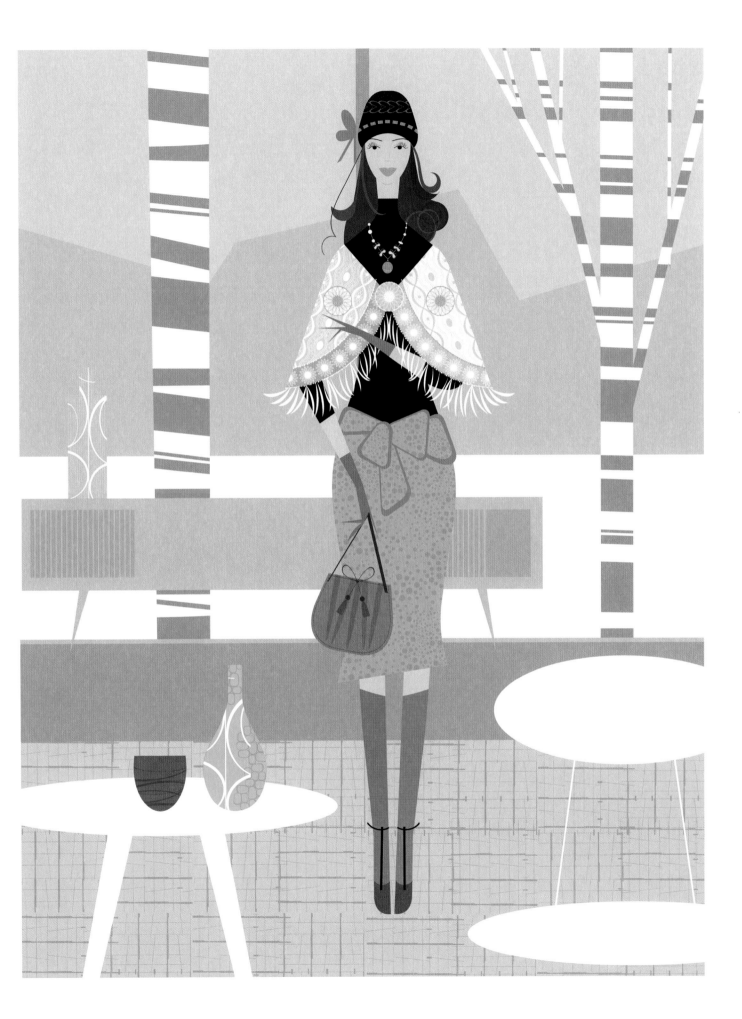

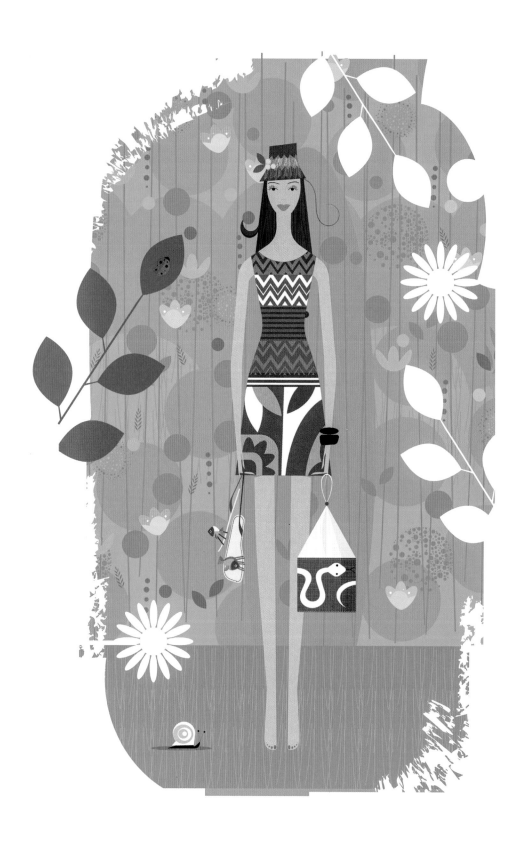

Garden, 2004
World, Tokyo, instore media for
Japanese boutique Qui est la?; digital

→   Packages, 2010
Clinique, gift bag; digital

"I had my eye on Bee for a while before I hired her to work on several projects. Her expression is the perfect balance between fashion and lifestyle."

MERRILEE HESTERFER-DIAZ
Director, Global Integrated Art Producer
Clinique, The Estée Lauder Companies

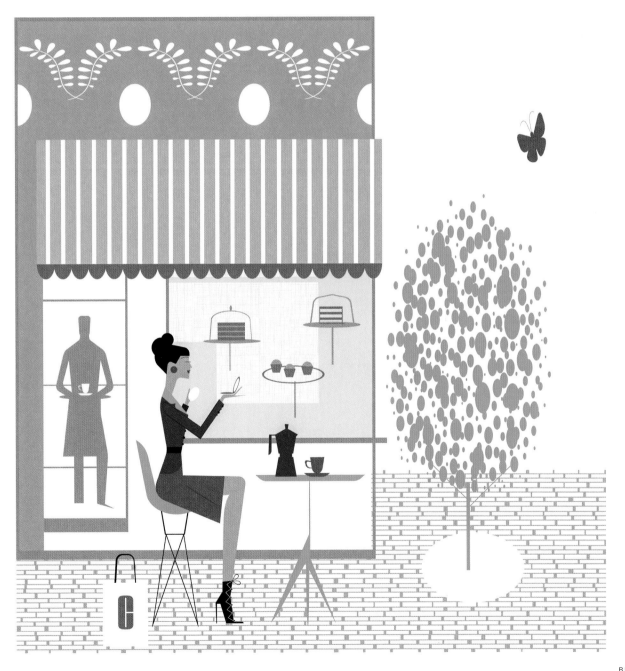

Gi Myao

1979 born in London | lives and works in London
www.gimyao.com

CLIENTS
Chanel, Harvey Nichols,
L'Oréal Paris, Zara

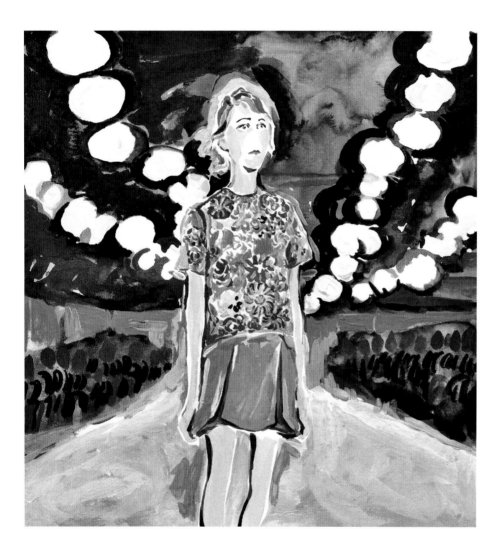

"Hand-drawn with details, it's touching and personal."

„Handgemalt und voller Details, das ist berührend und persönlich."

« Dessiné à la main avec des détails, c'est touchant et personnel. »

Christopher Kane Spring/
Summer 2012, Polaroid, 2011
Personal work, London Fashion Week;
gouache on paper

→　Are You Ready Girls?, 2011
Personal work; gouache on paper

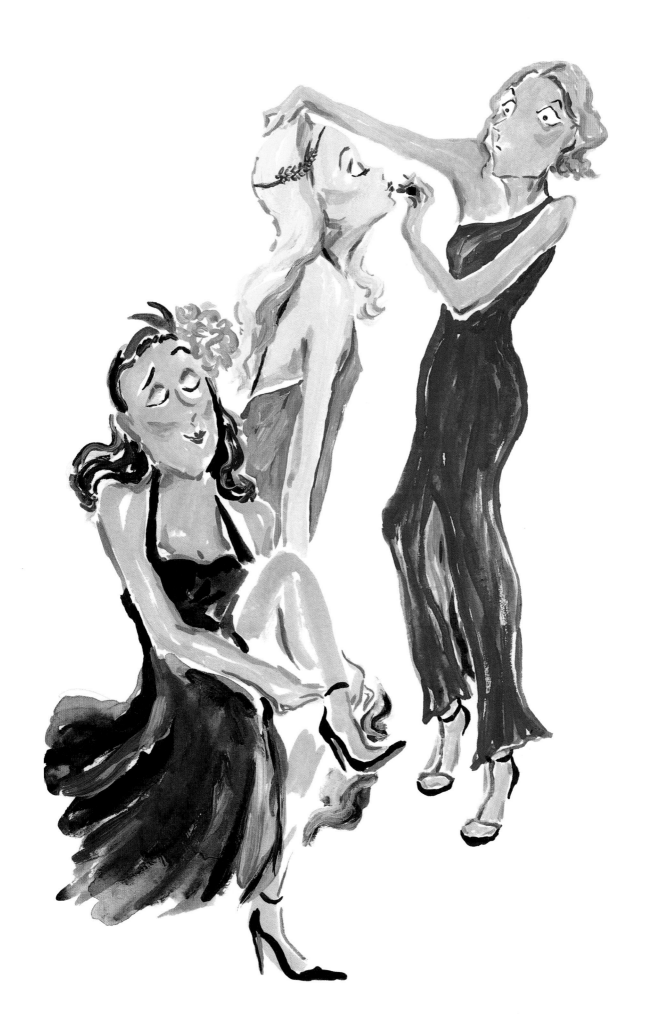

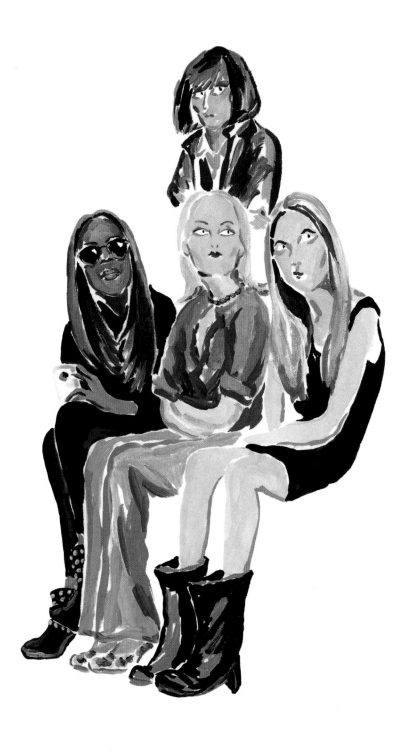

London Fashion Week Audience, 2011
Personal work; gouache on paper

↓   **The Way We Wore, 2010**
The Washington Post; gouache on paper

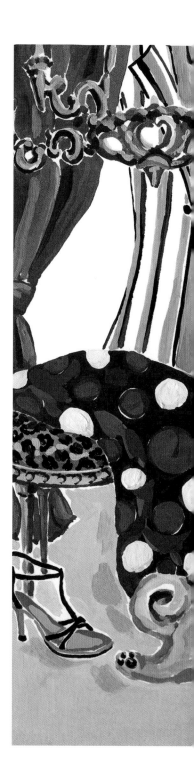

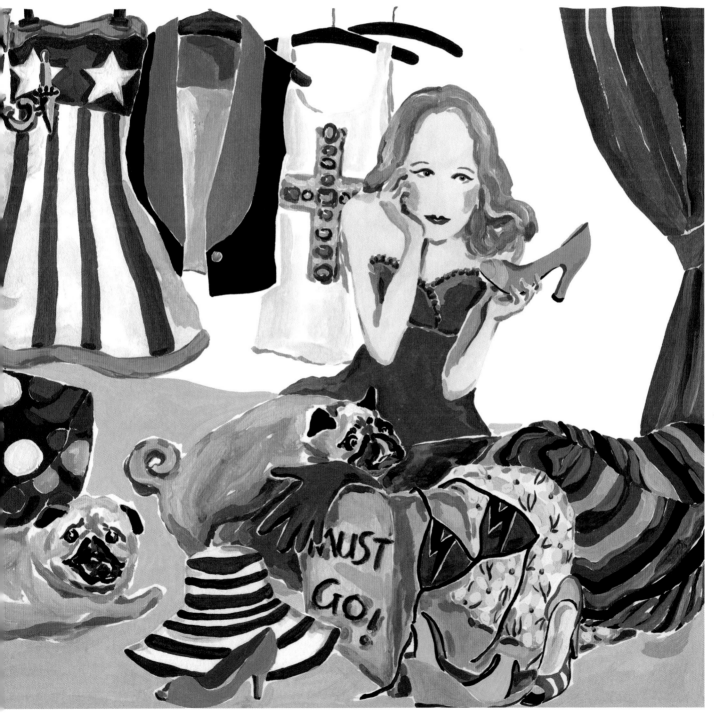

Zé Otavio

1983 born in São Paulo | lives and works in São Paulo
www.zeotavio.com

CLIENTS
Dercanvas, GQ Brazil,
Elle Brazil, Gloss magazine,
Capricho magazine

AGENT
Levy Creative Management
USA
levycreative.com

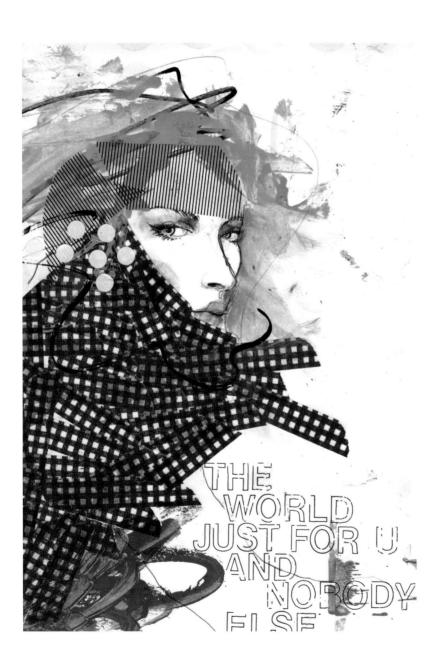

"A thin line between interesting
people on the streets and
urban subversion."

„Ein dünner Grat zwischen interessanten
Menschen auf der Straße und
urbaner Subversivität."

« Une ligne ténue entre les gens
intéressants dans la rue
et la subversion urbaine. »

The World Just For U, 2011
Personal work, ongoing project
E(femme)ra; mixed media

→   **V, 2011**
Personal work, ongoing project
E(femme)ra; mixed media

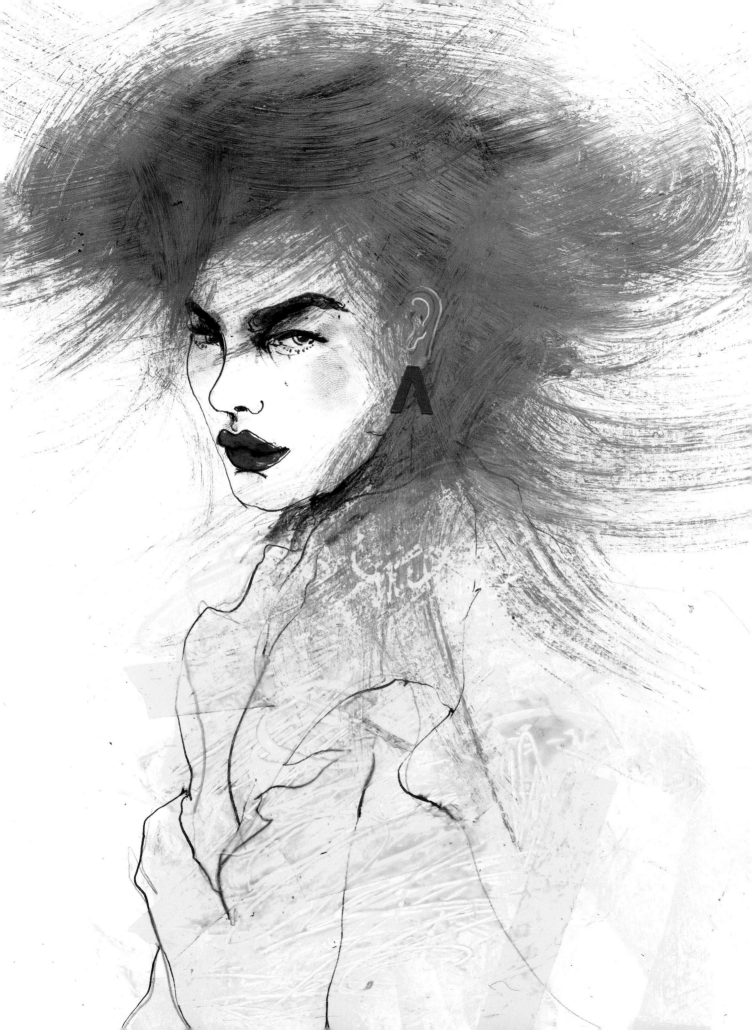

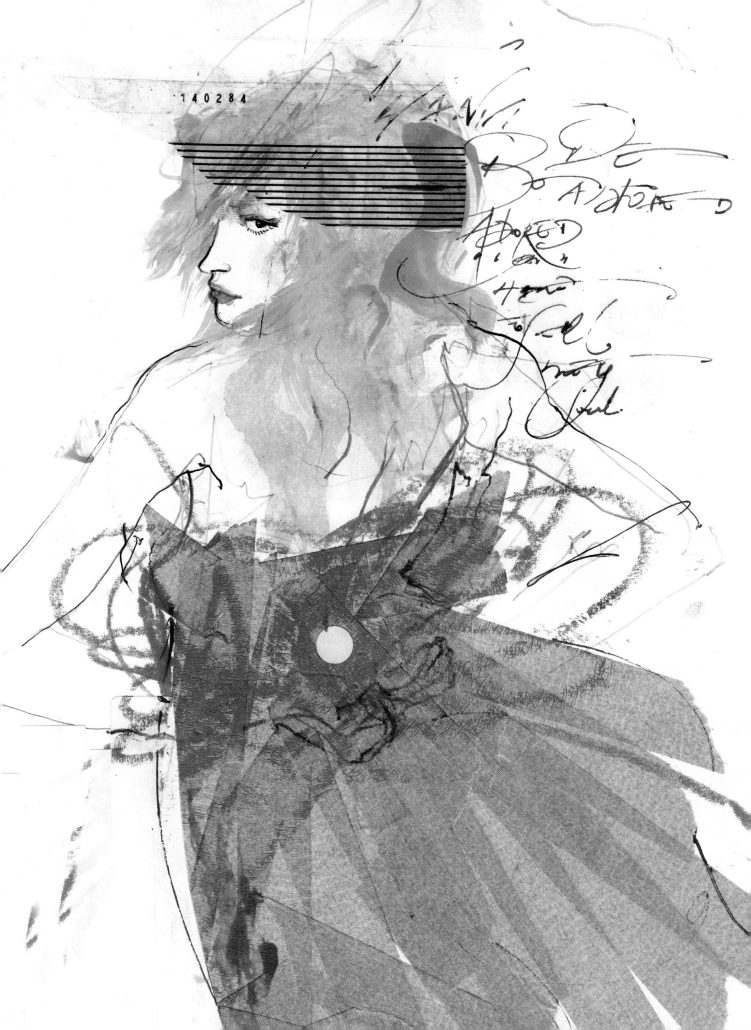

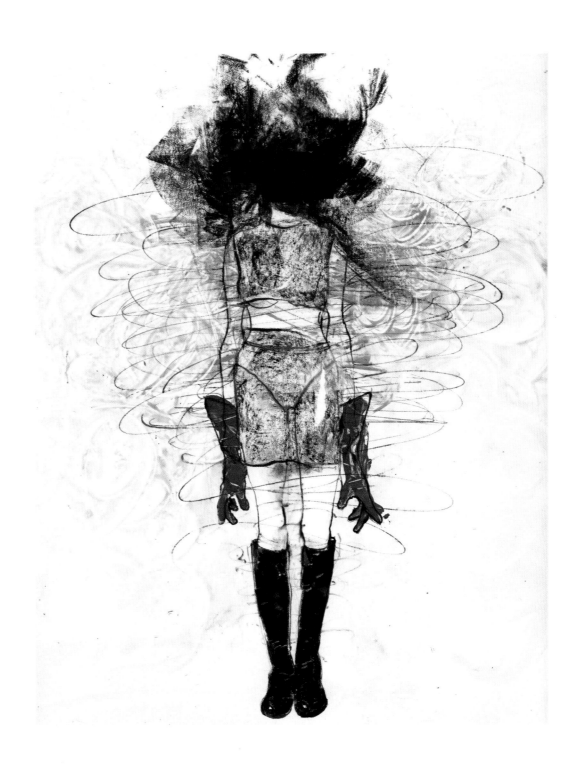

The Point of No Return, 2011
Personal work, ongoing project
E(femme)ra; mixed media

← **I Wanna Be Adored, 2011**
Personal work, ongoing project
E(femme)ra; mixed media

Mia Marie Overgaard

1978 born in Copenhagen | lives and works in Copenhagen
www.miaovergaard.com

CLIENTS
Amelia's Magazine, ASOS, Costume magazine, Mambo Australia, Gap, Marie Claire, Motilo.com, Stella/The Sunday Telegraph, The Wall Street Journal

AGENTS
Peppercookies
UK
peppercookies.com

Creative Syndicate
France
creative-syndicate.com

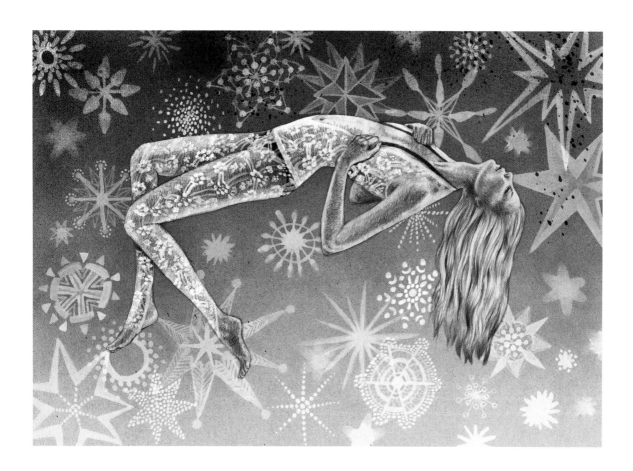

"The otherworldliness of fashion inspires me. Also the fact that fashion relates to the creation of identity, to see and to be seen, to reveal or to hide."

„Die Jenseitigkeit der Mode inspiriert mich. Auch die Tatsache, dass Mode mit der Erschaffung von Identität verwandt ist: sehen und gesehen werden, enthüllen oder verbergen."

« Ce qui m'inspire, c'est le surréalisme de la mode. Et puis la mode touche à la création de l'identité, voir et être vu, révéler ou cacher.»

Noir #1, 2010
Noir Spring/Summer 2010;
watercolor, ink, airbrush and digital

→   **Heroic, 2011**
Carlin International, trend book;
watercolor and digital

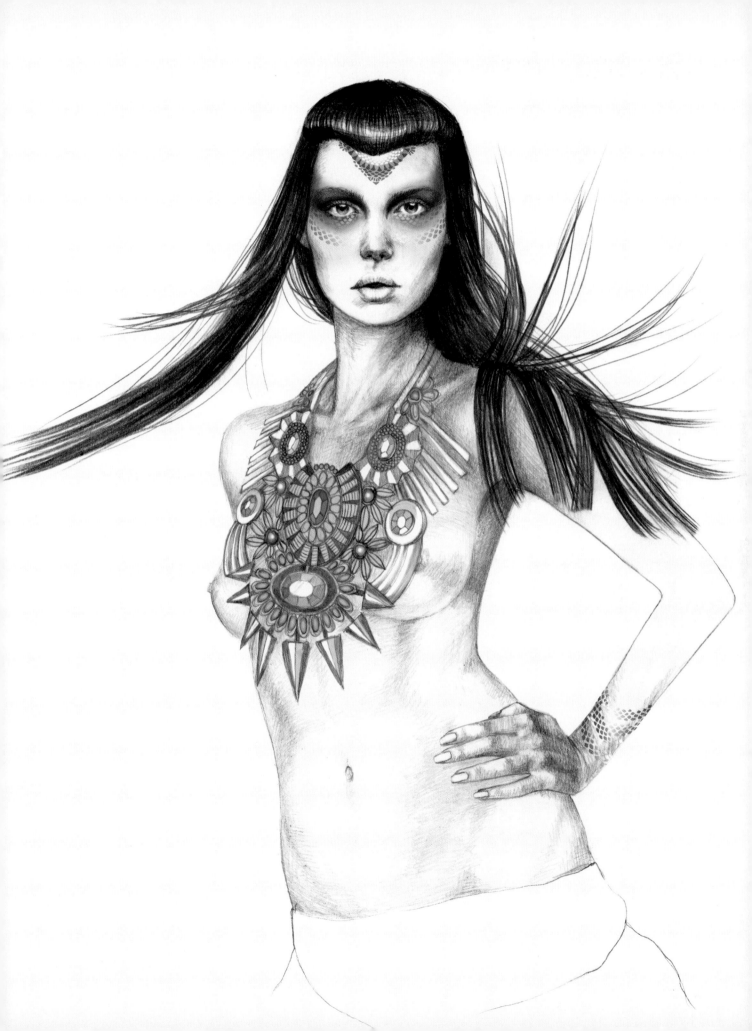

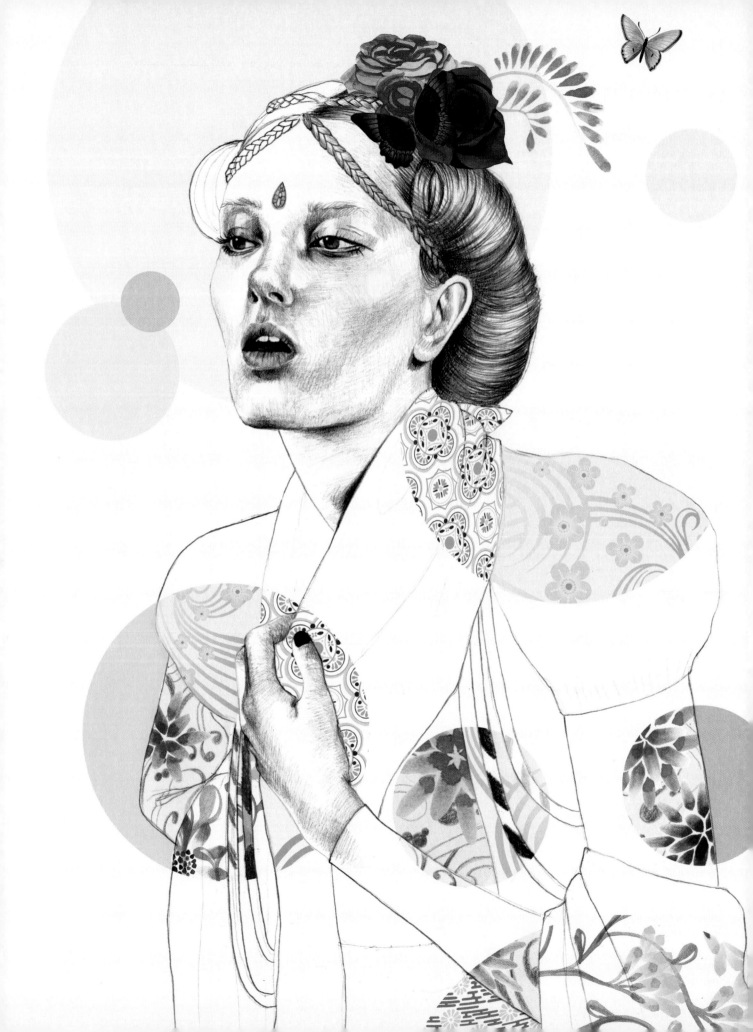

"Mia combines fashion and fantasy to perfection in delicate pencil and watercolor drawings, where people, animals and plants cohabit in chaotic beauty."

AMELIA GREGORY
Publisher and Art Director
Amelia's Magazine

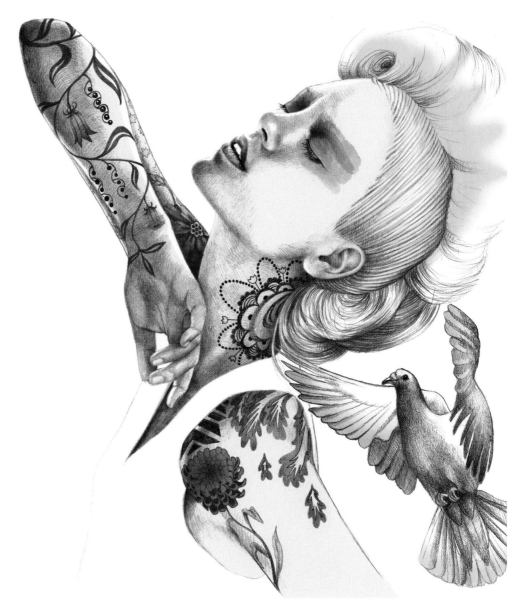

Promise, 2012
Carlin International, trend book;
watercolor and digital

←   Interlude, 2011
Carlin International, trend book;
watercolor and digital

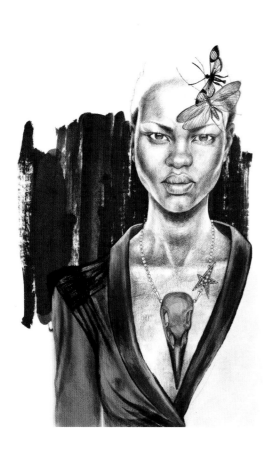

Noir #3, 2010
Noir Spring/Summer 2010;
ink and digital

→   Complicity, 2012
Carlin International, trend book;
watercolor and digital

↓   Manufacture, 2011
Carlin International, trend book;
watercolor and digital

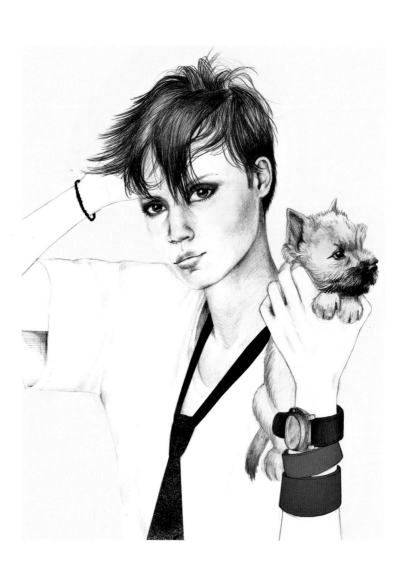

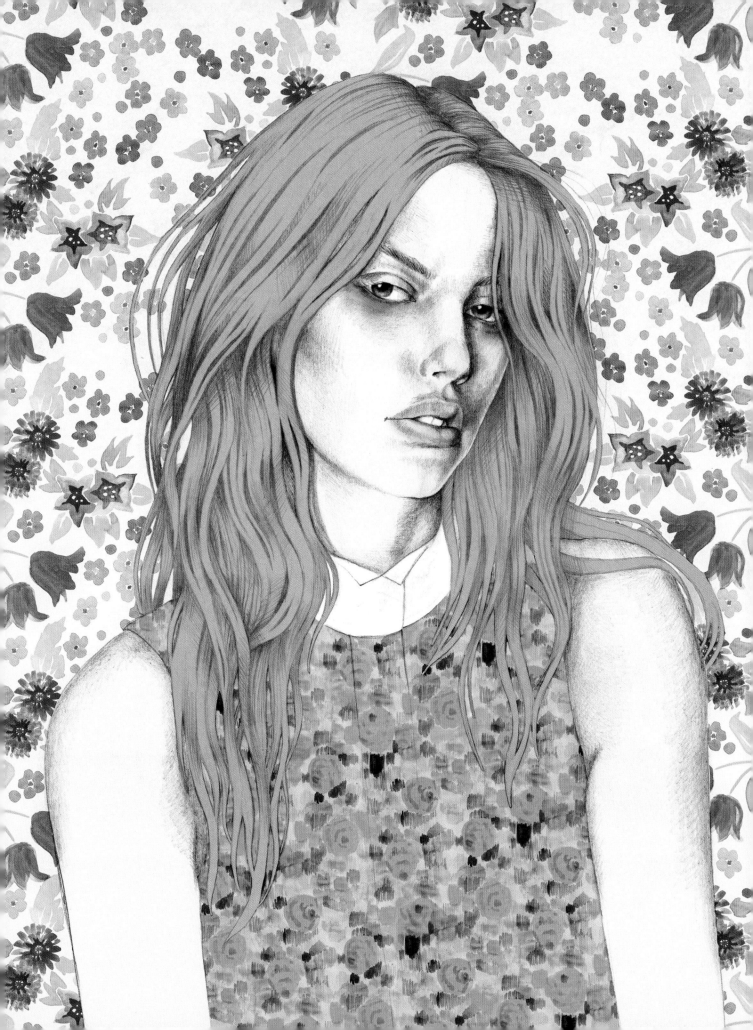

Sandrine Pagnoux

1976 born in Plessis-Bouchard, France | lives and works in Paris
www.sandrinepagnoux.com

CLIENTS
Nylon Guys magazine, Viktor magazine, Tiger magazine,
Rika magazine, Soon magazine, Marie Claire, Diesel, Harrods,
Le Coq Sportif, Nikita clothing, WestEast magazine

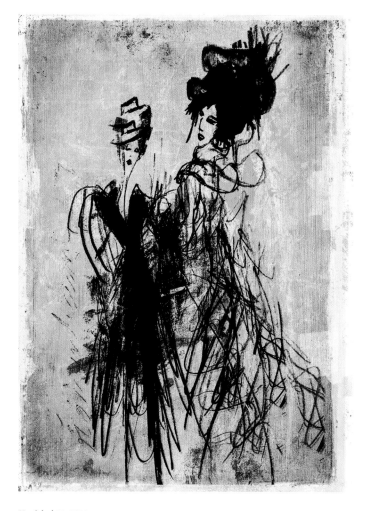

“My aesthetic is always strongly
influenced by fashion's movements
and models. Fashion is extremely
inspiring in my work.”

„Meine Ästhetik ist immer stark von den
Bewegungen der Mode und den Models
beeinflusst. Fashion inspiriert
meine Arbeit extrem.“

« Mon esthétique est toujours fortement
influencée par les mouvements
de la mode et les mannequins.
La mode me stimule beaucoup. »

Untitled #1, 2012
Viktor magazine, Creative Direction:
Alberto Tommaso Badalamenti;
hand-drawn and digital

→   Trouble in Mind, 2012
Nikita clothing, T-shirt print,
Spring/Summer 13, Art Direction:
David Young; hand-drawn and digital

→→   Untitled #2, 2011
Rika magazine, Fashion Design:
Ulrika Lundgren; hand-drawn
and digital

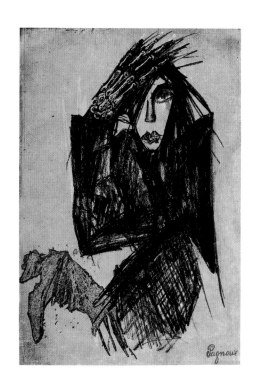

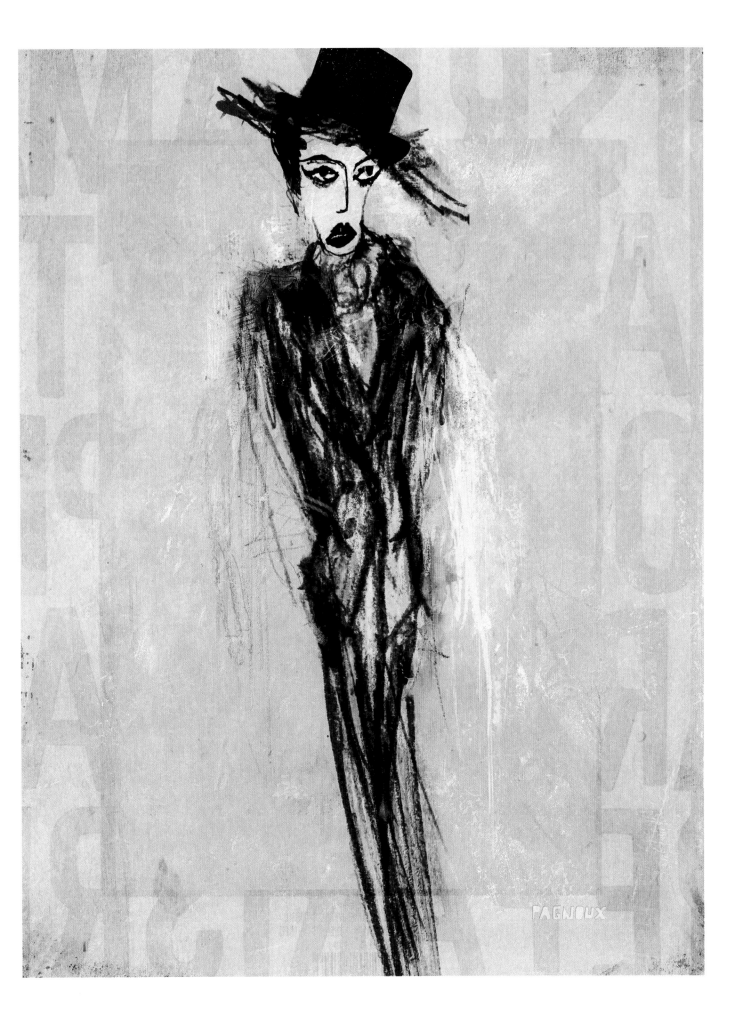

"Pagnoux uses my pictures and I love to see what she can do with them. It's always a great surprise and I'm proud to feature in her art."

SOPHIE ETCHART
Fashion Photographer

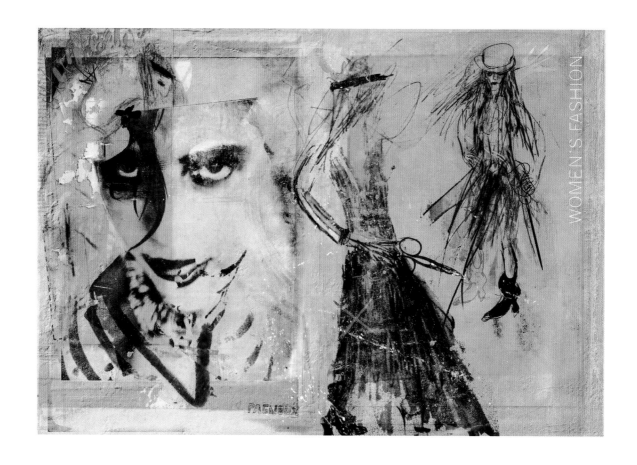

Women's Fashion, 2009
Soon magazine, Photography:
Sophie Etchart; hand-drawn,
collage and digital

→ **Something in the Air**, 2011
Personal work, Photography:
Sophie Etchart; hand-drawn, painting,
handwritten, digital collage and digital

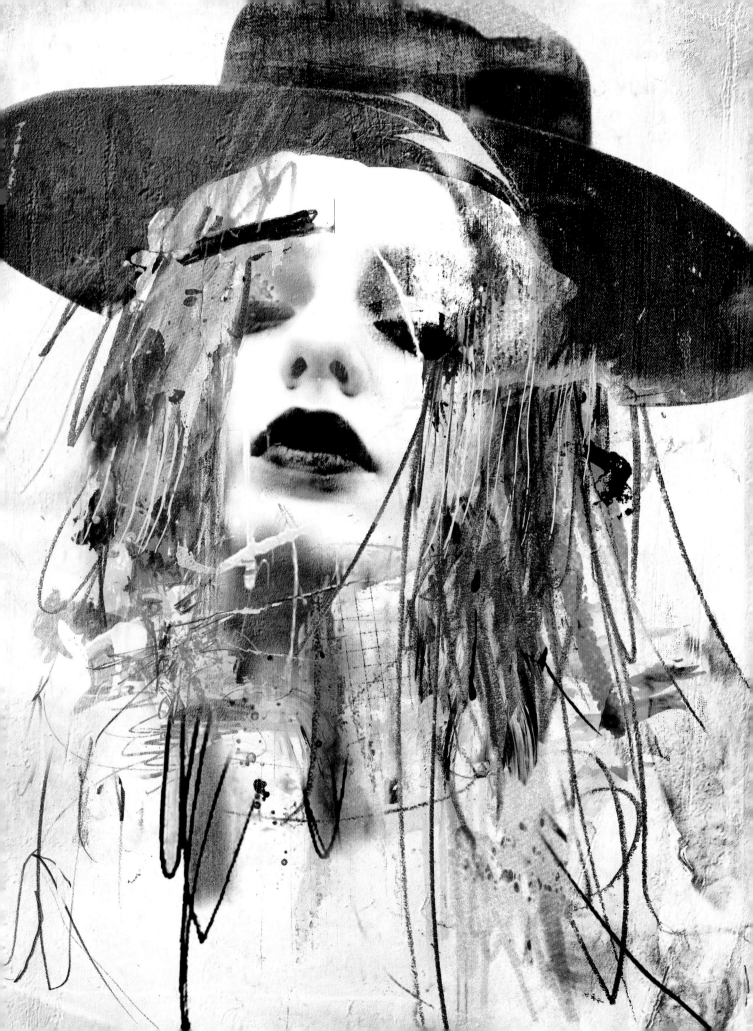

Julia Pelzer

1977 born in Hamburg | lives and works in Hamburg
www.juliapelzer.com

CLIENTS
The Sunday Telegraph,
Vogue, So Chic, Max
Mara, Meissner Porzellan

AGENT
SCHIERKE COM/
Germany
schierke.com

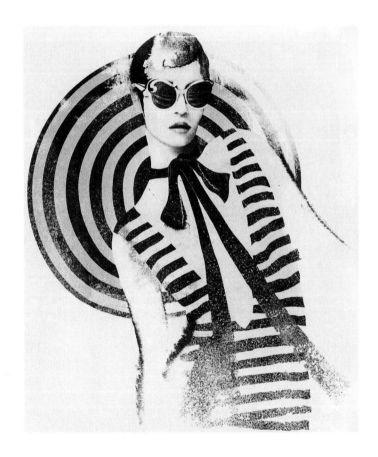

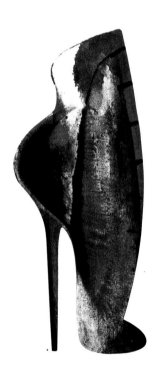

"My work always begins with the sensuality of a sheet of paper and sweeping ink-strokes. Only in this way can I create what I want to express – a promise of luxury and mystery."

„Die Sinnlichkeit eines Blattes Papier und geschwungener Tuschestriche steht immer am Anfang meiner Arbeit. Nur so entsteht das, was ich aussagen möchte: ein Versprechen von Luxus und Mysterium."

« Ça commence toujours par la sensualité du papier et de l'encre. C'est ainsi que je peux créer ce que je veux exprimer – une promesse de luxe et de mystère. »

Aloft, 2010
Personal work; watercolor and ink

← **Prada for Sunday Telegraph, 2011**
Charcoal and watercolor

→ **Sunday Telegraph, 2011**
Watercolor and colored pencil

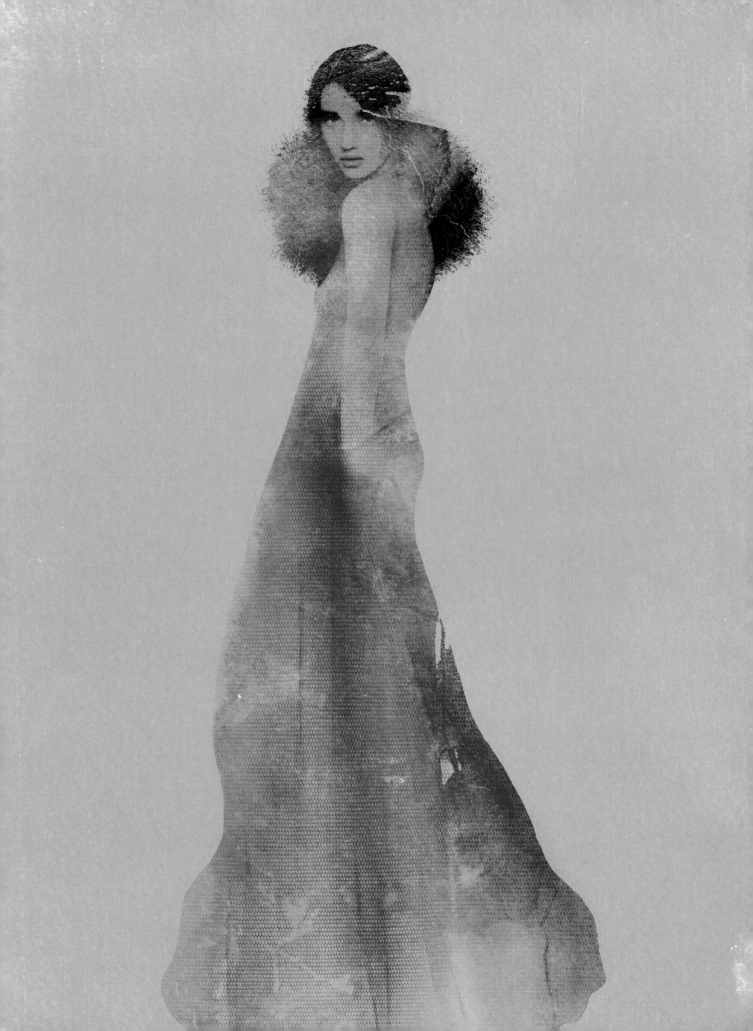

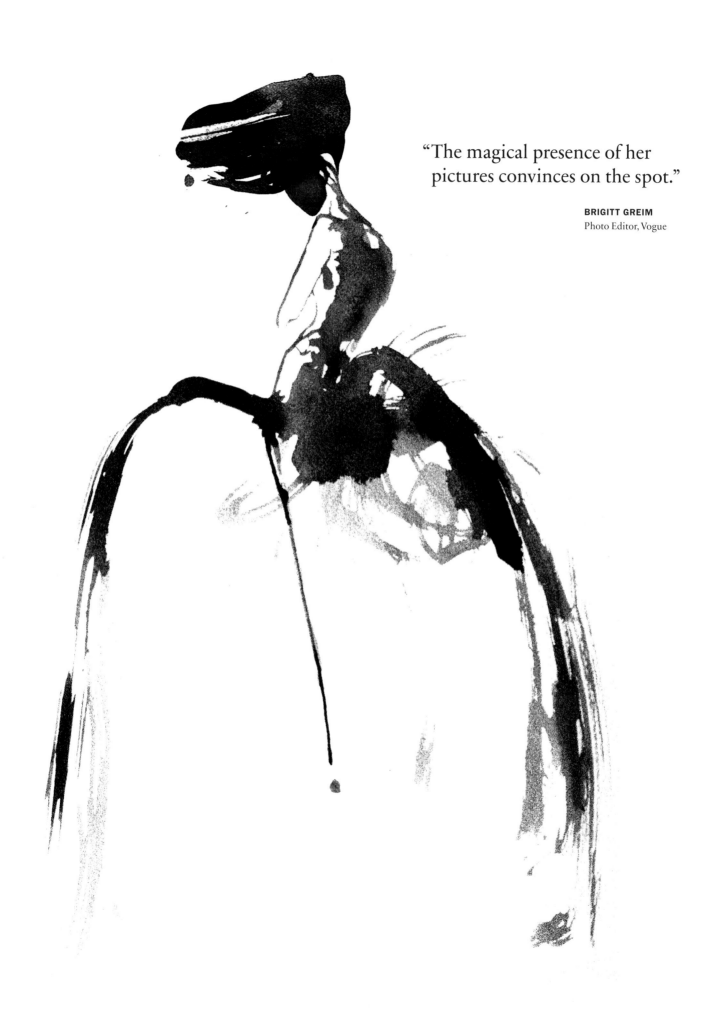

"The magical presence of her pictures convinces on the spot."

BRIGITT GREIM
Photo Editor, Vogue

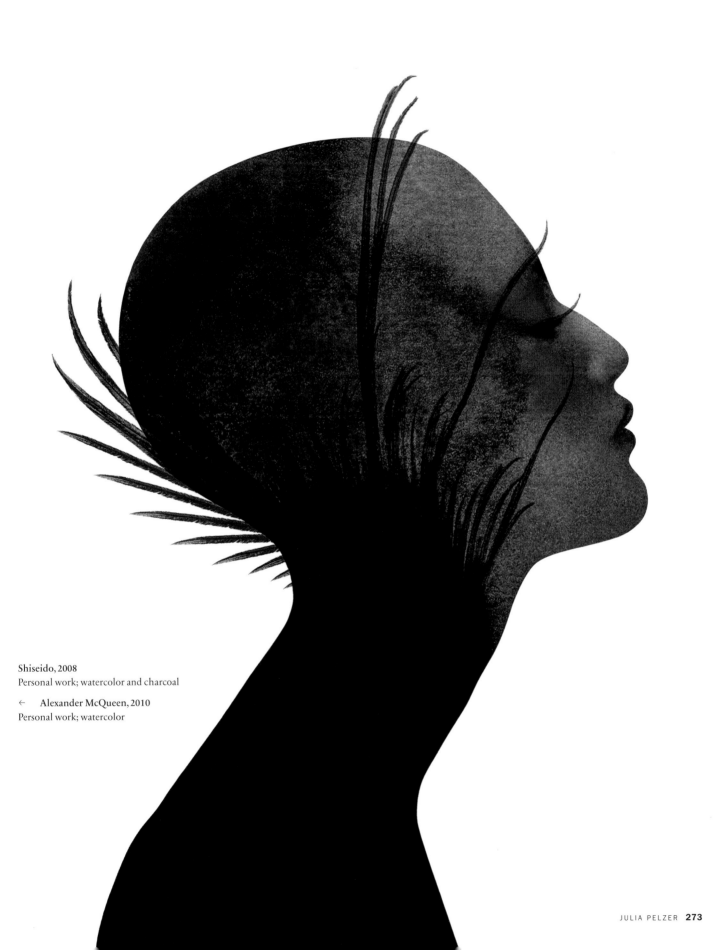

Shiseido, 2008
Personal work; watercolor and charcoal

←   Alexander McQueen, 2010
Personal work; watercolor

Gladys Perint Palmer

born in Budapest | lives and works in the USA
www.gladysperintpalmer.com

CLIENTS

Oscar de la Renta, Lancôme, Fendi, Christian Dior, Emporio Armani,
Vogue, The New York Times Magazine, Elle, Chanel, Shu Uemura,
Mercedes-Benz New York Fashion Week, Missoni,
Harper's Bazaar, Verdura, Lumière

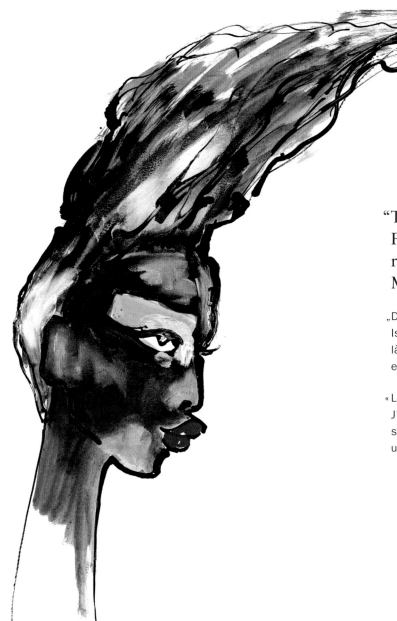

"The key word is Illustration not Fashion.
Fashion is great to draw when it is
ridiculous, sublime or outrageous.
My aim is to draw attitude, not frills."

„Der zentrale Begriff ist Illustration, nicht Mode.
Ist Mode lächerlich, vollendet oder skandalös,
lässt sie sich hervorragend zeichnen. Ich möchte
eine Haltung illustrieren, keinen Schnickschnack."

« Le mot clé est Illustration, et non Mode.
J'aime dessiner une mode ridicule,
sublime ou extravagante. Je veux dessiner
une attitude, pas des froufrous. »

Shena Moulton, make-up
Pat McGrath, 2011
Christian Dior Haute Couture,
Fall/Winter 2011–12; paint and
metallic marker

→   Alexandre Vauthier, 2011
Haute Couture, Fall/Winter 2011–12;
ink and gouache

274

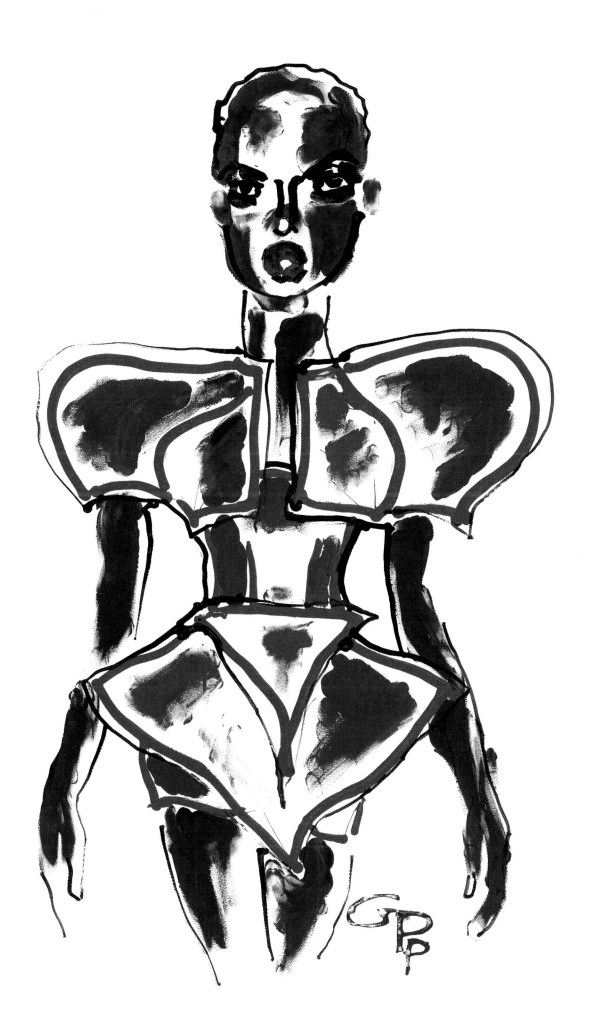

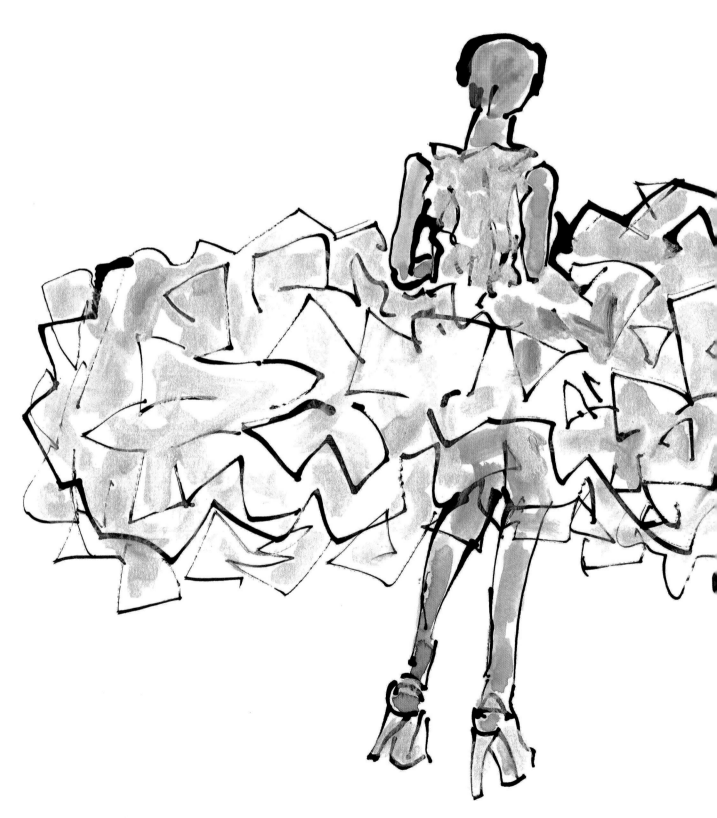

"There are many great illustrators... what makes a difference between Gladys's work and most of the others is that she does not draw a still subject, but her drawings have life because they capture a moment, a situation..."

VALENTINO GARAVANI
Fashion Designer

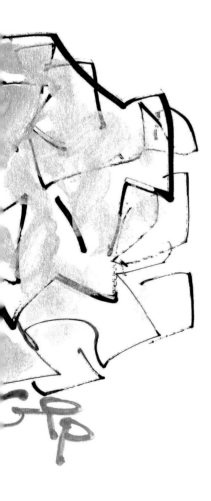

Iris van Herpen, 3d Printing, 2011
Galerie Nikki Diana Marquand,
place des Vosges, Paris; silver paint,
silver marker and ink

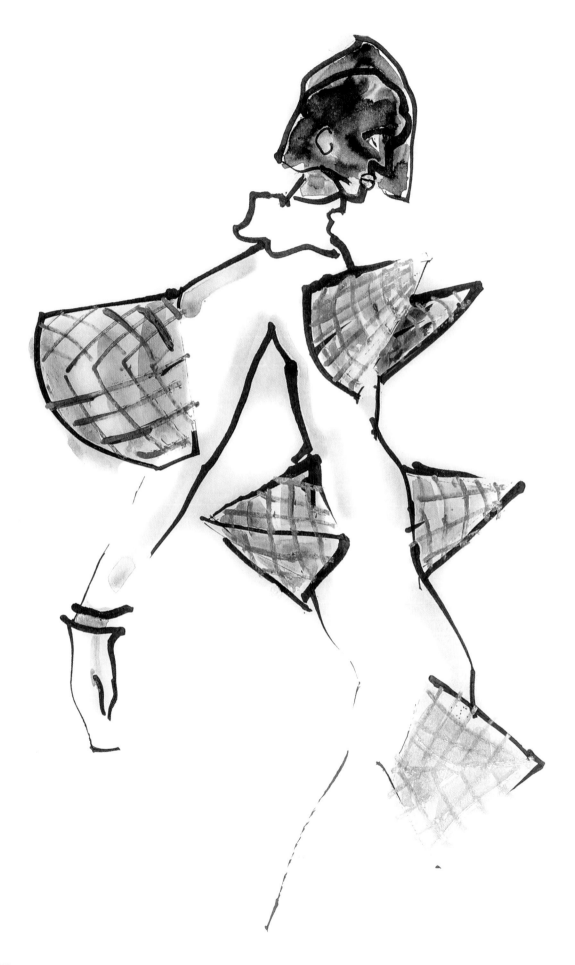

Wei Wei Sun, 2012
Valentino Haute Couture, Fall/Winter
2012–13; ink, wash and silver paint

←   Thom Browne, 2012
Watercolor and silver marker

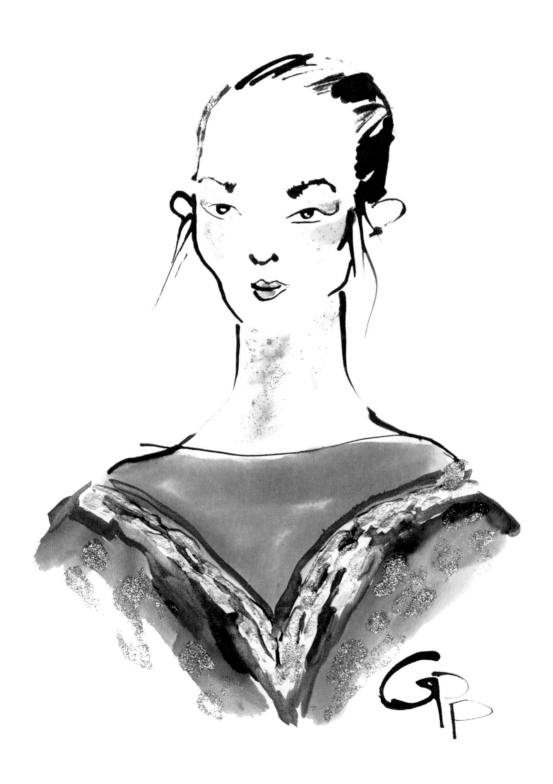

Marie Perron

1987 born in Paris | lives and works in Paris
www.marieperron.fr

CLIENTS
Dior, Boucheron, Shiseido, Lacoste, Ventilo,
Le Bon Marché, Glamour magazine (USA), Jalouse,
Cosmopolitan, Elle, 7000 magazine, Le Figaro

AGENT
Philippe Arnaud
France
philippearnaud.com

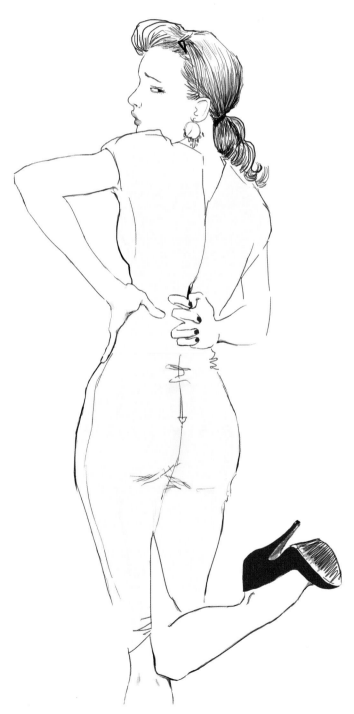

"The girls I draw are fashionable without
question. I used to be a fashion reporter,
drawing the girls on the catwalk.
I am also a style-tip columnist."

„Die Mädels, die ich zeichne, sind zweifellos
elegant. Ich habe als Modejournalistin gearbeitet,
die Girls auf dem Catwalk gezeichnet und schreibe
auch Kolumnen mit Style-Tipps."

« Les filles que je dessine sont très mode. J'ai été
journaliste de mode, je dessinais les podiums.
Je tiens aussi une rubrique de conseils de mode. »

Waiting For My Man, 2012
Cosmopolitan; pen and digital

→ **How to Chase After Girls, 2011**
Cosmopolitan; Liberty shirt and
Shetland knitwear; pen and digital

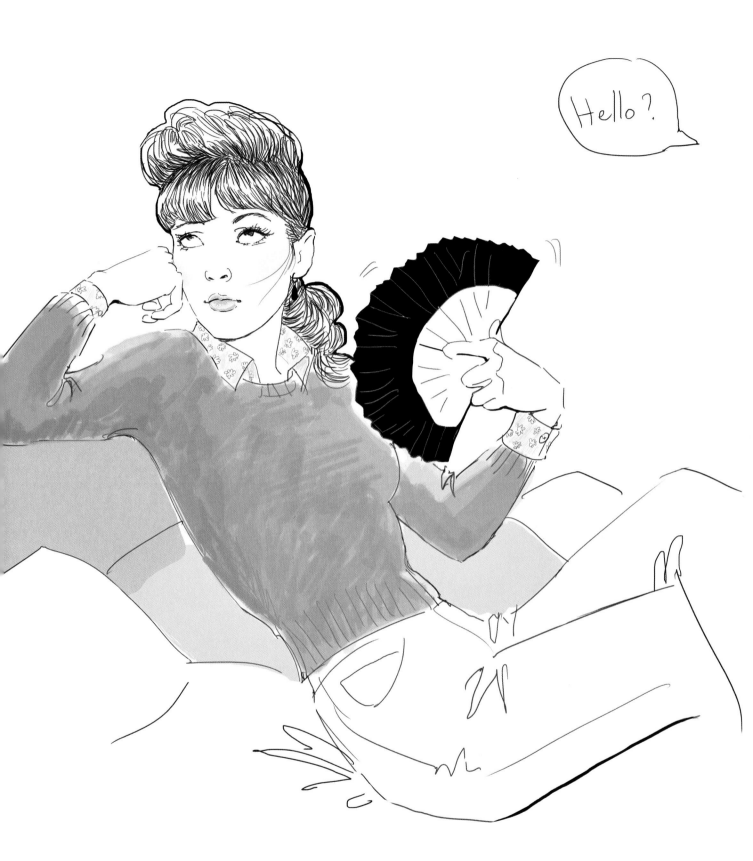

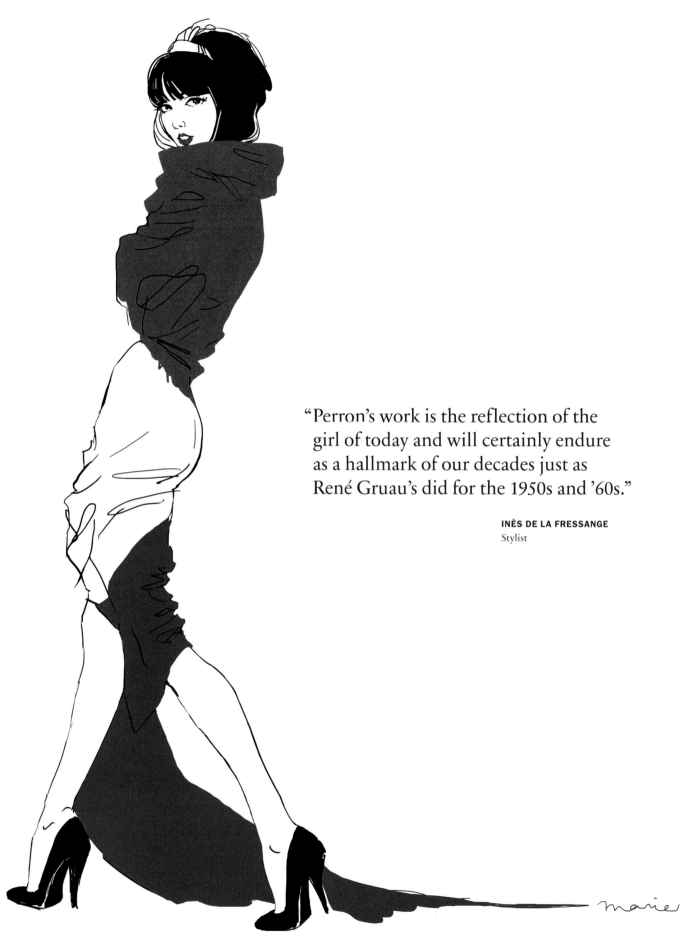

"Perron's work is the reflection of the girl of today and will certainly endure as a hallmark of our decades just as René Gruau's did for the 1950s and '60s."

INÈS DE LA FRESSANGE
Stylist

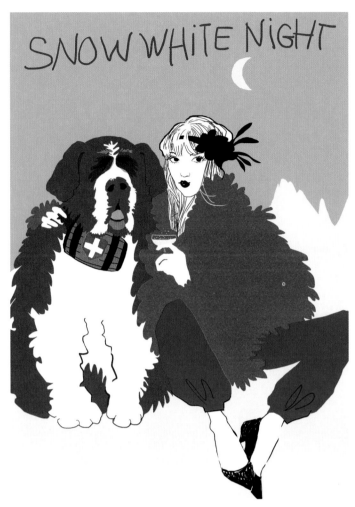

SNOW WHITE NIGHT

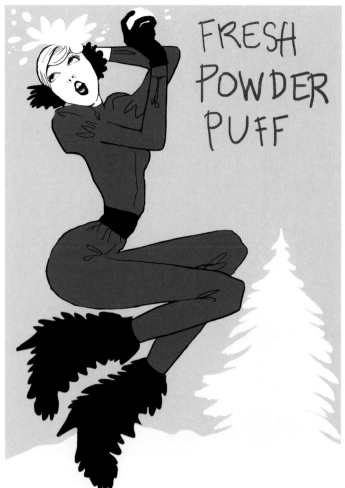

FRESH POWDER PUFF

**Snow White Night and
Fresh Powder Puff, 2012**
Cristal Festival, exhibition in Crans,
Montana, with fashion photographer
Steve Hiett; pen and digital

←   **Made in France, 2012**
Le Nouvel Observateur;
pen and digital

Stina Persson

born in Lund | lives and works in Stockholm
www.stinapersson.com

CLIENTS
Louis Vuitton, Free People, Reebok, Nike,
Vogue Japan, Levi's, Gap, Uniqlo, Microsoft,
Absolut Vodka, Nylon magazine, Mother

AGENTS
CWC International
USA
cwc-i.com

CWC Tokyo
Japan
cwctokyo.com

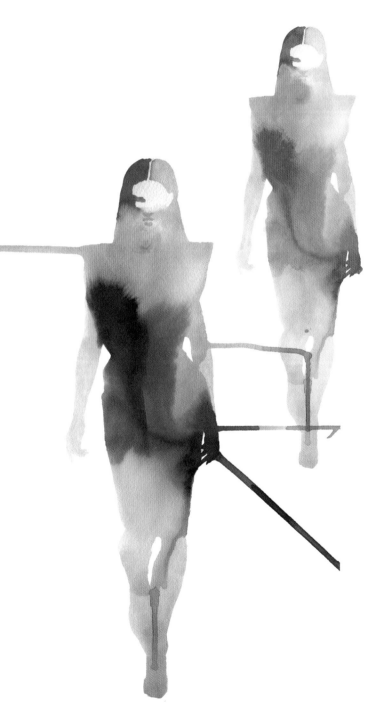

"I see my work as portraits. Portraits of oversized necklaces, printed dresses – and the intriguing women wearing them."

„Ich betrachte meine Arbeiten als Porträts: Porträts von übergroßen Halsketten, bedruckten Kleidern – und von den faszinierenden Frauen, die sie tragen."

« Je pense que je fais des portraits. Des portraits de colliers surdimensionnés, de robes imprimées – et des femmes fascinantes qui les portent. »

Pastel Catwalk, 2012
NK department store, Stockholm,
customer magazine; watercolor

→   **Louis Vuitton Sunglasses
Spring-Summer 2012**
Series of illustrations for Louis Vuitton,
website animation; watercolor
and photo collage

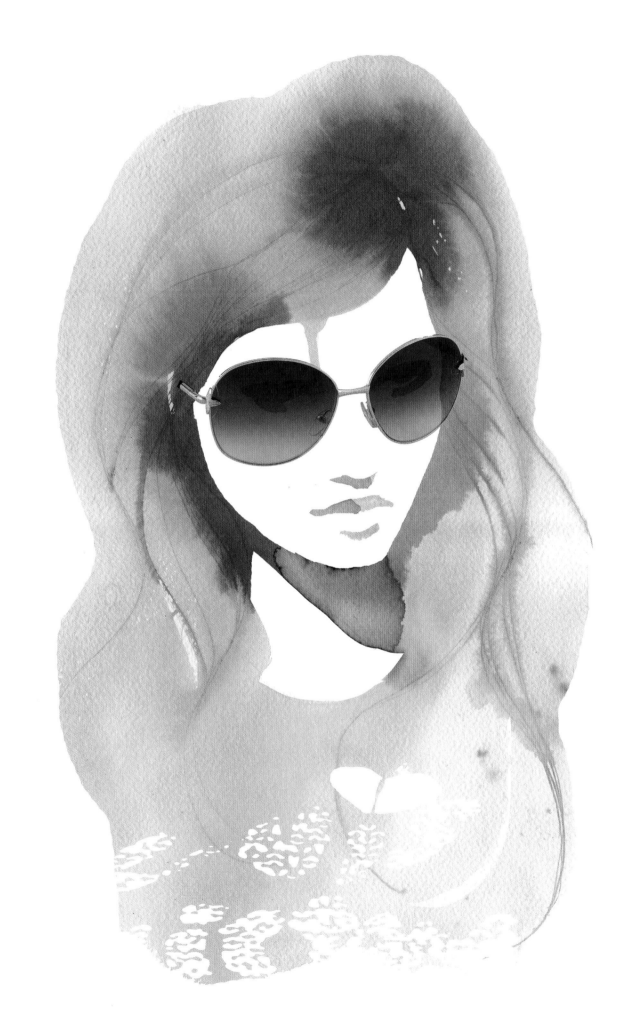

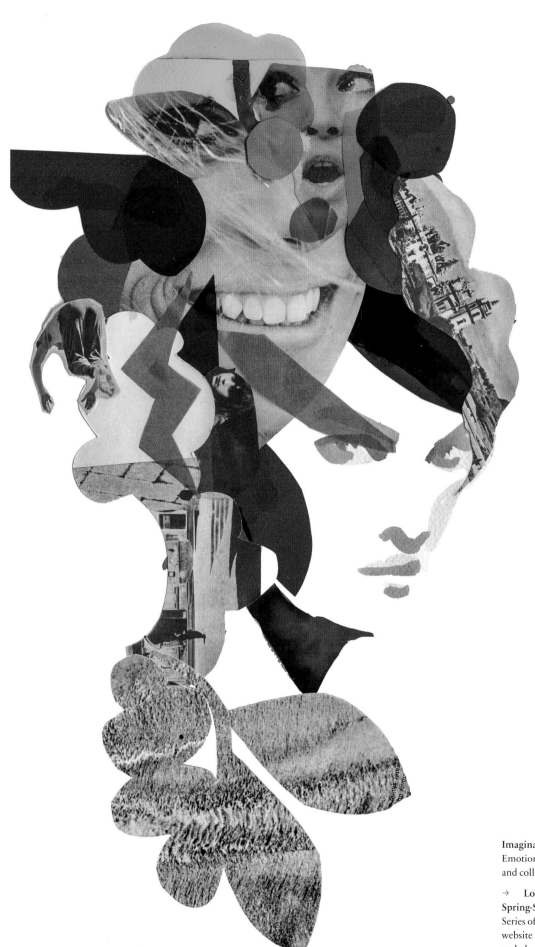

Imagination, 2012
Emotion magazine; watercolor
and collage

→ Louis Vuitton Fashion Jewelry,
Spring-Summer 2012
Series of illustrations for Louis Vuitton,
website animation; watercolor
and photo collage

"Using watercolors, Stina drew some beautiful and youthful silhouettes inspired by the Louis Vuitton Spring/Summer 2012 Fashion Show to illuminate the accessories collection, taking these fashionable jewels on a new digital journey."

LOUIS VUITTON
Digital Department

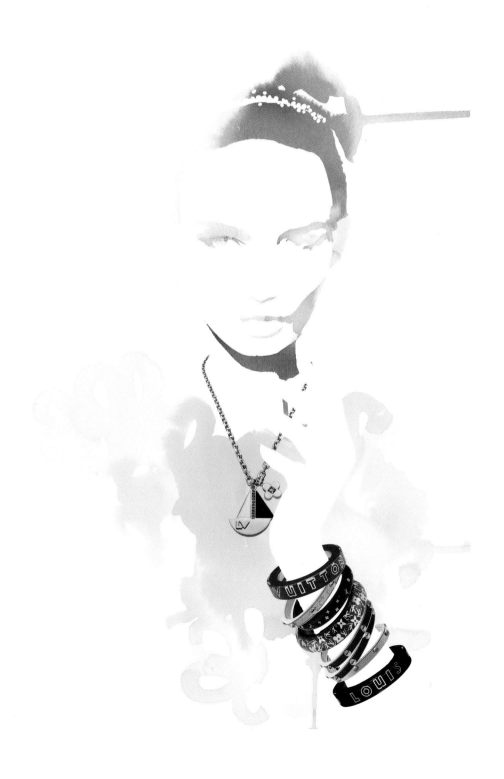

Erin Petson

1980 born in Middlesbrough | lives and works in London
www.erinpetson.com

CLIENTS
Dior, DVF, Moncler, Loro Piana, Swarovski, Victoria & Albert
Museum, Selfridges, Victoria Beckham/Mother, The Sunday Times
Style Magazine, Vogue Japan, The New York Times

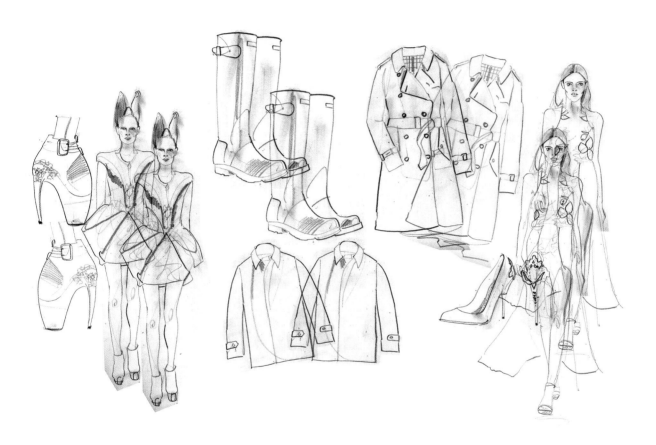

"I create ethereal, delicate, hand-drawn fashion-inspired
pieces – through line, texture and colour, I love to
inspire and capture my mind's eye."

„Durch Linien, Texturen und Farben schaffe ich ätherische, filigrane,
handgezeichnete, von der Mode inspirierte Werke. Ich liebe es
zu inspirieren und das einzufangen, was mein geistiges Auge sieht."

« Je dessine des images éthérées et délicates inspirées
par la mode. J'aime inspirer mon imagination avec les lignes,
les textures et les couleurs. »

GB Brands, 2012
Mother/Great campaign, animated
video interview with Victoria Beckham;
mixed media, pencil, acrylic, fabriano
paper and digital

→   **Versace, Fashion Face-Off
Top Trumps, 2012**
Sunday Times Style Magazine,
Top Trumps card game; mixed media,
pencil, acrylic, fabriano paper and digital

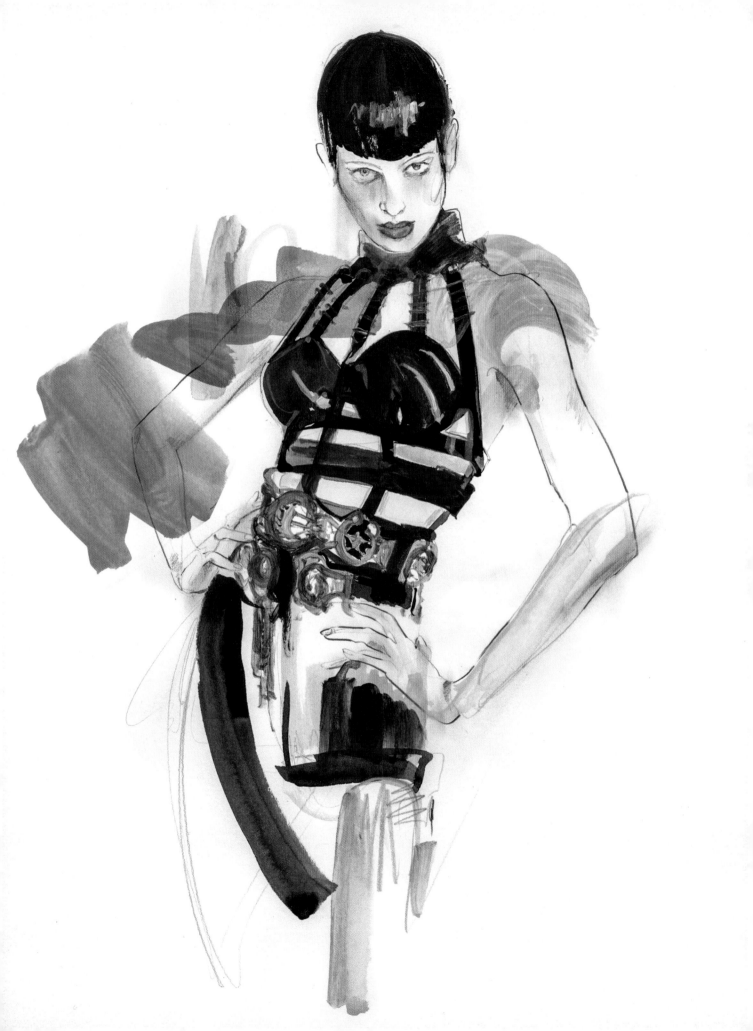

"I have long been drawn to the duality of Erin's work which seems to marry the fashion zeitgeist with something altogether more spiritual."

SARAH McCULLOUGH
Creative Concepts Manager
Selfridges London

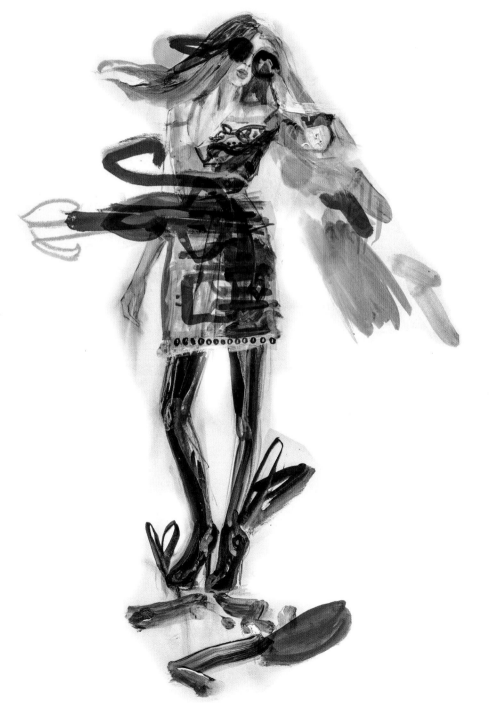

DVF Girl, 2011
Diane von Furstenberg/Sandbox
Studios, animated fashion video;
mixed media, pencil, acrylic,
fabriano paper and digital

→   **Riot Girl, 2012**
Elle Canada, fashion article;
mixed media, pencil, acrylic,
fabriano paper and digital

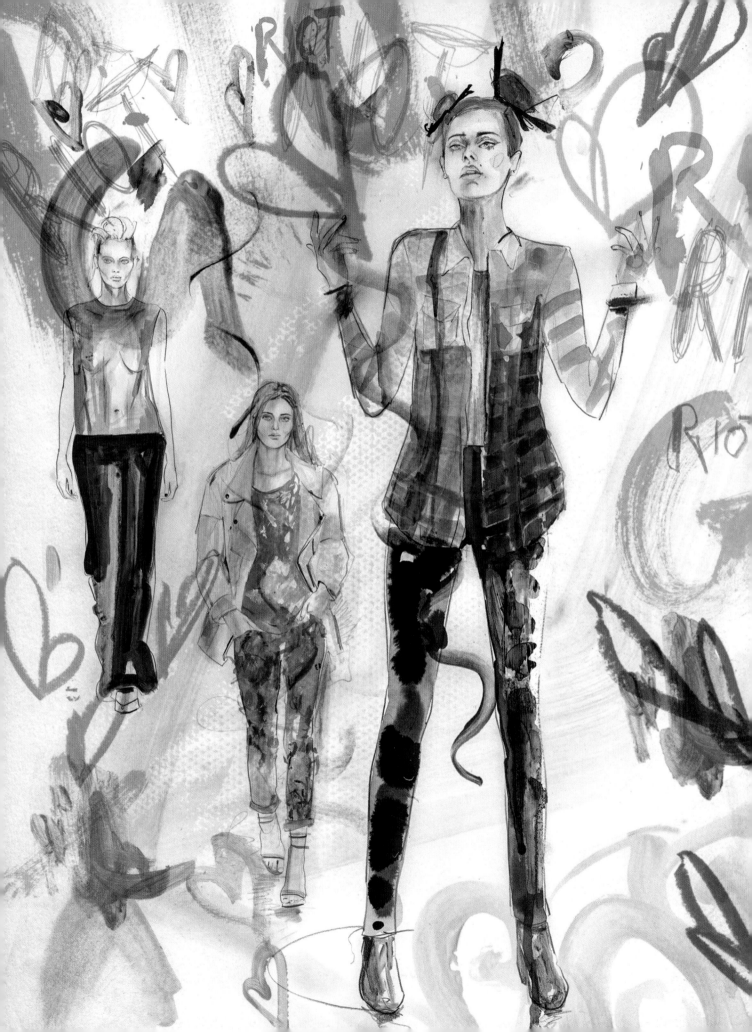

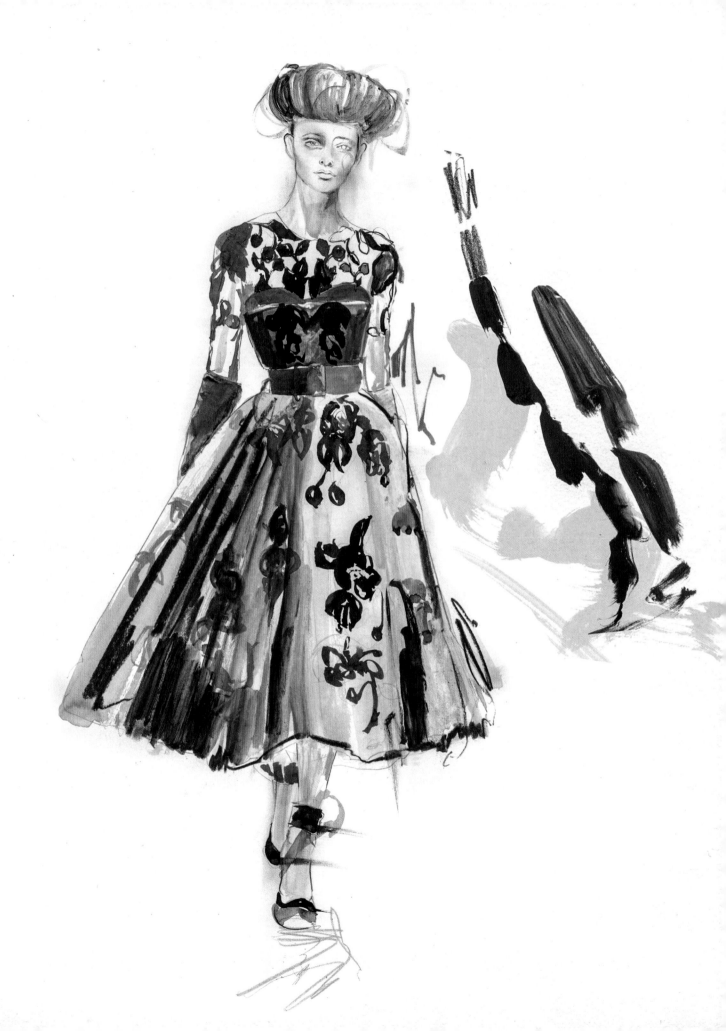

Ribbon, 2012
Swarovski, promotional book;
mixed media, hand-drawn, pencil,
acrylic, fabriano paper and digital

← **Catwalk Girl #2, 2012**
Quintessentially, online blog;
mixed media, hand-drawn, pencil,
acrylic, fabriano paper and digital

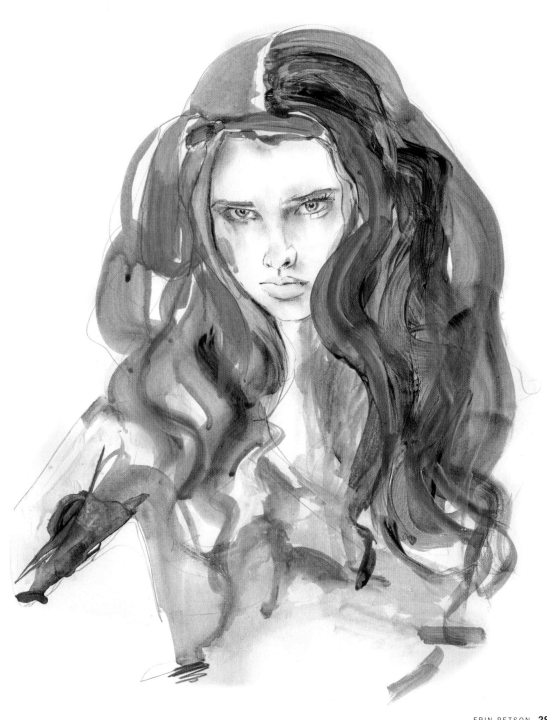

Sabine Pieper

1980 born in Germany | lives and works in Berlin
www.sabinepieper.com

CLIENTS
Elle UK, Vlisco,
Carlin International,
Mykromag

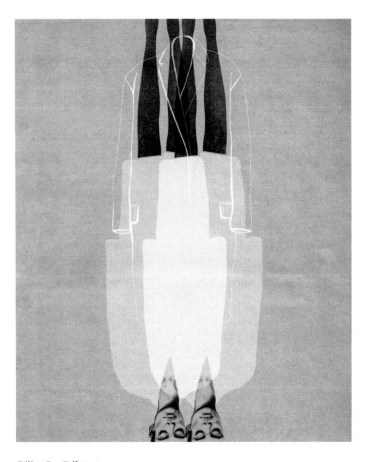

"For me, illustration is always a process
of trying and discovering, mixing
and melting, the opportunity to work
and create in a very playful way."

„Für mich ist Illustration stets der Prozess von
Ausprobieren und Entdecken, des Vermischens
und Verschmelzens – meine Chance, auf ganz
spielerische Weise zu arbeiten und zu kreieren."

« Pour moi, dans l'illustration il s'agit toujours
d'essayer et de découvrir, de mélanger et
de fondre, de travailler d'une façon très ludique. »

Céline Pre-Fall 2012
Personal work; pencil, watercolor
and digital

→   **Sœur, 2012**
Personal work; pencil on paper,
embroidery, watercolor, oil pastel
and digital

→ →   **Vlisco "Delicate Shades", 2011**
Vlisco & Deux d'Amsterdam,
Delicate Shades collection campaign,
Art Direction: Anneke Krull,
Production: Daphne Story, Production
Story/Photography: James Powel; pencil
and pen, ink, watercolor and digital

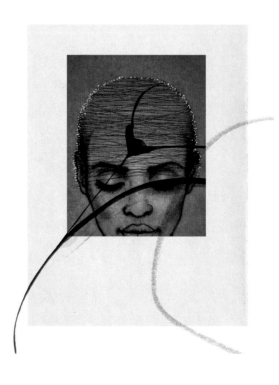

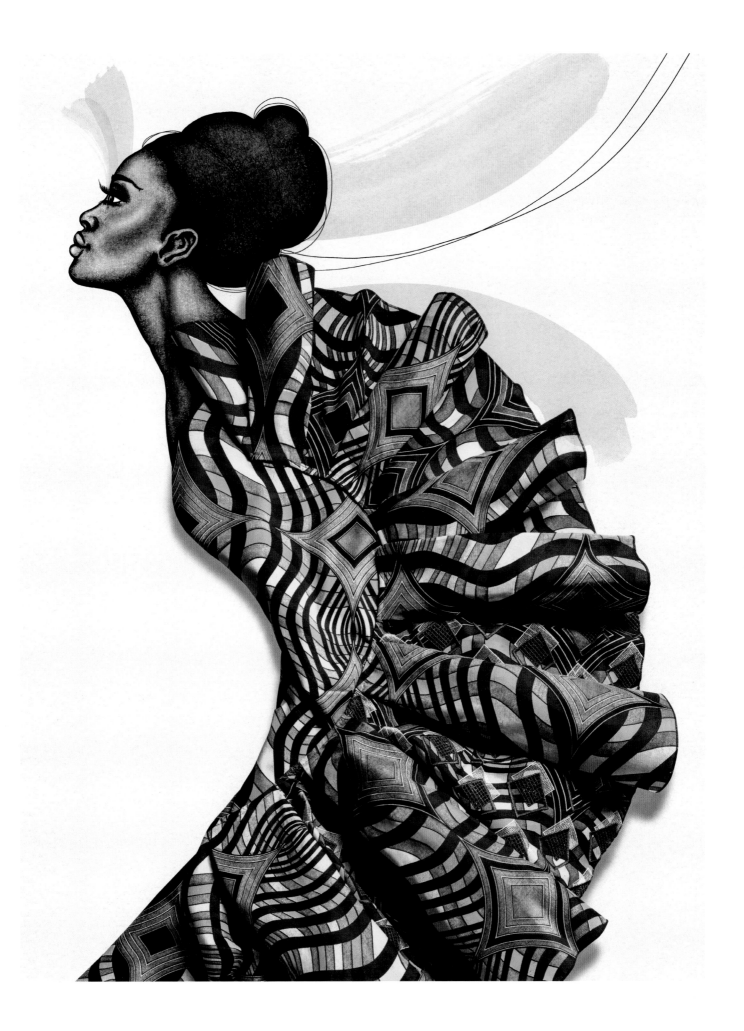

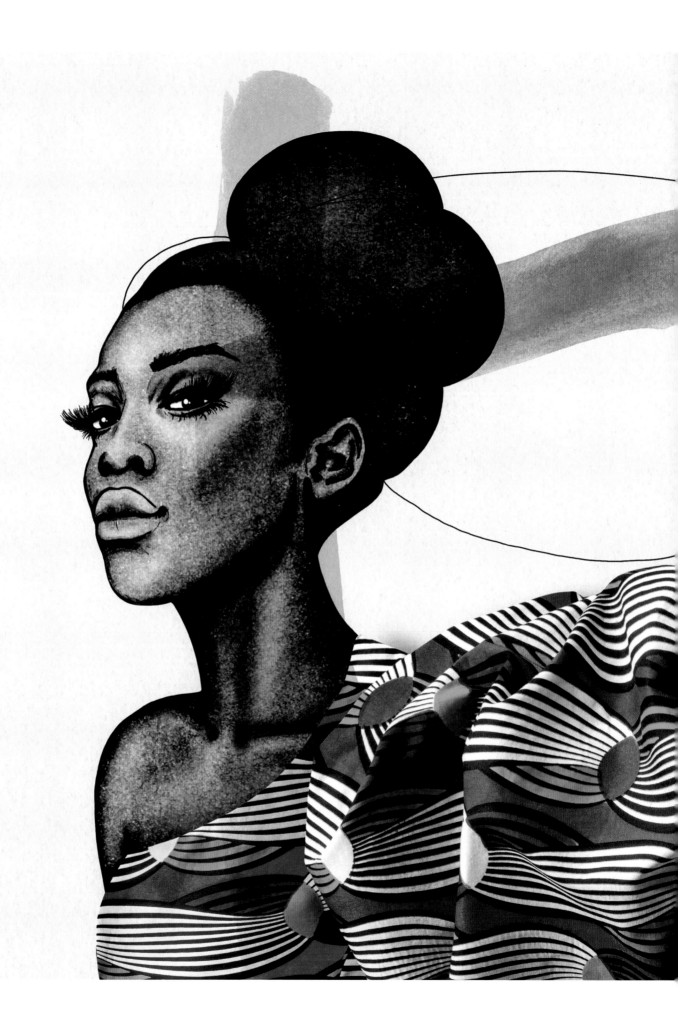

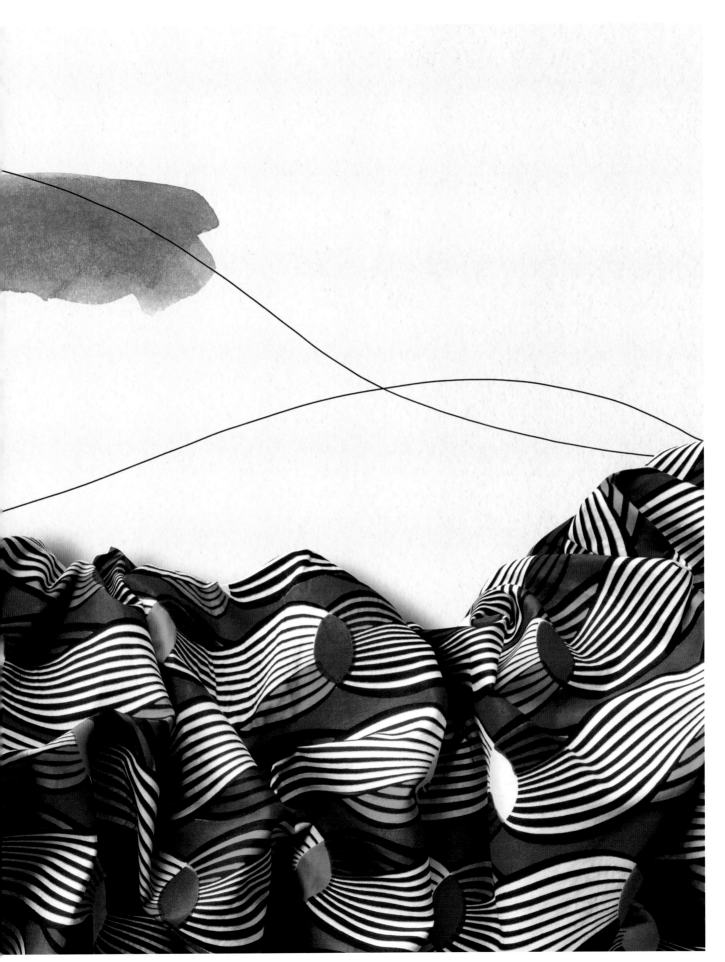

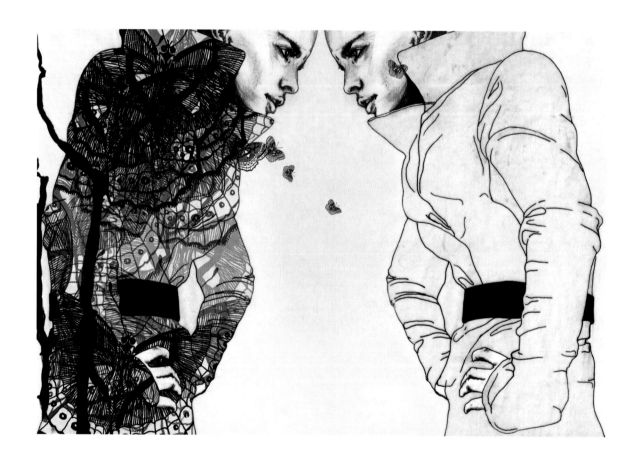

p.296 **Vlisco "Delicate Shades", 2011**
Vlisco & Deux d'Amsterdam,
Delicate Shades collection campaign,
Art Direction: Anneke Krull,
Production: Daphne Story, Production
Story/Photography: James Powel; pencil
and pen, ink, watercolor and digital

↑　　**Butterfly, 2009**
Personal work; pencil and pen on
paper, ink and digital

→　　**The Elle Girls, 2010**
Elle UK, mademoiselle column; pencil
and pen, ink, watercolor and digital

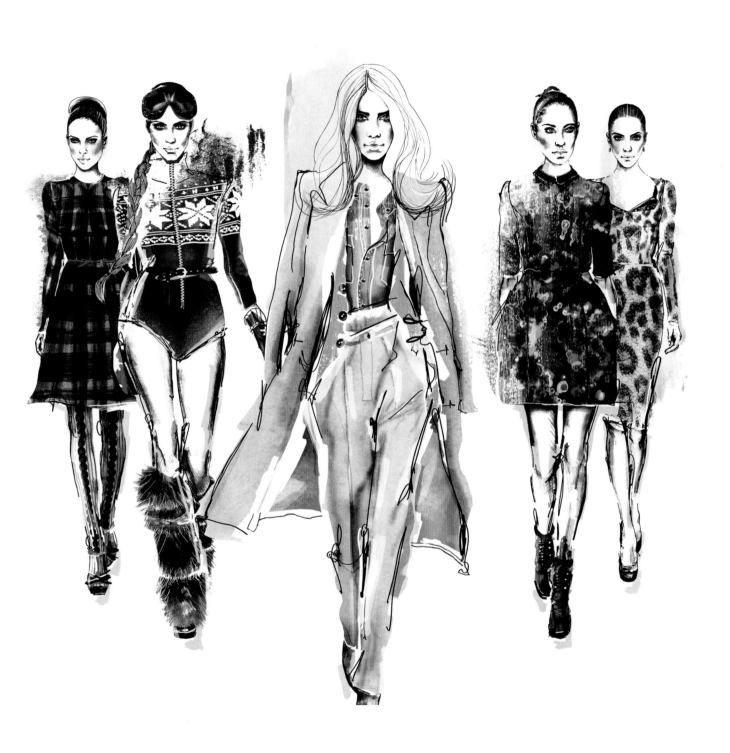

Bella Pilar

1972 born in New York | lives and works in Los Angeles
www.bellapilar.com

CLIENTS
Vogue Latin America/Mexico, L'Uomo Vogue, Bloomingdale's,
Mercedes-Benz New York Fashion Week, La Gardenia, Glamour
magazine, Savoir Flair, Coty, La Perla, Tiffany, LCX, Papyrus

AGENT
Magnet Reps
USA
magnetreps.com

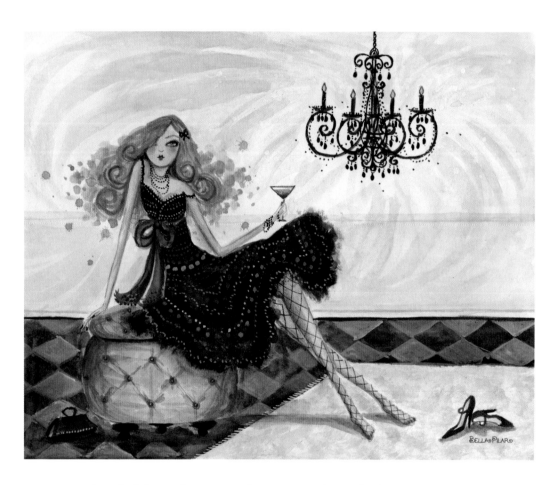

"I try to paint fashions for my girls to wear that I feel are timeless –
not dated, but more classic and everlasting. While I'm sketching
I ask myself, 'Will I still love this outfit years from now?'"

„Für meine Girls will ich tragbare Mode malen, die meinem Gefühl nach zeitlos ist –
nicht tagesaktuell, sondern eher klassisch und beständig. Beim Skizzieren
frage ich mich: ‚Gefällt mir dieses Outfit auch noch in ein paar Jahren?'"

« J'essaie de dessiner des vêtements intemporels – non pas désuets,
mais classiques. Je me demande ‹ Est-ce que j'aimerai toujours
cette tenue dans quelques années ? › »

Cosmo, 2008
Papyrus, postcard; gouache

→   Boardwalk, 2010
Personal work; gouache

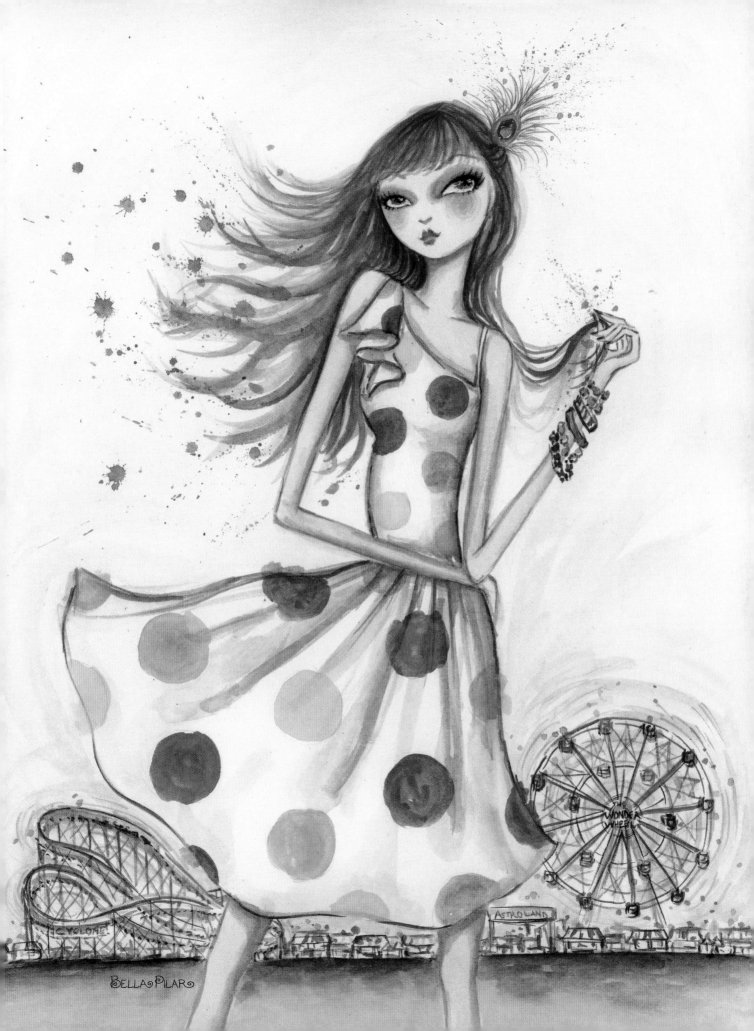

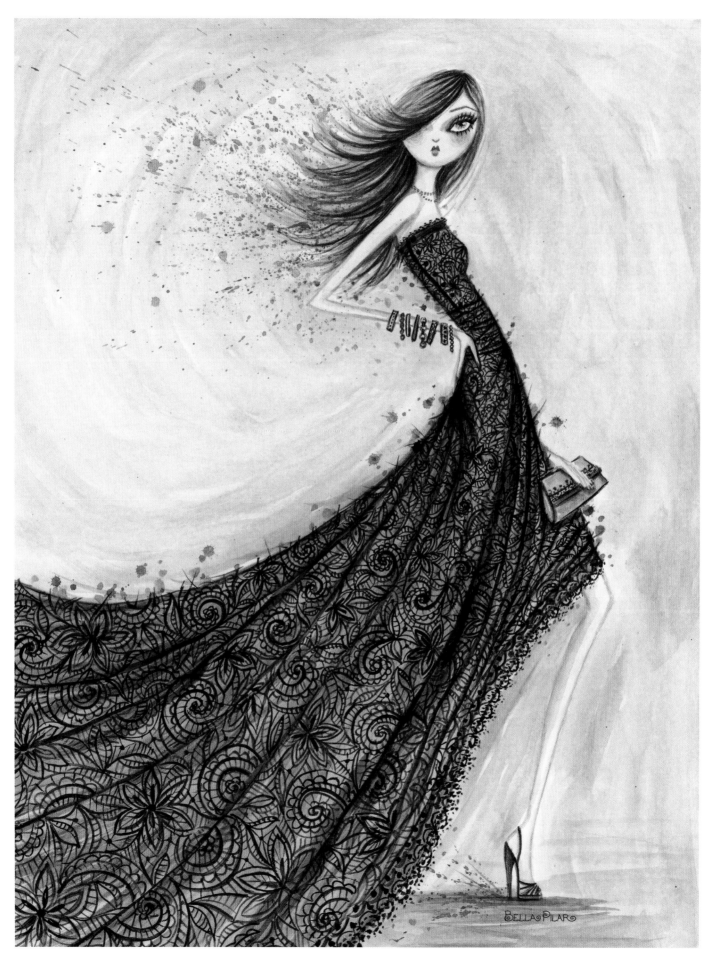

"Bella has an extremely fresh and unique eye for fashion. Her sophisticated sense of style has created a strong following of fans who adore her fashionable women."

DIANA RUHL
Vice President of Creative
Papyrus

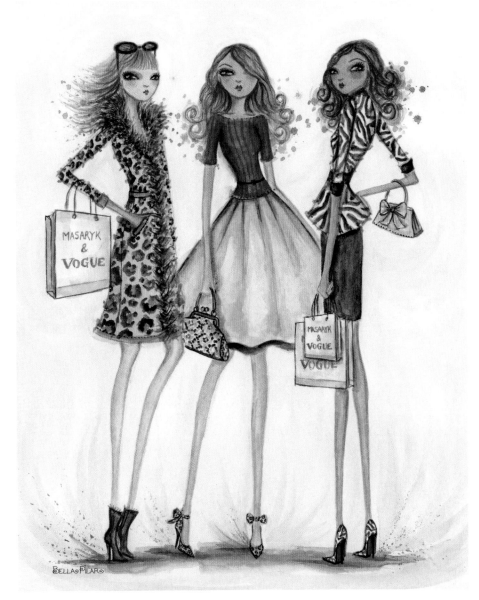

Vogue Girls, 2010
Vogue Latin America/Mexico,
T-shirts and tote bags, Art Direction:
Eva Hughes; gouache

← **Lovely Lace, 2012**
Papyrus and IMG/Mercedes-Benz
New York Fashion Week, schedule
of events and press lanyards, Creative
Direction: Diana Ruhl, Art Direction:
Richard Flores; gouache

Wendy Plovmand

1975 born in Copenhagen | lives and works in Copenhagen and London
www.wendyplovmand.com

CLIENTS
Guess, Topshop, Mads Nørgaard, Bruuns Bazaar,
By Malene Birger, Nylon magazine, Elle Girl,
Flair magazine, Organic Pharmacy, WWD

AGENTS
Traffic Creative
Management
USA
trafficnyc.com

Central Illustration
Agency
UK
centralillustration.com

"Feminine, detailed and playful with
a hint of the supernatural and
uncanny undertones."

„Feminin, detailverliebt und verspielt mit einer Prise
Übersinnlichem und seltsamen Untertönen."

« Mon travail est féminin, plein de détails
et ludique, avec une touche de
surnaturel et un soupçon de mystère. »

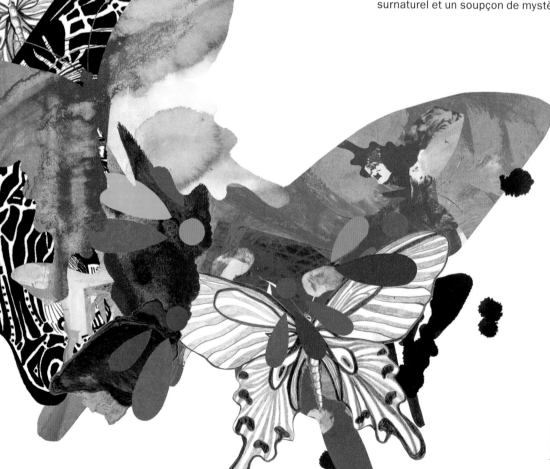

Butterflies, 2008
Eurowoman magazine, cover; pencil,
watercolor, ink, collage and digital

→   Elle Girl, 2008
Elle Girl Korea, cover; pencil,
watercolor, ink, collage and digital

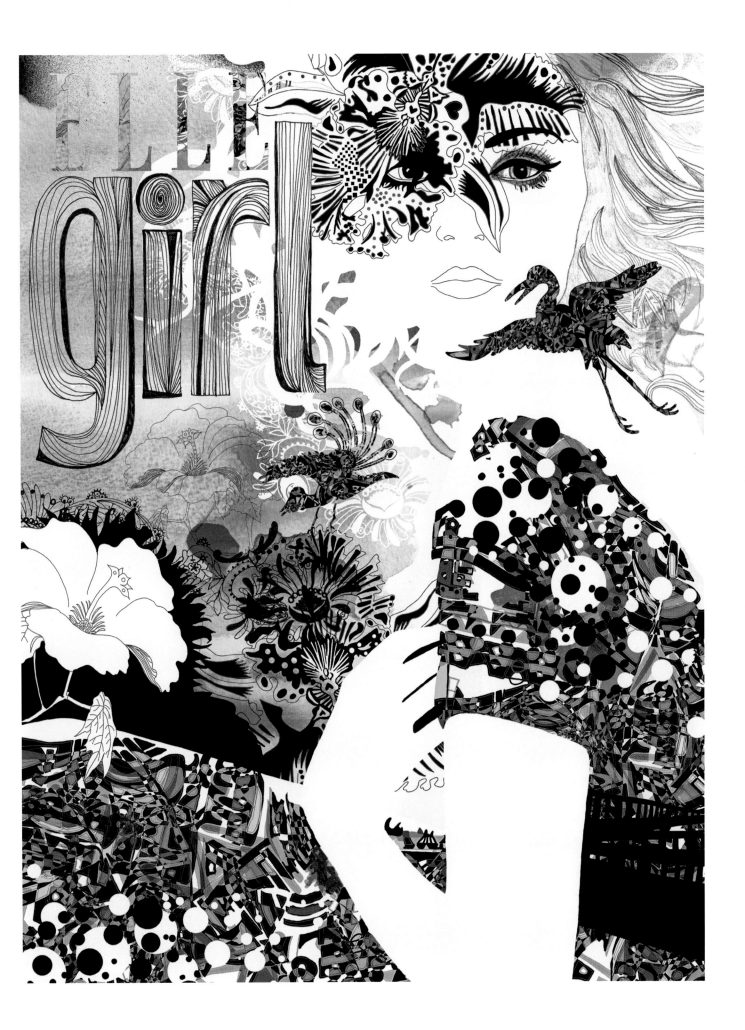

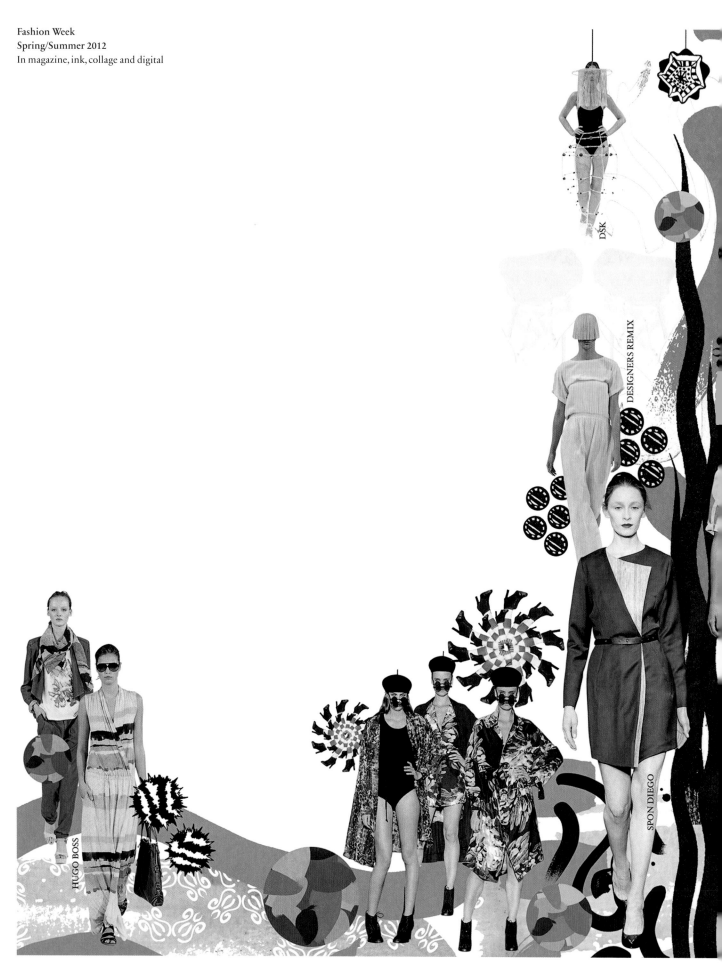

DSK

DESIGNERS REMIX

HUGO BOSS

SPON DIEGO

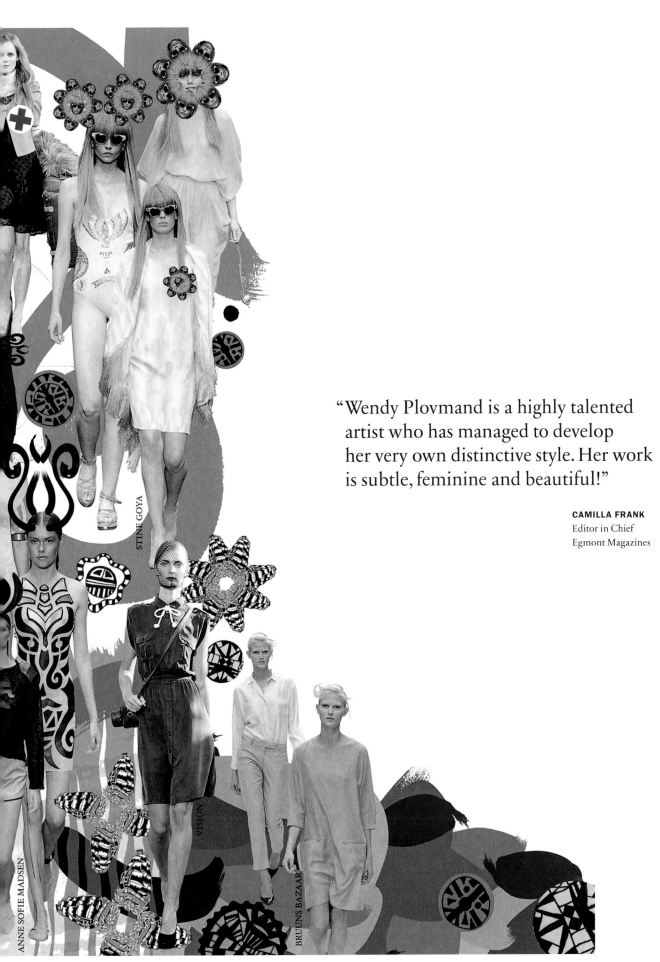

"Wendy Plovmand is a highly talented artist who has managed to develop her very own distinctive style. Her work is subtle, feminine and beautiful!"

CAMILLA FRANK
Editor in Chief
Egmont Magazines

Lucile Prache

1959 born in Paris | lives and works in Paris
www.lucileprache.com

CLIENTS
Promostyl, CTC, Longchamp, Cacharel,
Yves Saint Laurent, Corinne Sarrut, Marie Claire,
Et vous, Charles Jourdan, Galeries Lafayette

AGENTS
Traffic Creative
Management
USA
trafficnyc.com

Agence Virginie
France
virginie.fr

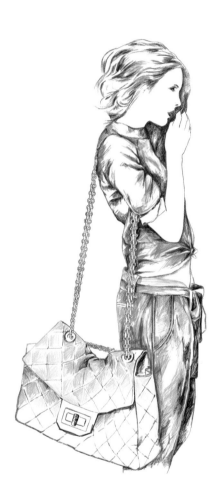

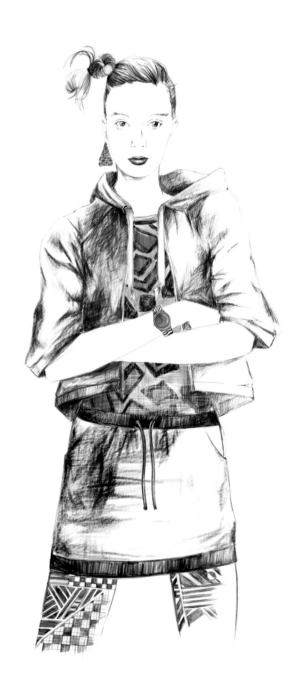

"Always wondering what is around the
corner next season, very exciting!"

„Stets auf der Suche danach, was die nächste
Saison bringt – sehr spannend!"

« Je me demande toujours ce qui va émerger
à la prochaine saison, c'est très excitant ! »

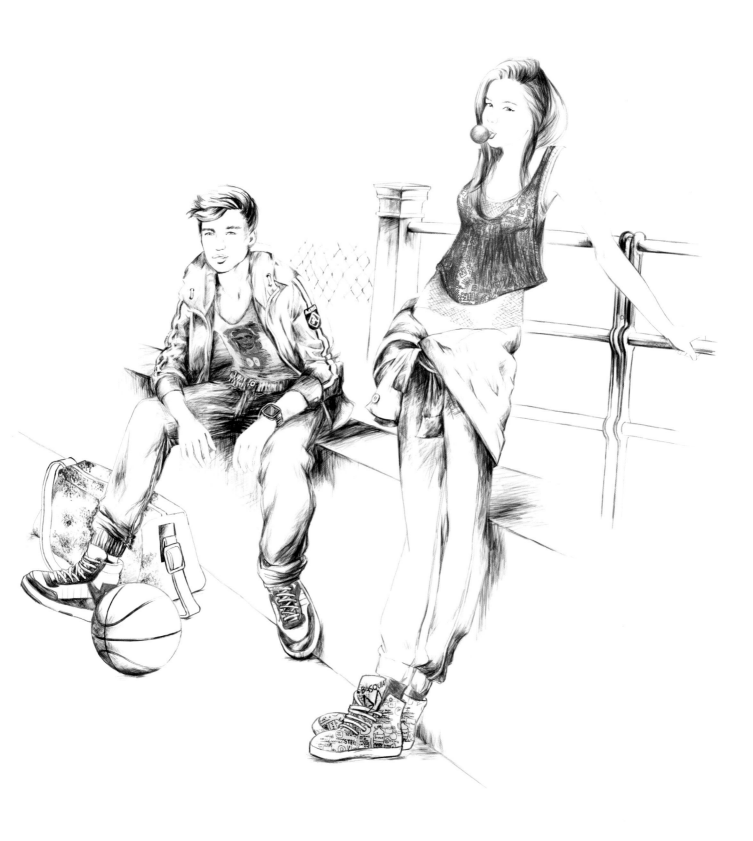

Untitled, 2011
Promostyl Paris, Styling:
Mio Gerallo, Karin Difonis; digital

←   Untitled, 2011
Promostyl Paris, Styling:
Mio Gerallo, Karin Difonis; digital

←←   Untitled, 2011
Personal work; digital

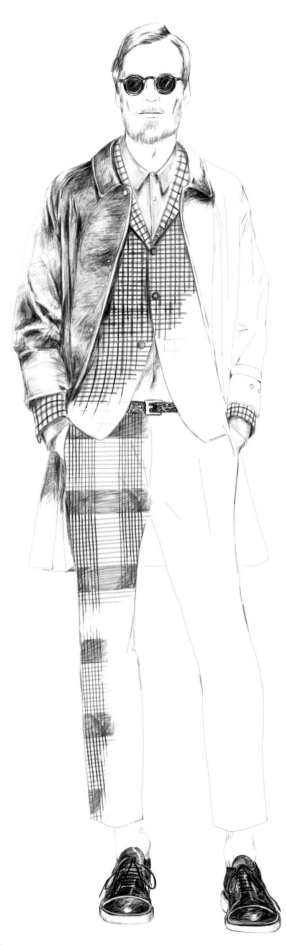

"Fashion is whimsical, trends are fleeting, Paris is beautiful and Lucile Prache's fashion illustrations are all three."

EMIAH C.
Writer, D2G Apparel

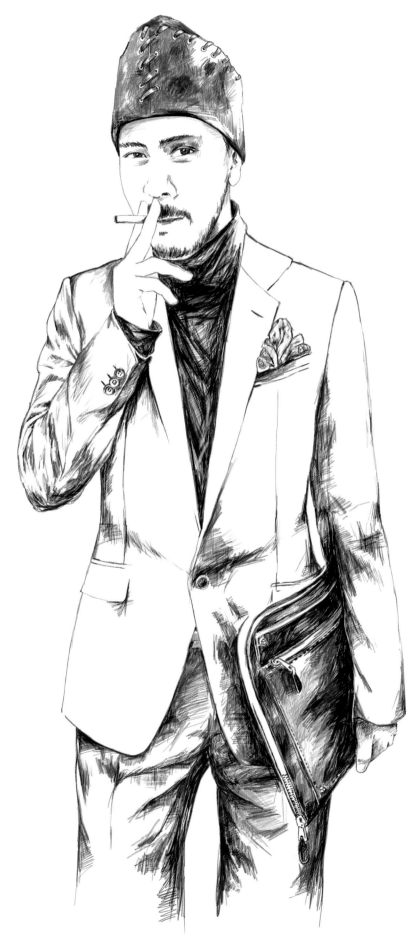

Untitled, 2011
Personal work; digital

← Untitled, 2011
Promostyl Paris, Styling: Marion
Hugoo, Murielle Froidefond; digital

Maria Raymondsdotter

1971 born in Stockholm | lives and works in Stockholm
www.raymondsdotter.com

CLIENTS
Farsta Centrum, Vogue USA, Elle UK,
Berns Salonger, Hotel Anglais,
Mama, Damernas Värld

AGENTS
Söderberg Agentur
Sweden
soderbergagentur.com

Central Illustration
Agency
UK
centralillustation.com

Snyder & the Swedes
USA
snyderandtheswedes.com

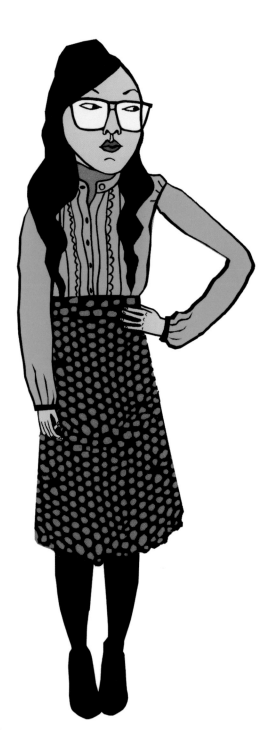

"I love people and their personal style.
Street fashion is what's most interesting.
My greatest hobby is people-watching."

„Ich liebe Menschen mit ihrem persönlichen Stil.
Dabei ist Street Fashion am spannendsten.
Mein liebstes Hobby: Menschen beobachten."

« J'aime les gens et leur style personnel.
La mode de la rue est ce qui m'intéresse
le plus. J'adore regarder les gens. »

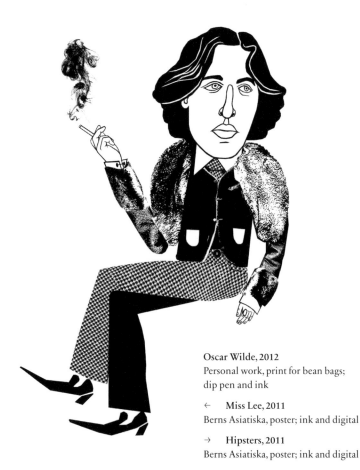

Oscar Wilde, 2012
Personal work, print for bean bags;
dip pen and ink

←   Miss Lee, 2011
Berns Asiatiska, poster; ink and digital

→   Hipsters, 2011
Berns Asiatiska, poster; ink and digital

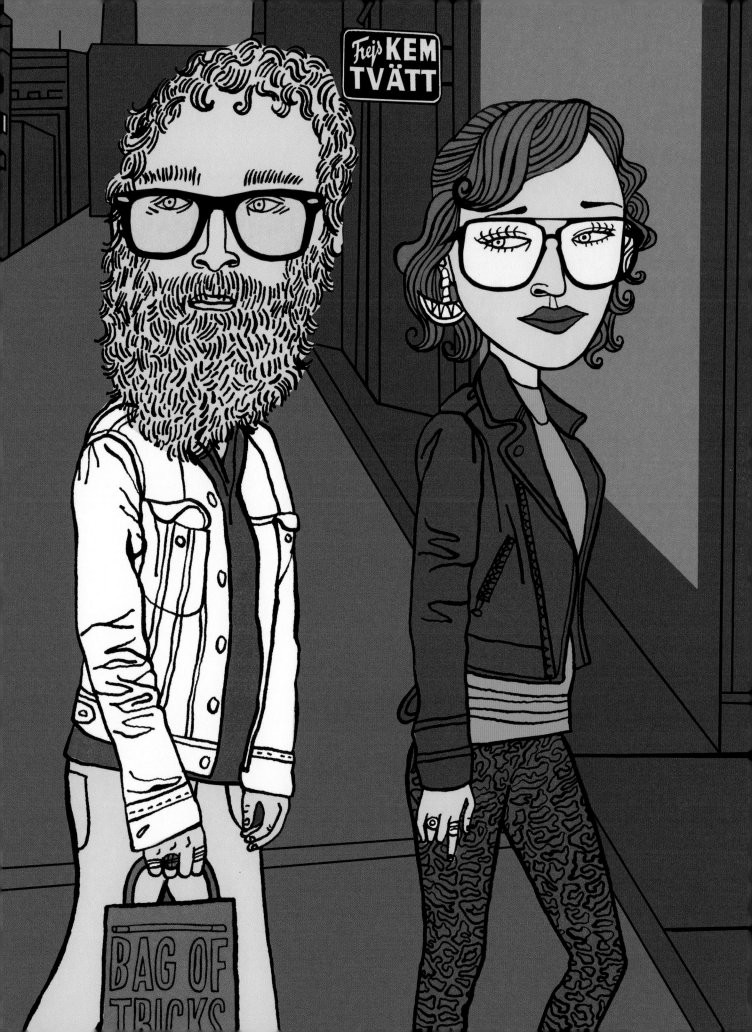

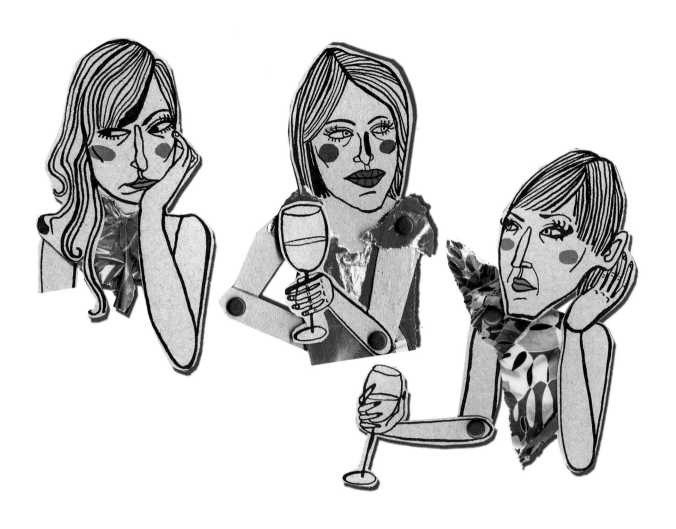

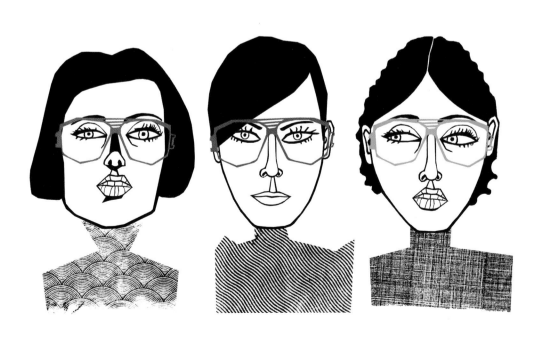

Katy, 2012
Personal work, series of 30 different
paper ladies, exhibition; collage

←   **Friends, 2011**
Damernas Värld magazine;
ink and collage

↙   **Specs, 2012**
Personal work; collage

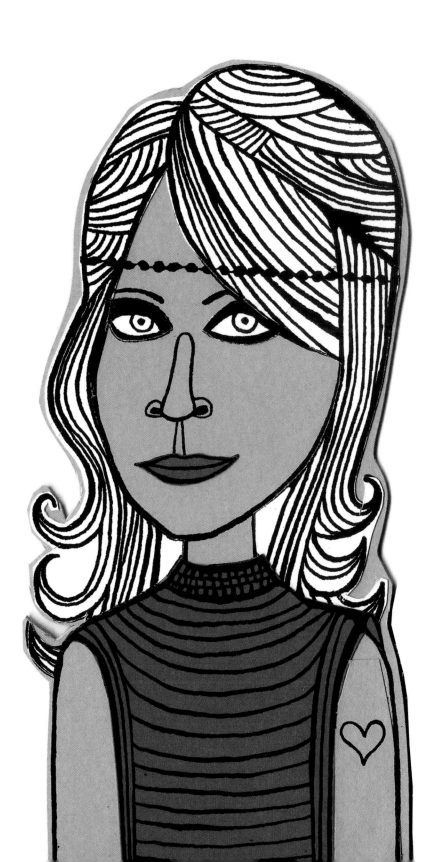

Katie Rodgers

1985 born in Atlanta | lives and works in Cambridge, USA
www.paperfashion.net

CLIENTS
Clé de Peau Beauté, Kate Spade,
Coach, Calypso St. Barth, Paul Mitchell,
Lucky magazine, Glamour magazine,
Elle Girl, Alicia Keys

AGENT
Digital Brand Architects
USA
thedigitalbrandarchitects.com

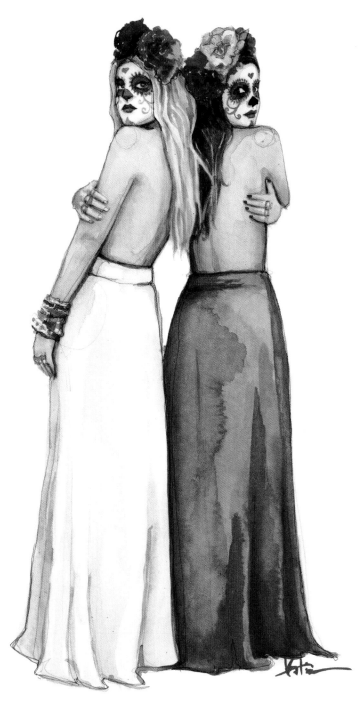

"I strive to create a whimsical world where fashion meets paper."

„Ich strebe danach, eine wunderliche Welt zu schaffen, in der sich Fashion und Papier begegnen."

« J'essaie de créer un monde fantasque où la mode rencontre le papier. »

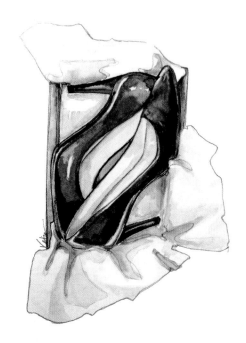

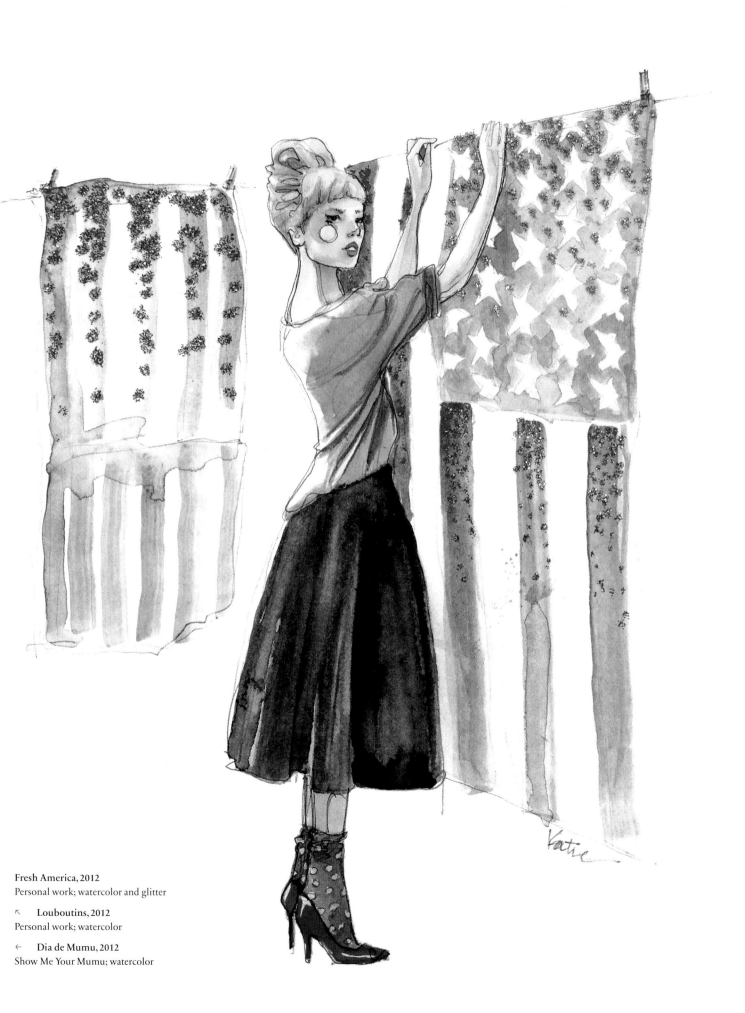

Fresh America, 2012
Personal work; watercolor and glitter

↖ **Louboutins, 2012**
Personal work; watercolor

← **Dia de Mumu, 2012**
Show Me Your Mumu; watercolor

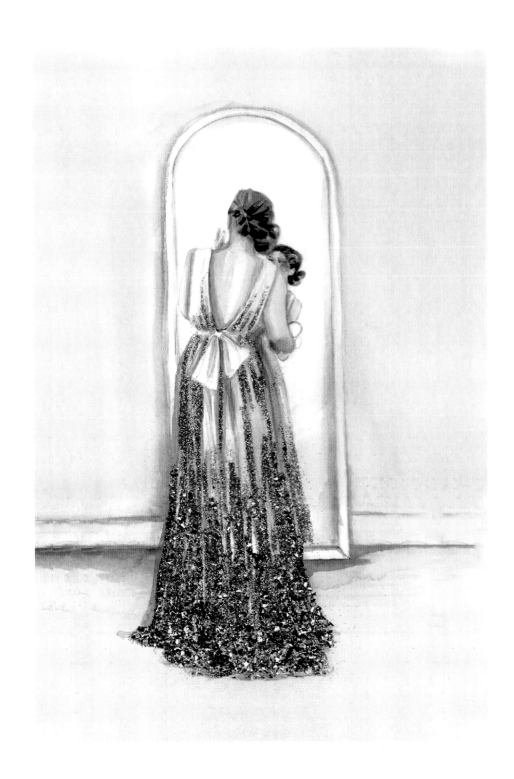

Getting Ready, 2012
Personal work; watercolor and glitter

→   Knitted, 2011
EmmaDime; watercolor and glitter

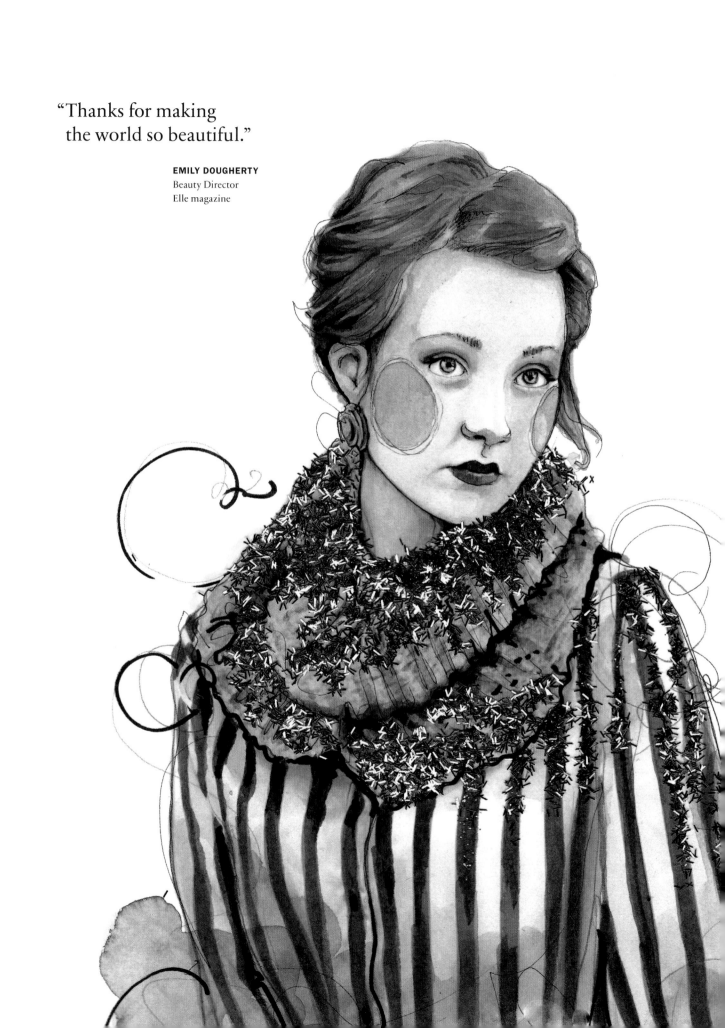

"Thanks for making
the world so beautiful."

EMILY DOUGHERTY
Beauty Director
Elle magazine

Masaki Ryo

born in Ishikawa Prefecture | lives and works in Tokyo
www.masakiryo.com

CLIENTS
World, Nice Claup, Atre, Canal 4°C, Vogue Japan,
Miss magazine, Rodeo Drive, Sonore de Toot,
La Senza, La Perla

AGENTS
CWC International
USA
cwc-i.com

CWC Tokyo
Japan
cwctokyo.com

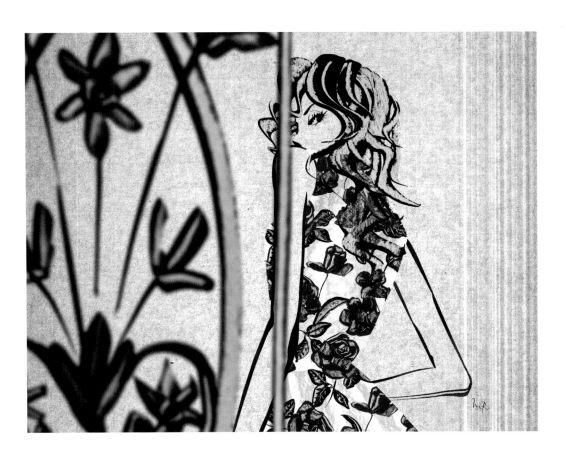

"While trying to depict the *au courant* beauty of fashion,
I place importance on still making the illustrations
unique and original in my own style."

„Zur Schönheit in der Mode will ich auf dem Laufenden bleiben und sie
abbilden. Dabei lege ich Wert darauf, die Illustrationen in meinem
eigenen Stil unverwechselbar und originell zu machen."

« Tout en essayant de représenter la beauté branchée de la mode,
je veux que mes illustrations soient uniques et originales,
avec mon style propre. »

Untitled, 2012
Personal work; acrylic and digital

→   Untitled, 2012
Personal work; acrylic and digital

p.322 Untitled, 2012
FedEx, advertising, featured in
Vogue Japan; acrylic and digital

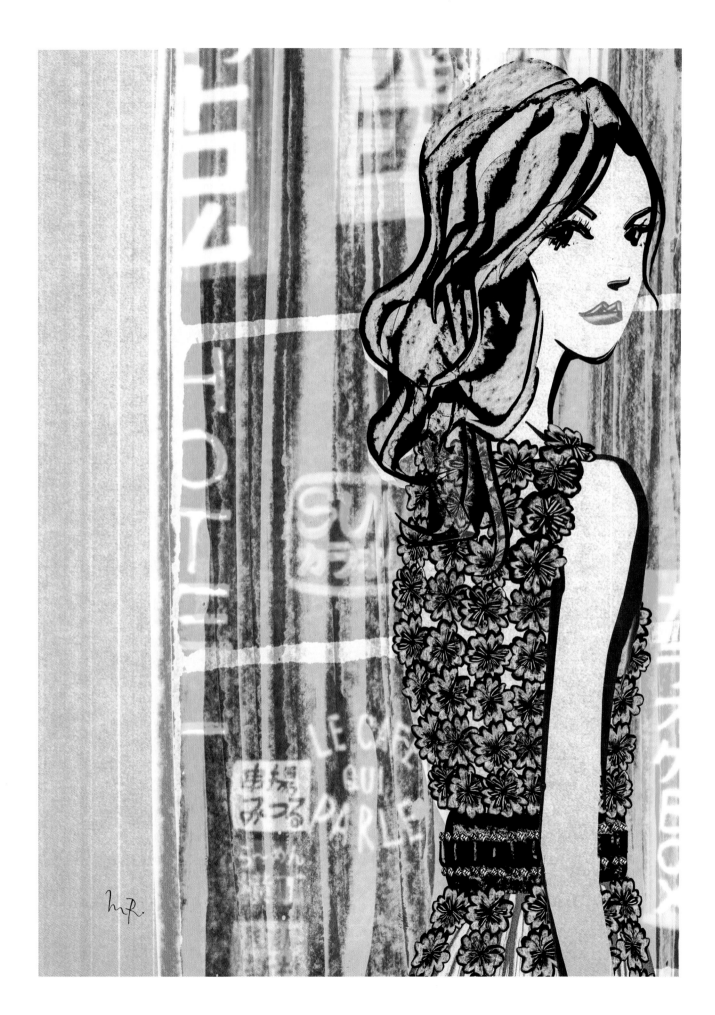

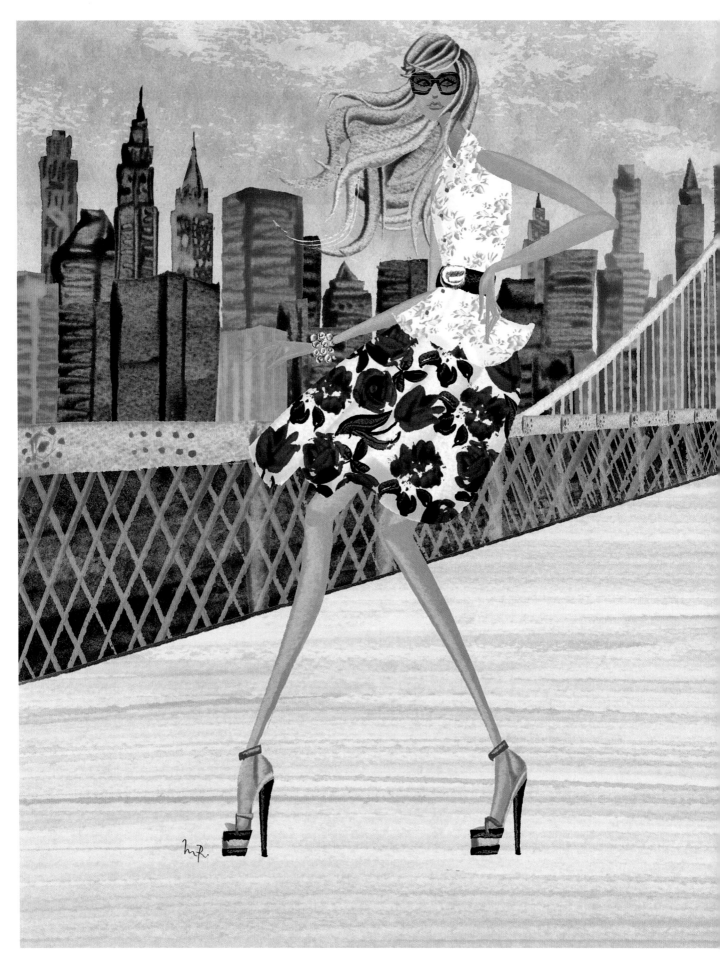

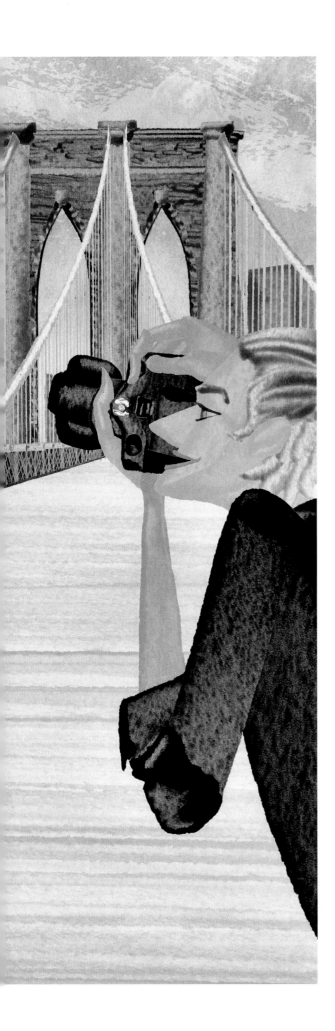

"His art is permeated by
his passion for fashion items."

MASAYA YAMAOKA
Art Director
Yamaoka-gumi / PIALA

Tomek Sadurski

1979 born in Poland | lives and works in Paris and Berlin
www.tomeksadurski.com

CLIENTS
Vanity Fair, L'Officiel Paris, FFW Mag São Paulo,
25 magazine, Andrea Crews, H&M,
Melissa Brasil, Lala Berlin

AGENT
SCHIERKE COM/
Germany
schierke.com

Beata Sadurska
Poland, USA
haanter.pl

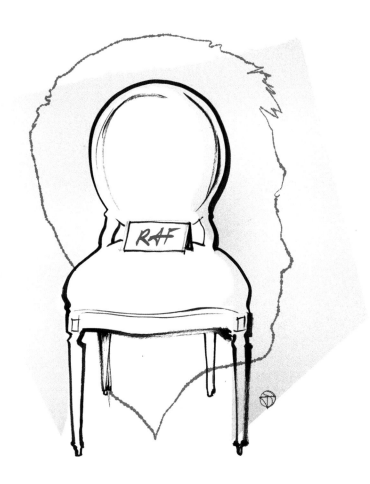

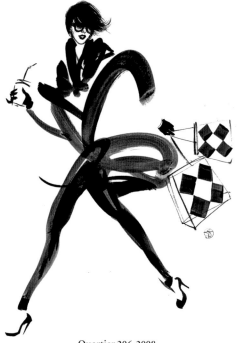

"The drawing in my works is a thread that binds together the different media into one."

„In meiner Arbeit werden die unterschiedlichen Medien
durch Zeichnungen zusammengeführt."

« Dans mon travail, le dessin est un fil qui rattache
les différentes techniques entre elles. »

Quartier 206, 2008
Acrylic and ink

↖ **Raf Goes Dior, 2012**
L'Officiel Paris; china ink and
digital collage

→ **Pani Magazine, 2010**
Quartier; watercolor, ink, acrylic paint
monotype and digital drawing

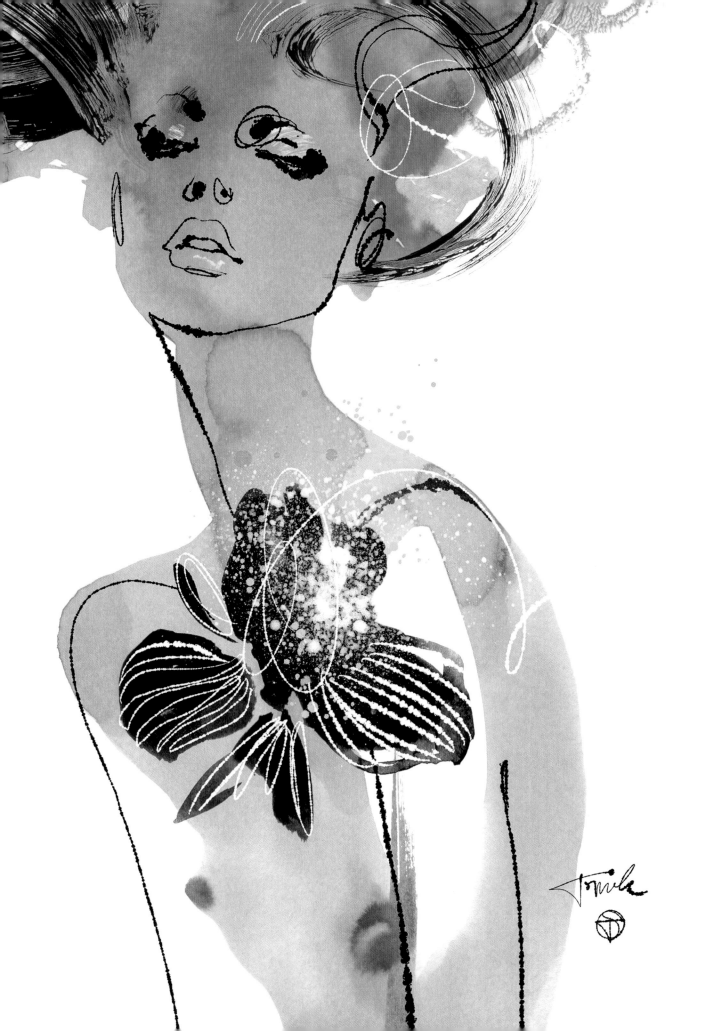

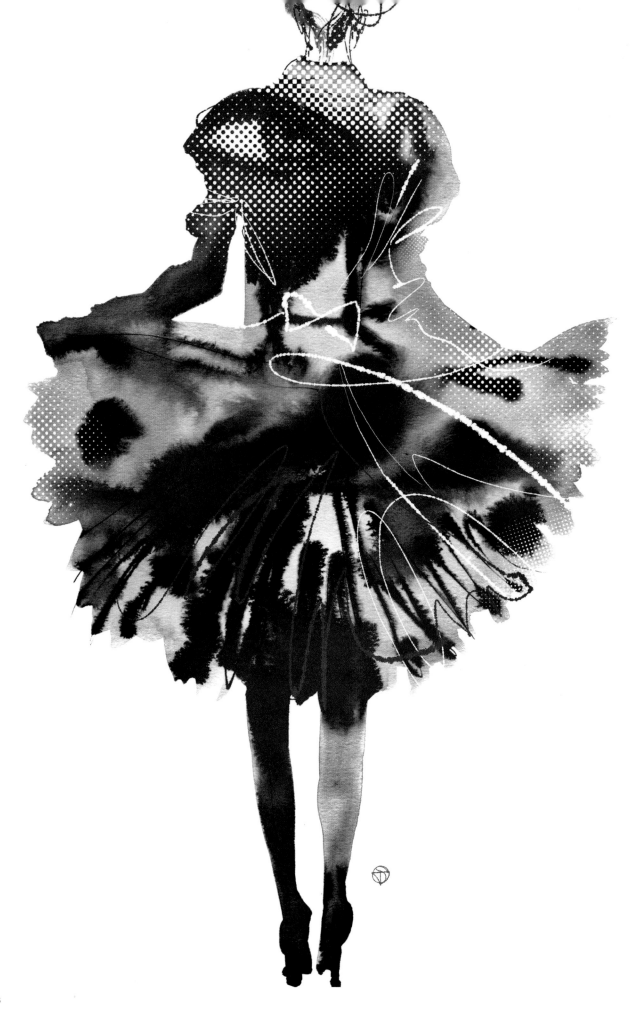

Abbey Lee, 2010
25 magazine, Photography: Marcin
Tyszka; pencil, ink, acrylic paint
monotype, digital drawing and collage

← Pleats, 2010
Watercolor, digital drawing and collage

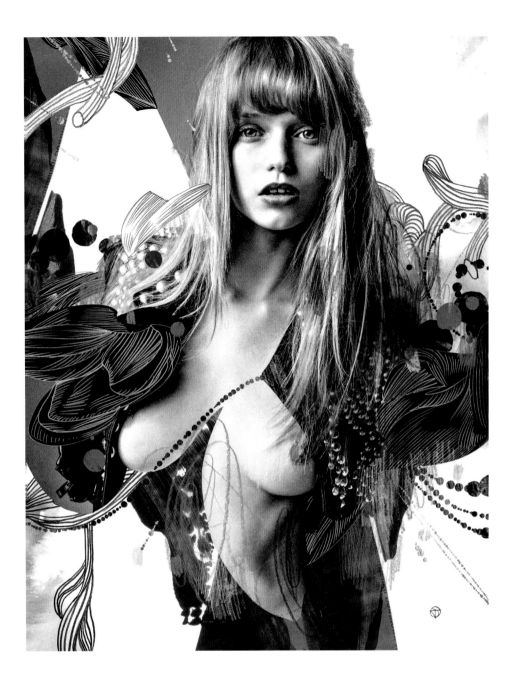

"Tomek Sadurski is a masterful fashion illustrator in the classic
style who unites artisanry with digital in his graphic works.
Best known for his collages and deconstructions, Sadurski
illustrates extraordinary images that reflect the *now*."

JINA KHAYYER
Fashion Journalist

Michael Sanderson

1986 born in Colorado Springs | lives and works in Portland and New York
www.michaelsanderson-newyork.com

CLIENTS
Victoria's Secret, Burkman Bros,
Hudson's Bay Company, Vogue Japan,
Miansai, IENA, commons&sense

AGENT
Taiko & Associates
Japan
ua-net.com/taiko

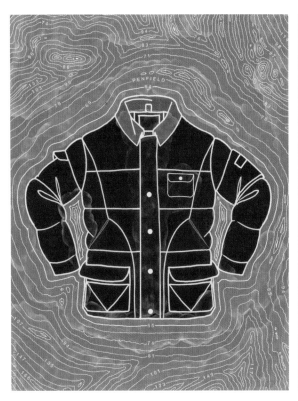 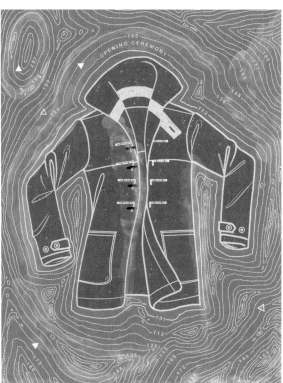

"What separates illustrators from photographers is their ability to work without limits to achieve a desired image – we create images, not capture them."

„Was Illustratoren von Fotografen unterscheidet, ist die Möglichkeit, ohne Limit zum erwünschten Ergebnis zu gelangen: Wir erschaffen Bilder und bilden nicht nur ab."

« Ce qui sépare les illustrateurs des photographes, c'est leur capacité à travailler sans limites pour obtenir le résultat désiré – nous créons les images. »

Hudson's Bay Co. Men's Fall
Preview Image #4 and #3, 2012
Hudson's Bay Co., Toronto, advertising;
ink and digital

→   commons&sense,
illustration #2, 2012
Editorial, Model: Genevieve Alder;
ink and digital

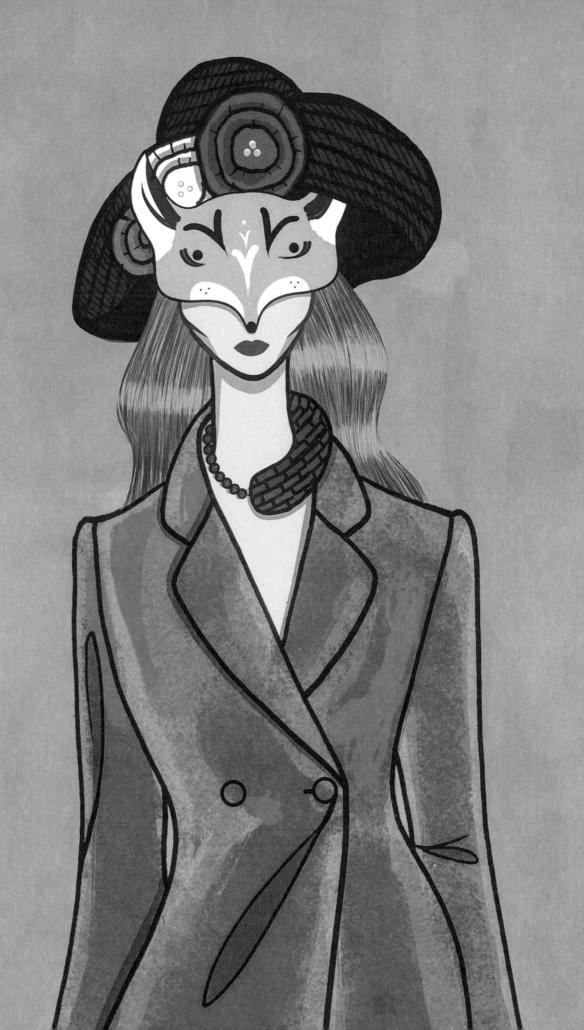

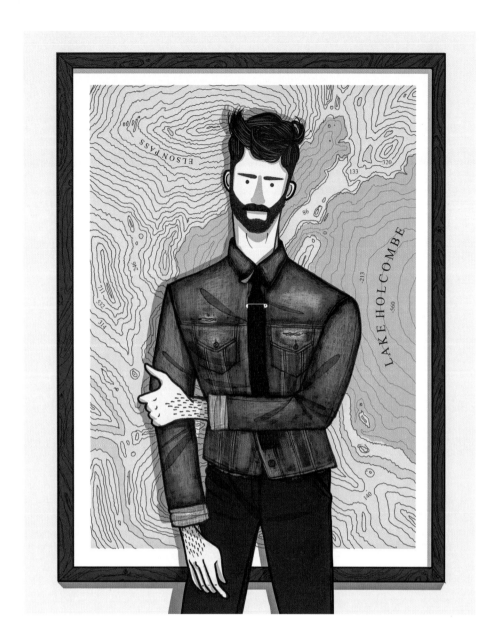

Hudson's Bay Co. Men's Fall
Preview Image #1, 2012
Hudson's Bay Co., Toronto, advertising,
Model: Holcombe Halsey;
ink and digital

→   Room Series Image #1, 2012
Personal work, advertising;
ink and digital

↘   Burkman Bros Fall 2013 Preview
Burkman Bros, advertising;
ink and digital

"Michael Sanderson is an illustrator on the way up.
His unique approach to the classic Pacific Northwest
style has the fashion world taking note."

SARAH YOUNGSON
Writer, Hudson's Bay Company

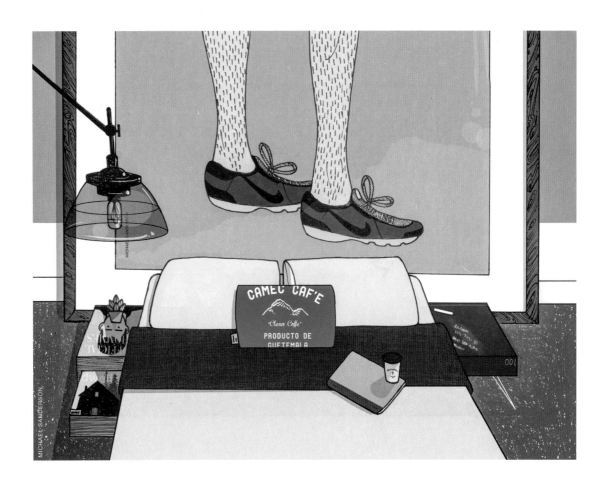

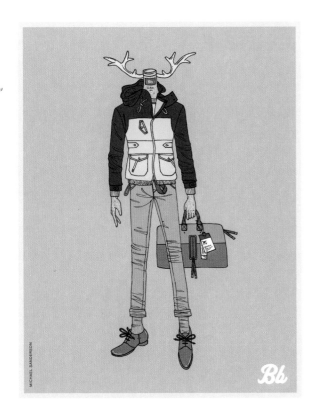

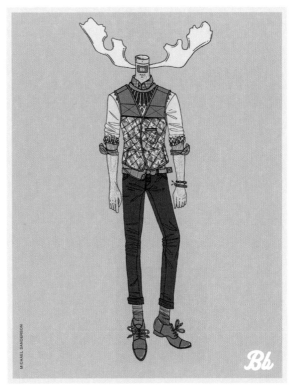

Paula Sanz Caballero

1969 born in Onteniente, Spain | lives and works in Alboraya, Spain
www.paulasanzcaballero.com

CLIENTS
WWD, Neiman Marcus, Inditex, Vogue,
The New Yorker, San Francisco Chronicle,
The Wall Street Journal, Ann Taylor,
Bloomingdale's, Marie Claire, Eckerle

AGENTS
2agenten
Germany
2agenten.com

Traffic Creative
Management
USA
trafficnyc.com

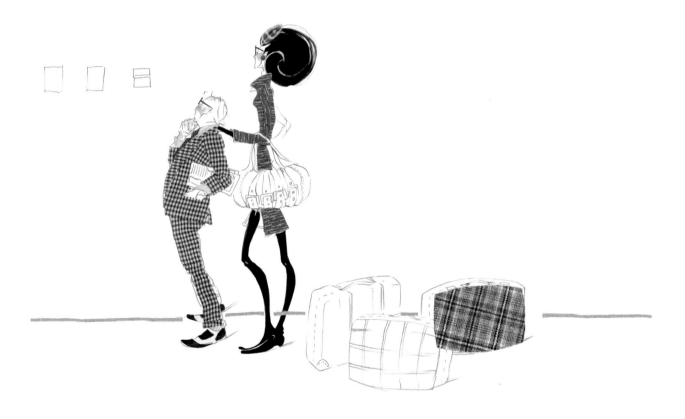

"The fashion that concerns me is the fashion that explains the character of the people wearing it."

„Mich interessiert Mode, die den Charakter
der Menschen erklärt, die sie tragen."

« La mode qui m'intéresse est celle qui révèle
le caractère des gens qui la portent. »

Aloisius and Leoparda Bohlhanseck, 2007
Personal work, exhibition; pencil
and fabrics on paper

→ **Monforte Aristides, 2007**
Personal work, exhibition; graphite,
oil and fabrics on canvas

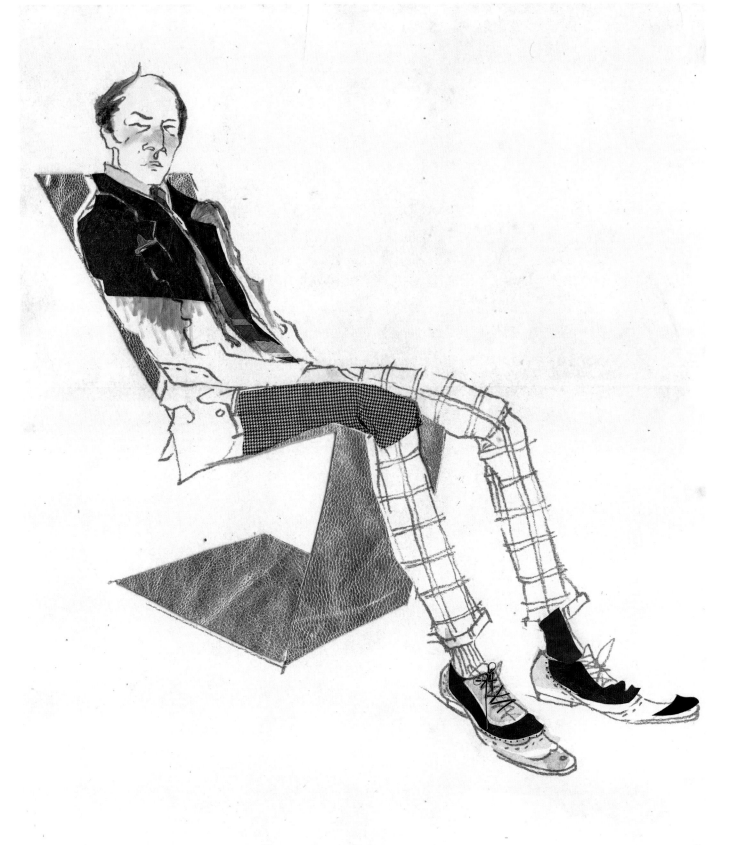

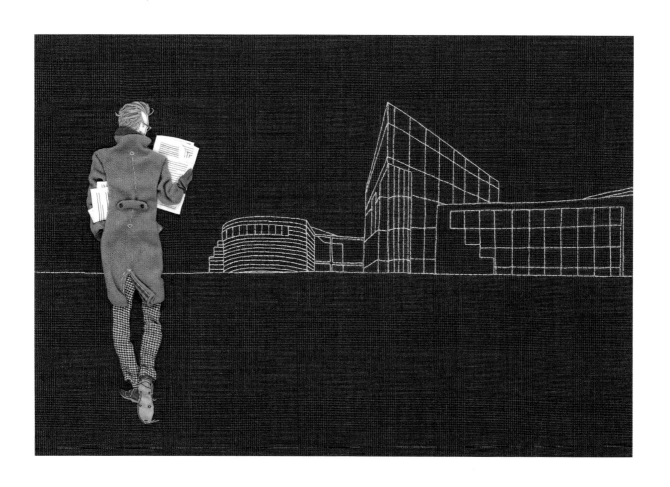

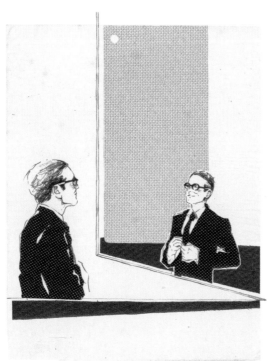

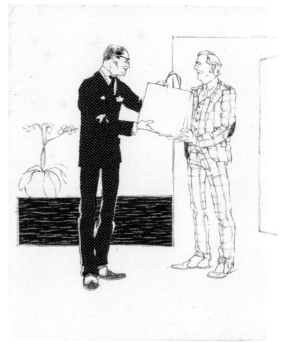

"Paula illustrates the most perfect people, but also
the truth they hide under their outfits – a sophistication
that oozes both love and irony from its seams."

DANIEL BORRÁS
Culture Editor, El Mundo

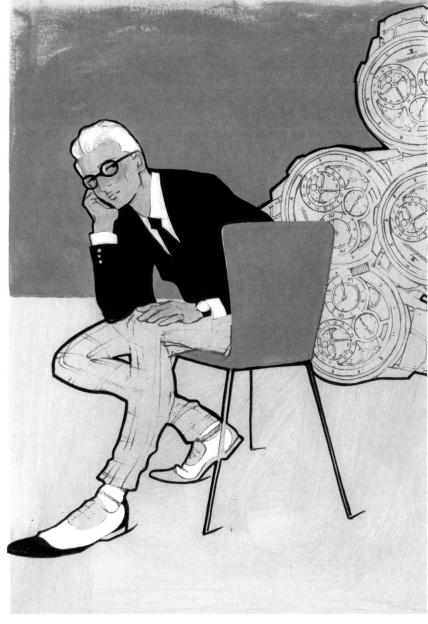

Seated Man Orange, 2010
Elsevier; acrylic on paper

↖   **Arteixo, 2010**
Inditex, annual report; embroidery

←   **Eckerle #6 and #5, 2007**
Eckerle; pencil and fabrics on paper

Marguerite Sauvage

1978 born in Paris | lives and works in Sydney and Paris
www.margueritesauvage.com

CLIENTS
Louis Vuitton, Longchamp, Paul & Joe, Azzaro,
John Lobb, ST Dupont, Swarovski, Christofle,
Galeries Lafayette, Old Navy, Victoria's Secret

AGENTS

Jacky Winter Group
Australia
jackywinter.com

Agence Virginie
France
virginie.fr

Magnet Reps
USA
magnereps.com

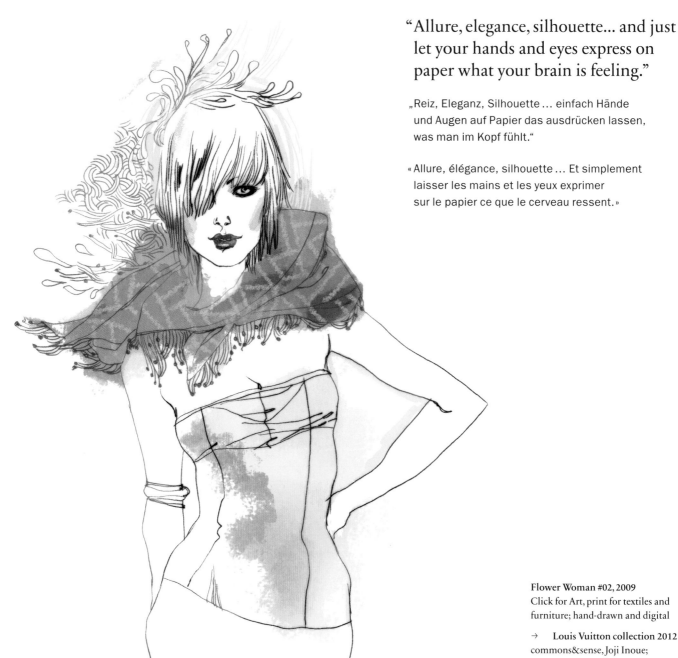

"Allure, elegance, silhouette... and just
let your hands and eyes express on
paper what your brain is feeling."

„Reiz, Eleganz, Silhouette … einfach Hände
und Augen auf Papier das ausdrücken lassen,
was man im Kopf fühlt."

« Allure, élégance, silhouette … Et simplement
laisser les mains et les yeux exprimer
sur le papier ce que le cerveau ressent. »

Flower Woman #02, 2009
Click for Art, print for textiles and
furniture; hand-drawn and digital

→   Louis Vuitton collection 2012
commons&sense, Joji Inoue;
hand-drawn and digital

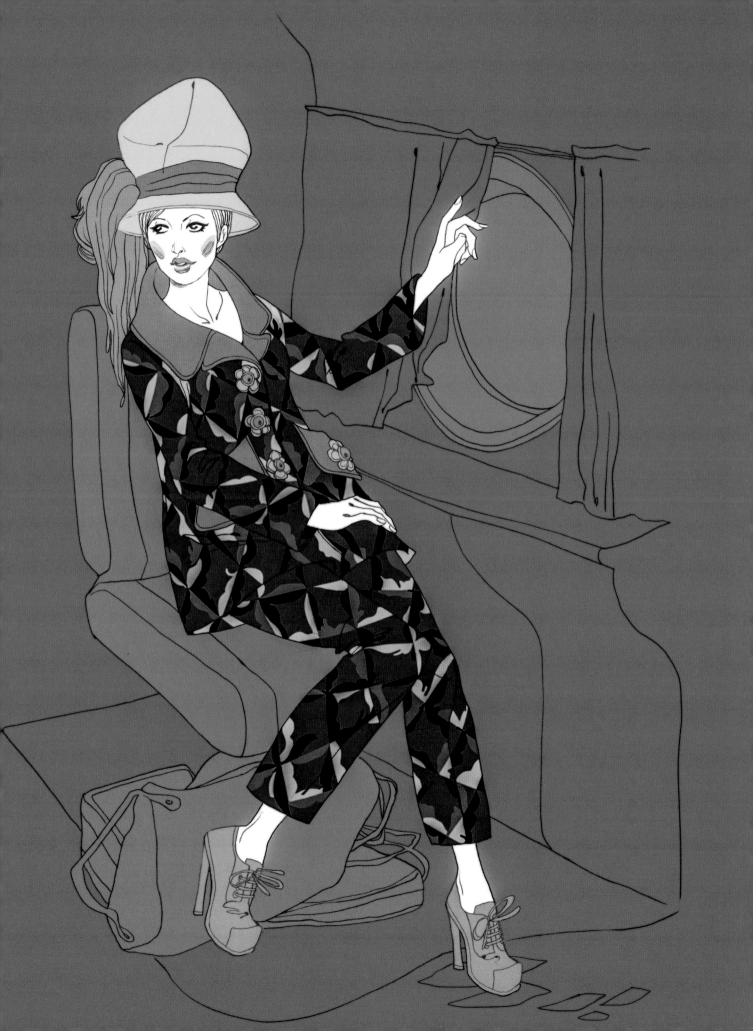

"One of today's most prolific fashion illustrators, blending traditional sensuality with truly modern and expressive line. Nothing short of magic!"

JEREMY WORTSMAN
Owner and Creative Director
Jacky Winter Group

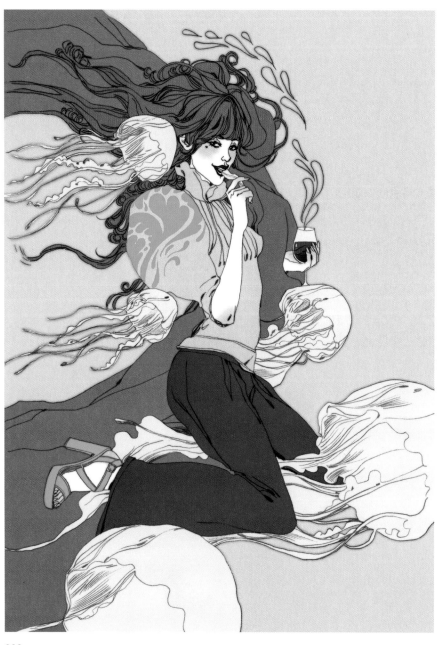

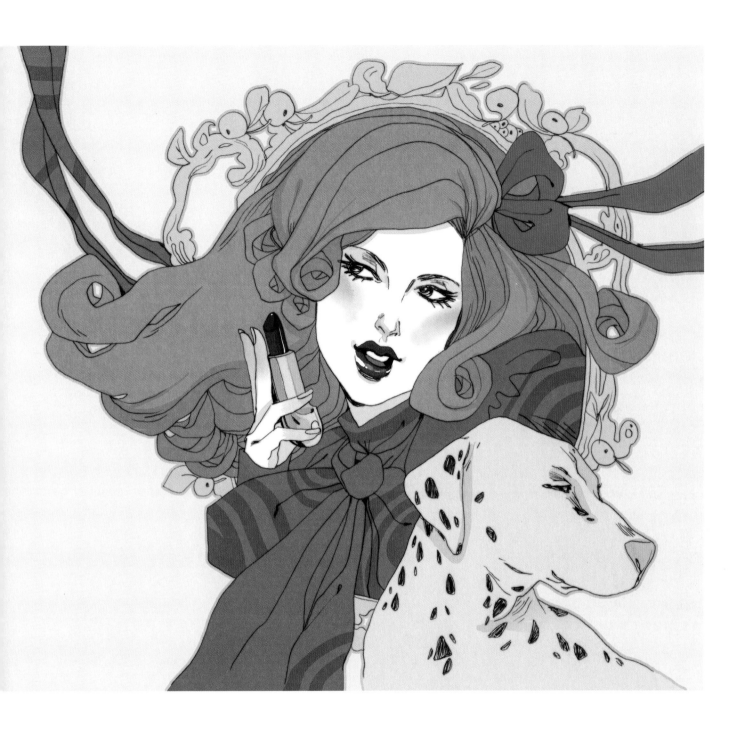

Lipstick and Style, 2011
commons&sense; hand-drawn
and digital

← Jelly-fish, 2010
Virginie, catalog; hand-drawn
and digital

Mariana Silva

1980 born in São Paulo | lives and works in Mexico City and, New York
www.marianasilva.com

CLIENTS
Diane von Furstenberg,
Tommy Hilfiger, OshKosh B'gosh,
Revisited Matters, Stephanie Salas

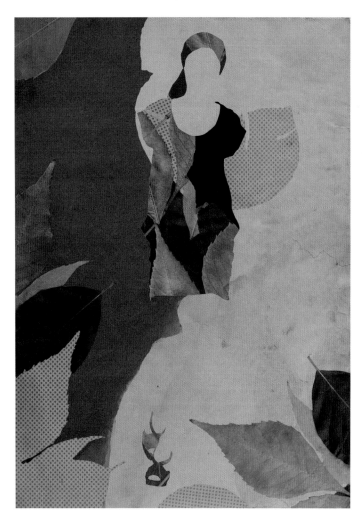

"When doing fashion illustration,
I enjoy creating patterns and
silhouettes to tell stories
inspired by nature."

„Um Fashion zu illustrieren, schaffe
ich gerne Muster und Silhouetten,
die von der Natur inspirierte
Geschichten erzählen."

« Quand je fais de l'illustration de
mode, j'aime créer des motifs et des
silhouettes pour raconter des
histoires inspirées de la nature. »

Leaves #2, 2011
Personal work, T-shirt print;
watercolor and digital

→   **Red #1, 2012**
Personal work, T-shirt print;
collage, watercolor and digital

→→   **Sins #3, 2011**
Personal work, T-shirt print;
collage, watercolor and digital

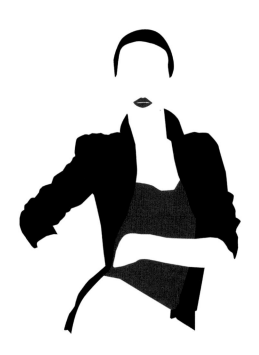

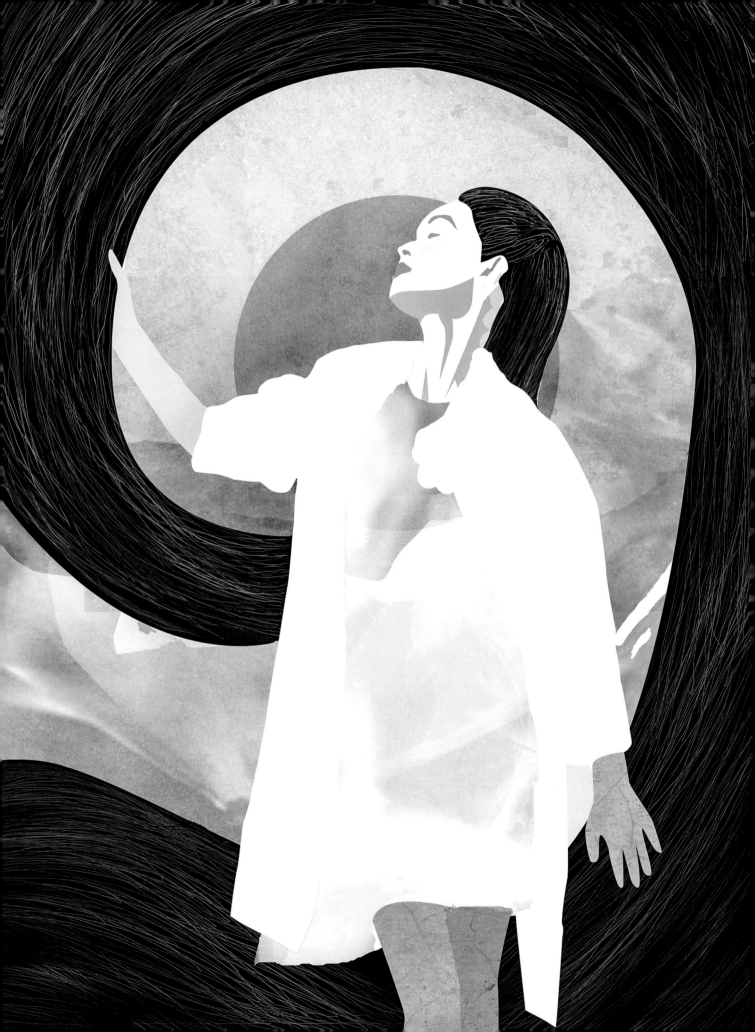

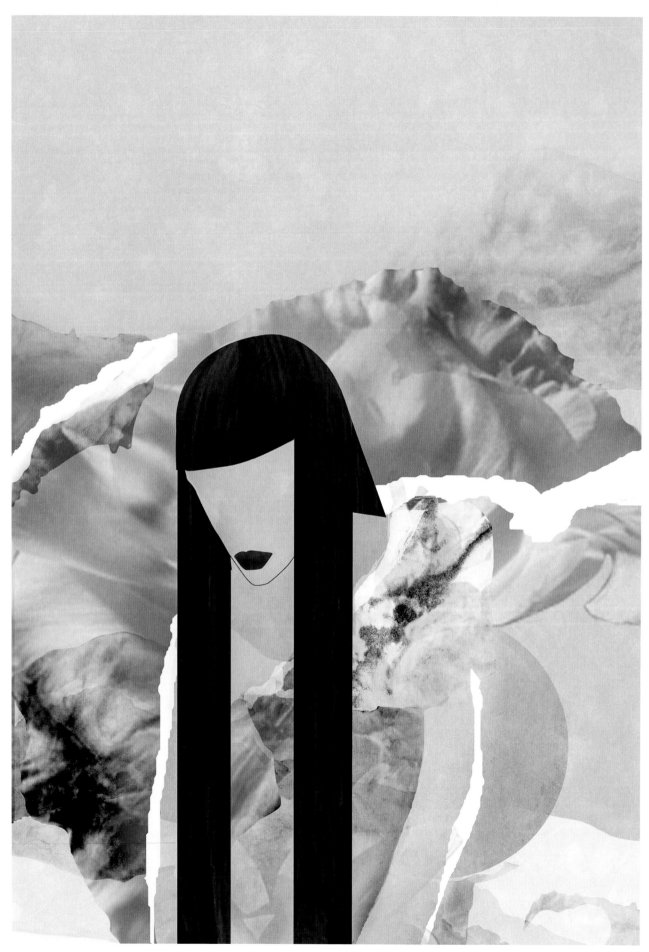

Sins #1 and #2, 2011
Personal work, T-shirt print;
collage, watercolor and digital

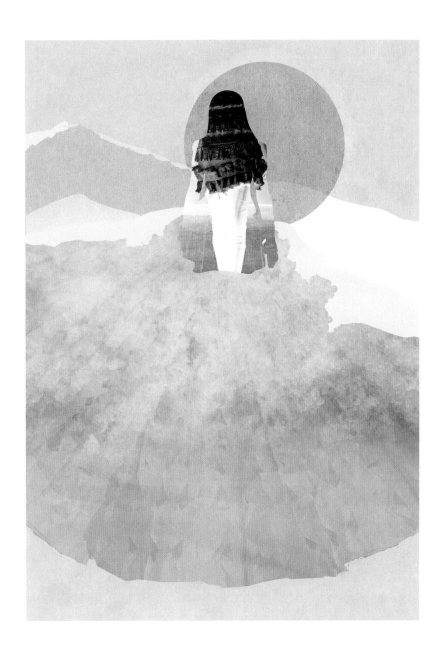

"Mariana's work is a strong, elegant, sophisticated maze.
Time is put on hold while all the details are contemplated
in a world inspired by simple beauty."

GINA WHITEHEAD
Agent and Partner
Artist & Agency

Kelly Smith

1985 born in Hobart, Australia | lives and works in Hobart
www.birdyandme.com.au

CLIENTS
Vogue Australia, H&M, Samantha Wills,
Net-a-Porter, InStyle UK, L'avion, Portmans,
Friend of Mine, ROC Eyewear

AGENT
Illustration Ltd
UK
illustrationweb.com

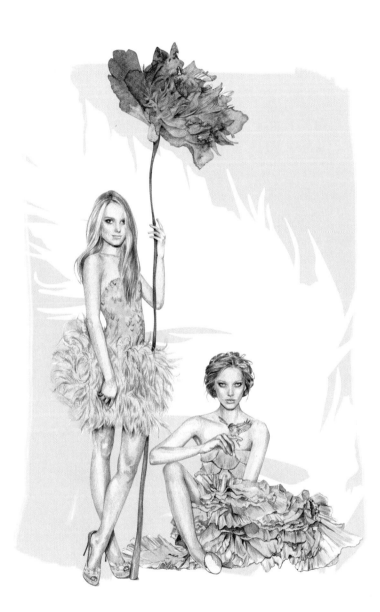

"Fashion illustration is, to me, about capturing the sense of whimsy and theatricality in a garment. It's all about color, texture and line."

„Für mich geht es bei Modeillustrationen darum, in Kleidungsstücken das Launische und Theatralische zu entdecken, und zwar mit Farbe, Textur und Linic."

«Pour moi, l'illustration de mode c'est capter la fantaisie et la théâtralité d'un vêtement. Tout est dans la couleur, la texture et le trait.»

L'avion, 2011
L'avion, print on silk scarf;
pencil, watercolor and digital

→ Interlude, 2012
Personal work; pencil and digital

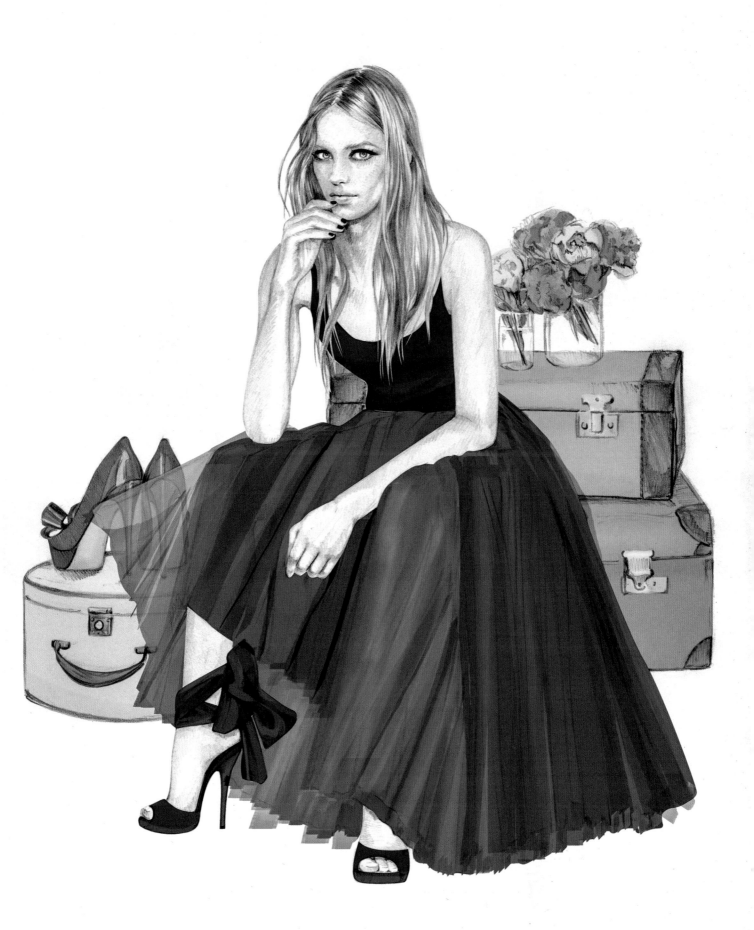

"Her ability to transport you into her beautiful world with whimsical pencil & watercolor illustrations is divinely intoxicating."

SAMANTHA WILLS
Designer and Director
Samantha Wills

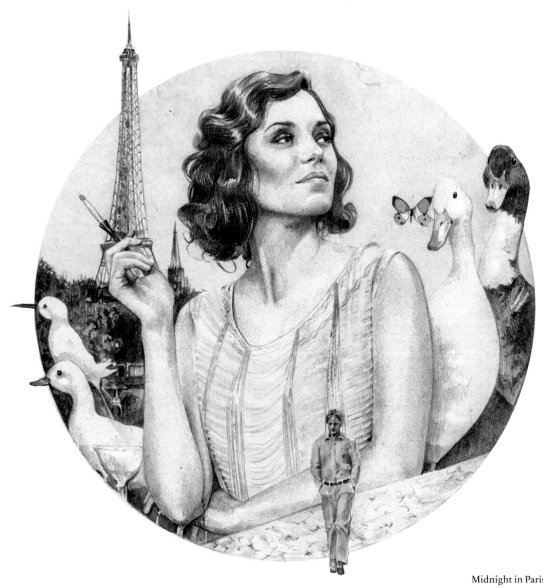

Midnight in Paris, 2011
Personal work, based on Marion Cotillard in Woody Allen's film *Midnight in Paris*; pencil and digital

→ Alexander McQueen
Couture Spring/Summer 2011
The Hub; pencil and digital

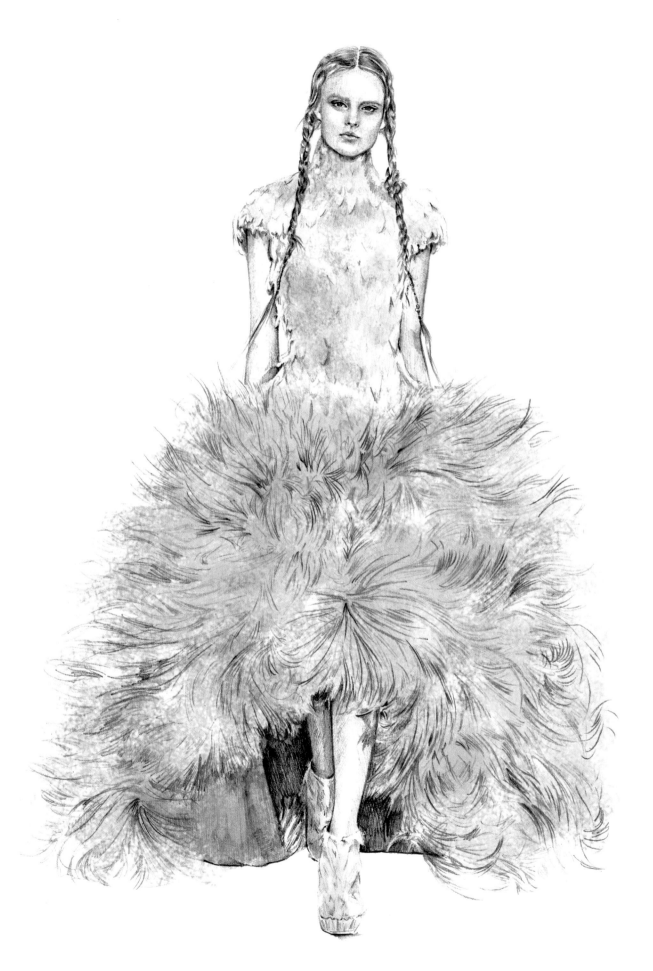

Deanna Staffo

1982 born in Pippa Passes, USA | lives and works in Baltimore
www.deannastaffo.com

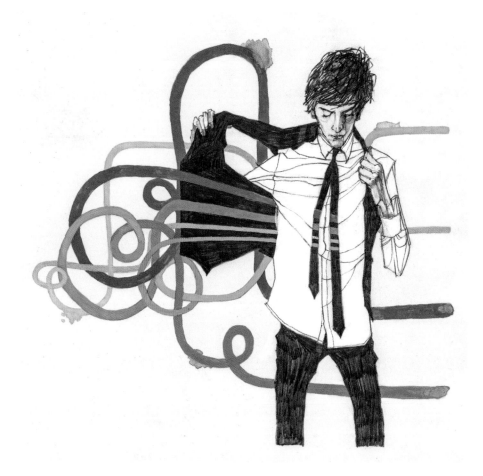

"I try to find a way to capture the mood of the clothing while also telling a little bit of a story beyond that."

„Ich versuche die Stimmung eines Kleidungsstückes einzufangen und gleichzeitig ein wenig die Geschichte dahinter zu erzählen."

« J'essaie de trouver le moyen de capter l'esprit du vêtement tout en racontant aussi une petite histoire au-delà de cela. »

He Explodes Rainbows, 2010
Personal work; graphite and acrylic

→   Dovima Handstand, 2010
Personal work; charcoal and acrylic

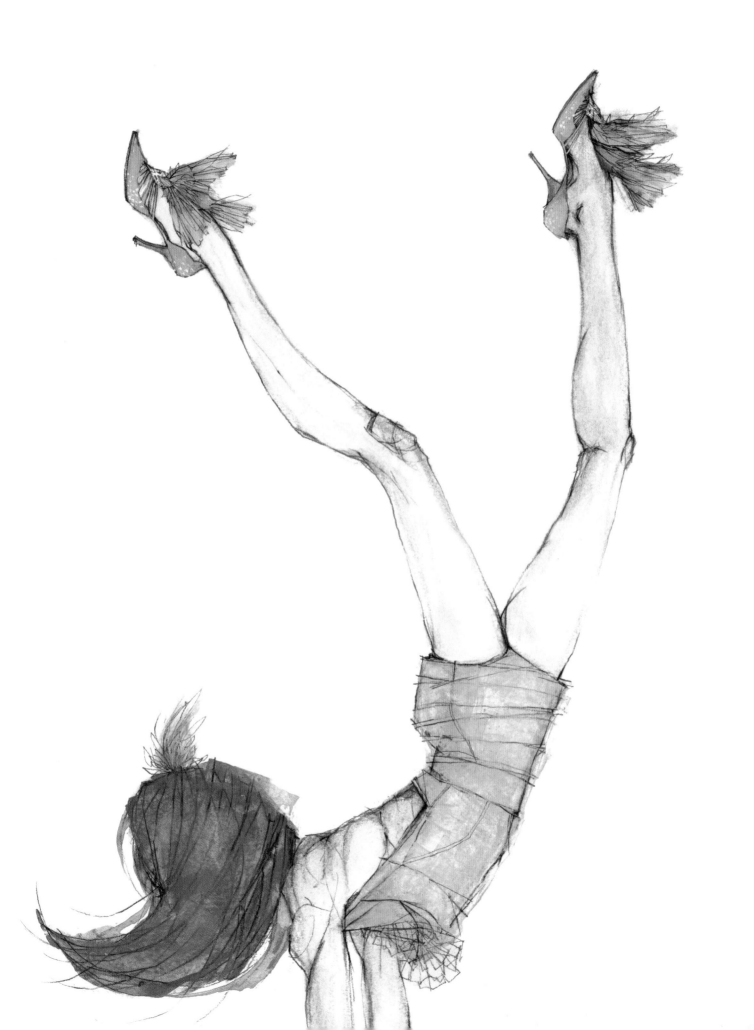

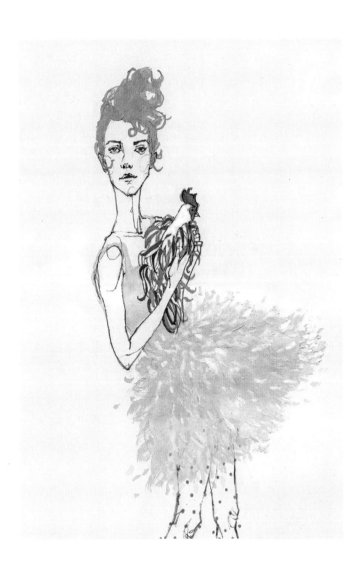

←   Rooster, 2010
Personal work; graphite and acrylic

→   Rabbit, 2011
Personal work; graphite and acrylic

↙   Yellow Scarf, 2011
Personal work; graphite and acrylic

↓   Bows and Braids, 2012
Personal work; graphite and acrylic

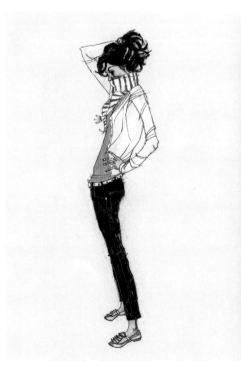

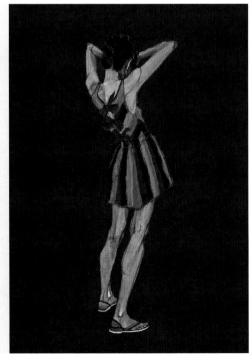

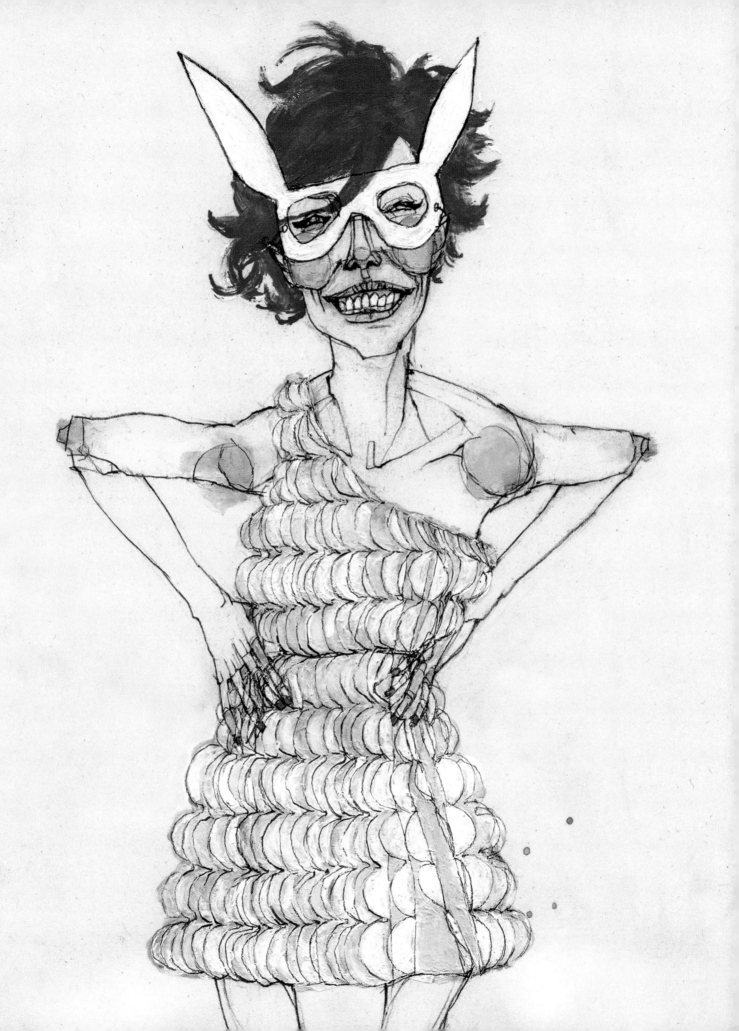

Izziyana Suhaimi

1986 born in Singapore | lives and works in Singapore
www.my-bones.tumblr.com

CLIENTS
Shop magazine,
Catalog magazine,
L'ile aux Ashby

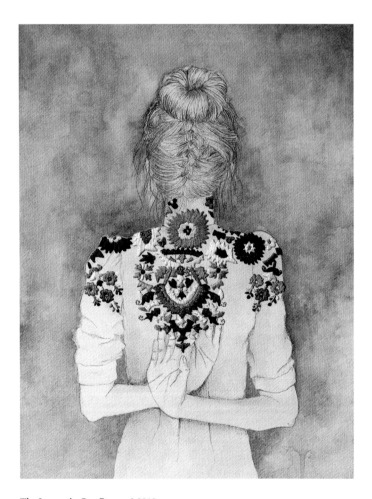

The Looms in Our Bones, 6, 2012
Personal work, exhibition; embroidery,
pencil and watercolor on paper

→   Untitled, 2012
Nylon magazine, Singapore,
interpretation of magazine cover;
embroidery and glitter on calico

→→ **Friends to Keep You Warm, 2011**
Personal work; embroidery, pen and
watercolor on paper

"A sense of wonder and
play, a little bit of mystery
and always having fun."

„Das Gefühl des Staunens und
Spielens, eine Prise Geheimnis
und immer viel Spaß."

«Une touche d'émerveillement
et de jeu, un peu de mystère,
toujours dans un esprit ludique.»

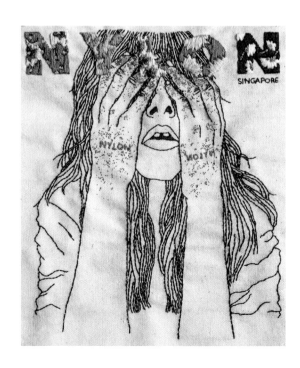

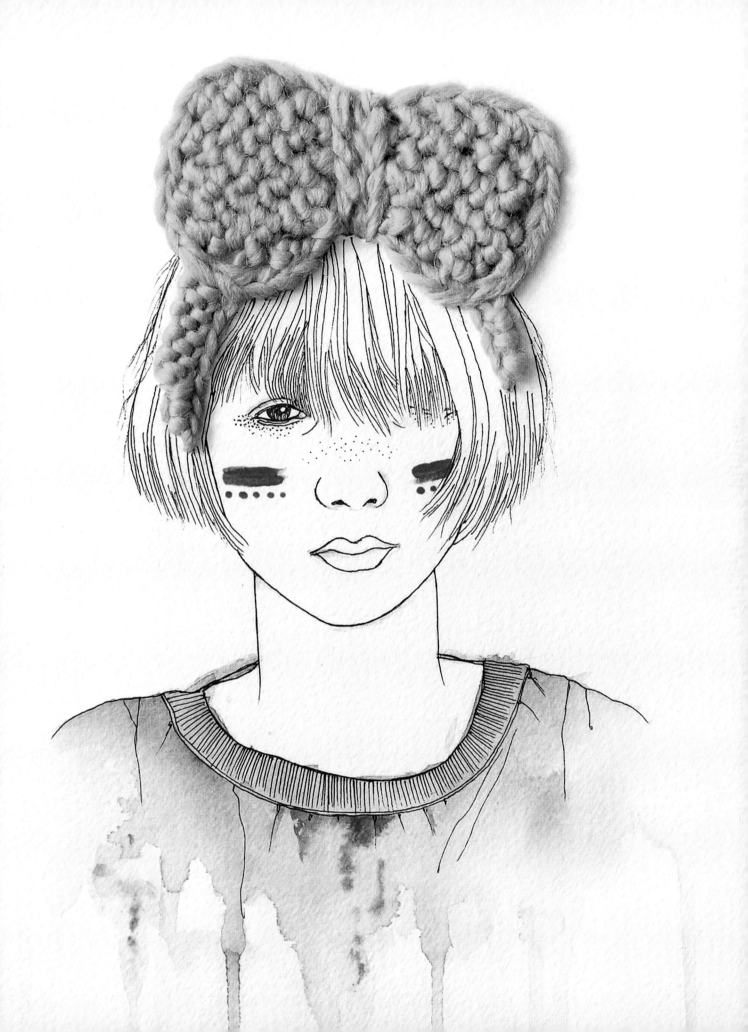

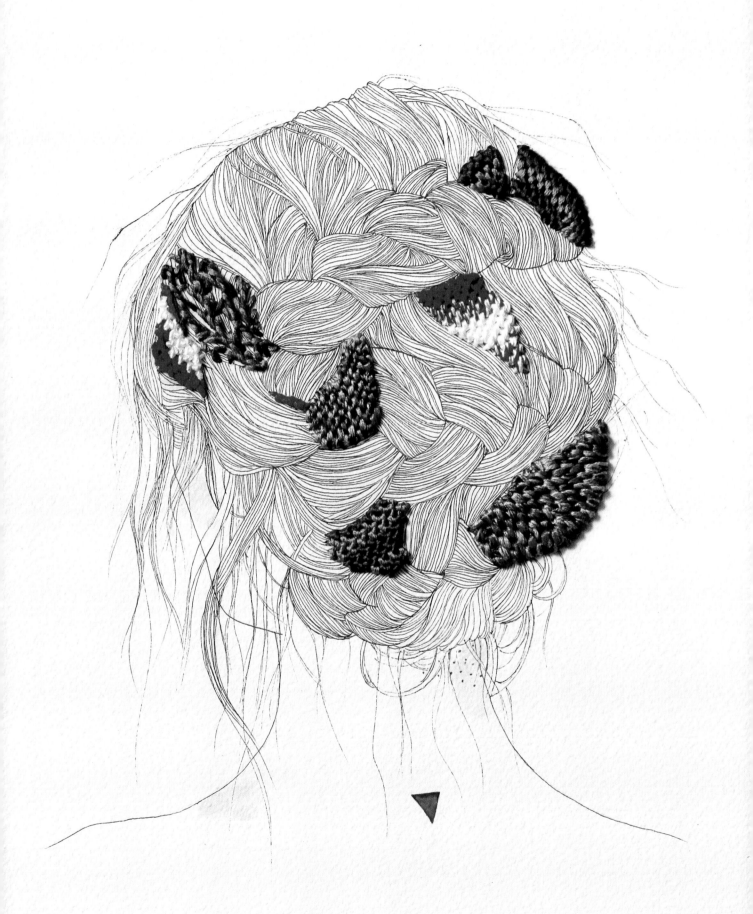

"A visual phenomenon that pushes the boundaries of the traditional and the new, a unique use of media which pulls the viewer in to examine the exquisite details."

ASH
Creative Director
Catalog magazine

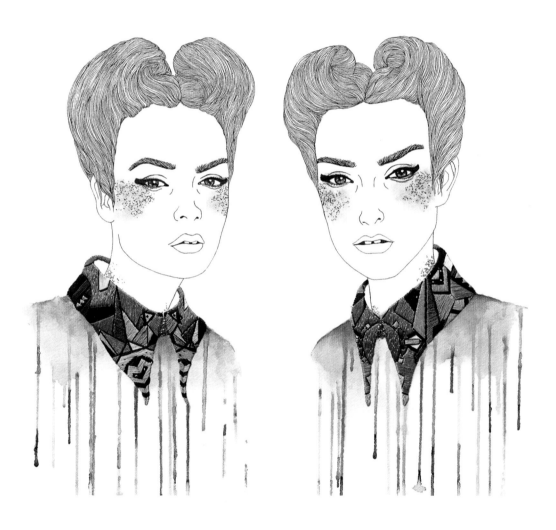

Friends to Keep You Warm, 2012
Collaboration with L'ile aux Ashby;
embroidery, pen, watercolor and
glitter on paper

←   **Friends to Keep You Warm, 2011**
Personal work; embroidery, pen and
watercolor on paper

Sandra Suy

1977 born in Barcelona | lives and works in Barcelona
www.sandrasuy.com

CLIENTS
The Economist, Van Cleef & Arpels, Chloé,
Elle, Glamour magazine, The Sunday Times, Zara,
L'Oréal, Max Factor, Triumph, Skoda, Pinko, H&M

AGENTS

Jelly London
UK
jellylondon.com

Ve Art
France
ve-art.com

2DM
Italy
2dm.it

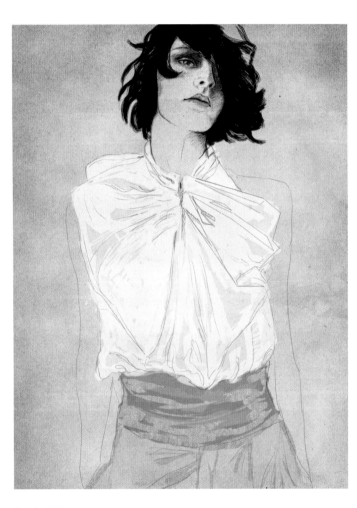

"Fashion is fun, creativity,
    it's a game for adults to play.
    I enjoy my job a lot!"

„Fashion ist Spaß, Kreativität,
    ein Spiel für Erwachsene.
    Ich genieße meine Arbeit zutiefst!"

« La mode, c'est le jeu, la créativité,
    c'est un jeu pour les adultes.
    J'aime beaucoup mon travail ! »

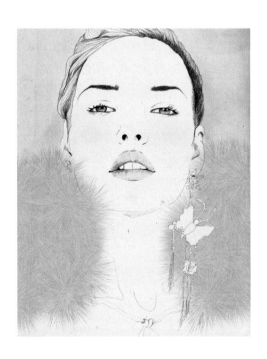

Lanvin, 2008
Personal work; mixed media
and digital

→   Adrienne, 2008
Personal work, utilized for
Zara Perfumes 2010–11;
mixed media and digital

→→ Gabrielle, 2008
Personal work; mixed media
and digital

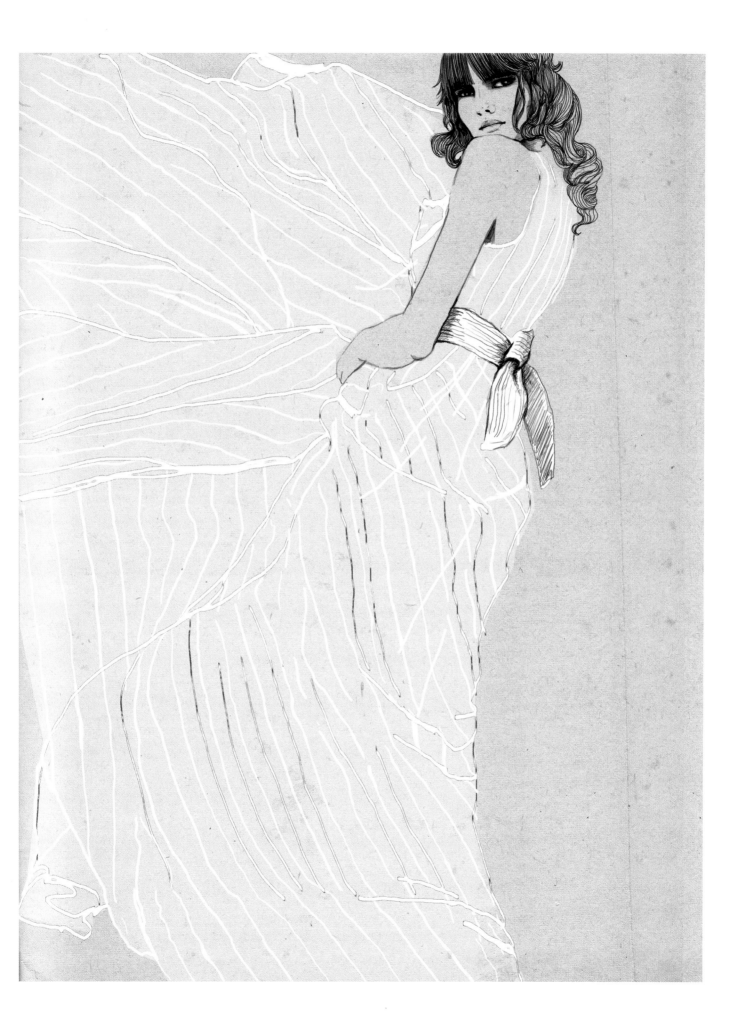

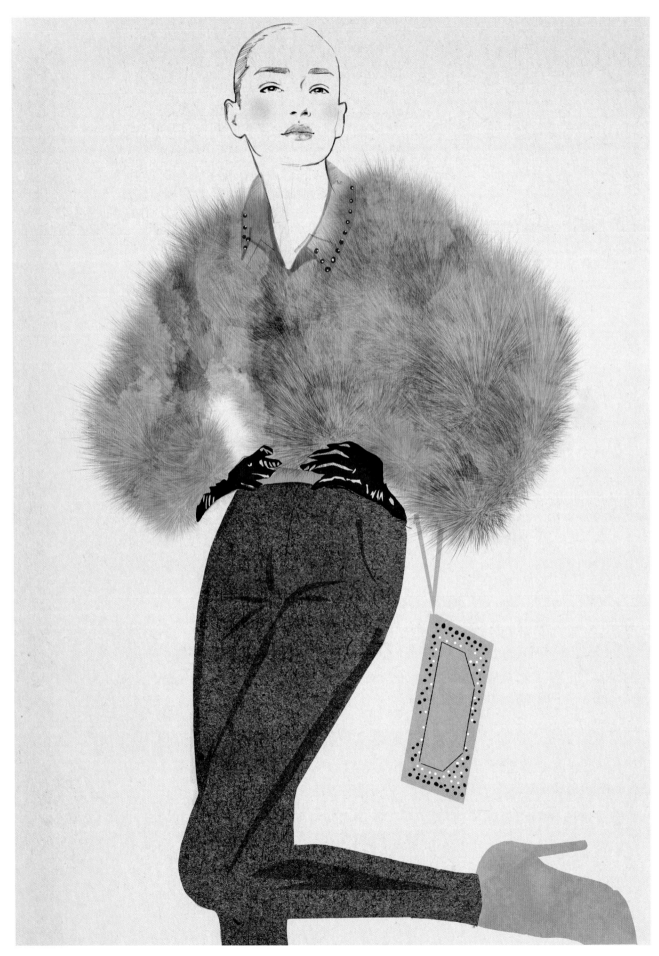

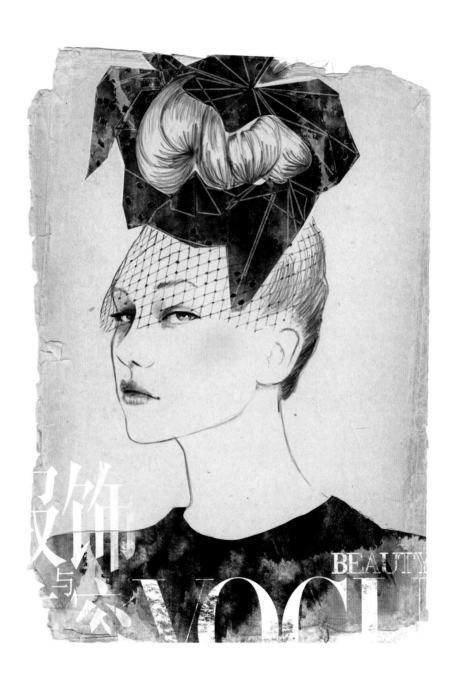

Vogue Japan, 2010
Personal work; mixed media
and digital

←   **Fur, 2012**
Pinko, lookbook; mixed media
and digital

Rush, 2009
Chew magazine; mixed media
and digital

↓   **Jeanne, 2008**
Personal work; mixed media
and digital

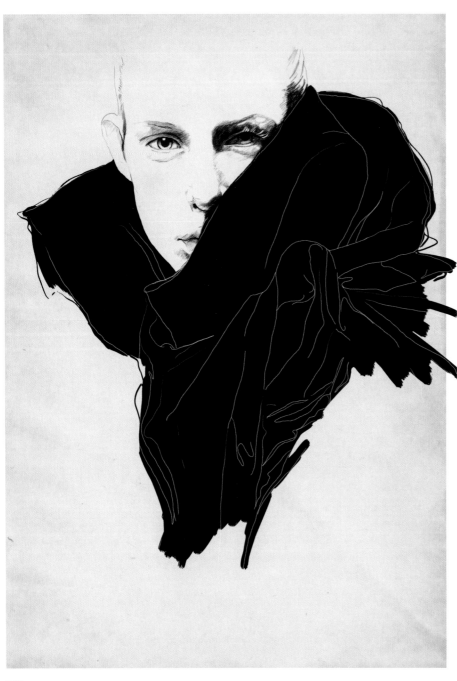

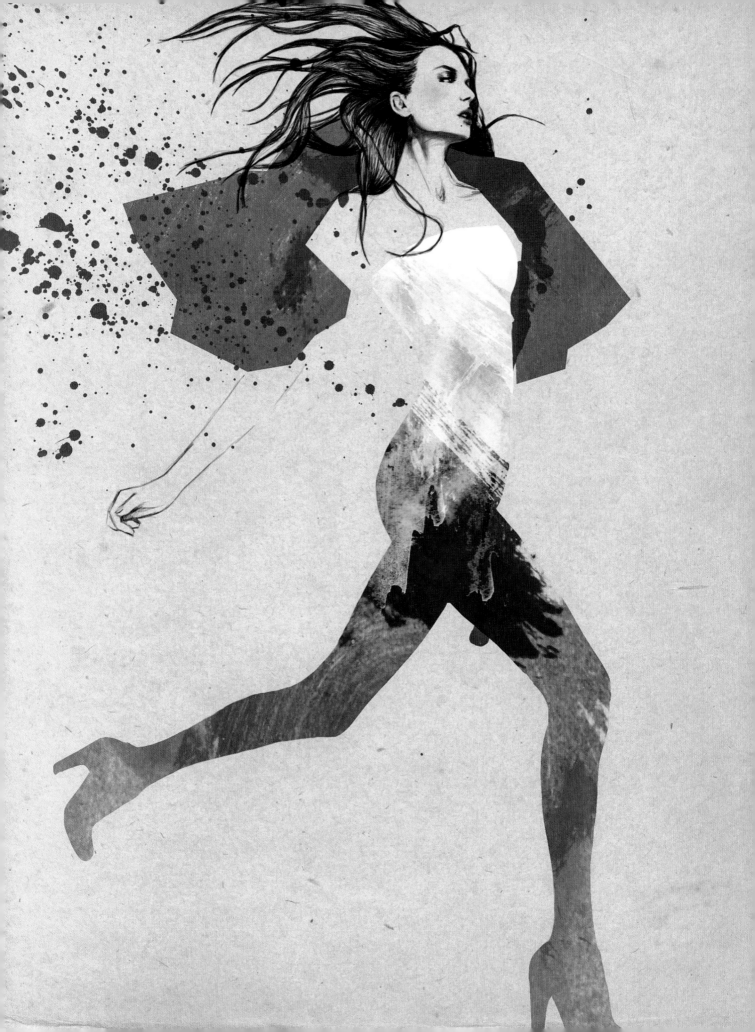

Hiroshi Tanabe

born in Japan | lives and works in New York
www.hiroshitanabe.com

CLIENTS
Anna Sui, Shiseido, The New York Times, Barneys,
The New Yorker, Lloyd & Co, Gap, LeSportsac,
Vogue UK, Ann Taylor, Rolling Stone

AGENT
Jed Root Inc
USA
jedroot.com

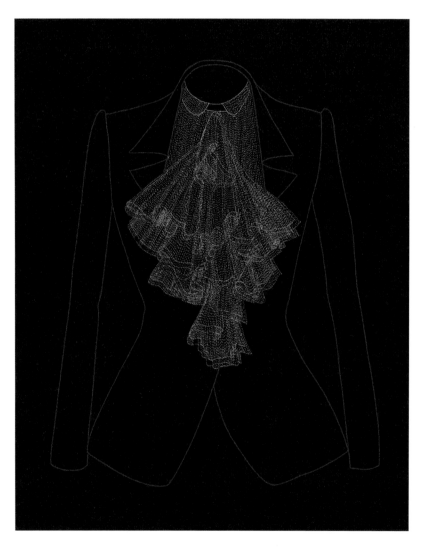

"Illustration can portray
fashion in ways that
are more exaggerated
and more personal."

„Illustrationen können Fashion
auf mehr als übertriebene und
persönliche Weise porträtieren."

« L'illustration peut donner une
image plus exagéréc ct plus
personnelle de la mode. »

Irene Cocktail Suit (c. 1950 USA), 2010
S magazine; pen and digital

→ Untitled, 2011
Shop Iza, website; pen and digital

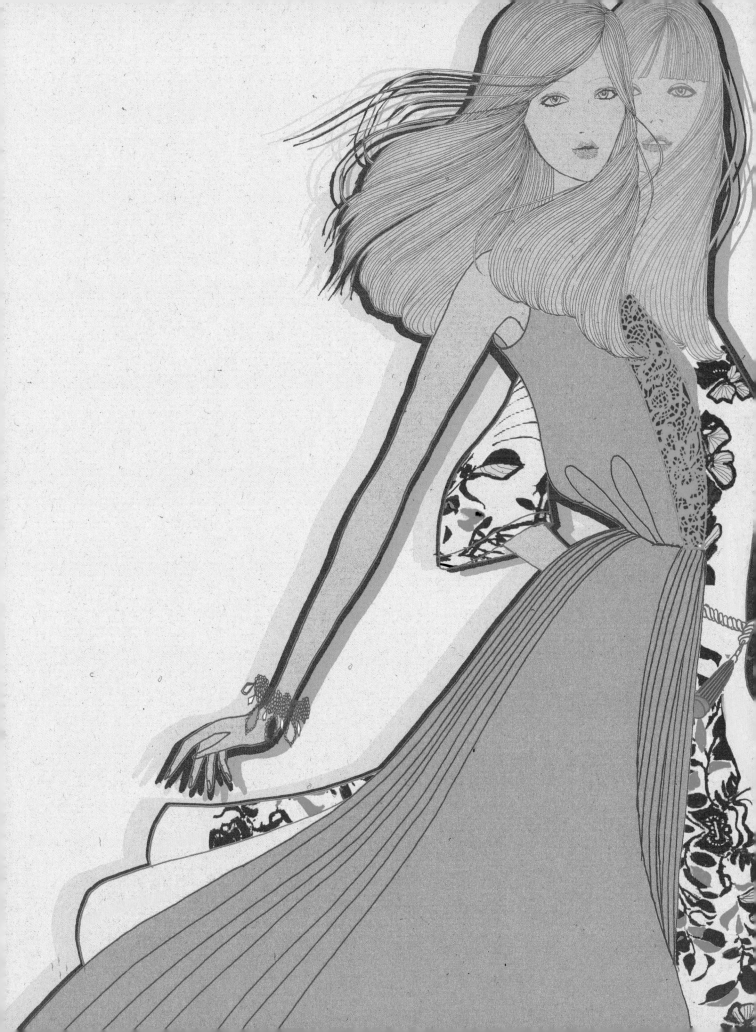

Untitled, 2011
Shop Iza, website; pen and digital

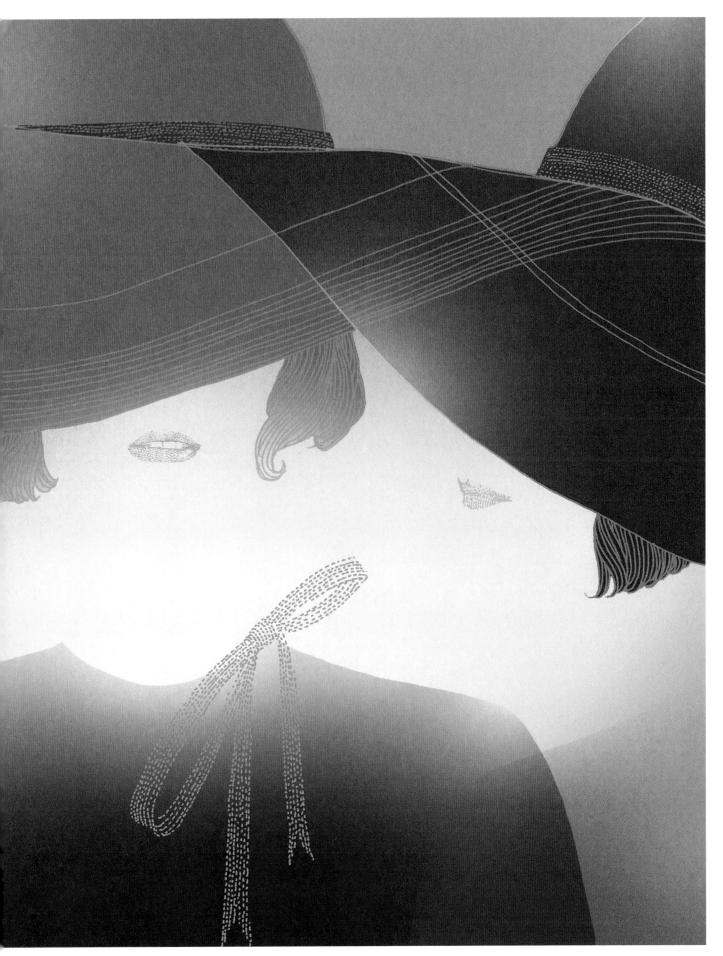

Eveline Tarunadjaja

1983 born in Surabaya, Indonesia | lives and works in Melbourne
www.lovexevol.com

CLIENTS
Gorman,
Anna Sui, Hurley

AGENT
CWC International
USA
cwc-i.com

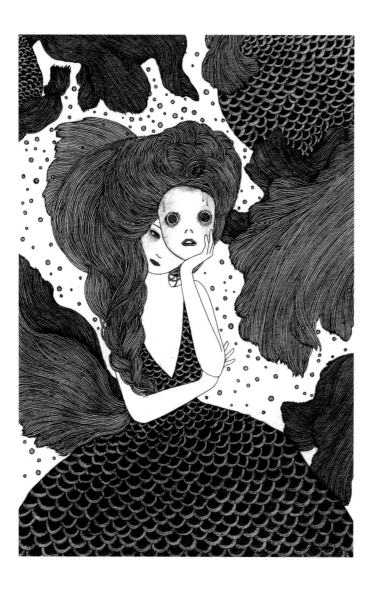

"I like drawing intricate patterns and textures to create images that are not just about fashion but also allude to a more intriguing story."

„Ich zeichne gerne komplizierte Muster und Strukturen für Bilder, bei denen es nicht nur um Mode geht, sondern die auch auf eine noch erstaunlichere Story hindeuten."

« J'aime dessiner des motifs et des textures complexes pour créer des images qui font allusion à une histoire plus intrigante que la mode elle-même. »

Skin, 2011
Personal work; ink and
watercolor on paper

→　Red Robin, 2011
Personal work; ink and
watercolor on paper

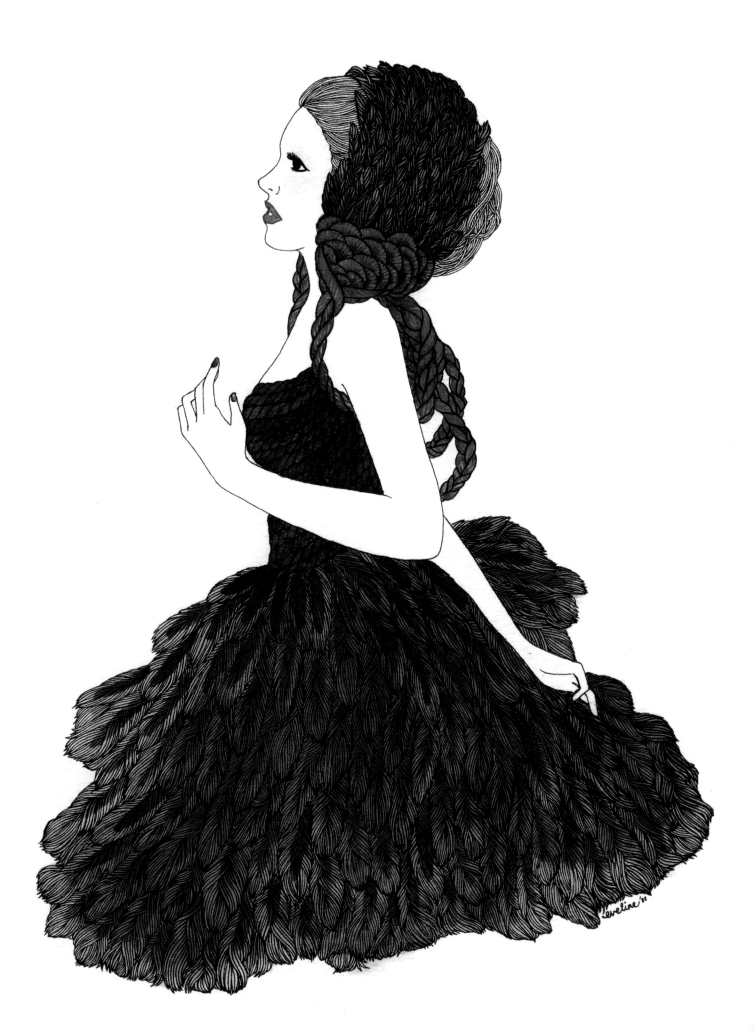

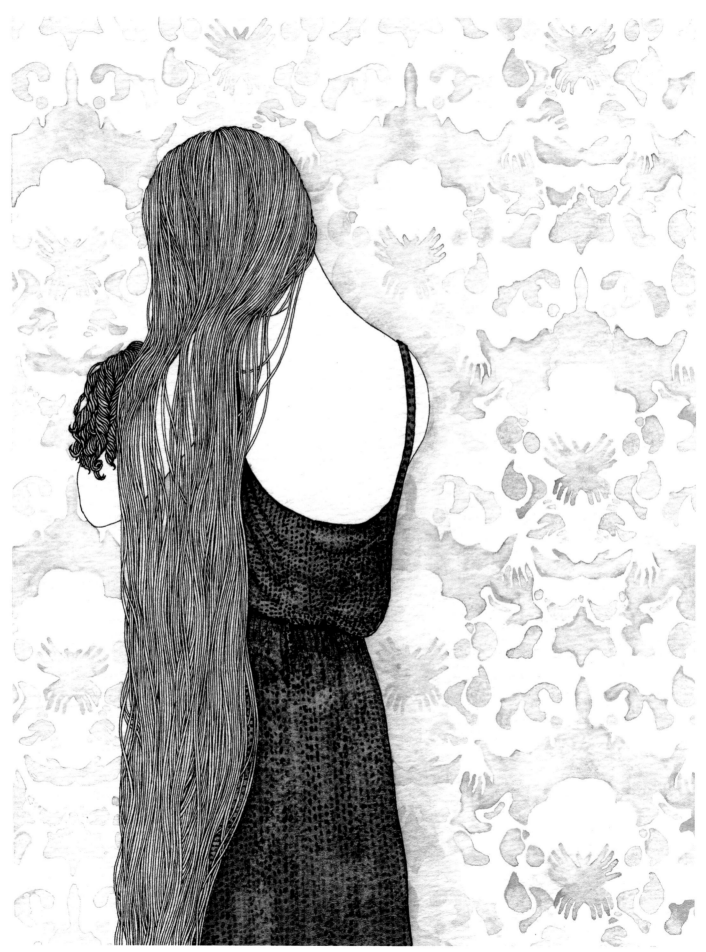

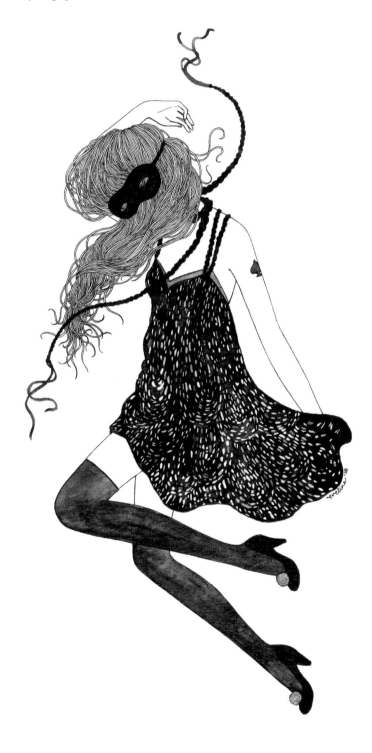

"Eveline's daily outfit series for our magazine resulted in a charmingly thoughtful, humorous piece that gave insight into a girl's everyday life."

KATE FINNIGAN
Style Director, Stella magazine,
The Sunday Telegraph

Masked, 2010
Personal work; ink and
watercolor on paper

← **Lullaby, 2011**
Personal work, exhibition;
ink and watercolor on paper

Luis Tinoco

1976 born in Barcelona | lives and works in Barcelona
www.luistinoco.com

CLIENTS
Flare, Glamour magazine, InStyle,
Yo Dona, Cosmopolitan, Top magazine,
Mia magazine, El País, +81, MTV,
Estée Lauder, Juicy Couture, Benetton

AGENTS
Lemonade
illustration agency
UK
lemonadeillustration.com

Make-up
Spain
agenciamakeup.com

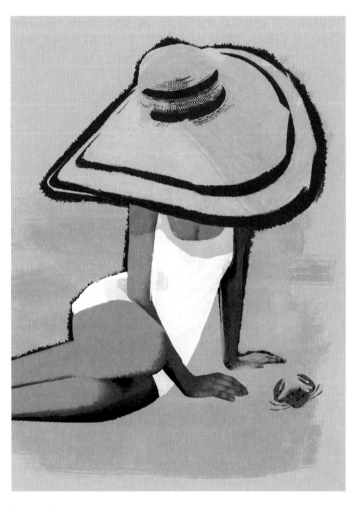

"I've been passionate about fashion
and illustration since I was a child.
The possibility of combining
my two favorite interests into
a career is marvelous."

„Seit Kindertagen beschäftige ich mich
leidenschaftlich mit Mode und Illustration.
Fabelhaft, diese beiden Lieblingsinteressen
beruflich kombinieren zu können!"

« Je me passionne pour la mode et l'illustration
depuis mon enfance. C'est fabuleux
de pouvoir combiner mes deux marottes
préférées dans mon métier. »

Summer Day, 2011
Juicy Couture, store display;
watercolor and digital

→ **Sasha Pivovarova, 2010**
Flare magazine; watercolor and digital

→→ **Aries, 2011**
Mia magazine; watercolor and digital

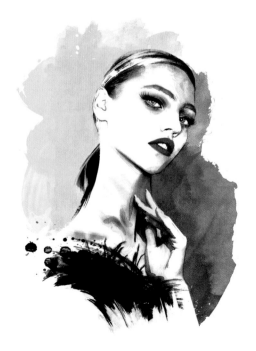

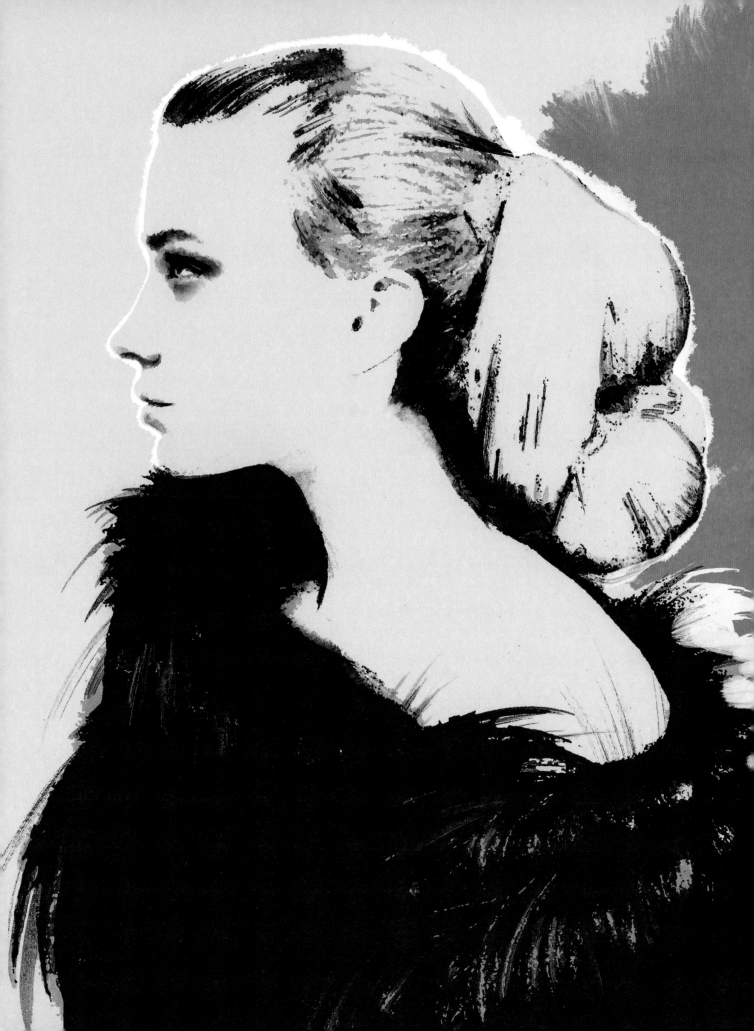

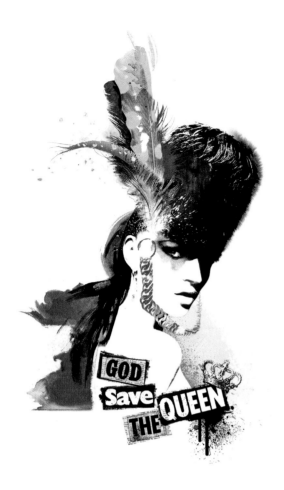

"Smart, intuitive, versatile and, of course, creative. Luis helps us in *Glamour* to communicate difficult concepts with the beauty required. A Friend."

JESÚS ALONSO
Art Director
Glamour magazine

Kate Moss
"God Save The Queen", 2008
Glamour magazine; watercolor
and digital

→   Agyness Deyn, 2009
Glamour magazine; watercolor
and digital

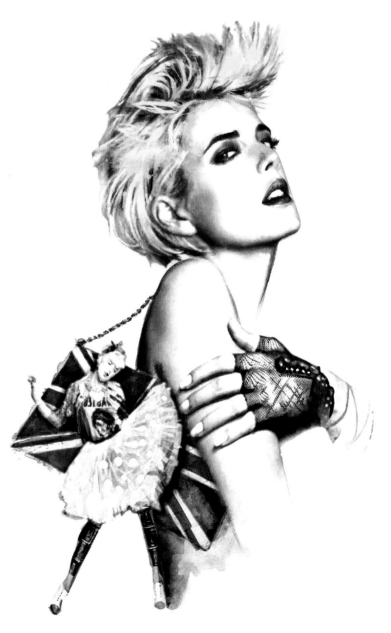

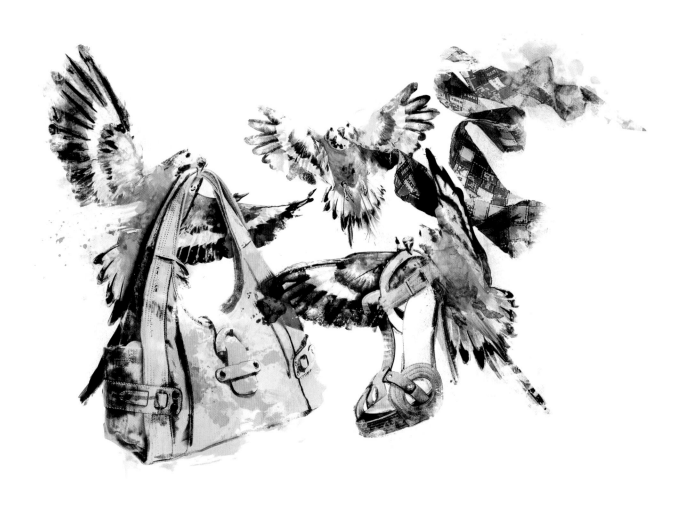

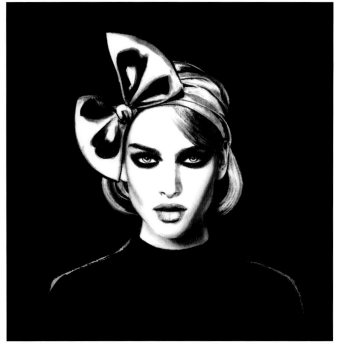

↑   **Summer Fashion Trends, 2009**
Top magazine, e-journal; watercolor
and digital

→   **Bow Girl, 2011**
Ontop "Head and Hair Accessories";
shop window and LED screen;
watercolor and digital

Fredrik Tjernström

1977 born in Uppsala | lives and works in Stockholm
www.fredriktjernstrom.com

CLIENTS
H&M, Oscar Jacobson,
Minimarket, Greta,
Fashion Tale magazine

AGENT
Agent Bauer
Sweden
agentbauer.com

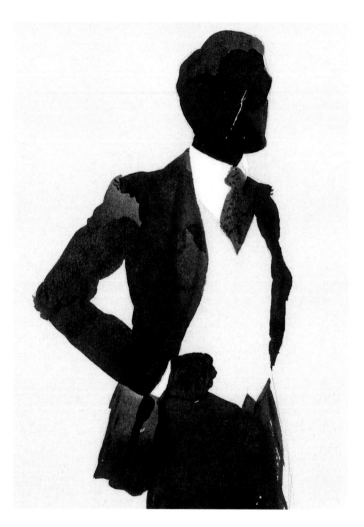

"My approach to fashion illustration is similar to my other work – I try to focus on detail and strong composition."

„Modeillustrationen gehe ich so an wie meine sonstige Arbeit: Ich konzentriere mich aufs Detail und die kraftvolle Komposition."

« Mon approche de l'illustration de mode est similaire à mes autres travaux – j'essaie de privilégier les détails et une composition solide. »

Brawler #4 and #1, 2010
Personal work; ink and gouache
on colored paper

→→ **Oscar Jacbson #1, 2012**
Oscar Jacobson, Art Direction:
Magnus Löwenhielm; ink and
gouache on colored paper

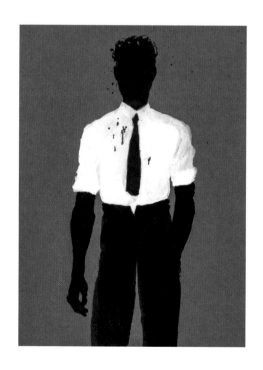

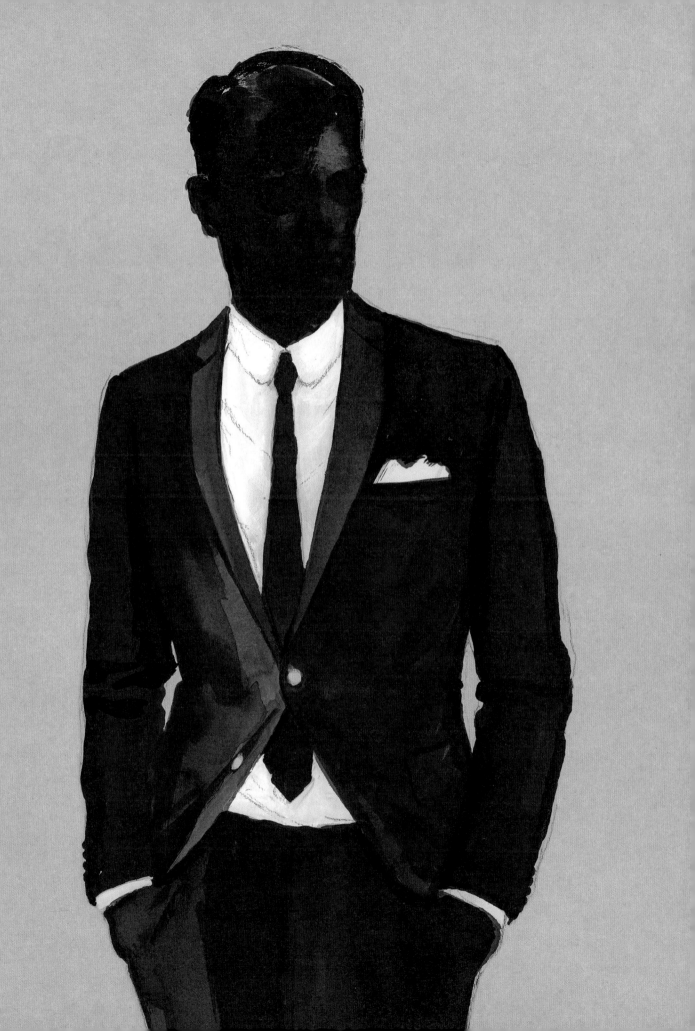

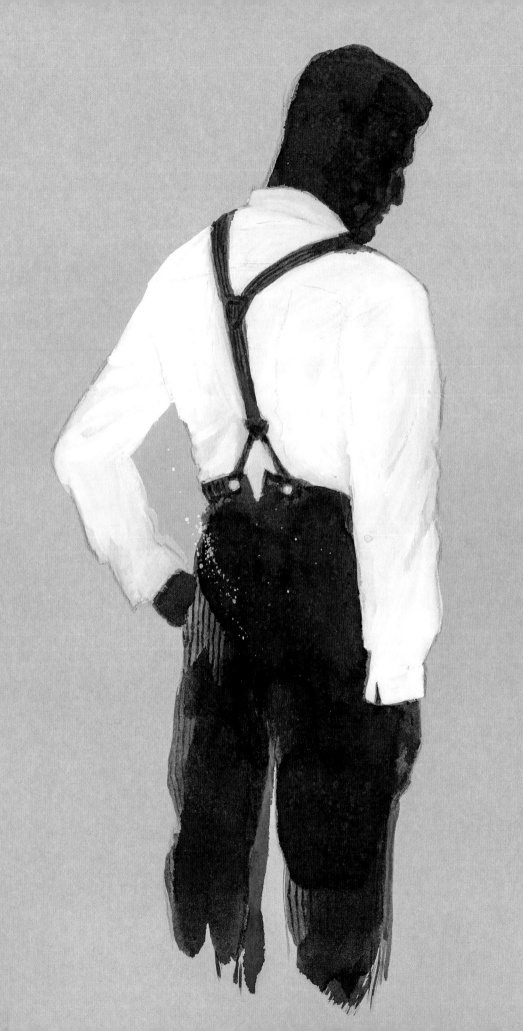

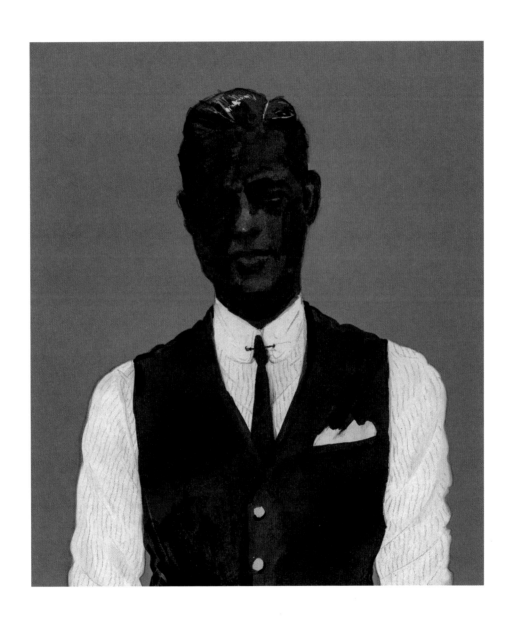

Oscar Jacobson #2, 2012
Oscar Jacobson, Art Direction:
Magnus Löwenhielm; ink and
gouache on colored paper

← **Brawler #3, 2010**
Personal work; ink and gouache
on colored paper

Ruben Toledo

1961 born in Havana | lives and works in New York

CLIENTS
Vogue, Interview, Paper magazine,
Harper's Bazaar, The New York Times,
The New Yorker, Visionaire,
Louis Vuitton, Nordstrom

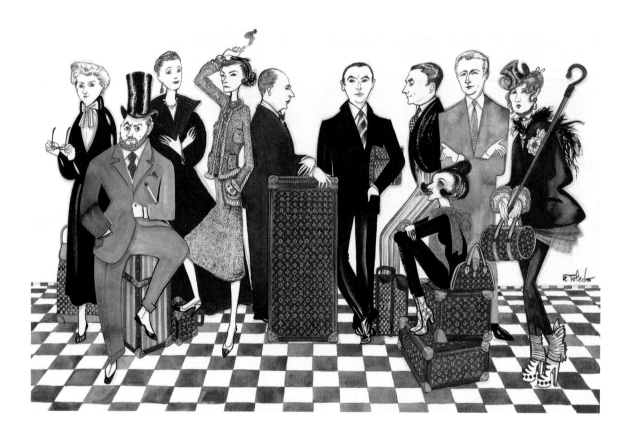

"For me, style is content. I let the clothes, the woman, the mood and the style form the composition. Clothing tells a story, and my focus is to listen and communicate that story through art."

„Stil ist für mich der Inhalt. Meine Kompositionen werden durch die Kleidung, die Frau, die Stimmung und den Stil geformt. Fashion erzählt eine Geschichte, und ich konzentriere mich darauf, diese Geschichte mittels Kunst zu erzählen."

«Pour moi, le style est un contenu. Je laisse les vêtements, la femme, l'atmosphère et le style former la composition. Les vêtements racontent une histoire, et je la retransmets à travers l'art.»

Designer Friends
From the series How Louis Vuitton entered the Fashion World, *Louis Vuitton The Birth of Modern Luxury*, Editions de La Martinière, Paris, 2005; watercolor

→   **Web Women, 2012**
Tiffany & Co., Internet watches; watercolor

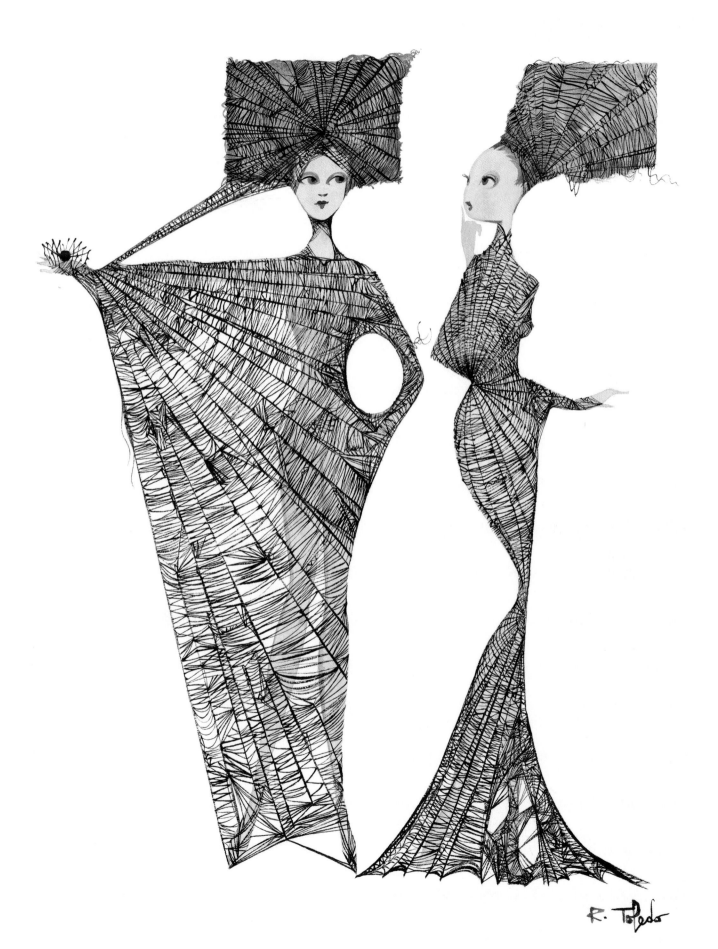

R. Toledo

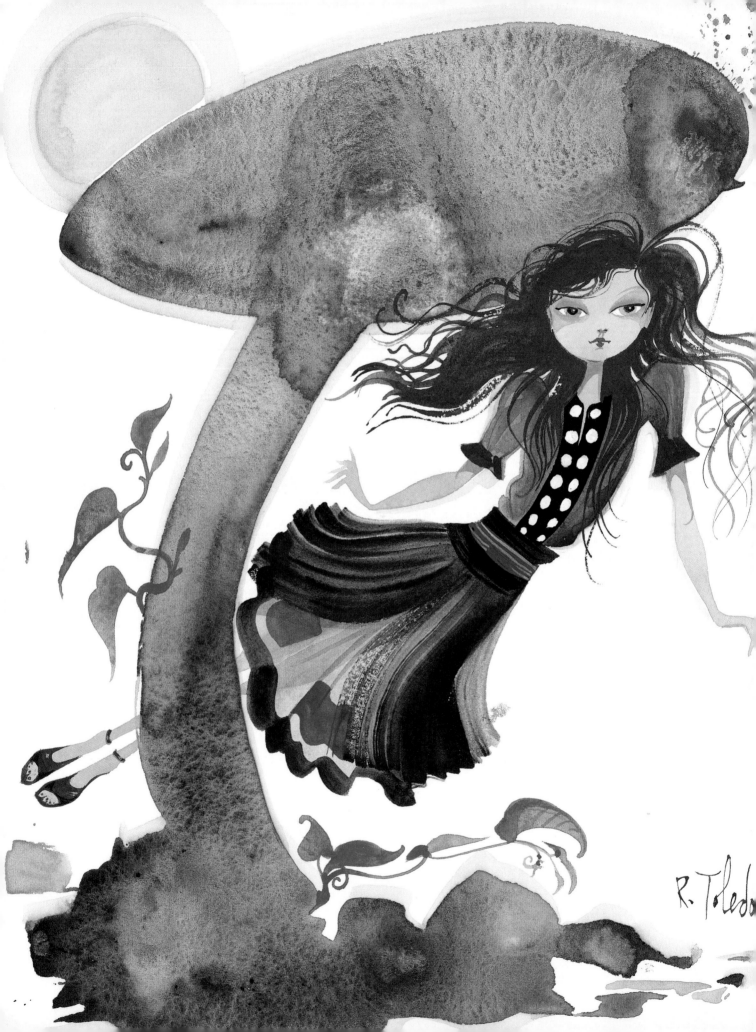

R. Toledo

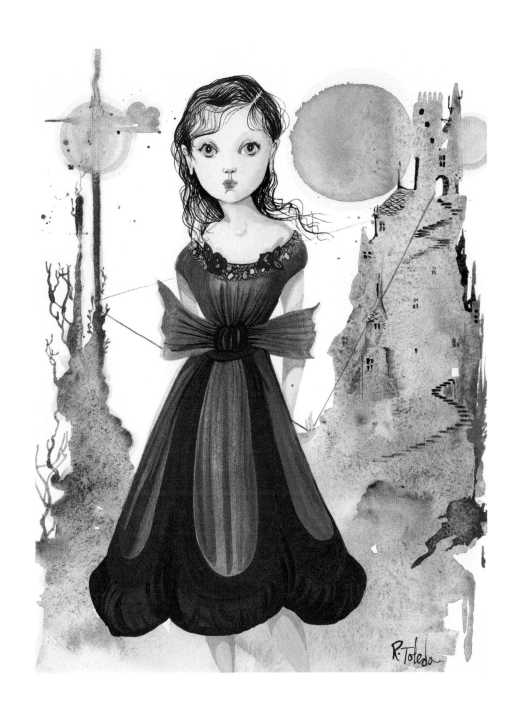

Castle, 2011
Interview magazine, Louis Vuitton;
watercolor

← Magic **Mushroom**, 2011
Interview magazine, Chloé;
watercolor

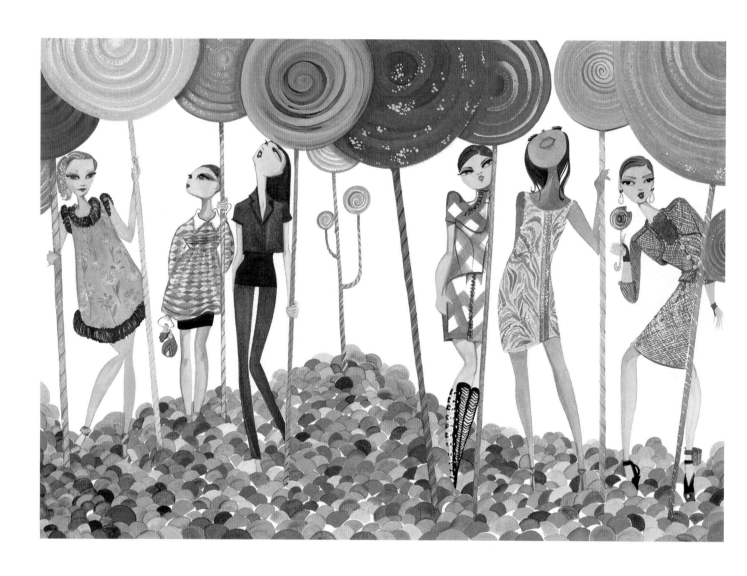

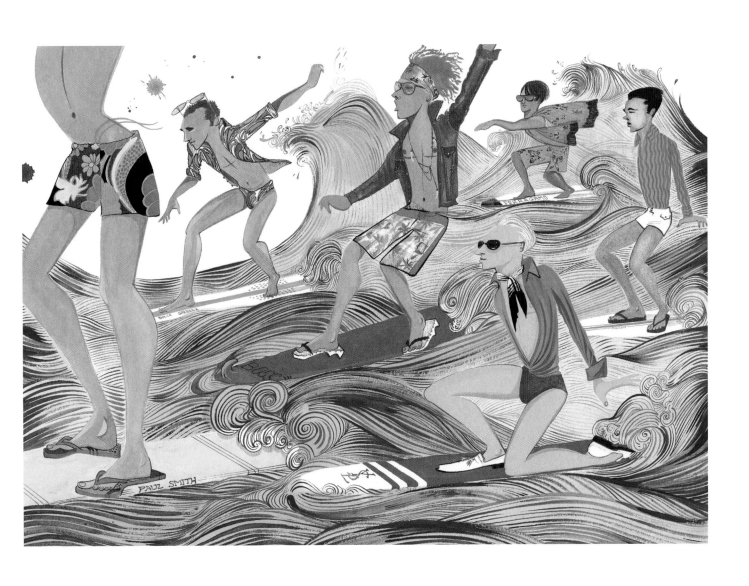

Surfers, 2013
Madame Figaro, Men's Spring/Summer
collection; watercolor

←   **Spring Time Candy Land, 2012**
Vogue Japan, left to right: Valentino,
Miu Miu, Jil Sander, Balenciaga,
Blumarine, Chanel; watercolor

Adrian Valencia

1975 born in Mendoza, Argentina | lives and works in London
www.adrianvalencia.com

CLIENTS
Vanity Fair Italy, InStyle Germany,
Links of London, Cartier, Montblanc

AGENT
Eastwing
UK
eastwing.co.uk

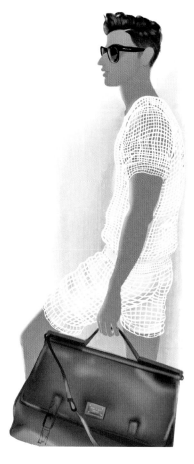

"I like the challenge of telling the story through a profile because I believe that the elements in the illustration become more interesting."

„Besonders liebe ich die Herausforderung, die Story anhand eines Profils zu erzählen, denn ich glaube, dass die Elemente einer Illustration dadurch interessanter werden."

« J'aime raconter une histoire à travers un profil parce que je pense que les éléments de l'illustration deviennent plus intéressants. »

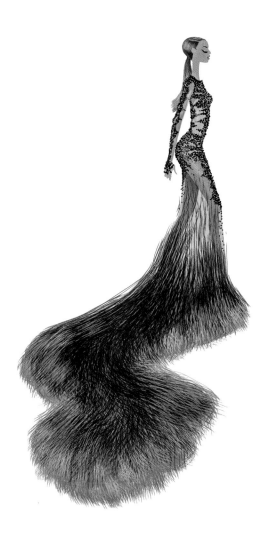

Dolce & Gabbana's Spring/ Summer 2012
Personal work, featured on D&G swide blog; digital

→   Untitled, 2012
Personal work, online blog; digital

→→ Teal Hair, 2011
Personal work, featured in
V magazine/Drawn This Way; digital

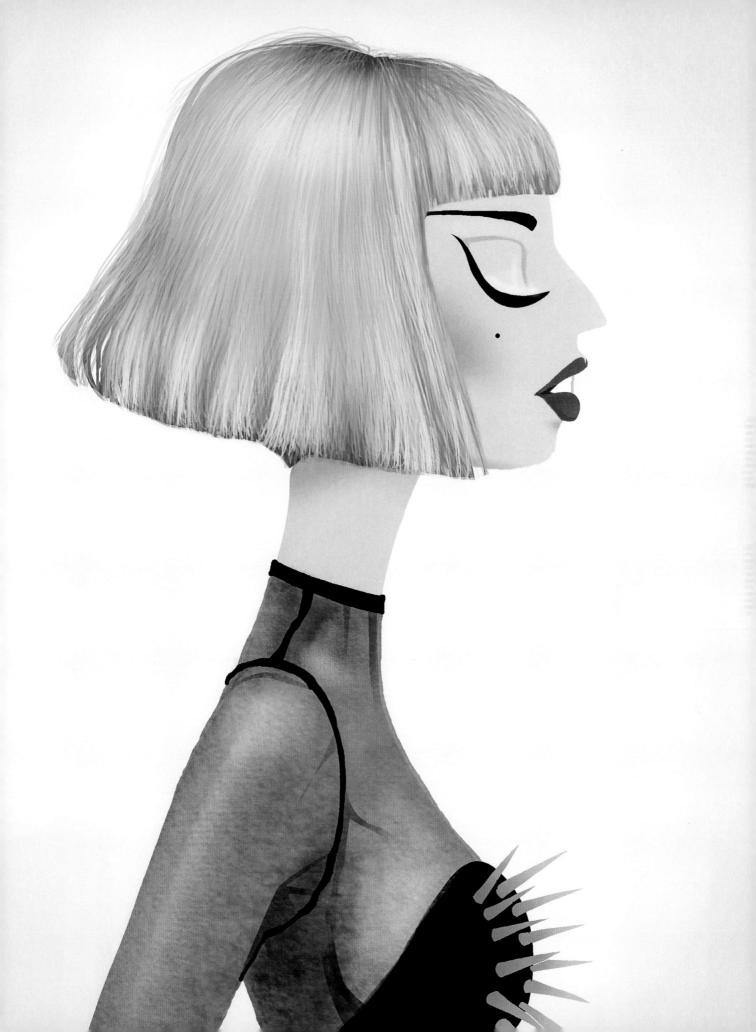

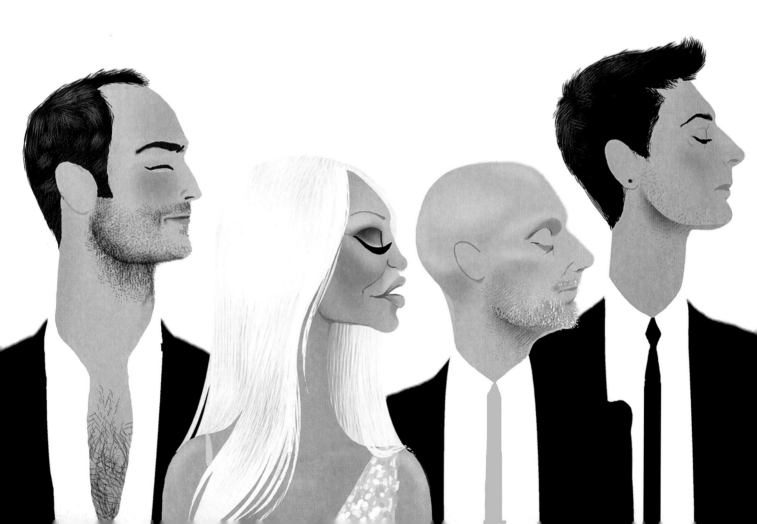

"We love working with Adrian because he draws the most friendly characters that still look extremely stylish even in the most precarious situations. He is 'InStyle' 100%."

ANNETTE WEBER
Editor in Chief, InStyle Germany

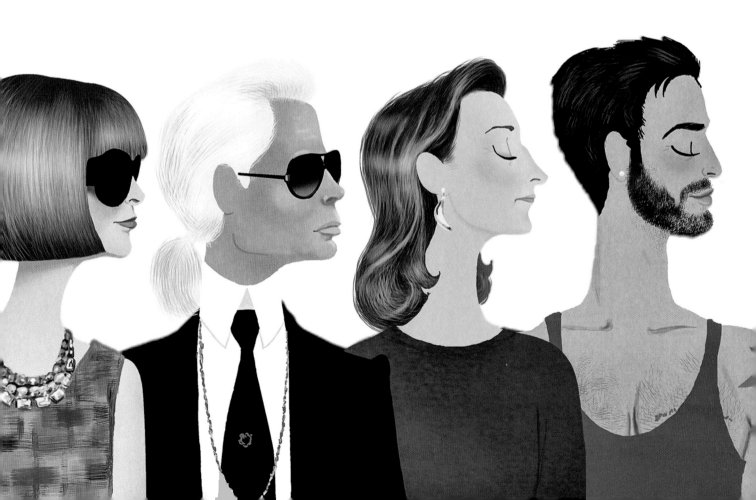

Annabelle Verhoye

born in Germany | lives and works in New York
www.annabelleverhoye.com

CLIENTS
The New Yorker, Vogue, Elle, Condé Nast Traveler,
Cosmopolitan, La Samaritaine, Catherine
Malandrino, Playboy, Walt Disney, InStyle

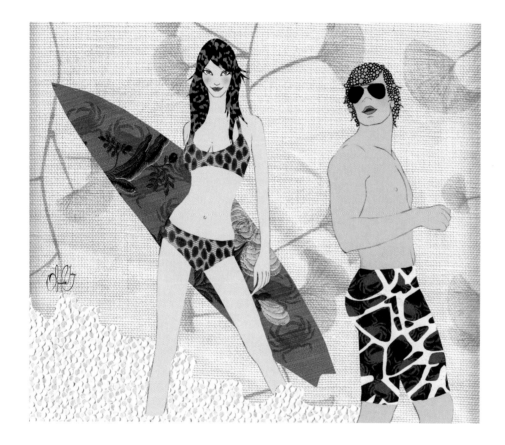

"My work seeks to create imagery in multiple dimensions
that is at the same time true to my subject's form.
I want people not only to see but to feel."

„In meiner Arbeit will ich Bilder in mehreren Dimensionen schaffen,
was gleichzeitig auf die Form meines Sujets zutrifft. Man soll
nicht nur betrachten, sondern auch fühlen."

« Je veux créer des images dans des dimensions multiples
tout en restant fidèle à la forme de mon sujet.
Je veux que les gens voient et ressentent. »

Cancer, 2011
Joy magazine; chine-collé

→   Pisces, 2011
Joy magazine; chine-collé

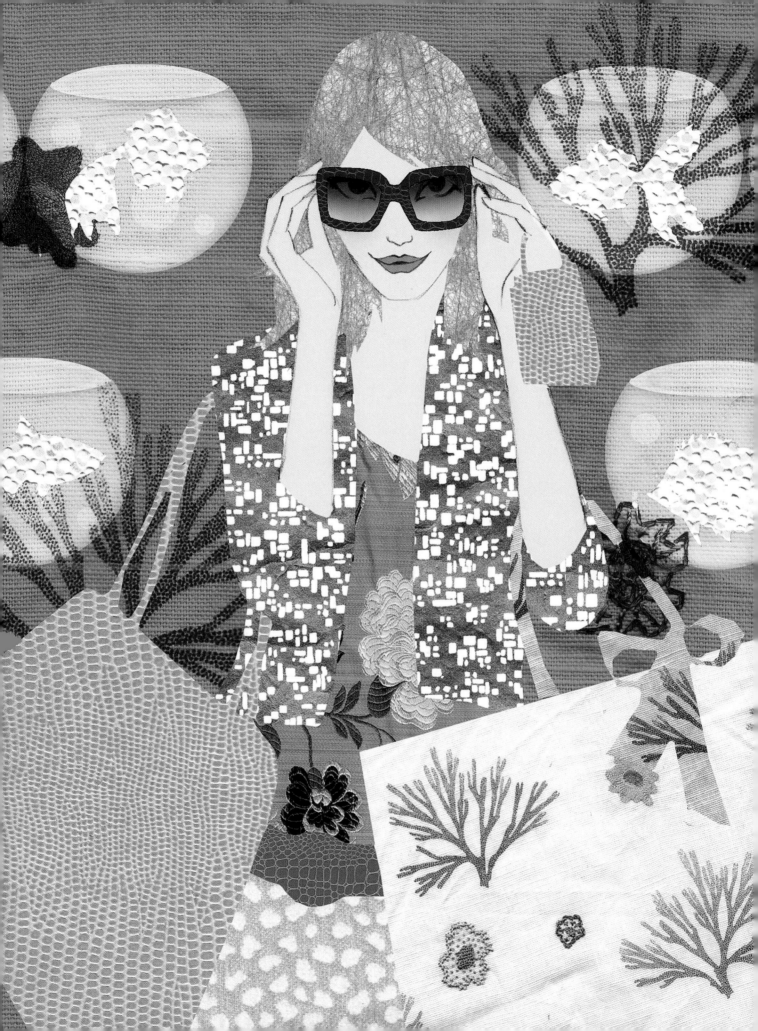

Angie Wang

1986 born in Shanghai | lives and works in Portland and Los Angeles
www.okchickadee.com

CLIENTS
Nylon magazine,
Escada, Zahia Dehar,
The New Yorker

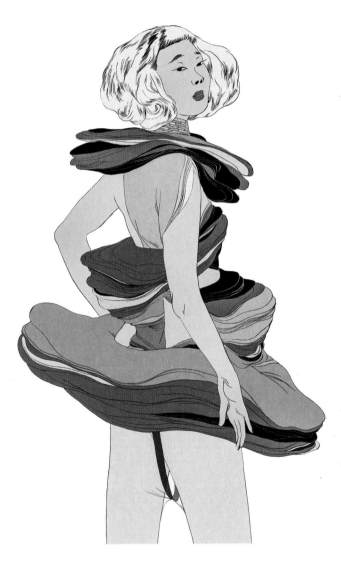

"It's important to me not to be afraid of ugliness, because to be fashionable is to be brave and willing to be ugly or weird."

„Für mich ist wichtig, nicht vor Hässlichem zurückzuschrecken. Modisch zu sein heißt tapfer zu sein und Mut zum Hässlichen oder Absonderlichen zu zeigen."

«Pour moi, il est important de ne pas avoir peur de la laideur, parce qu'être chic c'est avoir du courage et être prêt à être laid ou bizarre.»

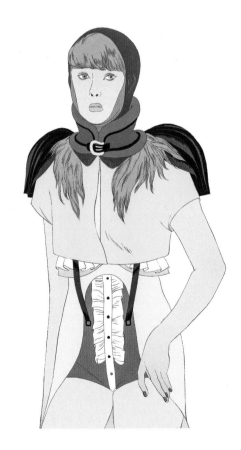

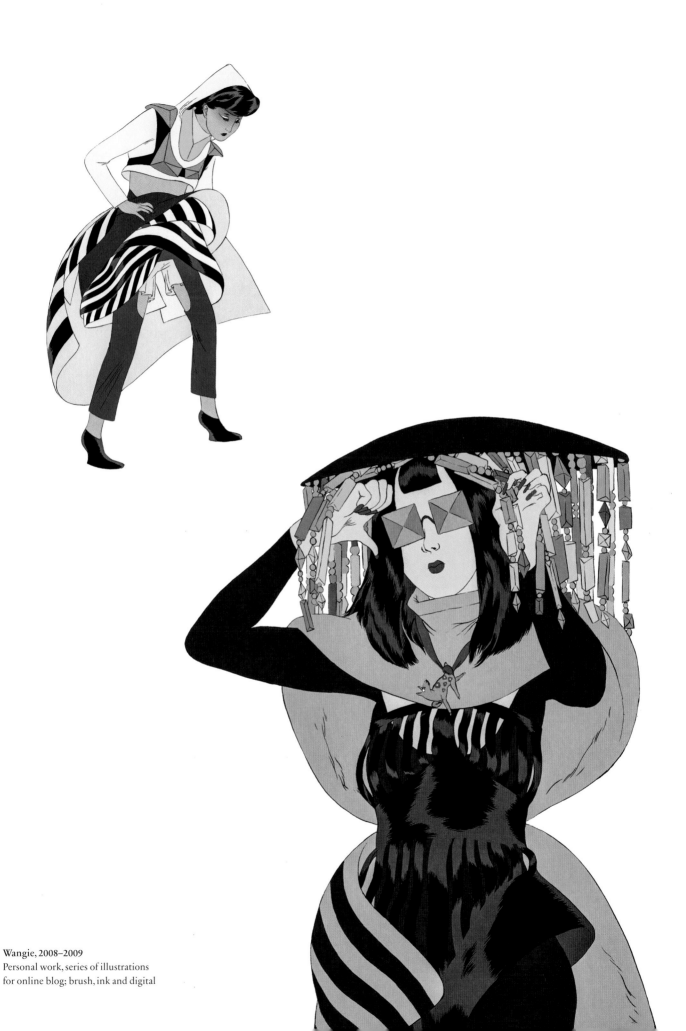

Wangie, 2008–2009
Personal work, series of illustrations
for online blog; brush, ink and digital

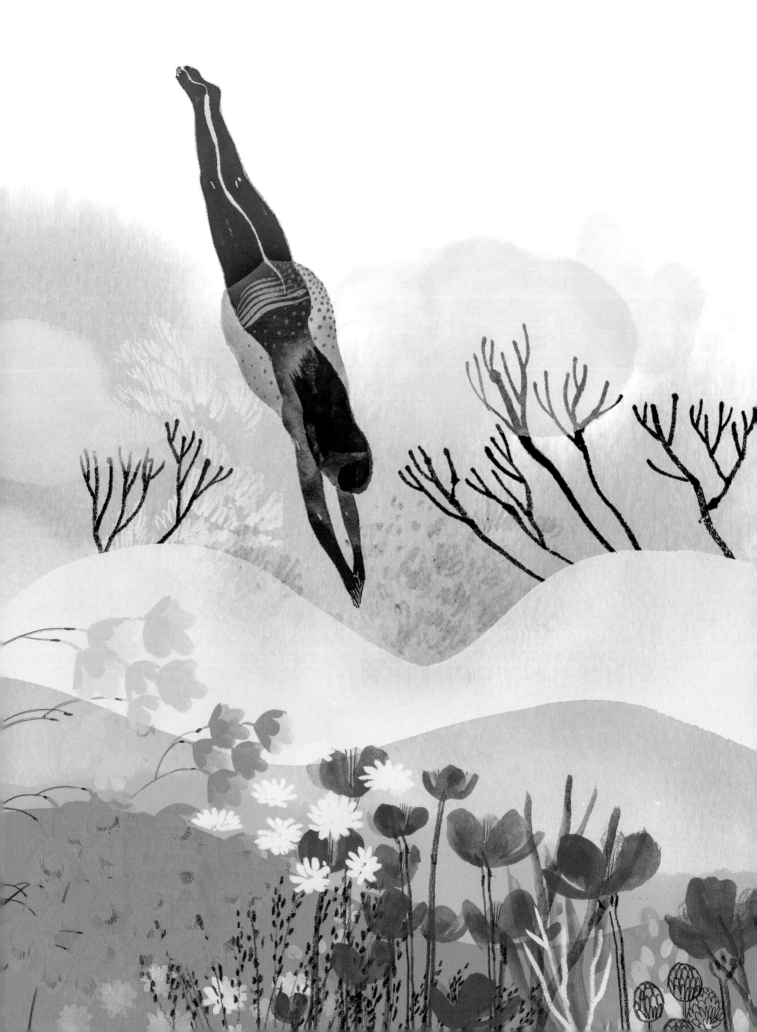

Rain Woman, 2012
Personal work; ink, watercolor,
brush and digital

← Spring, 2012
Personal work; ink, watercolor,
brush and digital

↓ Portrait of a Girl, 2012
Personal work; ink, watercolor,
brush and digital

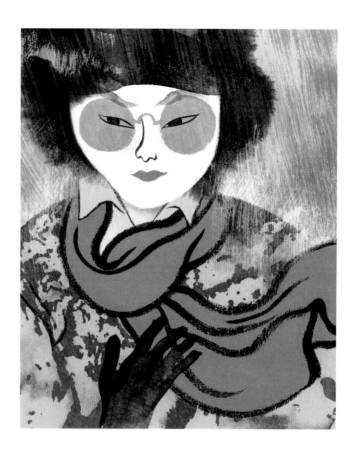

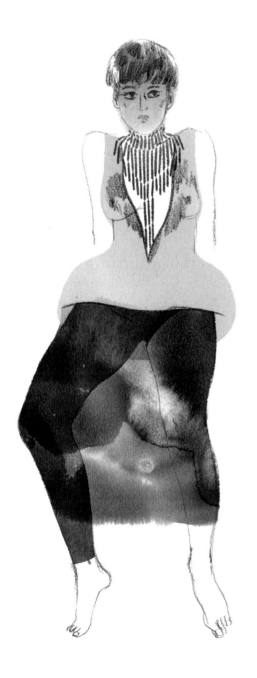

Autumn Whitehurst

1973 born in Providence | lives and works in Brooklyn
www.illustrationdivision.com/whitehurst

CLIENTS
RayBan, Victoria's Secret, Neiman Marcus,
Style.com, LeSportsac, Vogue Italy, Elle,
Nylon magazine, ST Fashion

AGENTS
Illustration Division
USA
illustrationdivision.com

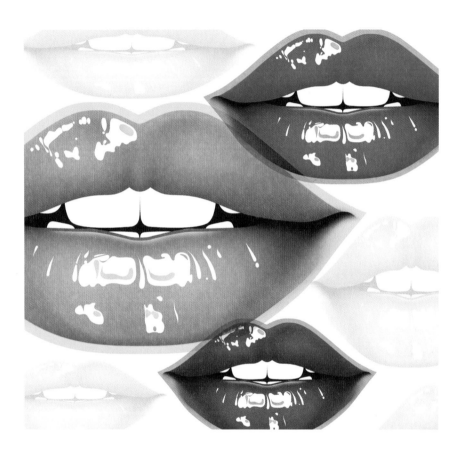

"My first love is color and form. When I'm working on
a fashion commission I try my best to marry these
elements to an idea to make the image sing."

„Meine besondere Liebe gilt der Farbe und der Form. Wenn ich an
Fashion-Aufträgen arbeite, versuche ich diese Elemente bestmöglich
in einer Idee zu verschmelzen, die dem Bild Leben einhaucht."

« J'aime la couleur et la forme. Lorsque je travaille sur
une commande de mode, j'essaie de marier ces éléments
avec une idée pour faire chanter l'image. »

Spring Brights, 2011
Telegraph magazine, Art Direction:
Gary Cochran; digital

→ Aquarius, 2010
Glamour magazine, Art Direction:
Will Hooks; digital

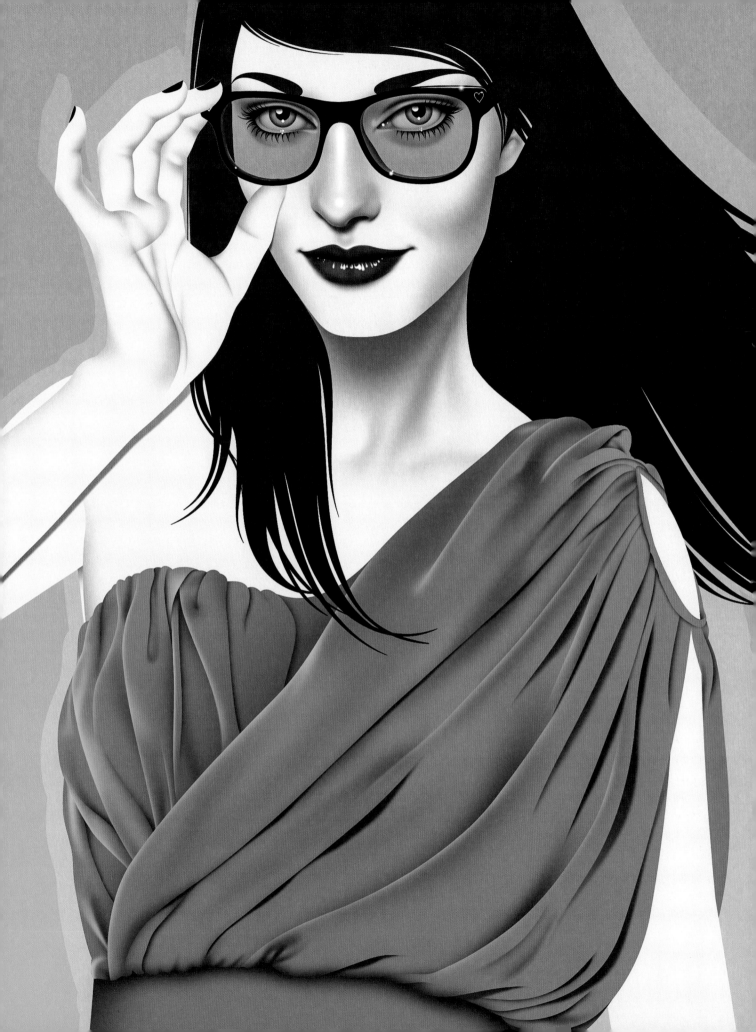

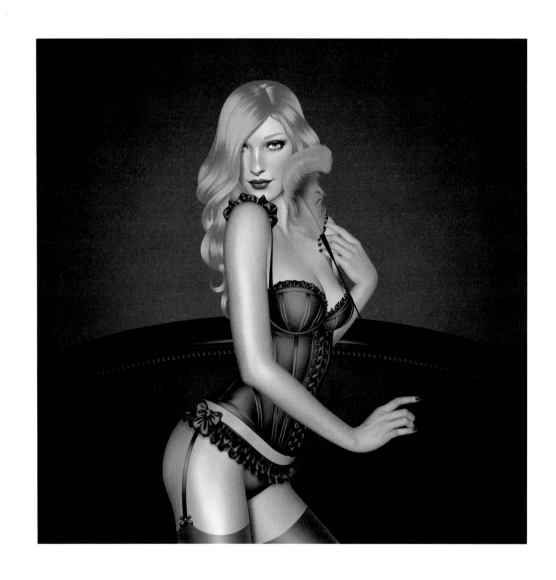

Victoria's Secret, 2010
Art Direction: Priscilla Ober; digital

→   X Factor-Lux, 2011
Art Department; digital

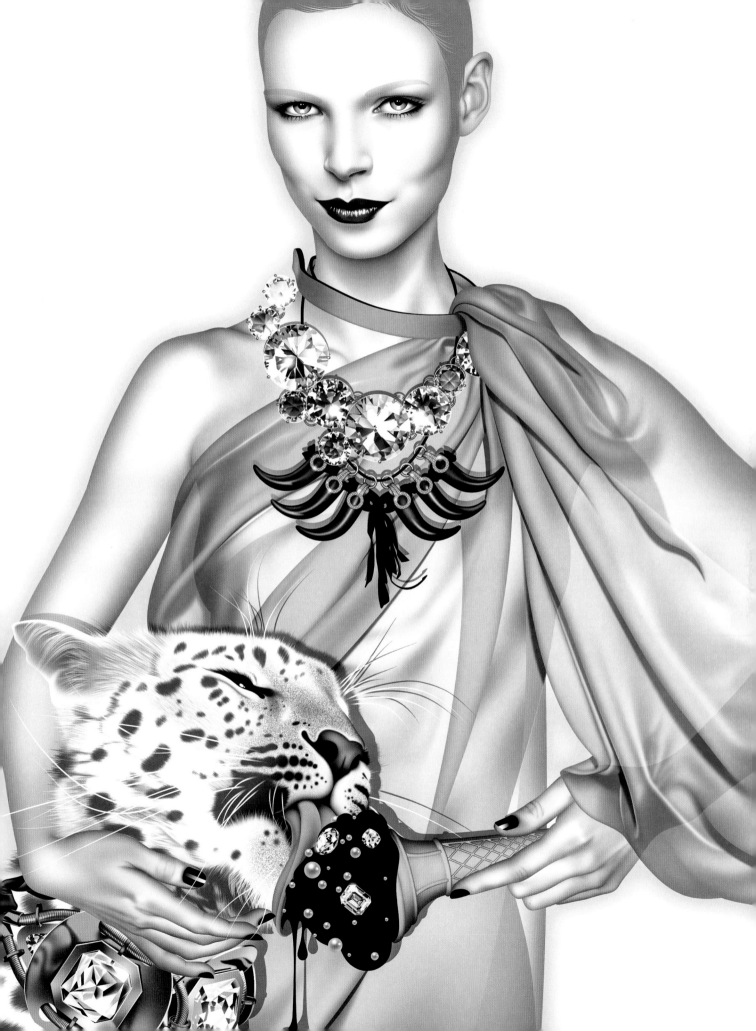

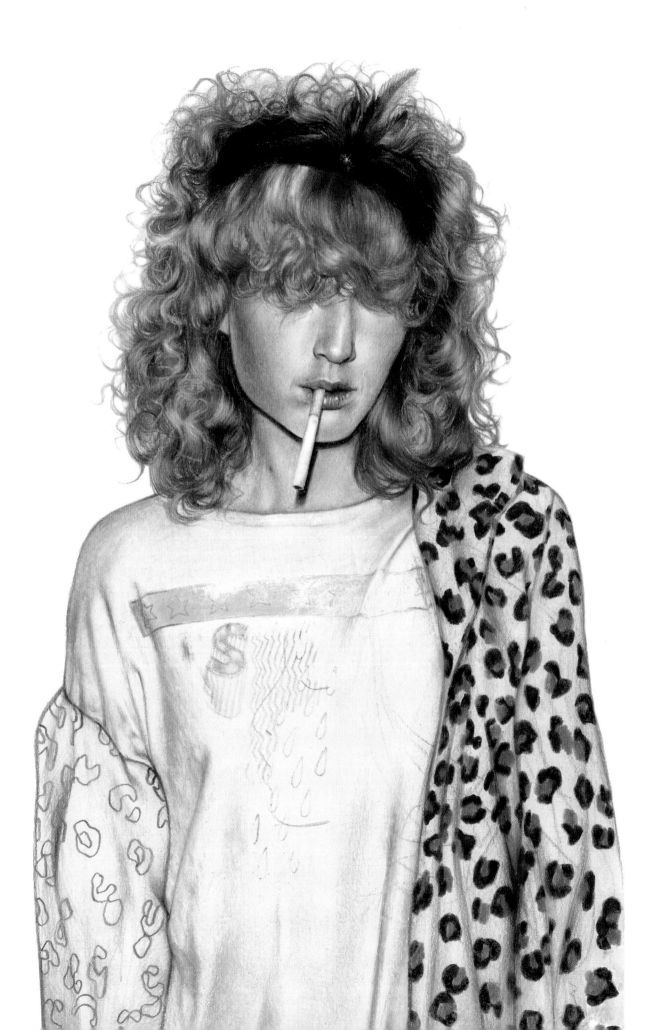

Acknowledgements

Danksagungen/Remerciements

The Illustration Now series has been a success from the beginning, but with this book on fashion illustration, we felt we were taking it a step further. To be able to achieve our objective, we aimed to put together a team of professionals who would bring not just credibility to the project, but more especially the pleasure of learning and discovering something new in a subject that has been explored in book form to a considerable extent.

Our team was eventually composed of historian Adelheid Rasche, who has produced an impeccable essay with an outstanding image selection, Steven Heller, who has taken part in all the books in this series, and Daniel Siciliano Bretas and Nora Dohrmann from our office in Cologne. Moreover, we received an invaluable and generous contribution from Margit J. Mayer, with whom we were in constant consultation regarding the selection of illustrators and who advised us on design, and Jonas Scheler, whose expertise from his studies in Fashion led to him recommending Ms. Rasche in the first place along with several of the illustrators.

Lastly, I also wish to offer my sincere thanks to all the illustrators for supplying the most astonishing work. On the production side we had Frauke Kaiser taking good care of this project, making sure the images were the best reflections of what the illustrators originally designed. I must also thank all the experts for sending comments, including many fashion designers, fashion design studios, journalists, stylists, fashion editors, agents, creative directors, and many others.

Julius Wiedemann

← Smoker, 2008
Minni Havas for T-bar,
T-shirt print; hand-drawn

© 2013 TASCHEN GmbH
Hohenzollernring 53, D-50672 Köln
www.taschen.com

To stay informed about upcoming TASCHEN titles, please
request our magazine at www.taschen.com/magazine or
write to TASCHEN, Hohenzollernring 53, D-50672 Cologne,
Germany, contact@taschen.com, Fax: +49 221 254919.
We will be happy to send you a free copy of our magazine
which is filled with information about all of our books.

EDITOR IN CHARGE
Julius Wiedemann

EDITORIAL COORDINATION
Daniel Siciliano Bretas

EDITORIAL ASSISTANT
Nora Dohrmann

DESIGN
Daniel Siciliano Bretas and Nora Dohrmann

PRODUCTION
Frauke Kaiser

ENGLISH REVISION
Chris Allen

FRENCH TRANSLATION
Aurélie Daniel for Delivering iBooks & Design, Barcelona

GERMAN TRANSLATION
Jürgen Dubau

Printed in Germany
ISBN 978-3-8365-4520-4

ESSAY BIBLIOGRAPHY

1. *Le Dessin sous toutes ses coutures: croquis, illustrations, modèles, 1760–1994*
(Paris: Palais Galliera Musée de la Mode et du Costume, Paris Musées, 1995)
2. Cally Blackman, *100 Years of Fashion Illustration* (London: Laurence King, 2007)
3. Laird Borrelli, *Illustrationen der Mode. Vol. 1: Internationale Modezeichner und ihre Arbeiten* (Munich: Stiebner Verlag, 2000)
4. Laird Borrelli, *Illustrationen der Mode. Vol. 2: Die Visionen der internationalen Modezeichner* (Munich: Stiebner Verlag, 2004)
5. Joëlle Chariau, *Drawing Fashion. A Century of Fashion Illustration* (Munich: Prestel Verlag, 2010)
6. Alice Mackrell, *An Illustrated History of Fashion. 500 Years of Fashion Illustration* (London: B.T. Batsford Ltd., 1997)
7. Roger and Mauricio Padilha, *Antonio Lopez – Fashion, Art, Sex & Disco* (New York: Rizzoli, 2012)
8. Adelheid Rasche, *Pailletten – Posen – Puderdosen. Modezeichnungen und Objekte der Zwanziger Jahre* (Berlin: Nicolai Verlag, 2009)
9. Adelheid Rasche (ed.), *Visions & Fashion, Bilder der Mode 1980/2010* (Bielefeld: Kerber Verlag, 2011)